DESERT WARRIORS

AUSTRALIAN P-40 PILOTS AT WAR
IN THE MIDDLE EAST AND NORTH AFRICA

1941 - 1943

Russell Brown

FIRST EDITION

BANNER BOOKS

First Published in 2000 by Banner Books
122 Walker Street, MARYBOROUGH
Queensland 4650
Australia

Design & Production by McTaggarts The Printers
63 Torquay Rd. HERVEY BAY
Queensland 4655.
mcprint@mctaggart.com.au

Cataloguing In Publication information

Brown, Russell, 1945-

Desert warriors : Australian P-40 pilots at war in the Middle East
and North Africa 1941-1943

Bibliography,
Includes index.
ISBN 1 875593 22 5.

1. World War, 1939-1945 - Aerial operations, Australian. 2.
P-40 (Fighter planes). I. Title.

940.544994

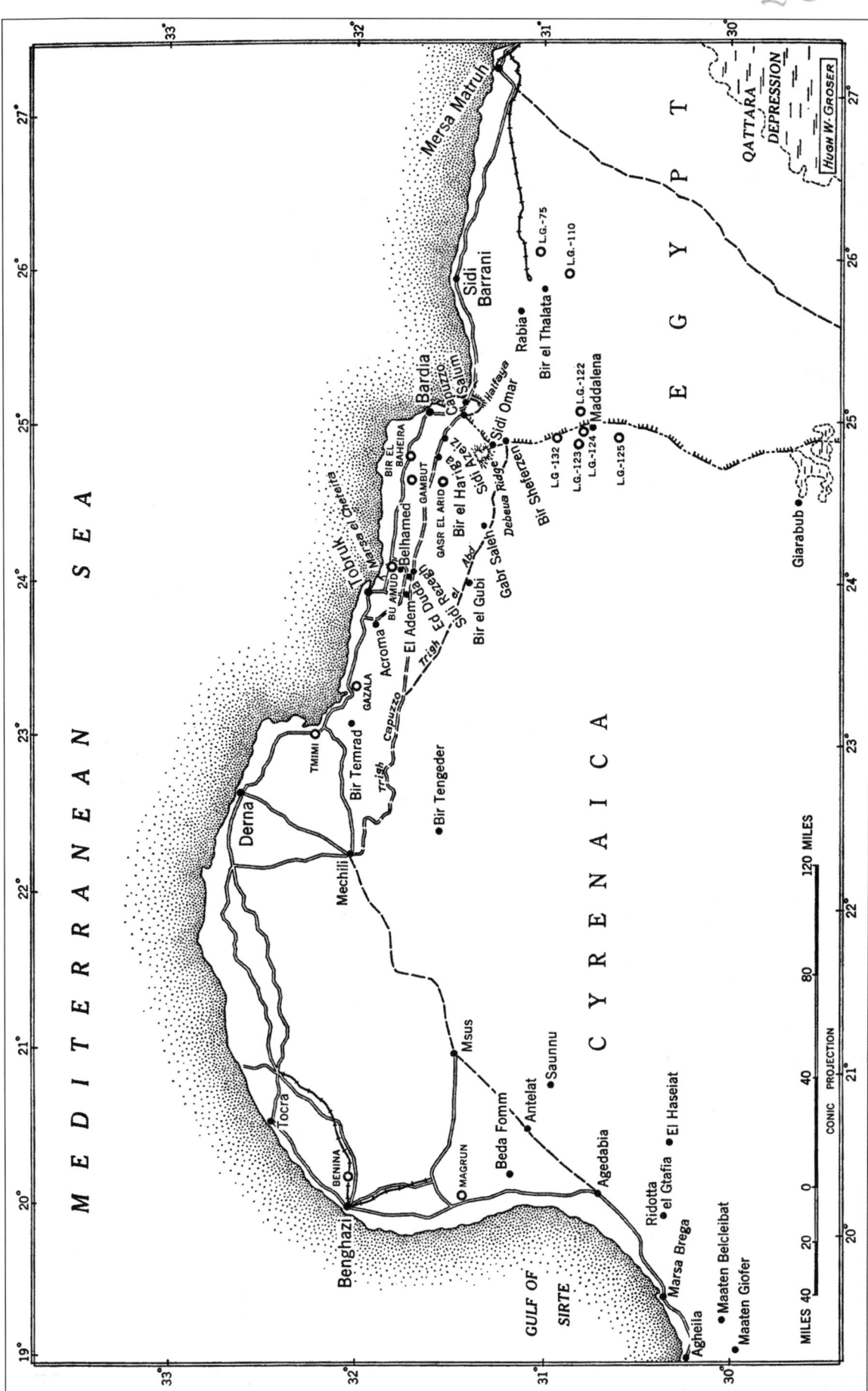

ZG-00

MEDITERRANEAN   SEA

E G Y P T

C Y R E N A I C A

GULF OF
SIRTE

QATTARA
DEPRESSION

Hugh W. Groser

Mersa Matruh

Sidi
Barrani

Rabia
Bir el Thalata

L.G.-75
L.G.-110

L.G.-122
Maddalena
L.G.-123
L.G.-124
L.G.-132
L.G.-125

Giarabub

Bardia
Capuzzo
Salum
Halfaya
Sidi Omar
Sidi Azeiz
Debeua Ridge
Bir Sheferzen

Bir el
Baheira
GAMBUT
Bir el Hariga
Gasr el Arido
Abd
Gabr Saleh

Tobruk
Mersa el Chereita
BU AMUD
Belhamed
El Adem
Sidi el Rezegh
Trigh Ed Duda
Bir el Gubi

Acroma
GAZALA
TMIMI
Bir Temrad
Trigh Capuzzo
Bir Tengeder

Derna

Mechili

Msus
Saunnu
Antelat

Beda Fomm
Agedabia

Ridotta
el Gtafia El Haseiat
Marsa Brega
Maaten Belcleibat
Maaten Giofer
Agheila

Tocra

BENINA
MAGRUN

Benghazi

MILES 40   20   0   40   80   120 MILES
CONIC PROJECTION

C ontents

Acknowledgements

After reading *These Eagles, RAAF Log* and *RAAF Saga* as a child, I developed an abiding interest in the history of the RAAF, and its fighter units in particular. I first met Alan Rawlinson and his wife Gwen in 1994, after he had been kind enough to answer some of my questions about 3 Squadron's activities by mail. Since then we have maintained regular contact, and it was talking with Alan which inspired me to begin this project.

By making available numerous photographs from his personal collection, and his private memoirs, which were intended for family consumption only, he has enabled me to give the story life and interest far beyond my original expectations, and my sincere thanks go to him and Gwen for their friendship and hospitality.

Special thanks to Peter Cuthbert, the tireless secretary of 3 Squadron RAAF Association, whose introduction to Alan set the ball rolling.

Since the work was started, I have made contact with a number of DAF pilots, and I owe them all my sincere gratitude for the material they have provided, and the help they have so readily and enthusiastically offered.

John Hooke of 3 Squadron, and his wife Pat have extended their hospitality, and John consented to a series of taped interviews, as well as making available his log book and several photographs.

Ron Cundy of 260 Squadron copied the relevant pages of his log book, provided photographs, and offered advice and encouragement.

Dave Borthwick of 450 Squadron provided a written account of his ordeal in the desert after being shot down and wounded.

Eric Bradbury wrote from Western Australia with details of his early days with 3 Squadron, and sent a photograph.

Tom Wood of 3 Squadron sent me a copy of his Air Force recollections, numerous photographs, and with his wife Merral, inadvertently became a volunteer proof reader. Since then Tom has made his log book available, and lent me several rare books, including *3 Squadron at War*.

A very kind invitation from Tom and his wife to attend 3 Squadron's reunion and annual dinner in Canberra was accepted with gratitude. My wife and I spent a memorable four days with the members of 3 Squadron, and were privileged to attend their memorial service and Squadron dinner. I am grateful to everyone who made us feel so welcome, and extend particular thanks to Tom Russell, who entrusted his album of photographs to me.

While we were in Canberra, Tom Wood suggested that we contact his old Flight Commander Keith Kildey, who kindly provided access to his log book and photo album, and patiently answered numerous questions concerning his activities during the desperate days of the retreat in 1942. Keith and his wife Marg put me in touch with Ian 'Joe' Lyons and Alan Righetti. Ian had lost his first log book, after his disastrous first (and only) operation with 3 Squadron, but his memory was clear, and his harrowing experience of 9 January 1942 is recorded first hand.

Alan Righetti responded to my request for information with an extract from his war diary, several rare photographs, and a fascinating excerpt from a wartime sketchbook which dealt with a German pilot whom he shot down on 30 December 1942.

Ken McRae, 3 Squadron's Engineering Officer, was another contact made in Canberra, and he very generously made available a collection of photographs of his ground crews at work, several of which will be put to use in the second volume.

Bob Whittle of 250 Squadron, and his wife Frankie, answered a long list of questions, and sent copies of log book pages, contemporary newspaper clippings and a magnificent selection of photographs, which filled a serious void concerning the activities of 250 Squadron in 1941.

Des Cormack of 250 Squadron, a fellow teacher, consented to an interview, provided photo copies of his log book, written recollections, and free access to his superb photo album, all of which enabled me to fill the gaps concerning 250 Squadron's activities in 1942.

Ted Lawler of 450 Squadron has provided a detailed account of the work of the ground crews, and numerous rare photographs of the ground crews at work. His fine contribution is included as an appendix.

Max Jenkins of 450 Squadron gave an impromptu telephone interview and consented to the use of a quote from his log book.

Gordon Steege, 450 Squadron's first Commanding Officer, sent a letter with details of the Squadron's training period, and his difficulties in finding experienced pilots. As well as this, he patiently answered numerous questions, and sent a splendid set of photographs depicting many of 450's original pilots. His material also merits its own appendix.

Through Gordon Steege, Snow Swift, a desert Beaufighter pilot with 272 Squadron, kindly offered two moving letters concerning the loss of PO 'Rusty' Kierath. Permission from the Kierath family to use them is gratefully acknowledged.

Janet Beck of RAAF Historical Records has given me tireless assistance, and apart from the mass of material she provided, always found time for a friendly chat. Janet was responsible for all of the items under the heading of RAAF Historical Records, as well as much detailed information concerning Australian pilots who served with RAF squadrons. Without her help, the book could not have been written.

Janet steered me towards Monica Walsh, Curator of Research at the RAAF Museum, Point Cook, who guided me through her meticulously catalogued collection of photographs, arranged the copying of my selections, and unearthed a diary and letters written by 3 and 450 Squadron ground crew members.

Particular thanks to Margaret Lewis and the helpful staff of the Research Centre at the Australian War Memorial, who found numerous rare documents and arranged for their photo copying.

Permission from the AWM to use maps from John Herington's *Air War Against Germany and Italy 1939-43* as end papers is gratefully acknowledged.

Lex McAulay of *Banner Books* has been an encouraging and enthusiastic editor, and put me in touch with Tom Wood, Eric Bradbury and Ted Lawler, as well as providing several rare photographs.

His advice and guidance has been invaluable. My sincere thanks go to Lex for his encouragement and his faith in the project.

George James, Hon Secretary of 450 Squadron Association, responded to my request for assistance with a copy of *OK - Recollections of the Desert Harassers, Memoirs of a Fighter Pilot,* by Alex Markle, the War Diary of Viv Herrett on computer disc, and numerous photographs, as well as a copy of Stan Watt's autobiography, which will be invaluable when I begin work on the next volume.

When I first got in touch with George, the book was three parts finished. The revisions and additions made possible by his information were a pleasure to work on.

In England, Bob O'Hara searched through the archives of The Public Records Office at Kew, and discovered a great quantity of material concerning 112 and 250 Squadrons, and also made it possible to clear up what I consider to have been an injustice done to 3 Squadron concerning their activities on 22 November 1941.

Fellow researcher and enthusiast Doug Norrie, who is working on his own book about 450 Squadron, offered numerous rare photographs of personnel from 3, 250 and 450 Squadrons, and I am very grateful for his generous assistance.

In the United States, Frank Olynyk was most helpful in tracking down missing victory claims for 450 Squadron, and John Beaman provided details which solved the mystery of 3 Squadron's encounter with a rare Focke-Wulf 190. My sincere thanks to both gentlemen.

For details of the activities of German and Italian fighter pilots, I am indebted to the works of Chris Shores, Hans Ring and William Hess, who wrote the definitive histories of the North African Campaign, *Fighters Over The Desert,* and *Fighters Over Tunisia.*

To the staff of the Stawell Library, Gail Wood, Anne Ellis, Vicky Carlyon and Caroline Clode, I extend my thanks for arranging the borrowing of several rare reference books, and unrestricted use of the microfilm reading machine. Now they know why I spent so much time peering through a magnifying glass in a dark corner.

My wife Lorraine has patiently read the text as it was prepared, and offered comments and encouragement throughout a project which has taken more than twenty months. Research trips to Canberra and Point Cook could not truly be considered as holidays, but she happily gave me the time I needed, and actively assisted with research at the AWM and the RAAF Museum, where she discovered numerous suitable photographs. Her patience and support have meant a great deal.

Juanita Franzi of Aero illustrations has put together an original selection of profile drawings of the Tomahawk and Kittyhawk. Her meticulous research and attention to detail has resulted in what I consider to be the finest drawings of the P-40 so far produced.

Finally, as a fledgling author, it was with some hesitation that I approached Wing Commander Bobby Gibbes, DSO, DFC & Bar, 3 Squadron's longest serving Commanding Officer, to write a foreword. He readily agreed, and his enthusiastic response was quite overwhelming. His revealing insight into the life of a desert fighter pilot is a moving piece of writing, and his comments about the confirmation of victory claims are of great significance.

My sincere thanks to everyone who has helped so willingly. I hope that the end result meets with your approval.

oreword

WING COMMANDER BOBBY GIBBES (Ret) DSO, DFC & Bar

When Russell Brown asked me if I would be willing to write a foreword for this book I readily agreed but I had no inkling as to what would be involved. When the quite huge draft of the book was received I was completely taken aback wondering if I could ever manage to read through it, let alone be able to honour my agreement. However, after checking the first few pages I realised that I had been given a wonderful opportunity to read this magnificent and accurate record of events which took place over sixty years ago. I have carried out comprehensive checks of events recorded against entries in my diaries and flying logbook and have not only confirmed from all records available to me, together with the re-awakening of memories of sixty years ago, much which had faded over the years and brought them crowding back once again. I congratulate Russell Brown on his research and thoroughness in accurately recording many details of combats and operations by the desert fighter squadrons and including in some cases, those of the enemy.

Russell has written of the young men who flew with me and of pilots in other squadrons, many of whom I still remember. I thought that I had hardened over the years but I found that I still tended to become tearful when reading the various pages and remembering the faces of those brave young men who perished in fighting for a cause which has helped to preserve our wonderful Australia of today. Most of these young men had never really lived and few had known marriage, the wonderful experience and joy at the arrival of children, watching them grow through schooling, marriage and in turn producing their own children - our grandchildren.

This is a wonderful and factual record and should be read by all those who have not known the trauma and fear which our Desert Warriors experienced and indeed by those too who survived. I admit to being terrified on many occasions and finding it nearly impossible to keep on flying. On one occasion after being shot down by the rear gunners of four bomber JU88s flying in diamond formation, I parachuted from the flaming torch which my aircraft had become and made a heavy landing in a high wind. I lay on the ground surveying the bend in my left leg and I was in agonising pain. I wondered if I was in enemy territory or on our side of the lines and was ashamed at feeling gladness, knowing that I would not now be killed in aerial combat, at least for some time.

There was a time when I suffered horrific nightmares and on wakening I would try to stay awake in fear of further frightening dreams. After the war these nightmares occurred less often and soon ceased altogether. Some pilots were less fortunate and in two cases of which I am aware, ended by taking their own lives.

I spent two years living in tents in the desert in continuous dusty conditions with water always in short supply. Despite the efforts of our dedicated and hard working ground crews, dust on the perspex of our aircraft caused scratches which made it difficult to see against the glare of the sun. We generally flew with our canopies open despite the cold air at altitude which penetrated the light tropical clothing needed in the hot conditions below. Despite the many hardships and discomforts, we enjoyed good health in the desert and a rewarding association with our fellow pilots and ground personnel.

Before ending this foreword, I would like to comment on bizarre statements made by some researchers after the war on the method of confirming victories by the RAF and USAAF pilots by suggesting that if they were considered honourable men their claims did not have to be substantiated by other witnesses. This was arrant nonsense and it was not possible for a desert pilot to have a victory confirmed without a witness. Our aircraft were not equipped with camera-guns so we had no photographic records of combats fought. It was so difficult to get confirmation that on one occasion I didn't bother to submit a "sortie report" even though I confirmed it myself afterwards when driving from the aerodrome of Bir Dufan to the area. I found the wreckage of a 109 with the body of the dead pilot still inside it. It had not burnt and the retreating Germans probably did not have time to locate and bury the pilot.

On an earlier occasion, after several attacks on a lone JU87 which damaged it badly, it was about to crash-land on very stony terrain when two 109s flew above me. I engaged them and did not have the time to watch the landing. I claimed it as a probable naming the place, terrain and heading of the aircraft when last seen. A day or so later, one of our top pilots, Sgt. pilot Cameron, reported a crashed Stuka, where and as I had claimed it. The RAF did not credit me with it as there had been a lot of action in the area and they could not be sure that it was the aircraft which I had claimed. Although I was disappointed at the time, in hindsight the RAF were correct.

After the war I became a friend of Erhard Braune, an ex-commanding officer of III/JG 27. In discussion with him on tactics etc., I asked him why the claims of some Luftwaffe pilots appeared unrealistic as they didn't add up with our known losses. He told me that these high claims helped the morale of the German population.

I commend Desert Warriors to those who are interested in the true history of the war in North Africa which saw the beginning of the end of the Axis forces in Europe and made it possible to concentrate our forces for the defeat of Japan.

Bobby Gibbes

Preface

Australian airmen made a significant contribution to the Allied victory in North Africa, and the later successful invasions of Sicily and Italy. This book deals in detail with the activities of 3 and 450 Squadrons RAAF, and the numerous Australian pilots who flew with 94, 112, 250 and 260 Squadrons RAF on Tomahawks and Kittyhawks.

There were many other Australian pilots with the RAF Hurricane and Spitfire squadrons, and the medium bomber units. The RAAF also contributed four bomber squadrons to the Desert Air Force: 454, which operated Blenheims and Baltimores; 458; Wellingtons; 459; Blenheims (briefly), Hudsons, Venturas and Baltimores; and 462 with Halifaxes. Anyone who was flown in an aircraft of No. 1 Air Ambulance Unit will have good cause to remember the service provided by this fine unit. 451 Squadron first operated Hurricanes in the Tactical Reconnaissance role, and later converted to Spitfires. The efforts and sacrifices of all these brave young men should not be forgotten.

Lest it be thought that undue emphasis has been given to 3 Squadron, it should be explained that more documentation of their activities was available than for 450 Squadron and all of the RAF units. Almost all of 3 Squadron's Combat Reports have been preserved, and are used throughout the book. There are *none* to be found for 450 Squadron! It was a good thing that 450's Operations Record Book provided such careful detail of their various combats. 112 Squadron's Intelligence Officer recorded the bare details of each pilot's actions in any particular combat, and then wrote a summary of the whole event. Thus there are few individual combat narratives available for this unit. Some Combat Reports from 250 Squadron were discovered, and these have been included.

To preserve the authenticity and immediacy of Combat Reports and extracts from Operations Record Books, no changes to spelling or grammar have been made.

Depending on the vintage of the reader, the way in which the Messerschmitt 109 is referred to will certainly cause confusion, and perhaps annoyance. Allied pilots invariably referred to the aircraft as the ME 109, and that is how it appears when contemporary quotations are used. However, in modern aviation literature, the term *Bf109* is used, as the aircraft was designed by Willi Messerschmitt but produced by the *Bayerische Flugzeugwerke*. It was not until later in the war that Professor Messerschmitt took control of the organisation, when its later products officially adopted the prefix 'Me'. (I have already been taken to task over this by one of my contributors, and hereby offer this explanation to all readers who remember that they shot down an ME 109 and *not* a Bf109.)

Finally, a word about the structure and time frame of the book. When I began working on it in 1998, the original intention was to cover the *air combat* experiences of Australia's Tomahawk and Kittyhawk pilots in the Middle East and Western Desert, and to briefly summarise the Mediterranean Campaigns, as there were very few occasions when enemy aircraft were encountered after the conclusion of the campaign in Tunisia. However, the great importance of the other tasks carried out by the Kittyhawk pilots could not be ignored, and the book grew in size.

Modern day fighter aircraft have to be able to carry out a multitude of roles: interception, air superiority and ground attack. It can be fairly argued that the first multi-role fighter of World War II was the Kittyhawk. This might not have been the designer's intention, but in the Western Desert, of necessity, this is exactly what happened. When first introduced in January 1942, it was the best fighter available, and despite its lack of performance, it was well used in this role, particularly as a bomber interceptor. But its pilots soon found themselves called upon to strafe the advancing *Afrika Korps,* to escort the increasing numbers of medium bombers, (often carrying bombs themselves while so doing), and to act as dive-bombers, a task they carried out with devastating effect.

Since my research began, I have been given a vast amount of material concerning the campaigns in Europe, and to do this justice, my intention is to produce a second volume, dealing with 3 and 450 Squadrons in Sicily and Italy.

C hapter 1   Introduction

At 1340 on 19 November 1940, four Gloster Gladiators of 3 Squadron RAAF took off from their base at Gerawla in Egypt on a tactical reconnaissance (Tac. R.) over the Italian lines. Twenty minutes later they were attacked by some eighteen Fiat CR42 fighters, and in the long dogfight which followed, they destroyed four Fiats for the loss of one Gladiator and its pilot, Sqn. Ldr. Peter Heath. 3 Squadron had begun its operational career in the Second World War, which it ended four years and six months later as one of the two pre-eminent fighter squadrons of the Desert Air Force.

On 10 June 1940 the Italian dictator Benito Mussolini declared war against Britain and France. On 15 July, 3 Squadron RAAF sailed from Sydney on the RMS *Orontes,* arriving at Port Tewfik, Egypt, on 23 August, becoming the first Australian Air Force unit to reach the Middle East.

On 16 September the squadron moved to Helwan, near Cairo, where it formed into three flights, two with Gloster Gladiators, and the third with Westland Lysanders. There were also five Gloster Gauntlets, intended for use as dive bombing trainers. The Gauntlets were the first to see action, but were soon withdrawn due to maintenance difficulties, and when the Lysander Flight re-equipped with Gladiators in early January, the squadron was operating as a pure fighter unit. It took part in General Sir Richard O'Connor's brilliant offensive, Operation *Compass,* which began on 9 December, and by 9 February 1941 had reached Agheila, capturing the ports of Tobruk and Benghazi in the process.

3 Squadron claimed sixteen enemy aircraft destroyed while flying Gladiators, and withdrew briefly to begin re-equipping with Hurricanes on 29 January.

Two factors now conspired against O'Connor: Churchill's order to divert some of his forces to the futile defence of Greece, and the arrival of the Germans.

Mussolini was forced to swallow his pride in the face of the possibility of total defeat in Tripolitania, and actually ask for the direct military assistance which had been offered by the Germans. It was not long in coming. General Erwin Rommel arrived on 12 February, in command of the *15th Panzer* and the *5th Light* Divisions, the advance elements of what was later to become famous as the *Afrika Korps.* Twelve days later the first exchange with British forces took place.

With 73 Squadron RAF, 3 Squadron's Hurricanes were made responsible for the air defence of Benghazi, and the area 200 miles south to the front at Agheila, and soon encountered their first German aircraft. On 15 February, FO John Saunders shot down the first German aircraft to fall to fighters in Africa, a Ju88 of III/KLG 1.

I/StG 1 and II/StG 2 also arrived in Africa to support Rommel, and 3 Squadron claimed the destruction of no fewer than eight Stukas of I/StG. 1 on 18 February: the first 'Stuka Party' of the desert war.

Rommel began his offensive on 24 March, and by 10 April had reached Tobruk, which was cut off three days later, thus beginning the famous siege. 3 Squadron evacuated its base at Benina on 3 April, and from then on fought a constant rear-guard action, claiming thirty-four German aircraft while flying Hurricanes.

> On 19 April 41, we handed over our remaining two serviceable Hurricanes to 274 Squadron RAF and were pulled out for a rest. . . . We had 14 days' leave at the Hotel Cecil in Alexandria, right on the foreshore. It took about four refills to reach the stage of having no brown ring of mud around the bath. Then clean uniforms, a cold beer, fresh food and the war and desert was far behind.[1]

The Desert War had a special nature and mystique all of its own, and no book about the subject would be complete without some mention of the unique environment in which the struggle took place. Alan Rawlinson, who was with 3 Squadron from the beginning, wrote the following description of desert conditions as a background to his story, and it provides a vivid picture of life for the men of the Desert Air Force.

> The coastal strip of the Western Desert, where all of the many campaigns were fought, was mainly firm, but with sandy patches in parts. The large sand dune areas were further to the south, away from the coast.

> The hard surfaces were dotted with low woody bush called camel thorn. The blowing sand gathers around these small bushes and gives them a lumpy character in the event of a forced landing. Airfields were easily established by just grading it. The summers were very hot and dry and the winters cold and dry. Winter rainfall resulted from cooler unstable sea air, but there was not a lot of it.

> Drinking water was always short and heavily chlorinated. Ancient wells were salt impregnated and fouled by both sides as the desert battles ebbed and flowed over hundreds of miles. Hard rations were routine - bully beef, M & V (meat and veg) beans, bacon, milk - all tinned. Powdered eggs and the ubiquitous hard army biscuits. On rare occasions we had fresh meat. More strictly raw meat, not very fresh and of doubtful origin. I recall seeing fresh fruit twice, once vividly. Seeing someone on a one-holer, nothing else in sight but the stark desert stretching to the horizon, sitting there peeling an orange!

> During stationary periods our Messes were sometimes made of wood, but usually they were canvas marquees called E.P.I.P.'s (English Patent Indian Pattern). Sometimes there was a concrete floor. We used trestle tables, folding chairs, camp stretchers and sleeping bags, enamel mugs and plates. For sleeping we had ridge poled tents, 2 or 3 per tent. Issue blankets - we bought the odd sheet. A small canvas basin on folding legs for washing, a larger one resting on the ground as a bath - if ever there was enough water or time. Salt water soap sometimes worked best.

> A cup of water in the morning did for teeth, rudimentary face wash and a cold shave. Talking of shaving, perhaps I should explain why Air Force people went in for large moustaches. Regulations state - "the upper lip may remain unshaven" - no mention of trimming or shaping. Once a week, fortnight, or possibly a month, depending on the water supply, a stand up wash in the open with about a quart of water. Latrines were two or four holers or squat slits when on the move (or a shovel!) Fine powdered dust caked into one's clothes and head, as the flying environment was always hot and sweaty. A breeze raised dust. Aircraft operations or engine tests made things unpleasant. Khamseens or Sirrocos occurred now and then.

> After a dust storm the aircraft flying controls were jammed solid. Pressure washing (pneumatic) was needed to clear them. Sometimes the aircraft were flown and turned upside down to shake out the dust. It was disconcerting to get a face full of dust in the middle of a dogfight.

> Aircraft servicing, particularly guns, was a very difficult task for our groundcrew. They achieved wonders in those appalling conditions, and we were rarely let down.

> Particularly on the move there were no lights after dark. We then ate from one kitchen, with rarely any tables or chairs. Sleeping bags on the ground, about 7 or 8 to a tent. We dug the tents in to about 18

inches as bombers were always roaming about dropping odd ones here or there to keep us awake. Being dug in we ignored them. A direct hit is rare in those conditions. We slept in clothes for days - and weeks on the move. In winter with flying suits (Sidcot), and flying boots as well, on occasions sleeping under the aircraft. Caked in dust and sweat for days, but strangely very lean and fit. When the dust was dry it was like a sort of talcum powder - well sort of.

As a newcomer to the desert, sandfly bites turned septic. Lots of small red spots with yellow heads. From then on immunity prevailed. Dysentery was rare - diarrhoea less so.

Flying conditions were good with odd exceptions like dust storms - or showers which produced slushy surfaces. It was a routine procedure from 1940 for Airfield Operations to send to HQ Desert Air Force, a dust rising signal when appropriate. Being an area where the weather was generally flyable - VFR - the prospect of dust storms was important information, also their extent and direction of movement. Aircraft operations and large ground movements encouraged the development of dust storms. They could persist for over 24 hours.

The fine powder penetrated any man made structure. The issue anti-gas goggles were helpful on the ground. Cockpit hoods were permanently scratched. In the sunny conditions they spangled hopelessly, and we flew with them open to achieve a clear view. Goggles were the same and we wore them "up" more to have them there in case of fire. Hoods could jam with dust, another preference for leaving them open. Parachutes were never left in the aircraft in case they were strafed. When aircraft numbers were small and the operational pressure great, some lesser unserviceabilities were accepted.[2]

We now come to the aircraft which is central to the story of both 3 and 450 Squadrons, and the many Australian pilots who flew with RAF units: the Curtiss P-40.

The P-40 series of aircraft owed their origin to the Hawk 75, which was designed in 1934, breaking new ground as the first all metal low wing monoplane fighter with a retractable undercarriage to enter service with the United States Army Air Corps. The initial contract for 210 Hawk 75s, designated P-36 in USAAC service, was let in July 1937. Compared with the European countries, which were hastily re-arming for the anticipated conflict, fighter development in the United States was slow, hampered by a lack of suitable in-line engines, as well as a lack of appreciation of the critically important role that fighters would be called upon to play in the coming war. Fighters designed in England, Germany and Japan had rendered the P-36 obsolete before the war broke out, and when the in-line liquid cooled Allison became available in 1936, Curtiss made the decision to install one in a P-36 airframe.

This machine, with the designation XP-40, was actually the tenth production P-36A, and first flew on October 14 1938, powered by an Allison V-1710 which produced 1,160 h.p. for take off, and 1,000 h.p. at 10,000 ft. After a fighter competition held in January 1939, the Air Corps issued a contract for 524 P-40s.

Having taken delivery of some 200 P-40s, the Air Corps deferred the remaining 324 to allow Curtiss to fulfil an urgent French contract for 140 H-81A-1s, (Curtiss's designation of the new fighter). None of these aircraft were destined to land in France before the country's collapse, and they were redirected to the RAF, which was, at that stage of the war, in desperate need of modern combat aircraft with which to face the expected invasion. However, the aircraft from the French contract were not initially suitable for combat, many still having French instrumentation and throttle modifications, while lacking armour plating, self sealing fuel tanks and bullet proof wind shields. Consequently, this initial batch of aircraft was issued to army cooperation squadrons and newly forming fighter squadrons to be used in the training role. The P-40B variant (H-81A-2) carried two extra wing guns and the necessary combat worthy refinements, and 110 were delivered to the RAF; none saw combat.

These were followed by an order for 930 P-40Cs (H-81A-3), which carried an additional 134 gallons of fuel in a new fuel system. These machines retained their American radios, and had four wing mounted .30 calibre machine guns, which were replaced by .303 Browning guns in

RAF service. Curtiss built 930 of this variant for the RAF, which gave it the designation of Tomahawk IIB. With added weight of extra guns, armour plate and an increased fuel load, the maximum speed had deteriorated from 357 mph at 15,000 ft. to 345 mph, while the empty weight had risen from 5,376 lbs. to 5,812. The normal loaded weight of the Tomahawk IIB stood at 7,459 lbs. , compared to the *maximum* loaded weight of 7,215 lbs. for the Tomahawk I. The climb rate had been reduced from 3,080 to 2,650 ft. per minute.

These reductions in performance were compensated to some degree by increased fire power, and an increase in the normal range from 650 to 730 miles. However they did not compare favourably to the Messerschmitt Bf109E, which was already in the process of being replaced on the Channel Coast by early examples of the Bf109F. Consequently, none of the Tomahawks issued to the Squadrons based in England flew operationally over Europe, apart from one unauthorised strafing sortie by a Tomahawk I of 410 Squadron RCAF in August of 1941.[3] By then however, the Tomahawk II had been well and truly blooded in the Middle East and Desert campaigns, and proved itself to be a worthy companion for the Hurricane, so much so that the pilots of JG 27 began to press for the introduction of the Bf109F.

The numerous Australian pilots fighting in the Desert first encountered the Tomahawk in early 1941, when 250 Squadron RAF was reformed in Palestine on 1 April from "K" Flight, a flight of Gladiators. Its initial equipment was the Tomahawk. 3 Squadron moved to Palestine and began to re-equip with Tomahawks in May. 112 Squadron RAF, which was one of the original desert squadrons, took its Gladiators to Greece, and returned to the desert after the fall of Crete. It too began to re-equip with Tomahawks on 14 June, when the first aircraft to arrive on strength crashed on landing! A day after the arrival of the second, its undercarriage collapsed after 'a perfectly normal landing',[4] and the squadron lost two inexperienced pilots to accidents in Tomahawks during their training period.

Will all these bullets really go in that little hole? One CO, two Flight Commanders and two junior officers trying to do the job of two competent armourers. From left: Fl. Lt. Hugh Chapman, PO Stan Wells, FO Gordon Wolsey, Fl. Lt. Dicky Martin and Sqn. Ldr. John Scoular of 250 Squadron. The Tomahawk carries a standard pattern of Temperate Land Scheme camouflage, Dark Green and Dark Earth. (Bob Whittle)

The Tomahawk had no specific vices, but it was quite different from the British fighters in use in the desert at the time, and took some getting used to. Neville Duke of 112 Squadron, fresh from flying Spitfires over France with 92 Squadron RAF, did not have a happy first encounter with it.

I pranged a Tomahawk on my first flight.

Before I went up on a fifteen minute "look-see", I sat in the big, American cockpit which seemed enormous, talking with other pilots and getting the value of their experience in these aircraft, and going over all the knobs and buttons. The aircraft seemed big and heavy and it certainly packed a powerful punch with two .5 inch machine-guns on top of the fuselage and four .3 inch machine-guns in the wings. These guns were cocked by levers, the breeches of the .5's protruded into the cockpit and, I was to discover later, gave off clouds of exciting smelling cordite when they were fired.

I took off quite normally but my first impressions were not very encouraging after being used to Spitfires. The performance of the Tomahawk seemed poor and its rate of climb was slow; but still it was fun to be flying again and to get a view of the desert from another angle. When I came in to land I did the normal three-point Spitfire landing, ground looped and ended in a heap. The next thing I knew was that I had broken off both undercarriage legs and the Tomahawk was sliding sideways into the sand, raising great clouds of dust, and both wheels were shooting off into the air of their own accord. . .

The following morning I took up a Tomahawk again, flew around for an hour and put it down all right, mastering the necessary "wheel landing" technique.[5]

In contrast, Bob Whittle, a stalwart of 250 Squadron, who, in common with most of his companions had never flown a Tomahawk before joining the unit, considered it to be an excellent aircraft, and had no difficulty landing it. 'I used three pointers - the others wheeled them on - tails down.'[6]

3 and 250 Squadrons had the benefit of the expertise of two American pilots, Lieuts. Lewis Meng and William Momyer, to help with their conversion, but it seems that 112 Squadron had to go it alone. A complete lack of technical manuals and instructions exacerbated the problems experienced. 250 Squadron had its share of accidents, mainly with swings and overshoots during take off and landing.

Not all the pilots of 250 were as accomplished as Bob Whittle. This is AK392, his first chosen Tomahawk. The comment on the original print read 'My 392 after Dave Gale (another Australian) had finished with it.' The aircraft carries Temperate Land Scheme camouflage.

(Bob Whittle)

While the Tomahawk had the disadvantages of inferior speed and rate of climb compared to the Bf109, it was rugged and reliable, and the best aircraft available at the time. But it was the tenacity and determination of its pilots, and the hard work and ingenuity of its dedicated ground crews which made it an effective fighting machine in the desert.

Chapter 2   P-40 into battle - 3 Squadron in Syria

3 Squadron RAAF moved to Lydda by 14 May, and its first two Tomahawks (AK407 and AK410) were delivered from 102 Maintenance Unit at Abusueir by Sqn. Ldr. Jeffrey and Fl. Lt. Perrin. FO Lindsay Knowles and PO Wilf Arthur brought AK388 and AK439 on the sixteenth. On 17 May, a Gauntlet was provided for refresher training for eight newly joined pilots posted in from the Middle East Pool on 30 April, and who had done no flying for approximately five months. These pilots were Sergeants P.J. Reid, M.J. Baillie, R.K. Wilson, G.E. Hiller, A.C. Cameron, D. Scott, H.M. Smeeton and M.P. Randell.

The unfamiliar new aircraft caused a certain amount of trouble. On 18 May FO Knowles swung on landing, the subsequent ground loop causing the starboard wing to strike the ground, inflicting damage which was not repairable in the squadron. The tail wheel of the Gauntlet was damaged on 19 May, which meant that the training for the newly joined pilots was curtailed. Tomahawks AK365 and AK366 were delivered on this date.

Next day Fl.Lt. Pelly found that the port undercarriage leg of his aircraft would not lock down, and it collapsed on landing, the damage once again being of sufficient magnitude to require repairs beyond the Squadron's capabilities. On the 21st AK354 was taken on charge, and AK388 was returned on 23 May. On 26 May FO Davidson failed to land straight down the runway in AK474, (its delivery flight) and veered, hitting AK365 which was parked along side.

Tomahawk troubles. On 26 May FO Davidson swung on landing in AK474 and hit AK365, which was parked near the runway at Lydda. (RAAF Museum)

Perhaps it was unfamiliarity with the layout of the American controls, (and poor design of the cockpit layout) which caused FO Bothwell to select 'Wheels Up' instead of 'Flaps Up' at the end of his landing run on 30 May. AK407 subsided beneath him, again requiring repairs beyond the squadron's resources. Lt Smith, a South African flying with the Australians, damaged AK440 on his way from the M.U. in a landing accident at Ismalia. By this stage of proceedings, thirteen Tomahawks had been taken on charge, of which six had been damaged in accidents. Lt Smith came to the attention of the maintenance engineers again several days later, when he attempted to land on an unfinished portion of the runway, where the port undercarriage leg struck a surveyor's peg and broke. He opened the throttle and flew several circuits, finally achieving a successful crash landing with no further damage.

Alan Rawlinson, by now one of 3 Squadron's Flight Commanders, recorded his impressions of the conversion and training period.

> We received our first Tomahawks and started flying, but had an unfortunate run of landing accidents. The advice given was to bring them in a bit faster than the Hurricane, wheel them on and let the tail come down later - no three pointers. The tail wheel had an amount of steer which helped when taxying and at low speeds after landing. Lydda airport had wide but not very long runways - a civil airport. The surface was concrete. It was our first experience of using runways.
>
> We started with about five aircraft, all of us doing a short flight and a few quick circuits, accepting the advice from our American friends. There were no pilots' notes or handbooks. After a few landings, the problems showed up. Undercarriage legs started to collapse after quite respectable landings. Pilot A or B appeared to land O.K., but the next pilot, C, after a perfect landing would have a leg collapse well after touch down. We sorted it out to a light radius rod at the top of the legs. On retraction, the legs came backwards and turned 90 degrees through a bevel gear which allowed the wheels to fit flat into a recess in the wings. The radius rod played a function here. However, when landing fast on the concrete surface in a tail up attitude, the legs were jarred backwards and, because of the bevel gear function, with a rotating tweak. The radius rod could not take it and broke. It was most annoying, damaging quite a few aircraft before we found the reason - and aircraft were in short supply. We reverted to three point landings and had some minor trouble on the runways in cross wind. The steering tail wheel contributed to this. So - we settled for slower tail down wheelers and had no more trouble.[1]

There were other unforseen troubles. 250 Squadron was reforming, and its equipment was also the Tomahawk. On 2 June, a twenty-nine year old Australian with the unit, PO Clive Caldwell, took off in AK398, and 'the hood blew off just after he had left the ground. . . Although he was momentarily knocked out, he landed the a/c safely'.[2] Lt. Momyer related: 'A number of canopies were flying off in flight which had caused a good deal of concern by (sic) the British. I checked a reported failure and found that the mechanics were failing to safety the canopy catch and also not putting the rear part of the canopy on the canopy track. . . .The technical orders covering the canopy arrived three months after they had the airplanes'.[3]

3 Squadron's difficulties came to the attention of Air Marshal Tedder, AOC-in-C, who 'wrote pessimistically to the Air Ministry on 3 June: "I am afraid that No.3 with their Tomahawks will not be ready for operations. The Australians are very unexpectedly making heavy weather over the Tomahawks, but I have applied a little ginger which, I hope, will have the necessary effect".'[4] His appreciation of the situation was a little harsh, in the light of Lt. Momyer's observations, who 'found the British working on their Tomahawks in a vacuum of information. "When I arrived, there were no technical orders or written instructions on American equipment in the entire Middle East Command. There were very few British mechanics who had ever seen American equipment". '[5]

3 Squadron's first and only training fatality occurred on 5 June when Sgt. Norman Evans crashed in an orange grove a short distance from the airfield. There were no witnesses to the accident other than several Arabs. What could be gleaned from them suggested that the aircraft struck the ground in an apparent spiral dive. It was thought possible that Sgt Evans blacked out from an earlier aerobatic manoeuvre.

On 7 June AK388 was delivered from Abusueir, and in spite of the training and maintenance difficulties, the Squadron was deemed to be ready for action, which was not long in coming.

'On the 7 June we were told there was to be an offensive move into Syria *the next day (Author's italics)* and were given our operational tasks. Never a dull moment. We only had eight Tomahawks. The only ammunition for our .5's was ball and armour piercing. No high explosive or incendiary'.[6]

Due to fears of increasing German influence in the area, and an indication that the Vichy French had made plans 'to withdraw troops into the Lebanon and pass Syria over to German control',[7] Operation *Exporter* was planned: advance into Vichy French Syria and secure the airfields at Damascus, Beirut and Rayak.

General Wavell was reluctant to take any action in this area, as he was preparing to launch his first offensive from Egypt towards Libya since the arrival of the *Afrika Korps*. He was overruled by the Chiefs of Staff and Winston Churchill, and plans for an advance by the Australian 7th Division, two cavalry regiments, the 5th Indian Infantry Brigade and a Free French force were put in place. Naval support for the left flank of the force as it advanced up the Lebanese coast was provided by the 15th Cruiser Squadron, consisting of HMS *Phoebe, Ajax* and *Coventry,* a landing support ship and eight destroyers. As part of the small number of squadrons available for air support, 3 Squadron RAAF were to take their new Tomahawks into action for the first time.

In the early hours of 8 June, five Tomahawks flown by Peter Jeffrey, (AK476) Jock Perrin, (AK427) PO John Saunders, (AK354) FO Bobby Gibbes, (AK393) and PO Eric Lane (AK366) took off to attack the French base at Rayak, which had already been attacked ineffectually by three Hurricanes of 80 Squadron RAF. The Tomahawks destroyed a D520 of GC III/6 and hit five more, damaging two of them seriously.

This was Bobby Gibbes' first combat experience, and very nearly his last, as he explained in his autobiography.

> I was selected for the morning show, together with five [sic] other pilots, the C.O. to lead. The thought of justifying my training by coming to grips with the enemy, was somehow satisfying, and at the same time, rather frightening. I think that I was afraid that I would not be able to conquer my fear of facing possible death. I was about to be put to the test.

> We were called before dawn and we hurriedly dressed and donned our flying gear. I needed no call as I had been awake for most of the night worrying about the morrow. During the final briefing, our target, together with formation details, and method of attack, were outlined by Peter Jeffrey, our commanding officer. We were going to strafe the Rayak aerodrome in Syria, a Vichy French Air Force base.

> On climbing into my Tomahawk, my fear started to abate and was being replaced by a growing excitement. It had gone completely by the time we started our engines and became airborne at first light. . .

> On nearing Rayak, we went into starboard echelon and dived down selecting aircraft parked on the ground as our targets. I shot up an old biplane, type unknown, and somehow, due to my inexperience and stupidity, I ended up under Jock's aircraft. He was shooting at a square building on the western side of the aerodrome, and I flew in a shower of his empty cartridge cases, within a foot or so of the surface of the field. I was not able to bank and turn away without colliding, and I tried desperately to skid from beneath him. He finally pulled up and I was able to clear his target by a few feet only. It was an awfully close shave, and Jock had no idea of how close we both went to joining our maker. I never told him. We had really tempted fate that day.[8]

No enemy aircraft were encountered for several days, and the squadron was occupied with ground attacks on aerodromes, troops and motor transport (M/T). On 9 June Fl. Lt. Alan Rawlinson experienced engine failure on take off in AK439 and force-landed ahead, wheels up, in a cultivated field. Subsequent examination revealed that the no. 2 connecting rod assembly had failed. On the 11th, Sgt. Smeeton returned to Lydda with a faulty engine and damaged AK435 on landing.

On 13 June, eight Tomahawks led by Sqn. Ldr. Jeffrey took off at 1450 to provide air cover for the cruiser squadron. The patrol arrived at the same time as a formation of Ju88s which were about to commence a bombing attack on the vessels. The Squadron's Operations Record Book (ORB) records that these aircraft carried Italian markings, but they were in fact from II/LG 1 based on Crete. After the speedy attack delivered by 3 Squadron, claims were submitted by Peter Jeffrey, (AK476) Jock Perrin (AK464) and John Saunders (AK427) while two more were claimed as damaged. In fact, two Ju88s failed to return, one from 4 Staffel (L1+DM) flown by Lt. Dickjobst, and one from 5 Staffel, flown by Lt. Bennewitz.[9]

Peter Jeffrey's combat report showed his approval of the Tomahawk's performance, if not the aircraft recognition abilities of the fleet's gunners.

> Saw enemy aircraft on starboard bow in line astern about to commence dive bombing of fleet from 15,000 ft. Turned towards them but was fired on by own A.A. so turned round it to intercept enemy on other side of A.A. Saw one Ju88 being attacked by two other Tomahawks and as they broke off the attacks I commenced making quarter and beam attacks.

> Starboard engine burst into flames and enemy made off towards BEYROUTH, attacked again and apparently put other engine out of action as enemy glided down and into the sea. Aircraft broke up badly on striking water.

> It appears that a Tomahawk can easily catch the JU. 88's (sic) and manoeuvre so as to make any attack desired by pilot. This is borne out by other pilots that took part in the combat.

Fl. Lt. Jock Perrin's appreciation of the action was succinct.

> I dived on one aircraft and carried out a stern attack, - overshot and turned. I then carried out a head on attack - The aircraft dived straight into the sea.

This might have been the same aircraft attacked by John Saunders, who reported:

> On sighting aircraft my flight leader climbed and then attacked. I followed and badly damaged one during a steep dive. Smoke was pouring from one engine. This a/c was immediately attacked by another one of our a/c.

> I sighted another making out to sea at about 40 ft. I made many attacks from all angles. Each time he attempted to turn inside me. Smoke was pouring from port engine and one wing. Shortly after he crashed about 10 miles out to sea. The crew of 4 were swimming near crashed a/c.

FO Frank Fischer also attacked one of the Junkers, noting that some dropped bombs as they were attacked, while others appeared to jettison bombs. The second machine he attacked had smoke coming from its starboard engine, and he then saw another Tomahawk attack this Ju88, which finally caught fire and went down into the sea. He formated on this aircraft and found it to be the CO.

These reports indicate that it was possible for pilots to attack the same aircraft without always being aware of the presence of their companions. If German records show that only two Ju88s were lost, clearly one of them must have been shared by at least two pilots.

At this point it should be made clear that this narrative is not an attempt to re-write history, or refute claims made by pilots in perfectly good faith, under the conditions which prevailed at the time of the events being described. Intelligence officers accepted or rejected claims on the information available to them at the time. In almost every theatre of aerial combat, over claiming was inevitably prevalent, as a result of several pilots attacking the same target within a very compressed time frame, and being totally unaware of their companions' actions.

To give a clear example of this, one only needs to refer to the action fought at approximately 1730 on 18 August 1940. On this day ZG 26 lost thirteen Bf110s in combat, and two more were written off in crash-landings in France. Nine were shot down in the early afternoon, and another four in the late afternoon. 85 Squadron claimed *six* Bf110s in the latter combat, as well as single claims by 56 and 54 Squadron pilots, both of whom were credited with victories. Four of 85 Squadron's claims were seen to go into the sea, and another was a 'flamer'. Both the 54 and 56 Squadron claims crashed on land. When it is possible to compare claims directly with admitted losses, it will be seen on occasions that they do not always correspond.[10]

The pilots of 3 Squadron had good reason to be pleased with their performance. Two more of the Ju 88s were damaged, (FO Gibbes claiming a probable) and no damage was sustained by any of the Tomahawks. The successful pilots, Peter Jeffrey, Jock Perrin and John Saunders were well seasoned in air combat, having already made claims for one, five and three enemy aircraft earlier in the year while the Squadron was flying Hurricanes.

On 15 June FO Saunders (AK464) took off at 1215 hrs. on a recce flight and returned to report 12 AFV (armoured fighting vehicles) and 40 M/T (motor transport vehicles). At 1740 hrs. seven Tomahawks took off to attack these, and encountered two Martin 167s of GB I/39. The Squadron immediately attacked and both aircraft were shot down, victories being awarded to Peter Jeffrey and FO Peter Turnbull, whose combat report follows.

> On sighting a/c climbed from 7 to 8000 ft, by which time the E/A. were under us and splitting up. I chased one eastwards and making three stern attacks, setting the stbd. engine on fire. He tried to get away after dropping his bombs - one man parachuted so I followed him until it crashed and burnt.
>
> I then caught up to the second E/A. and gave it a long burst after which it crashed, two men escaping.
>
> The a/c were mottle camouflaged, and are easy to identify on top by the white circle of the roundel.

FO Peter Turnbull already had four victories on Hurricanes, and a probable from the Squadron's Gladiator days.

Peter Jeffrey reported two people getting out from the aircraft which he attacked, and "saw the other Glenn Martin crash". It thus seems likely that his victim was No.111 which crashed near Deraa, Lt. Baron and two of his crew being wounded, while the other machine, No.118, crashed in flames, Sgt Chef Tanchoux's crew all being killed.[11]

The Tomahawks then carried out their strafing attack successfully and returned to base, where Alan Rawlinson suffered his second bout of mechanical trouble, finding that he could not lock down the undercarriage, and the aircraft was extensively damaged on landing.

No further contact was made with enemy aircraft until 19 June, when a flight of Tomahawks led by Fl. Lt. Rawlinson encountered eight Martin 167s from Escadrilles 6B and 7B. The Tomahawks had been escorting a Blenheim dropping leaflets. Alan Rawlinson's combat report relates what happened next.

> Enemy observed flying south ahead and to port . We were down sun and flying very slow (sic) covering the Blenheim. Opened up and passed over to the sun going down on the last formation. Enemy immediately dived to port, 6 of them closing formation. Some bombs were dropped. Engaged enemy at beam and developed into quarter and then stern at 300 yds. After a reasonable burst both .5's stopped Broke off and reloaded.
>
> Chased enemy at full throttle and eventually came within 250 yds. of a lone E/A. Gave him a good burst and tracers were seen to enter the fuselage - only .5 shooting. Enemy then S.E. of Beirut suburbs. Enemy a/c port wing went down and was diving steeply.
>
> Due to slow speed when enemy sighted (145) and down sun position the best advantage was lost. Great difficulty was found in catching them once they dived.

FO Bothwell also fired at the Martins, without observing any damage. He *did* however report that 'guns appeared to fire satisfactorily', an indication that the squadron had been experiencing difficulties with the reliability of their weapons. In fact, two of the Martins were hit; 7B-3 of Lt de V De Gail at the rear of the formation suffered severe damage, and 6B-6 of Ens de V Lacoste left the formation after being hit.[12] Nine days later, the same two units would clash again, with tragic results for the French.

On 23 June the Tomahawks had their first encounter with Vichy fighters during an airfield strafing operation. They attacked Qousseir airfield, which they identified as El Asir, in the Kousseir area.[13] They left an aircraft burning, set fire to a hangar, and then encountered nine D520s from GC III/6 which had been scrambled from Rayak to intercept. The Tomahawks held the height advantage, and dived on the Dewoitines, their initial attack setting fire to the D520 of Sous Lt Le Gloan, who left the fight rapidly. FO Bothwell (AK420) shot down two D520s, the aircraft of Lt Stenou and Sgt Savinel, both of whom were killed. Cne Richard claimed one Tomahawk destroyed. Sgt Reid in AK370 had his starboard wing holed by cannon fire, FO Lindsay Knowles (AK436) reported shooting the wingtip off one of the D520s and claimed a damaged.

On 25 June eight aircraft flew to LG H-4 and after refuelling took off at 1330 on an offensive patrol in the Palmyra area. After ten minutes, the Tomahawks encountered three LeO 451s from GB I/12, which were mis-identified as four Potez 63s, (an excusable error as both types were twin engined bombers with oval shaped fins carried on dihedral tailplanes.) All three were shot down, one each by FO John Jackson, (AK366) who had four earlier Hurricane victories to his credit, FO John Saunders,(AK393) his fifth victory, and Sgt Alan Cameron,(AK436) his first. Cameron was one of the replacement pilots from 30 April whose training for the Tomahawk began on the old Gauntlet.

FO Jewell reported setting the starboard engine of one alight, and this was last seen losing height. It was later confirmed as having crashed and he was credited with a victory, but as there were only three French machines in the formation, he must have attacked one of the aircraft shot down by the other three pilots. Five of the twelve crew men were killed.

At 0605 on 26 June, Fl. Lt. Alan Rawlinson led nine Tomahawks on a devastating low level attack on the enemy airfields at Homs, Qousseir and Rayak.

> These airfield attacks were always carefully planned. All large stationery targets, particularly airfields, were usually well defended with flak of all sizes. I planned to approach Homs airfield from the east, down a long west facing mountain slope, just as the sun appeared over the mountain ridge top behind us. It went well. We came down the slope, keeping the speed at 200 mph in a spread out vic so as to cover the whole airfield in one pass, with the sun behind us and at a speed which allowed for better sighting and longer bursts of fire.
>
> There were railway lines running north and south right along the eastern boundary fence of the airfield. Our line of approach took us across the railway at right angles. It all went perfectly. The Dewoitine D520 fighters were lined up with ground crews all over them doing daily inspections. It was about 8 am and a beautiful morning.
>
> I opened up on the nearest aircraft in the line, but just a little too early. My fire hit the top of a train and something at the fence line, which was set alight. I lifted my sight onto the first aircraft, firing, then on to the next and so on through the first line of about eight all told. The first aircraft burned, but I had no time to assess the damage to the rest. Ground crews were going in all directions. I went down right on the deck, straight ahead away from the target area; then pulled up slightly for the rest of the formation to see and follow me, turning south down the main road. I looked back at the target and saw a large grey mushroom shaped cloud rising up to a couple of thousand feet. It was confirmed later that the fire on the fence line was fuel which set alight to the train loaded with explosives and it blew up.
>
> We continued on with the strafe down the road to [Qousseir] airfield where I hit a transport, a tent and a dump, and at Rayak I damaged another Dewoitine. On the road south I hit a staff car, two transports and an armoured fighting vehicle.[14]

Seven D520s were lost to ground attack during the campaign, six of them to 3 Squadron during this operation.

There were no operations on 27 June, but the next day 3 Squadron had its second encounter with the Martin 167s of Flotille 4F. Nine Tomahawks led by Alan Rawlinson took off for Damascus-Mezze where they refuelled, taking off again at 1015 to escort Blenheims on a bombing raid. Five minutes earlier six Martin 167s from Escadrilles 6B and 7B had taken off, in two sections.

Following is Alan Rawlinson's translation from *L'Aviation de Vichy Au Combat - La Campagne de Syrie 8 juin - 14 juillet 1941,* by Christian J.Ehrengardt and Christopher Shores, which tells the tragic story from the French point of view.

Every war brings many tragedies. The Syrian Campaign was no exception. But in the course of this one, no aviation drama compares to that which struck the L'Aeronavale on the 28th June 1941.

It was 1010 when six Glenn Martins of 4F Flotilla took off in two sections, each with a crew of four.

7B-5 Lt deV Laine	6B-3 Lt de V Ziegler
7B-4 OE Le Friant	6B-4 Ens de V Playe
	6B-6 Ens de V Lacoste
	7B-6 Lt de V De Gail

The first section of two aircraft was to bomb troops assembled at the Iraq Petroleum Bay, south west of Palmyra.

The second section was to attack another concentration at the North Oasis of Mohammed Ben Ali.

Early that afternoon(sic) nine Tomahawks of No.3 RAAF Squadron left Jenin for Damascus-Mezze airfield, refuelled, and left to provide an escort to a formation of Blenheims over Palmyra. After the Blenheims bombed, the Australians returned to the area. They saw clouds of smoke from the bombs dropped by L'Aeronavale. It was 1145.

The Tomahawks suddenly appeared behind the French, spreading out into three groups of two aircraft, and then made their first pass. It was an ideal situation as they didn't have to worry about French fighters in the area. They were able to open fire calmly and with determination.

In less than three minutes all six bombers fell in flames and the wreckage was scattered over the desert.

6B-3, 6B-4, 6B-6 and 7B-4 crashed to earth. There were no survivors.

7B-6, hit by the first burst, tried to escape down to ground level, but was caught and mercilessly attacked. Quartermaster Sarotte was able to escape by parachute. Sergeant Major Guerat, bleeding, also had the chance. They were both taken prisoner.

Lieutenant Laine in 7B-5 did a quick turn to the right. He was surprised not to see his No.2, Friant. Tightly held in his seat, he sadly tried to find the other Glenns. He could not see the column of black smoke descending. Intrigued, he searched to his rear. His blood ran cold. Three P-40s have caught him. In a fraction of a second, he knows that Friant has gone down. Two fighters were along side, while the third was in a good position to open fire. The first burst destroys the rear fuselage and the left engine starts to burn. Another burst destroys his instrument panel. Laine calls his two machine gunners without response. His R/T is destroyed. They are both dead or wounded. Laine did appreciate the fire power of the P-40.

He dived to earth to avoid another attack. The fighter's second attack hits the right wing. The aircraft becomes uncontrollable. Laine hesitates a moment. He is too low to bale out. The risk is great as he doesn't know the other two men in the back are not in a state to jump. Ensign Massicot is jammed in his cupola and has more troubles than in the cabin. He chooses to put down on the ground quickly. The Glenn Martin's left wing is burning and he puts down on a sand dune, losing speed quickly. It is a hard jolt. Massicot is ejected through the plexiglass cupola and suffers multiple fractures. Laine is half stunned as he hits the instrument panel but remains conscious and tries to get out of the wreckage quickly. He opens the window and jumps through the flames. Unfortunately he has trouble with the automatic parachute cable and falls on his knees in the inferno. In spite of the flames he reaches Massicot to save Quarter Master Libouban and Quarter Master Parmentir. At that moment the rear of the fuselage is shaken by exploding 10 kg. bombs which blocks his path and stops him from reaching the other two injured people who may have been killed in the last attack.

Laine has two burnt legs from ankle to thigh and his right arm in tatters. His brow is bleeding freely and his face swollen.

Massicot has a bullet in his back as well as burns and multiple fractures. In this condition, these two men, alone in the desert, without water start to walk north. They are fortunate to be rescued by some Bedouins who take them to T4.[15]

The attack by 3 Squadron's Tomahawks on lightly armed and unescorted bombers illustrates the futility of sending such aircraft out without fighter cover. Similar disasters were to befall the Marylands of the SAAF later in the desert war.

Alan Rawlinson (AK446) was responsible for the destruction of 6B-3, 6B-4, (the first two aircraft to fall) and 7B-5, the last, graphically described in the translation. FO Peter Turnbull (AK476) accounted for 6B-6 in the initial attack, and then 7B-6, while Sgt. Rex Wilson (AK429) shot down OE Le Friant's 7B-4, Lt Laine's No.2.

The other Australian pilots who took part in this action were Sgt. Randall, (AK427) FO E Jackson (AK464) Sgt. Baillie, (AK420) FO Arthur, (AK378) FO Tom Trimble (AM398) and FO Knowles, (AK436) who somehow found himself in front of Lt Laine's 7B-5 and attacked it from about the 2 o'clock position, passing so close over the top of Alan Rawlinson that the roar of his engine could be heard!

The Tomahawks landed back at Damascus-Mezze for refuelling, but when they took off to return to Jenin, Sgt. Michael Randall suffered engine failure, and was killed when the aircraft crashed.

On 29 June, eight Tomahawks took off from Rosh Pinna for Damascus where they refuelled at 1745 to carry out a low flying attack on Qousseir. Here they found a number of Martins, three of

3 Squadron pilots at Rosh Pinna in northern Palestine during the Syrian campaign. Left to right: Sgts. Rex Wilson, Dudley Parker, Derek Scott, Geoffrey Hiller; FOs Bill Kloster, Peter Turnbull; Fl. Lt. Jock Perrin; Sqn. Ldr. Peter Jeffrey; Sgt. Alan 'Tiny' Cameron; Fl. Lt. Alan Rawlinson, Sqn. Ldr. John Laver (Medical Officer, partly obscured); FOs John Saunders, Wally Jewell; Fl. Lt. Lindsay Knowles; FO Tom Trimble. (Alan Rawlinson)

which were destroyed by strafing. A fourth was damaged as well as a Farman and a D338. A Glenn Martin was seen in the air during this attack, and FO Arthur and FO Knowles gave chase, pursuing the unfortunate Frenchmen for 30 minutes, before Knowles (AK436) shot it down into the sea 20 odd miles west of Beirut. Sous Lt Lefroid and his crew were killed.

The squadron was occupied with ground attack duties for the next ten days, encountering no enemy activity in the air, but on 10 July they were involved in a fierce clash with the D520s of Esc 1 AC. Seven Tomahawks took off at 1025 to escort twelve Blenheims of 45 Squadron RAF, tasked to bomb an ammunition dump near Hamana, south of Beirut. The Tomahawks were considerably higher than the Blenheims, which carried out their attack successfully, but the explosions were seen by the D520 pilots, who were in a position to attack the bombers head on from below. Before the Australians could react, three Blenheims were shot down and another so badly damaged that it crash-landed on return. The burning Blenheims alerted the Tomahawk pilots to the situation and they dived to repel the attack. They believed that they had destroyed all five D520s, two being awarded to FO Turnbull (AK386), and one each to FO John Jackson (AM378), PO Lane(AK526) and Sgt Hiller (AK476). French records show that only two Dewoitines failed to return, one pilot losing his life and the other baling out successfully.

Fl. Lt. Alan Rawlinson preparing to take off in AM386 for his last patrol of the Syrian campaign; 1645 hours on 10 July. (Alan Rawlinson)

11 July proved to be the last day of hostilities, as well as the day when 3 Squadron lost its first Tomahawk in combat. In the morning six Tomahawks flew up to Palmyra where they were joined by a dozen Hurricanes from two British units. After refuelling the formation left at 1200 to strafe the airfields around Aleppo. At roughly the same time, nine D520s of GC II/3 set off to escort three LeO 451s. Lt Lete experienced engine trouble and lagged behind his companions. Flying alone, he spotted some of the Tomahawks and attacked successfully, shooting down FO Frank Fischer, who had been acting as "swinger"(in the terminology of 3's ORB), ie. weaving behind the others to warn them of impending attack. That this technique was less than successful on many occasions is now well appreciated. However it was an accepted tactic at the time, and it

took the needless loss of many a good pilot before more effective alternatives were found. * Lete was attacked by both FO John Jackson and FO Bobby Gibbes(AK464), who pursued the Dewoitine until it crash-landed. Jackson and Gibbes were jointly responsible, but they agreed to toss a coin for the victory, which Gibbes won![16] Thus it was recorded as his first victory, Jackson by now being credited with six, two of which were in Tomahawks.

The Squadron believed that Fischer had been killed, but he rejoined the squadron when the fighting was over after having been assisted and concealed from French troops by friendly Arabs.

During a final strafing attack on some vehicles and guns, FO Lindsay Knowles was hit by AA fire and crash-landed his Tomahawk in friendly territory.

3 Squadron had proven that the Tomahawk was an effective fighter, being more than a match for the D520, which had given the Hurricanes a difficult time. Ten Hurricanes were lost to the French fighter, while only two of the eleven D520s lost fell to Hurricanes, four to 'X' Flight's Gladiators (in exchange for only one lost Gladiator) and five to the Tomahawks.

For the remainder of July and all of August, 3 Squadron remained in the Middle East, finally based at Rayak, where they were not involved in further combat operations. Fl. Lt. Jock Perrin left the unit to return to Australia. FOs John Jackson, Lindsay Knowles, Peter Turnbull and John Saunders were all promoted to Fl. Lt., back dated to 1 July. The unit had a core of experienced and successful pilots to continue the battle. On 1 September orders were received for a move to the Desert, and on 8 September, the Squadron started to settle in at their new base; LG 102 at Sidi Heneish.

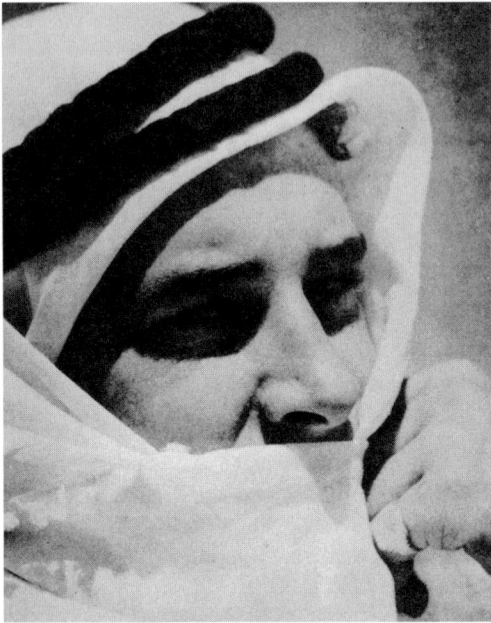

FO Frank Fischer after returning from being shot down during the last operation of the Syrian campaign. The Squadron reported him as missing, believed killed, but he was hidden by friendly Arabs until the fighting was over. (Alan Rawlinson)

* Bob Whittle of 250 Squadron actually enjoyed the 'weaver's trade'. In response to a question about its effectiveness or dangers, he said "Being a weaver was an exciting part of the formation - having first contact with the enemy!"

AM386, named *Sweet FA* by Alan Rawlinson. A new aircraft, it was only flown operationally in Syria on seven occasions by Rawlinson and Peter Turnbull, before losing its starboard tailplane while Fl. Lt. Rawlinson was flying aerobatics on 22 August. He carried out a skilful landing without flaps at 150 mph, but the excessive speed caused it to tip on to its nose in a drainage ditch at the end of the runway.
(Alan Rawlinson)

SUMMARY OF 3 SQUADRON'S OPERATIONS IN THE SYRIAN CAMPAIGN

AIR COMBAT VICTORIES		E/A DESTROYED or DAMAGED BY STRAFING		
Ju88	2	D520	7	24
LeO 451	3	LeO 451	7	7
D520	5	M-167F	3	1
Martin 167F	9	Pz25TOE	3	
		Misc.		3
Total	19 (24 claims)	Totals	20	35

(9 more French aircraft were destroyed by
other British fighter units, against 17 claims)

LOSSES - AIR COMBAT	GROUND FIRE	DAMAGED (Air Combat)
1 FO Fischer 11 July	1 Sgt. Baillie 26 June	1 Sgt Reid 23 June
	2 FO Knowles 11 July	

(Fischer returned to the unit after cessation of hostilities.)

(Baillie and Knowles crash-landed in friendly territory; Reid brought his damaged aircraft back to base.)

C hapter 3   Tomahawks in the Desert

When the Desert war began in June 1940, the RAF in the Middle East was little more than a second line force, with no immediate possibility of reinforcement, or re-equipment with more modern aircraft. The RAF had suffered significant losses of aircrews and aircraft in France, and the Battle of Britain was yet to begin. When it did, production of fighters increased significantly, but the training establishments were stretched to the limit to meet the demands of the hard pressed fighter squadrons.

The most modern fighters available to Air Commodore Raymond Collishaw, commanding 202 Group, were the Gloster Gladiators of 33, 80 and 112 Squadrons. Only one squadron of Blenheim IVs was available, the remainder of the bomber force consisting of four Blenheim I Squadrons. The sole Hurricane in the Desert (nick-named *Collie's Battleship*) belonged to 80 Squadron. Nevertheless, these units quickly established air superiority over the considerably greater numbers of *Regia Aeronautica* aircraft, and were able to provide excellent air support to General Richard O'Connor's forces when Operation *Compass* began on 9 December 1940.

By then, the trans-Africa supply route from Takoradi on the Gold Coast had been established, and on 28 November, 73 Squadron left there with the first Hurricanes bound for Egypt. Ironically, the dominance of the RAF and the success of O'Connor's Western Desert Force led to the arrival of the Luftwaffe, and the pendulum swung in favour of the Axis forces. The departure for Greece of 80 Squadron in November, followed by 112 in January 1941, and 33 during February, had already weakened the RAF's desert fighter force, and by the time Rommel had invested Tobruk in April, only three Hurricane squadrons, 73 and 274 RAF, and 3 RAAF were available to support the ground forces.

Initial German deployments were I/StG 1 and II/StG 2, (Ju87s) III/ZG 26, (Bf110s) and III/KLG 1 (Ju88s). The aircrews of these units were confident and experienced, and far more dangerous opponents than their Italian allies. I/JG 27 flew its first operation on 19 April, and immediately established a degree of superiority over the hard pressed Hurricane units, which nevertheless continued to take their toll of Axis aircraft, although they were almost always outnumbered and at a height disadvantage.

When the first Tomahawks began to arrive at Takoradi in March, they caused a bottleneck. By the end of April, there were over 200, all lacking spares and tool kits. It was to be some considerable time before they would be deployed in any numbers, but the RAF was making great strides in adapting to the difficult conditions of the desert environment, and problems were steadily overcome.

It was at Beaverbrook's suggestion that Air Vice-Marshal G. G. Dawson, one of his assistants at the Ministry of Aircraft Production, was sent out to the Middle East in mid-May to investigate and advise on the whole question of maintenance and repair. This was welcomed by Tedder, who knew Dawson from his own days at the ministry. And Dawson, as well as being an engineer specialist, was a "ball of fire". The impetus which he lost no time in imparting in all directions quickly transformed the repair and salvage arrangements of the Command. The Maintenance Units were expanded and increased; local resources and civilian labour was exploited [and] salvage units were given a long-needed mobility.[1]

250 Squadron RAF re-formed with Tomahawks on 1 April 1941. Based at Aqir in Palestine, they became operational on 11 May, when 'ten pilots and aircraft were at once ordered to Amriya for the air defence of Alexandria'.[2] The remainder of the Squadron joined them on 25 May, the whole unit moving to Lake Maryut on the outskirts of Alexandria.

At 0815 on 29 May, four Tomahawks took off to intercept an intruder, which turned out to be a Ju88, ten miles from Alexandria, on a bearing of 30 degrees. FO G.B. Smither (RAF) attacked, and left it with a smoking port engine. The engagement was inconclusive, as the Ju88 could not be found after the first attack due to poor visibility. The Tomahawks were above 26,000 feet, and PO Archie Wilson blacked out due to oxygen failure. He regained consciousness to find the aircraft

> diving over the vertical at full power sans the cockpit canopy, which had just blown off. As I tried to reach for the engine controls I was subjected to very violent buffeting followed by what I can only think must have been a degree of structural failure as suddenly, despite the erstwhile security of my harness, I was dragged out of the cockpit over the fuselage striking something solid, possibly part of the tail section, and then oblivion.

When he regained consciousness, he had difficulty with the 'D' Ring, as the parachute was a Battle of Britain relic used by 250's CO, John Scoular, as a seat cushion in the ops room, and had not been re-packed since 1940! After a struggle he got it to work, and hit the water seconds after the canopy deployed.

Sgt. Bob Whittle, his No.2, stayed with him and his 'prompt action' in giving an accurate bearing to control enabled them to send out a Sunderland flying boat of 230 Squadron to pick up Wilson some forty-two miles off the coast. He spent over two hours in the water before being rescued. *

Amongst the pilots of 250 Squadron there were numerous Australians: another of these was Sgt. Tom Paxton from Sydney, * who has a claim to fame. In company with FO Hamlyn on 8 June, Paxton (AK398) shared in the destruction of a Cant Z1007 of 211[a] Squadriglia over Alexandria, to record the first air combat victory of a Curtiss fighter of the P-40 series, preceding the kills scored by 3 RAAF in Syria by five days.

On 11 June 250 Squadron moved forward to 'Sidi Haneish, to take part in the impending army campaign designed to relieve Tobruk',[3] Operation *Battleaxe,* which opened on 14 June.

---

* After the war, Archie Wilson became Chief of Staff of the Rhodesian Air Force, and retired as Air Marshal A.O.G. Wilson ICD OBE DFC (US). He emigrated to Australia, and maintained his friendship with Bob Whittle, whose wife Frankie provided a letter to the Caterpillar Club written by AM Wilson in 1989, which gave the details of his bale out.

* There is some doubt whether Tom Paxton was in fact an Australian citizen, or merely resident in Australia for a period long enough for his colleagues to have regarded him as such. His service number indicates that he joined the RAFVR, and his loss is not recorded on the AWM Roll of Honour Data Base. The Commonwealth War Graves Commission lists his parents' address in England. Notwithstanding these facts, both volumes of 'Aces High' record him as an Australian.

For three days No.250 flew a series of standing patrols over the battlefield, meeting very few enemy aircraft; but when, on 18th June, the land battle swung very much in the enemy's favour, Tedder intervened and ordered all fighters to concentrate on ground strafing. This was done, the Tomahawks of No. 250 concentrating on the main Capuzzo-El Adem roads. Although effective this was relatively costly, as four pilots, including one Australian were lost on one such operation. [4]

On this day 250 lost one aircraft to AA, and three pilots to the Bf109s of JG27, including PO Donald Munro (AK383), who baled out. The squadron considered that he was fired on during his parachute descent.

The squadron's CO, Sqn.Ldr. John Scoular, a veteran from 73 Squadron in France, shot down a G-50 on 25 June, for what John Rawlings calls 'first confirmed victory'.[5] (The ORB noted that the Cant attacked by Paxton and Hamlyn on 8 June was finally destroyed by shore batteries when it appeared to be about to force-land. Hamlyn also engaged a Ju88 on 10 June, which was recorded by the squadron as inconclusive, although it was left with both engines smoking.)

On the following day, 250 was in the thick of the action. Escorting Blenheims to Gazala, they were met by thirty Axis fighters between Capuzzo and Tobruk. A number of Australian pilots were involved in this action. PO Jim Kent damaged a Bf109, shot down a G-50 and strafed a staff car for good measure. Sgt G.C.(Charlie) Coward destroyed a Bf109, as did PO Clive Caldwell in AK419. (By this time he had recorded 47 hours on the Tomahawk.)

I took off from Sidi Barrani East at 1245 hrs on escort duty to Gazala. On return from Gazala 10 E/A ME109's were sighted which attacked us and immediately dived away. We proceeded past Tobruk and came upon a large dogfight of approx 40 machines below us in the Capuzzo area. I singled out a ME109 and dived on him from the rear. I closed with range and gave him two bursts of fire with all guns. The ME109 continued with the dive, crashed in flames approx 3 miles west of Capuzzo. I climbed up to find another machine but they had all disappeared.

Three Australian pilots of 250 Squadron: from left, Sgt. 'Charlie' Coward, an engineering Warrant Officer known as 'Tubby', Sgt. Mick Ryan and Sgt. Richard 'Slinger' Nitschke. The nick name 'Slinger' came from a successful Australian fast bowler called Nitschke who had an unusual slinging action. (Bob Whittle)

Tom Paxton (AK446) claimed another Bf109, (finally recorded by the squadron as a probable), while Sgt. David Gale (AK349) was shot down and killed.

250 Squadron maintained an informal diary of day to day events. Its tone suggests that it was kept by the CO, with occasional input from the Adjutant. This day's events warranted considerable attention, and it seems clear that Clive Caldwell relieved some apparent frustration caused by having not previously encountered the enemy in the air.

The patrol came back in two(s) and threes, with stories of bringing down M.E. 109's & G.50's, also beating up a staff car, all of which was most exciting. P/O Caldwell shot down an ME109, having shouted over the R/T for five minutes 109, 109, 109 - it is hopeless to try and record here his account . . . each sentence is accompanied by suitable actions and as one follows another so quickly, the listener is not sure where he is - suffice it to say that he has at last seen an E/A in the air and also shot it down.

Then Sgt. Paxton in his very deliberate English, shouts that he has got a 109, in actual fact the 109 is on his tail about two spans away and he brought it right in front of our formation, still shouting that he has got one! Our total bag was 4 Me 109's and 1 G 50, also a staff car.

Tom Paxton did not score again with 250 Squadron before being posted to 30 Squadron, flying Hurricanes. With this unit he shot down a Ju88 in January and a He111 in February. The Squadron was then sent to Ceylon, flying off the aircraft carrier *Indomitable*. Tom Paxton was involved in the interception of the first attack by Japanese carrier based aircraft on Colombo. He shot down two Zeros before being forced to bale out of his burning aircraft. Suffering from second degree burns, he was taken to hospital, but died of shock two days later on 7 April 1942.

Clive Caldwell (AK346) and Sgt. Bob Whittle (AK423) shared one of the two Bf110s of III/ZG 26 which failed to return on 30 June. This combat took place while 250 and 73 Squadrons were escorting a Tobruk convoy. They found an Axis formation consisting of twenty Ju87s and some thirty fighters; G-50s, Bf109s and Bf110s. Jim Kent was shot down and killed by Oblt. Franzisket of I/JG 27.[6] Caldwell destroyed two Ju87s.

In company with Sgt. Whittle I attacked a ME110 at approx 15,000 ft. Sgt. Whittle attacked first from astern and disengaged. I attacked rear quarter and astern and before disengaging observed smoke pouring from starboard engine. Whittle again attacked and saw the E/A continuing dive apparently out of control & smoke coming from starboard engine.

I then observed 2 G.50's approx. 5,000 ft below me heading W. I attacked from above, full deflection. I was unable to observe result of attack.

Losing height to approx. 2,000 ft. I attacked a Ju87 flying above us as it climbed from its own attack, smoke began to come from it, and it quickly caught alight, crashing into the sea in flames.

I then attacked another Ju87 as it was making a turn towards its target. After two bursts from my guns I saw smoke begin to come from it and it also caught fire and went into the sea within 1/2 ml. of the first one.

The ME110 went down approx 6 mls. N.W. of the ships. Time 1735 hrs.

The 2 Ju87s both went down into the sea within 1/2 mile of each other approx 1 ml. to the E.S.E. of the ships and would be plainly visible to personnel aboard them. Time 1743 hrs, 1746 hrs.

Caldwell's log book later noted that all three aircraft were *'confirmed in sea near ships'* but curiously did not acknowledge that he shared the 110 with Bob Whittle. The ORB noted Whittle's part in the attack on the 110, initially recording it as 'badly damaged at 18,000 ft; it was almost certainly destroyed.'

Bob Whittle also claimed an Italian aircraft probable, (mis-identifying a G-50 as a 'Probable Savoia')[7] and a Bf109 as damaged. At this time he had a total of only 5.25 operational hours from eight sorties. Like Clive Caldwell on the 26th, he was successful in his first combat. He was to establish himself as an extremely valuable member of the Squadron in the months to come.

Sgt. Bob Whittle with full flying gear returning
after a successful combat. (Bob Whittle)

250 Squadron were then involved in uneventful convoy escorts for several days, but on 7 July flew a wing sweep with several other squadrons over Bardia. No enemy aircraft were encountered, but

Caldwell, who had become separated from his companions, claimed that he shot down one of two G-50s seen returning to their airfield, and, on his way home, strafed car parks near Salum and killed a number of enemy soldiers. Caldwell was already developing an uncanny gunnery sense which was to bring him great success, and he assiduously practised this by low level firing at his own aircraft's shadow when other targets were lacking.[8]

(His log book noted that this aircraft was confirmed by 73 Sqn and PRU - author)

Caldwell's personal papers contain the following note concerning the development of the 'shadow shooting' technique.

I was not happy with my shooting, and indeed I thought that the average fighter pilot was a poor shot, until I discovered the concept of 'shadow' shooting. When we flew low over the desert, the early morning sun cast racing shadows on the sand. When I first tried to hit a colleague's shadow, I missed; I fired over the shadow and well behind, but with more practice and self correcting I soon mastered the art of deflection shooting with fixed guns.

Later Tedder sent a directive [to] all fighter squadrons of the DAF referred to as the method introduced by P.O. Caldwell of 250 Squadron.

Caldwell damaged Bf109s on 12 July and 3 August, and scored his next success on 16 August, when he shared in the destruction of a G-50 while on a convoy patrol. Caldwell and Whittle claimed Bf109s damaged and probable respectively on 18 August, again while covering ships. Twelve of 250's Tomahawks met twenty Bf109s escorting six bomb carrying Bf110s which immediately jettisoned their bombs when attacked. The Messerschmitts shot down Sgt. Joseph McCullough (AK554), who was killed, and damaged another Tomahawk.

A valuable collection of photographs which gives a good
impression of living conditions in the Western Desert.

250 Squadron Sergeants' Mess.

The pilots' mess after the Sergeants' and Officers' messes were combined.

Washing clothes in salt water.

Western Desert luncheon *al fresco*.

Dug in sleeping accommodation, Bob Whittle on right.

Part of the Squadron's camp.

(All photographs Bob Whittle)

Caldwell claimed a probable Bf109 on 28 August, once again over shipping, and came very close to losing his life on the following day. 250 Squadron was again on convoy escort north of Sidi Barrani when they were attacked by I/JG 27. Caldwell (AK493), who was acting as weaver, was attacked by Lt. Werner Schroer and his wing man, and his Tomahawk caught fire. Caldwell prepared to bale out and Schroer, (not unreasonably in the circumstances) claimed a victory, one of 61 claimed in the desert of his eventual total of 114. He was the second highest scoring German pilot in the Desert after Hans Joachim Marseille.

Clive Caldwell's combat report tells the story in full.

At approximately 1905 hours whilst acting as weaver for my formation I was attacked by two M.E.109's, apparently simultaneously, one coming from astern, the other from port side, neither of which I saw personally. Bullets from astern damaged tail, tail trimming gear, fuselage and starboard main plane; while the aileron on that side was destroyed and a sizeable hole made in the trailing edge and flap some four feet in board from the aileron, evidently by cannon shells, a quantity of splinters from which pierced the cowling and side of the cockpit, some entering my legs and right side. Fire from the port side, seemingly almost full deflection shots damaged the fuselage, a number of bullets entering my left shoulder and hip, small pieces of glass embedding in my face, my helmet and goggles being pulled askew across my nose and eyes - no doubt by a near miss. As a result of the hits on the main plane and probable excessive avoiding action, the aircraft spun out of control. Checking the spin, I blacked out when pulling out of the ensuing dive, recovering to find flames in the cockpit.

Pulling the pin from the safety harness I started to climb out to abandon the aircraft, when the fire, evidently caused by burning oil and not petrol as I thought, died out, so I decided to remain and attempt a landing.

Looking behind me as I crossed the coast at about 500 ft, some 6 miles East of Sidi Barrani and going SouthEast, I saw a number of planes maneouvring (sic) off the point of Barrani in a manner suggesting an engagement. As my plane appeared to answer controls reasonably well, apart from turns, oil pressure and temperature being satisfactory despite quantity of oil freely splashed over floor, sides and windscreen, I made a gradual turn and climbed back toward the said aircraft finally carrying out an attack on what I believed was a M.E. 109 which took severe avoiding action. Having previously lost the pin to my harness, I was holding the straps with my left hand for security, which together with the damage already sustained by the machine [made] it unadvisable (sic) to attempt much in the way of quick changes of attitude so I carried on to very low level, and continued on to my base, arriving at 2010 hours. Oil temperature and pressure remaining satisfactory all the way, - Using half flap only, because of damage to starboard flap, I landed to find the starboard tyre flat as a result of a bullet hole. By use of left brake and rudder I was fortunate in bring the aircraft to rest without damage.

The Messerschmitt he attacked was at first noted in his log book as *ATTACKED & DAMAGED E/ A NEAR SIDI B.* Nor did he claim it as destroyed in his combat report. A later note beneath this shows _SHOT DOWN ME109F CONFIRMED_ presumably by sources outside the squadron. It was his fifth confirmed individual victory. He was taken to hospital, where doctors removed bullets and shrapnel from his neck, shoulder, back and leg, and perspex splinters from his face. The following day's log book entry dryly noted *SELF U/S.* By this time he had accumulated 133 hours on the Tomahawk, of which the last 65 were flown in August.

He returned to his unit only three days later, and was in combat again on 1 September, when he noted in his log book *JUMPED BY ME109s. SELF NEARLY BOUGHT IT. VERY BAD.*

The 250 Squadron diary recorded this combat in some detail several days after the event.

It is regretted that owing to an error, no record was made of the occasion when Killer Caldwell became at (sic) the wrong end of 2 Me 109Fs. This officer was weaving behind the formation at the time of the incident, but has so far failed to give an accurate explanation of what happened. His only comment was: "I didn't think it could ever happen to me." "Like bloody hell!"

Fortunately in spite of 5 cannon shells in the wings, and a number of bullet holes in his tyres etc, he was able to fly the aircraft back to base and make a successful landing, having in the process shot down one of the M.E.s before leaving the scene of action.

"I didn't think it could ever happen to me."
Clive Caldwell and AK493 with visible battle
damage after his engagement with Werner
Schroer on 29 August. (Bob Whittle)

*It may be added that he was himself wounded at
the outset, while numerous bullets removed much
of the glass from in front of and behind his head,
in all several dozen piercing the aircraft round
about the cockpit and fuselage.*

*Sum total of the affair. Killer collected 3 wounds,
the aircraft lost one aileron, one rudder control,
one flat tyre, one flap U/S and holed, approx 100
small holes and 5 large ones, was on fire, which
was extinguished. In return, 1 Me109F destroyed.*

112 Squadron RAF moved to LG 102 on 8
September, the same day as 3, and the two
units were to work together with great success
in the months to come. Operations for 3 re-
commenced on 13 September, when 'B Flight
carried out flying practice in new tactical
formation, ie. 'fluid pairs'. This formation,
primarily used to combat the 'hit and run' tactics
of Me109s, allows greater manoeuvrability and
can be used for both offensive and defensive
action'.[9] This was basically the same formation
as that used by the Germans, two *rotten,* which
formed a *schwarm,* tactics first developed in
the Spanish Civil War by Werner Molders, and
which remained unchanged throughout the war.
It took Fighter Command a long time to discard
the 'vic' of three aircraft which restricted
manoeuvrability, and the individual pilot's ability

AK493 and Clive Caldwell, showing damage to the fin and fuselage just ahead of it, the trailing edge
of starboard wing and flap, the flat tyre, and the shredded aileron. The staining in front of the roundel
is probably hydraulic fluid. The hydraulic tank is situated immediately behind and beneath the rear
view panel. Bob Whittle called it 'a remarkable escape.' Note the lack of squadron codes, and the
Desert Camouflage scheme in standard pattern. (Bob Whittle.)

to search, as much effort was spent maintaining the close formation which was required. To be fair, the vic formation had been developed for the purpose of attacking unescorted bombers, before the *Luftwaffe* had bases close enough to England to permit the use of escort fighters. When the Battle of Britain began, it was seen as unwise to attempt to bring about a major change in formation tactics in the middle of a struggle for survival, but the 'finger four' formation adopted by the Tangmere Wing in 1941 soon became standard for the rest of Fighter Command in England. It seems strange that the improved tactics adopted in Europe were not passed on sooner to the fighter units of the Desert Air Force. It would appear that 3 Squadron did not have the opportunity to use its new formation for long, because, as Robin Brown explains:

> To combat the Messerschmitt threat new tactics were devised. Instead of flying straight and level during offensive sweeps with a couple of aircraft weaving in the rear, the whole squadron now weaved. 'I should hate to tackle one of these formations' wrote Tedder, 'which look like a swarm of angry bees'. *Oberleutnant* Werner Schroer of JG 27 described them rather differently: 'bunches of grapes' - presumably since they were so easy to pick off.[10]

Schroer and his comrades however, had the very great advantage of being able to accept or reject combat at will. The Bf109 had a superior climb rate and maximum speed to the Hurricane and the Tomahawk, and the Germans would only commit themselves to combat if they had the advantage of superior altitude. The shape of the formation perhaps becomes of less significance if the combat inevitably begins with an attack from above.

3 Squadron pilots at LG 102, Sidi Heneish, September 1941. Seated on Tomahawk, left to right: Sgt. Rex Wilson, FO 'Robbie'Roberts, FO Roy Bothwell, Fl. Lt. Wilf Arthur. Standing, left to right: FO Bobby Gibbes, FO Bruce Evans, Sgt. Frank Reid, Sgt. Dudley Parker, Sgt. Alan Cameron, Sgt. Derek Scott, Sgt. Wal Mailey, FO Lawton Lees, FO Frank Fischer, Sqn. Ldr. Peter Jeffrey, Fl. Lt. Alan Rawlinson, Fl. Lt. Lindsay Knowles, FO Malcolm Watson, FO Eric Lane. Kneeling, left to right: Sgt. Ron Simes, FO Wally Jewell, FO Tom Trimble, PO Bill Kloster. The Tomahawk still carries Temperate Land Scheme camouflage of Dark Green and Dark Earth. (Alan Rawlinson)

Operations began in earnest for 3 Squadron at 1815 hours on 14 September, when five Tomahawks set off to strafe Gambut. FO Roberts (AK439) encountered a Ju88 when about to attack, and after a burst from his guns the E/A was seen to be emitting thick black smoke. PO 'Sammy' Lees (AK456) also attacked this aircraft, avoided an attack by a 109 from his starboard quarter, and then 'dived at 110 coming head on from below, and gave him a burst'. The 110 crash-landed, but this was unseen by any of the Australians, and no claim was submitted. * While the strafe was in progress, several more Bf109s arrived and attacked from above. As Lees withdrew, he was harassed by two of these, and suffered damage to his starboard elevator, the right rudder pedal and port aileron, which was blown off. This caused the aircraft 'to flick onto [its] back out of steep left hand turn'. He then 'dived out and squashed onto ground at approximately 200 M.P.H'. Lees returned to the unit on the 18th. He kept the Tomahawk in the air until about thirty miles east of Gambut, where he crash-landed. He walked until he met an Allied patrol south of Sollum. FO Burbury (AK464) was shot down and captured.

On the afternoon of the 14th, General Brett of the United States Army Air Corps visited 3 and 250 squadrons, and discussed the performance of the Tomahawk with Peter Jeffrey and 250's new CO, Teddy Morris.

15 September saw the temporary departure of FO Jewell and PO Lane, on attachment to 7th Armoured Division at Minquar-Ou-Im to obtain experience in Army manoeuvres and tactics. This was a sign of things to come. Under the newly appointed AOC-in-C, AVM Arthur Tedder, and AVM Arthur Coningham, the new commander of the Western Desert Air Force, inter-service cooperation was about to be elevated to a completely new plane.

> His talent for cooperation was displayed at once: he and his like sounding army colleague set up their headquarters side by side for the coming battle, they and their staffs even sharing the same Mess - a good beginning. And, shrewdly, Coningham promptly revised what he saw as exaggerated decentralisation in the new Air Support system. He perceived in good time that the true Air Support Control must be his own advanced Headquarters: only at the centre, beside the Army Commander, could there be a picture of the whole battle which would make the Air role truly effective.[11]

On 18 September, as well as the welcome return of FO Lees, Lindsay Knowles, John Saunders and Wilf Arthur returned to the unit from 71 OTU, after a spell of instructing which they had commenced after the cessation of hostilities in Syria.

First blood in the Desert for 3's Tomahawks was drawn on 24 September by Fl.Lt. Saunders. At 1245 an offensive patrol was flown over the Sofafi - Sidi Omar area without

'Cleo II', one of several 3 Squadron Tomahawks to carry individual names, with pilot, tentatively identified as PO Eric Lane, at Sidi Heneish, circa September 1941. The drawing is clearly on a replacement cowling panel.
(Alex Archer, 3 Squadron, via Doug Norrie)

---

* The aircraft was Bf110E 2F+GA, belonging to the Stabstaffel of StG 3. Its pilot, Oblt. Gerd was wounded.

contact with enemy aircraft, but on the way back, Saunders spotted a Ju88, and, with Sgt. Hiller, left the formation to attack it.

> Another Tomahawk and myself dived down and attacked Ju88 after making circuit above. Made couple attacks from astern and then lost own and enemy aircraft in cloud. Sighted enemy again in bad shape and attempted to head it back by head on attacks. After fight aircraft port engine was in flames and appeared out of control.

> About five ME 109's immediately attacked and fight followed. I got in about three bursts but did not seem to effect (sic) them. Received shell in own wing fracturing oil pipe line. Took cover in clouds and made for home. On coming out of clouds I was jumped by one ME 109 and my engine stopped. Made crashed (sic) landing after dive and 109 straffed (sic) until own aircraft was burning.

Saunders was taken to hospital and treated for shrapnel wounds and a broken toe.

Clive Caldwell was in action again on 27 September. At 1535, ten 250 Squadron aircraft led by Sqn. Ldr. Morris took off with a further twelve from 3 Squadron, to escort nine Marylands of 21 SAAF to Bardia. 250 Squadron was attacked by Bf109s. One Maryland and a Tomahawk were shot down while one Bf109 was destroyed by Sgt. H.N. Humphries (AK221), and another was attacked by Caldwell (AK324). The German pilots claimed two Marylands.

Surprisingly, 3 Squadron saw none of this action, but Clive Caldwell's combat report reveals the probable reason. Inexplicably, the bomber formation split up, and 3 Squadron must have stayed with the group which was not attacked.

> When about to cross the coast just north of Bardia, at 16,000 feet, while acting as weaver for my formation, I observed aircraft taking off from Menastu and Gambut dromes, others climbing for height out to sea, and noted several M.E. 109.s above in the sun and warned my leader by R/T. The bombers had split up and were consequently attacked by E/A, of which there were some 12 to 14 in the sky, mostly of the M.E. 109 F type.

> One of our aircraft (Sgt. Humphries - author) carried out an attack on one E/A. which was subsequently seen to go down, the pilot baling out over the sea. One Maryland burst into flames and went down into the sea, possibly as a result of A/A fire, which was fairly nearing (sic) and accurate in respect to height. None of the crew were seen to get out.

> The bombers having now left the area, 6 aircraft led by the C.O., with myself weaving behind, lost height on a course of approx. 140 deg., crossing the coast again near Bug Bug. (sic) At a position approx. 15 miles S.S.E. of Bug Bug, at a height of 6,000 feet we were attacked from out of the sun by 2 M.E. 109.s, F type, 2 more giving them cover from above. Their approach was unobserved until they were almost within range, and as I gave warning, they opened fire from about 200 yards, diving past. One attacked me, his tracer passing over my fuselage, the other attacking PO Wells on the outside of the vic. I managed to turn in on this machine, and carried out an attack from above on his starboard beam, firing about a few seconds bursts of all guns and seeing several explosive bullets hit the engine cowling and forward parts of the fuselage near the cockpit. The E/A pulled steeply up past my nose at a distance of not more than 30 yards, and I lost sight of it, while PO Wells' machine went down in flames and exploded on hitting the ground.

> The M.E.s above manoeuvred for position, but did not come down and engage us. Three E/A were seen finally to leave after the incident, climbing away into the sun. . .

Both combat report and log book entry initially recorded only a damaged claim, but his log book later noted that 'THIS E/A WAS CONFIRMED AS DESTROYED BY 7TH F.A. DATE 4/10/41'

Caldwell shot down another Bf109 on 28 September, north west of Bardia. It was his ninetieth operational sortie.

At 1200, PO Caldwell (AK324) and Sgt. Humphries (AK221) took off as weavers above a further four 250 Squadron aircraft, to provide top cover for 33 and 112 Squadrons, who, with a mixed formation of Hurricanes and Martlets of the RNFS, were escorting a large formation of Marylands.

Four Australian pilots of 250 Squadron: from left, Sgts. Noel Humphries, who flew with Swiss Air after the war, Charlie Coward, Bob Whittle and Mick Ryan. (Bob Whittle)

His combat reports at this time indicate that his situational awareness was, by now, particularly acute. He seemed to have the time to take in everything that was going on in the sky around him, and make a swift decision about how to deal with it.

When crossing the coast at Bardia at approx. 15,000 feet, while acting as weaver for my formation, which was providing top cover for Maryland bombers and their fighter escort, enemy fighters appeared, attacking a fighter formation on our left, while other E/A approached us from above, but did not attack.

Seeing the bombers heading north, having dropped their load, I lost height toward them, and when about 4 miles astern of them, observed an M.E.109 climbing steeply from below and in front of me, evidently using speed gained from a dive. The pilot of the M.E. obviously did not see me, and I fired my first burst with all guns at a range of about 350 yards, and got in a second short burst at a range of less than 200 yards. The E/A continued in its steep climb for a brief space, then appeared to fall off the top in an uncontrolled manner, going down in a long curve at a sharp angle. As other E/A were in the vicinity, I did not watch its descent, but made several steep turns to review the local situation, during which I observed two explosions, followed by considerable black smoke, on the ground below.

These explosions were separated by about 15 seconds in time, and approx. 4 miles in distance, at a position approx. 10 to 12 miles N.W. of Bardia. A few minutes earlier, I also observed an explosion followed by black smoke at a position approx. 7 to 8 miles West of Bardia.

Each of the explosions were of the kind made by crashing aircraft.

His combat report claimed a probable, and the log book later noted that it was confirmed by the bombers.

250 Squadron's diary recorded the event, later offering an amusing comment about the negative effects of leave.

Sept 28. A check on serviceability revealed a full operational strength of 6 A/C. These six, the CO in the lead, took off at midday to provide top cover over 18 Marylands and 32 other fighters for a second go at Bardia Harbour.

A most successful show, all aircraft returning. The CO and Ham acting as shepherd to two stragglers and keeping harm away from them. Caldwell saw a 109 climbing up from below him and fighting down a strong sense of unreality (because of the fact that it was below him - author) managed to shoot it down. P/O Cole with Sgts Nitschke & Coward returned from leave all looking as though they should be going off to a rest home. Experience is showing that nearly everyone, upon returning from leave is practically a non-effective for the first few days.

Bob Whittle's original caption for this photograph was 'Borrowed transport, W Desert 1941, 250 Squadron.' A close examination of the vehicle suggests that they would not have been in a hurry to return it to the original owners! (Bob Whittle)

On 30 September Caldwell damaged another 109 during a long shipping protection patrol. His total hours for September were 68.20.

A new intake of pilots for 3 Squadron arrived on 29 September and amongst their number was PO Nicky Barr, who was soon to become one of the Squadron's most successful and aggressive pilots. PO Peter Giddy and PO Lou Spence joined the Squadron on 1 October, and Fl.Lt. John Jackson proceeded to HQ. RAF Middle East to await transport back to Australia, where he was to lead 75 Squadron with distinction in the defence of Port Moresby in early 1942.

Alan Rawlinson and Peter Turnbull were both awarded the DFC on 10 October for 'courage, determination and devotion to duty'.[12]

At 1400 on 3 October, 112 Squadron provided high cover for the escort of a Tac. R. Hurricane of 451 Squadron RAAF to the west of Sidi Omar. When they returned, they had the sun at their backs and were bounced by six Bf109s of II/JG 27. Sgt. Ian Stirrat (AK502) was attacked by two 109s and killed.

On 4 October, the 250 Squadron diary was still concerned with the adverse effects of leave, with good cause, as the following entry reveals.

> *Sgt. Creighton and Sgt. Twemlow pushed off on seven days leave, no doubt filled with determination to undermine their health as far as is humanly possible while time and cash permit. Sgt. Cable returned from leave accompanied by Sgt Cornall, (both Australians - what else! author) who was released from jail apparently just in time to come back to work. Reliable information shows that Cornall was the victim of circumstances.*

On 11 October, 3 Squadron was visited by AVM Coningham, who addressed the pilots and outlined plans for future offensive operations.

> The dinner that followed had considerable significance as it marked the merging of the officers and sergeant pilots in the one mess.

> This radical idea, as far as the R.A.F. was concerned, was initiated by C.O. Peter Jeffrey, as he felt it was vital that all flying personnel should be together as much as possible and thus be able to discuss tactics and operations with a united viewpoint.* The development was resisted by R.A.F. squadrons, but

Fl. Lts. Alan Rawlinson and Peter Turnbull, shortly after both pilots were awarded the DFC on 10 October 1941. (Alan Rawlinson)

eventually spread throughout all the Desert Air Force squadrons. A.V.M. "Mary" Coningham (his nickname springing from the word "Maori" as he was a New Zealander) fully approved of the combined pilots' mess after joining the No. 3 pilots on this occasion, and this development which originated with No. 3 undoubtedly played a big part in the wonderful spirit that prevailed in the Desert Air Force until the end of the war.[13]

12 October was a day of heavy combat for 3 Squadron, after which there would have been no illusions about the difficulty of fighting the Bf109 in a Tomahawk. Twelve aircraft took off at 0730 in company with twelve from 2 SAAF to carry out a protective patrol over forward troops. Bf109s from I/JG 27 attacked and immediately shot down the weaver from the South African squadron. A general dogfight followed, during which Sgt Alan Cameron in AK506 scored his second victory.

> We were on patrol at 10,000 feet near Sidi Omar. I was flying No. 2 to the leader. Aircraft were reported 7 o'clock and the leader went into a medium left turn. Somebody screamed out 'duck' and I pulled round hard behind the leader. Two aircraft were firing at us from behind and I used a steep diving turn to evade them. I saw a Tomahawk with a 109 on its tail in a shallow dive. The cross on the side of the fuselage was conspicuous, also square wing tips. I pulled in behind and gave the 109 a squirt from the port quarter. I then lost sight of the Tomahawk. The 109 behaved as if the pilot was hit, ie. put his nose straight down very hard. I overhauled him quite easily, and from then on was throttled back to keep

---

Some time after the war I discussed the idea of a pilots' mess with Peter, as I believed that it was his idea. He assured me that the idea was put up to him by our squadron MO John Laver, but that he had implemented it. As a matter of interest, the RAF squadrons were ordered to do the same, which they did, but part of their bars was the preserve of Officers, and Sgt. Pilots had to drink at the other end. All formalities were dropped inside our pilots' mess and officers and sergeants addressed each other by their first names or nicknames and only the CO got 'Sir'.(Correspondence with Bobby Gibbes)

Several hairs of the dog. The pilots' mess of 250 Squadron, 'the morning after a visit from a neighbouring South African squadron.' It can be safely assumed that no operational flying was scheduled for this day. (Bob Whittle)

behind. I gave him two long bursts at short range and could see my tracers going into him. He hit the ground I think near Sidi Omar and I pulled out hard. The fight was still proceeding up sun and I climbed back into it. I saw a Tomahawk with its nose up in the air firing at a 109 above. I pulled back and gave him a squirt at long range, did not observe any results. I saw another aircraft flying away very slowly, pursued it and found it was a Tomahawk badly shot up, undercarriage semi retracted. Sergeant Scott was the pilot. My wireless was gone so we flew back slowly together to Sidi Barrani.

Wilf Arthur (AN314 Y) claimed a probable and a damaged, Gibbes claimed a damaged and FO Jewell left a 109 'with white smoke and petrol streaming from him', claiming a probable, but the Squadron was roughly handled by the Bf109s, having two aircraft badly damaged and losing one pilot.

FO Roberts was hit by cannon shells in the elevator and port wing which caused him to force land inside Allied lines. His aircraft was recovered for repair. Sgt. Scott's Tomahawk was extensively holed by fire from enemy aircraft but he was able to get away and crash land with wheels up at LG 05. Sgt Parker's aircraft was set on fire and he baled out. During his descent he was fired on by an ME 109F and was shot out of his parachute and killed.[14]

Parker was the victim of Lt. Sinner, whose fire:

hit the cockpit on the left side. Cannon shells set the tank behind the cockpit ablaze, and Parker then baled out; possibly he was already badly wounded or else fell through a burst of fire, but when he reached the ground he was dead. It was thought at the time that he had been shot on his parachute, but it is most unlikely that in the heat of a dogfight any pilot would have been able to leave the fight and concentrate on such a difficult target as a man swaying beneath a parachute. Immediately after seeing Parker bale, Sinner was attacked by two Tomahawks, (sustaining some damage, according to Marseille's biographer Franz Kurowski) pulled his Bf109E nearly vertical, and stalled. He pulled out of the ensuing dive when he reached a lower defensive circle of Hurricanes, nosed down at top speed for Gambut and was first back to base.[15]

Whether or not Sgt Parker was deliberately killed in his parachute, 3 Squadron had no doubts. [*] It was not uncommon for the German pilots to strafe crash-landed aircraft *and* their pilots, so such an act cannot be ruled out. Allied pilots also strafed downed opponents on occasions, perhaps in response to this practice of some of the *Luftwaffe's* pilots.

The other German pilots to claim victories in this fight were Oblt. Franzisket with one and Lt. Marseille with two, both in the later stages of the battle, according to Kurowski,[16] so they must have been Roberts and Scott. It might have been possible to observe Roberts' crash landing, but somewhat more difficult in Scott's case! 3 Squadron had had its first encounter with the 'Star of Africa'.

24. Fl. Lt. Lindsay Knowles speaking to his ground crew in front of AN355 R. This aircraft, carrying Temperate Land Scheme camouflage, was flown at first by Alan Rawlinson, and later by Lindsay Knowles on a regular basis, after Rawlinson had departed for a brief spell at 71 OTU. It was lost on 12 October when Sgt. Dudley Parker was shot down and killed in his parachute.
(RAAF Museum)

On the same day, 112 Squadron had a savage encounter with a mixed formation of G50s and Bf109s over Sofafi, its Australian members at the centre of the action. PO R.J.D. Jeffries destroyed a Bf109F, while PO F.E. Parker and Sgt. Rudolph Leu were shot down by Lt. Korner and Hpt. Gerlitz. Sgt. C.F. McWilliam suffered damage to his aircraft, and Sgt. W.E. Carson was wounded. Parker and Leu were found later that evening by the Coldstream Guards and returned to 112 several days later.

On 23 September, the *Luftwaffe* fighter force had been strengthened by the arrival of II/JG27, under Hpt. Wolfgang Lippert. He brought with him a core of highly experienced pilots. Lippert himself had twenty five victories, four of which were gained during the Spanish Civil War. 4, 5 and 6 Staffeln were commanded by Oblt. Gustav Rodel,(twenty victories), Oblt. Ernst Dullberg, (seven) and Oblt. Strossner. Obfw. Otto Schulz had nine victories, and was to become the unit's most successful pilot before his death in action in 1942. Other well qualified pilots were Oblt. Emmerich Fluder, a Battle of Britain veteran with five victories, and Obfw. Karl-Heinz Bendert, with six.[17]

To counter the increasing strength of JG 27 the RAF squadrons were now formed into three wings, 258 Wing consisting of 3 RAAF, 2 SAAF, 112 and 250 Squadrons RAF. A wing sweep in company with 238 Squadron's Hurricanes and the Tomahawks of. 2 SAAF and 112 Squadron was flown on 20 October.

---

[*] *Dudley Parker was shot down, set on fire and parachuted. As we were over our own territory we expected Dudley to return to us within a few days, but a South African Padre visited the squadron and told us Dudley's fate. Four 109s detached themselves from the combat above and dived down and shot him out of his parachute. (I had driven off the 109 which was shooting at Dudley.) (Correspondence with Bobby Gibbes)*

Although Marseille's biographer identifies Parker as Lt. Sinner's victim, he makes no mention of the fact that he was killed, merely that 'he was able to get out in time'.

Experiments with fighter formations of varying sizes during this preparatory phase also lead to the decision to form operational flying wings of two squadrons, thus creating two operational wings within each administrative wing. All fighter squadrons were also made fully mobile, No 3. on 3rd November being divided into three groups - No. 1 servicing party, No 2 servicing party, and rear party (headquarters, work shops, stores and transport). While No.1 party was on the move to a forward airfield, the aircraft were maintained by No. 2 party which quickly followed the flying complement when it moved, relieving No 1 party so that it could again advance. This arrangement ensured that the squadron could operate continuously when the land battle became fluid.[18]

Peter Jeffrey was promoted to Wing Commander to lead No. 2 Operational Wing, formed on 3 November, consisting of 3 and 112 Squadrons. This brought about the recall of Sqn. Ldr. Alan Rawlinson from 71 OTU to command 3 Squadron. Planning for the forthcoming Operation *Crusader* was almost complete.

250 Squadron was active on 30 October, flying a Wing Sweep from LG110 with 238 Squadron's Hurricanes. Sgt. Bob Whittle, flying AM392, which he named *Nux Vomica, (deadly poison)* shot down a Bf109 fifteen miles south west of Sollum, and the squadron claimed another 109 as a probable. Sgt. Clifton Cornall* was shot down fifteen miles west of Bardia and captured, while PO Cole's aircraft was damaged. One of the 238 Squadron Hurricanes was shot down, but the Germans believed that they had destroyed four aircraft, Obfw. Schulz claiming three!

AM392 was first flown operationally by Bob Whittle on 4 August. It was his regular aircraft for three months, although it was of course flown by other pilots. This photograph shows it shortly after delivery, and before the application of Squadron codes. The name indicates that ownership has already been claimed. (Bob Whittle)

Sgt. Cornall was released from captivity when the Italians surrendered in September 1943 and repatriated to Australia. Tragically, he was killed with the rank of Flying Oficer in a take-off accident in a Wackett trainer at 3WAGS Maryborough on 12 January 1944.

Almost three months later, *Nux Vomica* is carrying full squadron code letters, and showing signs of wear and tear. Ground crew in foreground. (Bob Whittle)

C hapter 4   Operation Crusader

Operation *Crusader* was the third British offensive to be attempted against Rommel's *Afrika Korps*, and the most effective up to that time. Previously, an attempt to retake Halfaya Pass, Operation *Brevity* on 15 May had been repulsed, and a month later, Operation *Battleaxe*, an attempt to relieve Tobruk was easily contained by the Germans, whose counter attack threw the British back to their start line. *Crusader,* to commence on 18 November was 'a major British offensive intended to defeat the Axis in Cyrenaica and relieve Tobruk'.[1]

> The main aims of the RAF between 14th October and 12th November (D minus 6)was to weaken enemy air strength by attacks on Axis shipping, supply organisations and lines of communication; neutralising enemy airfields especially those used by German fighters and dive bombers; and winning air superiority over the triangle formed by Bardia, Tobruk and Maddalena, in which area German fighters were most likely to be encountered.[2]

The activities of the squadrons have been recounted up to the end of October, and the period from then until 12 November 'was somewhat uneventful for No. 3 despite their forward location. During early November, operations consisted almost entirely of patrol and interception duties over Eighth Army units moving into position for the offensive, and ...all were uneventful'.[3] At this point the squadron was still based at LG 102 at Sidi Heneish, although many of their sorties had begun from LG 110 at Sidi Barrani. That they had met no German fighter opposition was most probably an indication that the Germans were conserving their resources for another attack on Tobruk, which had been planned to commence five days after the opening of *Crusader*.

Both 258 and 262 Wings moved forward again to Sidi Barrani on 12 November, and then to Maddalena on the 18th without ceasing operations. In the last week before the opening of the offensive the squadrons were relatively inactive, but a wing sweep lead by Peter Jeffrey was flown between moves; however no enemy aircraft were found.

Two wing sweeps were flown on the 19th, both of which were unopposed, but at 1420 FO Frank Fischer found the trouble the rest of his unit had been looking for. During the sweep he had been forced to return with oil covering most of his windscreen, and on the way found four Bf109s of II/ JG 27 strafing LG 132, the new base of 451 Tac. R. Squadron RAAF. In spite of his difficulties, Fischer attacked these single handed and shot one down. The others responded with vigour, and his Tomahawk took hits from Uffz. Reuter.

> I dropped out of formation owing to oil flowing into the cockpit. Just east of aerodrome on the wire from which 451 Squadron are operating, I looked back and saw three aircraft diving on the drome firing.

I turned back and dived on the first ME 109 then noticed a fourth in its dive. I did a stern attack on the 1st aircraft and got a very good burst in. Then turned and did head on attacks at the other three. I was then hit so rolled on back and dived to the deck.

Three 109's (sic) pressed home their attack and finally shot me down in a crash landing. They then straffed (sic) the aircraft *and myself* (author's italics) and set it on fire.

Later an army captain reported to 451 Squadron that a 109 crashed and burnt and that he had seen it.

Fischer escaped with shrapnel wounds and was awarded the DFC for his action.

On 20 November ten aircraft from 112 Squadron and ten from 3, led by Wg. Cdr. Jeffrey, took off at 0620 hours on an offensive sweep. They encountered half a dozen Bf110s from III/ZG 26 and at once attacked. Sgt. Ronald Simes in AM507 destroyed one, and other members of the squadron shared a second with Peter Jeffrey (AN224). 112 Squadron's Australians were also involved. Sgt. K.F. Carson (AN303) made two attacks on a Bf110 which took no evasive action, and went down with smoke pouring from it. Sgt. Leu shared another with two English pilots and PO Robert ('Butch') Jeffries attacked one, which caused it to stream glycol or petrol from both engines. Its rear gunner scored some hits on AN413 K, and Jeffries broke off the attack, claiming a probable.

Typical desert open air maintenance on 3 Squadron Tomahawks during Operation *Crusader*.
(RAAF Museum)

250 Squadron was also active on the 20th. At 1100 hours they provided top cover to Hurricanes of the RNFS on a fighter sweep over the Gambut - El Adem area. At 1210 they encountered twelve Ju87s of I/St.G 1 escorted by fifteen Bf109s. Flying his one hundredth operation, Sgt. Bob Whittle (AN313, a new *Nux Vomica*) waded into the Stukas, claiming one destroyed, one probable and two damaged. Two of these were later confirmed by Sub Lt. Penny of the RN Fighter Unit, bringing his total for the day to three and one damaged. A man of few words, his combat report was remarkably brief.

Squadron dash, engaged 109s in dogfight, self attacked JU.87's after they had jettisoned bombs. 3 attacks. 2 Beam and 1 quarter. Own casualties nil. E/A. One destroyed. One probably destroyed. Two badly damaged in wings and fuselage.

Sgt Richard Nitschke, a jackeroo in more peaceful times, had not long been with 250 Squadron and saw his first action on this day. He was credited with two Ju87s and a damaged Bf109 in the same engagement as Whittle. His Tomahawk was in turn hit by the Bf109s and he was forced to crash-land.

3 Squadron was not engaged on the 21st, but the Australians of 112 were busy. Eleven Tomahawks patrolling the Gambut - Tobruk area encountered two CR42s on their way home at 500 ft near El Adem. Sgt. Leu (AK509) forced one down to ground level where it crashed in flames, and the other, which crash-landed, was shared between PO Jeffries (AK541), Sgt. K.F. Carson (AK436) and PO Neville Duke, who noted 'The two other Tomahawks began chasing him and shooting him up, but I had no stomach for this sort of thing and concentrated on setting fire to his machine.'[4]

22 November saw a day of intensive aerial combat, after which

> the German Air Force never challenged our fighter force in straight forward combat again during the campaign, but resorted instead to raider tactics with small numbers of aircraft.[5]

However, the Desert Air Force, and 3 Squadron in particular, paid a heavy price for their successes, as Alan Rawlinson relates.

> AM on 22 November I led the Squadron as an escort to six Blenheims bombing enemy concentrations at Bir-el-Gobi, about 30 miles south east of El Adem. The Wing routine was for the bombers to fly over our airfield and carry out two orbits. This allowed time for the second squadron of the wing to take off and form up on the others. Each squadron of 12 aircraft took off together in one big echelon, across the wind so the dust blew away from the following aircraft and making only one cloud of dust. On this squadron operation the bombers flew only one orbit and headed out north west for the front. Our twelve Tomahawks got off and chased after them. I split my Squadron in air - 6 for Close Escort ie. 3 on each flank. I led the other six as top cover in 3 pairs. The Blenheims were a bit too slow for the Tomahawks. We were always throttled back to a speed which put us at a tactical disadvantage when enemy fighters attacked.

> The Blenheims bombed the target and were heading back east when we ran into about 15 ME109Fs head on and above. A number of JU87s were down on the deck, spread out and flying west. We had passed these Stukas on our way out to the target. They were later seen dive bombing our troops about 10 miles south of our formation. With the top cover I pulled up into a head on attack as the 109Fs came down firing. I fired at one from slightly below, was hitting him in the belly and knocking pieces from him. He pulled up slightly and passed close over head. I was then attacked by 3 109Fs from the south and others cut us off from our bombers and the close escort. It was a neat tactic which kept us, the top cover, in that situation for a minute or so too long. I looked over to the Blenheims and saw four black fires rising from the ground to the rear of the formation. Later we learned that they were 3 of our Tomahawks. Johnny Saunders, Mal Watson and Eric Lane were all killed, and one of 2 ME109s shot down by Derek Scott.

> After we returned from this sortie, the OC 11 Squadron, Wg. Cdr. Kellett, rang us and spoke to Wg. Cdr. Peter Jeffrey. He thanked the squadron on the excellent escort cover, saying that they had no casualties. He expressed regret at our heavy losses.[6]

This account of the action is at odds with a long held belief that 3 Squadron was escorting Blenheims of 45 Squadron to attack the Acroma - El Adem road, and that four of the Blenheims were shot down by the attacking Messerschmitts, but it is perfectly correct.

11 Squadron's Operations Record Book shows that *five* aircraft led by Wg. Cdr. R. Kellett took off at 0910, to attack

> dispersed M.T. and A.F.V.'s at pin-point 413379 near BIR EL GUBI(sic) from 5,000 feet. Bombs were observed to fall across M.T. and 4 direct hits were obtained.

> 10 ME.109's were seen over the target area, two of which were seen to attack the formation from the rear. One of them suddenly pulled up and exposed the belly and SGT. FISHER, rear gunner of P/O. RECHNER'S aircraft fired at point blank range and afterwards the aircraft was seen to go down with

black smoke pouring from it, and then crashed. The remainder of the ME.109's were then engaged by escorting Tomahawks. Slight Heavy and Light A.A. encountered over the target but inaccurate. All aircraft returned safely.[7]

The Operations Record Book of 45 Squadron reveals that the unit did indeed lose four aircraft during the day, but this happened during an unescorted 'cloud cover raid' in the afternoon. The following entry clarifies the situation beyond doubt.

Six aircraft left to bomb tanks and M.T. between Acroma and El Adem. They should have been over the target area at 1335 hrs. but owing to flying out of their way to avoid squalls they didn't arrive until 1405 hrs and ran into about 20 Me's 109. (sic) Two of our aircraft were seen to fall in flames, two were unaccounted for and two returned badly damaged by cannon fire (Cat. 2) Bombs were jettisoned. W/ Cmdr. Wallis, Sgt. Wood, Sgt. Melly and Sgt. O'Neill with their crews were missing.[8]

I/JG 27 claimed four Tomahawks and four Blenheims, and it seems that they were all recorded as being made during a single engagement. If this is so, it may have led to the assumption that 3 and 45 Squadrons were flying together, which is not the case.

Sgt. Derek Scott originally claimed two probable Bf109s in the morning combat, which were later confirmed by 11 Squadron.

Alan Rawlinson's memoirs provide vivid details of one of the longest dogfights of the war, which took place later in the afternoon.

PM on the 22 November the Wing flew a fighter sweep with 23 Tomahawks to the El Adem - Tobruk area. Peter Jeffrey was leading with 112 Squadron. I was behind and below with 3 Squadron. We had also, Wg. Cdr. Fred E. Rosier RAF with us in a Hurricane. He was going into Tobruk and using us as an escort.

Briefing by the Wing Leader, Wg. Cdr. Peter Jeffrey. "We are to fly an offensive sweep to Bir el Gobi - El Adem - Tobruk and over the Battle area. Call sign, "Lester Leader". Height 15,000 ft".

3 Squadron formation take off, Operation *Crusader*. The aircraft are widely spread to avoid dust. All appear to be carrying individual letters and wearing desert camouflage. The nearest aircraft is finished in a reverse mirror pattern. (RAAF Museum)

I will lead the Wing with 112 Squadron, 3 will follow close behind in our normal Wing battle formation. Turn signal will be given by pressing the RT transmitter button. One - left, two - right, three - straighten up. If we meet enemy fighters we will try and pull them into a dogfight. The usual plan - stay in the fight until all the enemy have gone, form up and return to base". The Wing Leader then briefs 112 Squadron over the telephone.

I brief 3 Squadron. "Right. Standard formation. Line abreast. 6x No.1s in the front line, No.2s behind and below their No.1s in a following line-abreast, no straggling". Stragglers are easily shot down. A line abreast puts all the No.1s up with the formation leader and not following him, as in a Vee formation. Followers tend to fall behind their leader and become stragglers. No.2s have a better chance of retaining their proper position behind their No.1s without the tendency to straggle. Apart from the leader, each aircraft weaves slightly, side to side, searching constantly. I have chosen my pilots - some old hands as No.1s but too many new inexperienced ones as No.2s. I brief No.2s. "Stick to your No.1s as a long as possible - even in a dogfight. Do what he does. If you get separated, never fly straight. Survive this operation before trying to be too aggressive. Right, let's go".

We move out to our aircraft, carrying parachutes and helmets, making sure that the RT plug is not dragging in the dirt. Then put on the parachute - some preferred to put the parachute into the aircraft first , with the help of the ground crew. Others prefer to put the parachute on first while the ground crew hold the helmet and goggles. Click, click - click , click, as the four metal harness lugs are clipped into the quick release box, which is positioned about the solar plexus. A quick wiggle and a shake to make sure the harness is snug and fits comfortably about those important parts of male anatomy. Then up onto the wing alongside the fuselage making use of the hand and feet holds. Grab the side of the cockpit - the crewman holding the aircraft harness straps clear of the seat. A quick scan of the aircraft from that position and step into the cockpit. Then sit back into the seat, allowing the parachute pack to slip into the seat recess. Take the aircraft harness straps from the crewman, putting the hole of one onto the pin of the other. Pick up the lower left and right aircraft harness straps from the cockpit floor and do the same. With the aircraft harness in the locked position, pull down on the tightening strops to give firm restraint.

You have now "put on your aircraft" or more to the point "put on your gun platform". A quick visual cockpit check - many things done at the same time. No loose items about, screw drivers, spanners etc, all levers and switches in the correct position - fuel, flaps, undercarriage, ignition switches - stick and rudder free and correct movement. Ready for start up, "All Clear" to the ground crew. They give thumbs up - OK. Fuel on, electrics and circuits set, fuel gauges, undercarriage and flap indicators "on".

Start up. Open throttle a little, pitch full fine, brakes on and locked. "All Clear" - "Contact". Press the starter button. The Allison engine had an inertial starting system- a step between the starter trolley power and the engine - which "whirred up" to a high sounding hum. At the right moment the engage switch is made and the engine is turned over quickly, giving out a broken note until it fires. Small spurts of blue/white smoke flow from the exhaust ports, which clear as the engine runs - a smooth healthy, powerful roar. Radiator flaps closed, check flaps - a quick part down and up - and left that way. Check flight instruments, gun sight etc. Gun firing button "off". Open up the power, a quick magneto check - left and right. Airscrew pitch a little back to "coarse" then back to "full fine" for taxy and take off, wave away chocks. Brakes off.

I taxy out and position myself on the downwind edge of a cross wind runway. The rest of the squadron stack alongside in one long echelon toward the wind. The Wing Leader has done the same with the lead squadron on the other runway. He runs up to full power on the brakes. I give my run up signal - circling my hand above my head. A quick squadron RT check - "Lester Leader over". They reply "2 - 3 - 4 - 5 etc", no more, not even an "Our Father". There is no air traffic control in the desert war. As the lead squadron passes the runway intersection I give my "take off" signal by hitting the top of the windscreen with my right hand -1 - 2 - 3. On 3, brakes off, open up evenly but quickly to full power. Up comes the tail, keep her straight and steady for the benefit of the formation. A quick glance at the instruments. A nice firm throaty roar from the engine. Lift off, select wheels up, touch the brakes to stop the wheels spinning and juddering in their wing recess. Ease back the throttle to climb power and airscrew pitch to 2,600 rpm. The formation is right there in open formation which they fly without direct reference - all searching the sky for enemy aircraft and checking their positioning as part of their search scan. All the time bobbing about in the hot rising air. The Wing is formed up and climbing out on a north west course in a minute. A quick RT check - Wing Leader to me, nothing more.

Over Bir el Gobi the Wing turns north for Tobruk, at height and at cruise power, all weaving and silent. The RT crackles - each and every pilot's heart races - frightening. Suddenly the RT speaks, quiet and clear: "Twenty plus fighters 10 o'clock above coming down". "Roger, I've got 'em." from the Wing Leader. Our aim is to draw them into a dogfight at our best height and speed condition, as we can out manoeuvre them. Usually they came down fast, picking a target, firing and going straight through and away. "Peck and Piss Off" we called it.

After a short pause, the Wing turns slowly to the left - the whole 23 aircraft pour into the turn. "keep 'em turning" from the Wing Leader as the two forces meet. Turns are tightened and our 23 aircraft spray out through the 20 plus ME109Fs, the heavy white tracers of their 20mm's reaching out for targets. Many targets, many 109s, everyone tightening turns to evade an attacker or to sight a target. The two forces explode into a savage dogfight. It is a tremendous sight. "There's a 109 on your tail" screams the RT - no call sign obviously. Every Tomahawk takes evasive action accepting that he is the target - up, down, pull tighter, flick in a high speed stall, necks stretched, all with that empty feeling of suspense, waiting for the 20mm's to strike.

But the fight is on. Tracers lace the sky and cordite smoke trails out. It is a mass of aircraft being fired at or firing at others. Some burning, some trailing fuel. The smell of cordite ever present. But it is the heavy white tracers of the 109s' 20mm's which take precedence. Throttles are whacked back and forward for some tactical advantage - leave revs at 2,600 rpm, gun stoppages are cleared automatically by the reload handles in the cockpit alongside the .5 breeches.

On this occasion, as the ME109s were trying to get a sight on us, we their targets, were turning and tightening it up a bit. The 109s being very fast and trying to achieve the proper angle off, were pulling a lot of G. Their tracers were going past behind one's tail. Then they overshot, found that they had lost a lot of speed and had been pulled into the dogfight. It was a good opportunity for the Tomahawks to get at grips with the 109s. I adopted my usual habit of yawing and slipping as I turned, which allowed a better 360 degree search. I was in a left hand turn just a little out from the centre of this swirling mass.

I picked up a 109 coming down into the fight from my high port quarter. He was fast and turning into me. Streamers were coming from his wingtips. I gently eased back on the stick, tightening my turn as he pulled tighter, trying to make a kill. Committed, he opened fire too soon. The heavy white tracer of his 20mm's went past behind me outside of my turn. I lifted my nose and rolled to the left - into my turn - as he went past behind and below me. I came out of my roll and was able to turn down onto him at about 100 yards range. I had a good bead on him and fired two good bursts which hit him in the cockpit and centre-section. I lost sight of him under my nose but two of my pilots reported that he burst into flames. From Flg. Off. R.H. Gibbes' diary extract - "I was trying to get a shot at it when a Tomahawk dived from somewhere above with a lot of speed and firing from about 100 yards, hit it cleanly in about the cockpit area. The Messerschmitt disintegrated in a ball of flame. I could only admire such magnificent shooting. I think the Tomahawk was flown by Alan Rawlinson". That is good confirmation.

I had gun stoppages which needed clearing so I reverted to my slipping and yawing turn. In addition to assisting my all around search this was a good defence manoeuvre against an unseen attack. If I was a target doing a "proper" turn, the attacker would pull his sight through my fore and aft axis and then take that line ahead to get his lead, or angle off - just like duck or skeet shooting. The yaw and slip gives the target aircraft a different flight path to the visual impression, thus producing a slight error for the attacker. In a dogfight it is not so apparent to the attacker. Always encourage survival - dead pilots don't destroy the enemy.

Another observation based on experience of then 12 months combat, was that targets tend to present themselves in a dogfight. In the early days one tended to tear about looking for targets which were usually fleeting, and often you found yourself to be a target. But back to the fight. The next 109 came down and was turning in behind me. I carried out much the same procedure as before but did not complete a roll in order to follow him. His tracers were going past outside of my turn. I was able to pick him up as he overshot and, from about 250 yards, fired short bursts until the guns stopped. The 109 went down in a slow spiral as I lost sight of it. I was sure that I had hit it, but the dogfight was too intense - other priorities took over.

A third 109 came down from astern and I could see him pulling in tightly until I lost sight of him beneath me. As I had cleared the gun stoppages I rolled over further into my left turn and picked him up again.

He was fast and pulling away. I had lost a bit of speed so decided to improve this by closing the hood and cleaning up the aircraft outline. I gave him a long burst from astern - I had been able to pull into the astern position because of the Tomahawk's better manoeuvrability but he was pulling away. By contrast he had opened fire during his attack on me but he could not pull inside my turn - his tracers went past behind me as before. It is easy to see if an attacker has you in his sights from his head-on aspect. However, when I fired I was blinded by grit and dust from the .5s with their breeches in the cockpit. I pulled out of the fight, weaving madly as I thought I had been hit. When my eyes cleared I could see no damage so I went back into the fight. I saw a Tomahawk going down steeply from the dogfight in a south westerly direction. It was not burning or trailing smoke but it was too far below to see any damage.

The fight was still raging. I picked up a pair of 109s coming down and turning into the fight. Again I closed the hood and chose one of them as a target. They were slightly above and I gave him a long burst from the beam, developing into the rear quarter. It didn't get that far as I was once more blinded by rubbish from the guns. I opened the hood and pulled away from where I thought was the centre of the dogfight. My eyes were stinging and sore. I was weaving, slipping and yawing - trying not to be an easy target. Again I could see no damage to my aircraft. The guns were still giving trouble, only 2 of the 4 x.3 wing guns were operating and my reflector sight was not working. I searched for the dogfight but it had dispersed - the sky was empty. Later I knew that it had deteriorated into a defensive circle of our remaining Tomahawks with the 109s diving through them from above in their old familiar fashion.

The fight lasted 65 minutes - one of the longest specific dogfights ever. Many of our survivors landed at a forward airfield low on fuel, returning to base next morning. Lindsay Knowles and Lees were killed. Roberts and Bill Kloster were shot down and taken prisoners of war. Ron Simes was shot down and walked home. On top of the morning's fight we had lost 8 aircraft for the day. The German losses on the day were about even.

At one point in the dogfight I saw two aircraft at the top of the turmoil carry out a head-on attack. The 109 was coming down at about 30 degrees, the Tomahawk was climbing up at him. Both of them were firing, the smoke from their guns streaming back behind them and their tracers streaking straight ahead. They were closing fast and both of them were being torn to pieces by each other's fire. They kept on firing until the disintegrating mass collided. It all happened in a flash. The dogfight just absorbed the scene and went on its own frenzied way. It was all so intense you could feel it. . .

After landing it was found that my hood was jammed, possibly by dust, and could not close completely. The rubbish from my guns was sucked up out of the gap and into my eyes en route - a cause so simple but the outcome could have been fatal. [9]

Contemporary reports and claims by the pilots of 2 Wing amounted to three Messerschmitts destroyed with a number of probables and damaged. In fact the German losses amounted to somewhat more than this, five aircraft being lost in the battle and another crash-landing when it returned to base with its pilot wounded.

3 Squadron lost five aircraft, 112 Squadron one, and Wg. Cdr. Jeffrey force-landed.

It is worth examining these losses and claims in more detail. Claims were submitted by Oblt. Fluder, (two), Hpt Lippert, Fw. Bendert, Ofhr. Woiditch, Fw. Glessinger and Obfw. Schulz, which equals the losses of No. 2 Wing exactly; however one of the Tomahawks lost was involved in a collision.

Of the German pilots who submitted claims, five were recognised aces. 2 Wing was fighting against seasoned veterans who enjoyed the added advantage of superior equipment. Hpt. Wolfgang Lippert, the Gruppenkommandeur of II/JG 27 had twenty five victories on arrival in the theatre, and ended with a final score of twenty nine. Fw. Karl-Heinz Bendert claimed thirty six victories in the Desert and ended the war as an Oberleutnant with fifty four, including nine Flying Fortresses. Ofhr. Franz Woiditch ended the war as an Oberleutnant, having subsequently served with JG 52 and JG 400 ,with a score of 110 victories. Obfw. Otto Schulz claimed forty two victories in the Desert before his death in action on 17 June 1942, when he was shot down by Sgt. James Edwards, a rising Canadian ace of 260 Squadron. Schulz numbered Neville Duke and Nicky Barr amongst his victims. Oblt. Fluder took part in the Battle of Britain and had scored eight victories by the time of his death in combat with 5 SAAF Squadron on 31 May 1942. He was the *Staffelkapitan* of 6/JG 27 from January 1942. Fw. Glessinger was killed in combat with 250 Squadron the following day.

PO Neville Duke of 112 Squadron was the only non-Australian to submit a claim. He shot down the Bf109 flown by Ofhr. Wascott of I Gruppe, who baled out and became a PoW. Duke's reflector sight had failed and he scored his victory using the ring and bead sight with which the Tomahawk was fitted. He already had two Bf109s from combats in Europe, and the shared CR42 mentioned earlier. He ended the war with a total of twenty six and two shared destroyed plus numerous probables and damaged.[10]

PO Jack Bartle (AK538), one of the Australians serving with 112 Squadron made his first claim, (the only other Bf109 to fall to 112 Squadron.) His victim may have been Fw. Hillert of I Gruppe, who crash-landed and became a PoW. Duke and Bartle would have been fighting together, both German pilots came from the same unit and both were captured.

Of the other four German aircraft which were lost, one was involved in a collision with Fl.Lt. Lindsay Knowles of 3 Squadron. Knowles failed to return from this battle, and it was only recently that Tom Trimble confirmed that the collision seen by several members of the Squadron involved Lindsay Knowles. His machine passed so close to Trimble that his serial number was easily read. Oddly, considering the collision, no German pilots lost their lives in the fight, but Lt. Scheppa was taken to an Italian hospital with unspecified injuries, so perhaps it was he who survived the collision with Lindsay Knowles.

Although claiming only one confirmed victory after the fight, it is likely that Rawlinson was responsible for the loss of at least two German aircraft.

> At the time I claimed a 109F destroyed, 1 probable and 2 damaged. Post war study of enemy records now show that it was 2 109Fs destroyed and 2 damaged.[11]

Sgt. Ron Simes (AM507, Z) also claimed a victory when he returned, which was 'confirmed by the 11th Hussars and 3 Recce Co. of the South Africans, amongst whom he crash-landed.'[12]

The other two German pilots shot down in the combat were Uffz. Tanier and Uffz. Reuter, (Frank Fischer's victor on the 20th) both of II Gruppe. Reuter was an 'experte' with twenty one victories at the time of his capture in May 1942.

However, the sixth and last loss is the most intriguing of all. Oblt. Ernst Dullberg, the *Staffelkapitan* of 5/JG 27, was wounded in the combat and crash-landed at base. He was hit by the fire of a Tomahawk which he saw closing in on him in a wide turn, but thought it was too far away to be dangerous. It opened fire from what he called 'an Olympic distance' and hit his fighter twice, one shot going through his Mae West life jacket, the other hitting the cockpit and wounding him in the left foot.[13]

This Tomahawk could well have been flown by Alan Rawlinson. While dealing with his gun stoppages and reflector sight problems, he noticed a 109 in the distance and took a long shot at it, using the ring and bead sight. He saw no sign of his fire striking it, and therefore did not submit a claim for a damaged. This brief instant is not mentioned in his written account of the combat. Years later, when reading *Fighters Over The Desert,* Alan Rawlinson recalled the incident, and wondered if his long shot at the 109 was connected with Dullberg's comments. Given the circumstances, and the fact that no other similar claims for damaged E/A were submitted by the squadron, it seems more than likely that it was. 112 Squadron made no claims apart from the victories to Duke and Bartle.

The losses sustained by 2 Wing were tragic. 3 Squadron had lost eight aircraft and seven pilots in the day's operations, and did not operate again until 24 November.

112 Squadron fared better: Sgt. Henry Burney was the squadron's only loss, but returned to the unit in company with Wg. Cdr. Rosier, who enterprisingly landed his Hurricane in an attempt to pick him up. A tyre burst and the aircraft had to be abandoned. The two pilots walked thirty miles to meet Allied soldiers and returned on the 25th.

The pilots who took part in the action on the afternoon of 22 November are listed below, in 3 Squadron's Operations Record Book. (Take off time was 1540.)

AN244 W/C. Jeffrey	landed in our lines and returned unit next day	
AN410 F/L. Knowles	missing	
AN389 F/L. Arthur	1745 *(landing time)*	Landed LG 134
AN441 P/O. Jackson	1745	Landed LG 134
AK382 F/O. Trimble	1745	Landed LG 134
AN373 F/O. Roberts	missing*	
AK390 P/O. Kloster	missing	
AK506 F/O. Manford	1555 R.T.B.	magneto trouble
AN305 P/O. Lees	missing	
AM476 SGT. Wilson	1610 R.T.B.	magneto trouble
AK378 SGT. Baillie	1745	Landed LG 131
AM507 SGT. Simes	missing	
AN365 S/L. Rawlinson	1715	Landed LG 122
AN224 F/O. Gibbes	1748	Landed LG 134

At 1130 hours on 23 November, 250 Squadron provided ten Tomahawks as top cover for Hurricanes of the RNFS patrolling over South African troops advancing on the Sidi Rezegh area. They encountered six Ju88s escorted by twelve Bf109s and twelve G-50s. The 109s attacked the Hurricanes before they could interfere with the bombers, and were in turn engaged by 250 Squadron, who fought them for twelve minutes. Clive Caldwell, now promoted to Flight Lieutenant, and flying Tomahawk AK498 LD-C, destroyed one Messerschmitt, as did Sgts. Bill Cable and Bob Whittle, who also claimed two more damaged. Sqn. Ldr. Morris's Tomahawk was damaged and one pilot shot down.

At 1530, five aircraft of 250 Squadron took off as top cover for a mixed force of Hurricanes escorting nine Blenheims to Trigh Capuzzo. This force was attacked all the way to its target, and both sides suffered casualties. Sgt Coward was hit by flak and crash-landed successfully, while Caldwell engaged Hpt. Wolfgang Lippert, *Gruppenkommandeur* of II/JG 27 at 1600.

When in the vicinity of Ben Eira, a number of Tomahawk fighters were seen approaching from ahead and above. As they passed on our starboard side, I observed other aircraft above and below them, one of which turned to attack our formation. I was able to turn head on up to this attack and saw the E/A open fire at a range of about 300 yds. Opening fire at the same time myself the E/A pulled out of its dive and I was able to put [in] a very satisfying burst with all guns as he did so. He fired a short burst at nothing at all, half turned over and went down steeply. I followed him over, but had to pull away quickly as a result of which I spun my machine, recovered too harshly, and flicked over the opposite way, losing sight of the E/A, and finally regaining full control at about 4,500 feet. While trying to climb back to the formation, I observed a fire on the ground and saw a ME.109 dive through the rear of the escort to below my level. As he pulled out of his dive to regain height in the apparent safe region at the rear, I was able to turn on to him and deliver an attack. He saw me and turned down and my first burst was

---

* *Australian War Memorial files AWM 54 779/3/29 contain debriefs of PoWs recorded after their return or release at the end of the war. During the dogfight, FO Roberts' aircraft was holed in the oil tank by six bullets, his windscreen was shattered, and he was struck in the head by a piece of the canopy. Unconscious for some seconds, he recovered to force-land successfully on the undercarriage. He left the aircraft intact as per orders and started walking back, but he was captured after fifteen miles.*

The day's work completed, Sgt Bob Whittle's ground crew relax with their aircraft, *Nux Vomica*.
(Bob Whittle)

from the rear quarter above at a range of about 400 yds. He went to ground level then flying directly into the sun. I was able to close the range to approx. 200 yds. and chased for a period of 2 to 3 minutes, firing five bursts in all. My reflector sight was useless against the glare, and I was using my ring and bead sight. Two fragments came away from the E/A, which was still flying with apparent efficiency when last seen.

Caldwell initially claimed the first 109 as a probable, but,

From subsequent enquiry it was seen that the first ME.109 was destroyed, several pilots having observed the incident and the result.

Lippert baled out over Allied territory. In doing so he

broke both his legs when he struck the vertical stabiliser. He was found by British troops and after being administered first aid, was taken to General Hospital 119 in Egypt. There both legs became infected, necessitating an immediate amputation.

Lippert defended himself in a futile attempt to save his legs.... When it became clear that there was no alternative, he agreed to the amputation. He died from an embolism ten minutes after the operation without ever regaining consciousness.[14]

On 24 November Rommel counter attacked, and his tanks advanced so rapidly that they overran the headquarters of XXX Corps. Early in the afternoon 3 Squadron was escorting Marylands, and

on the way home we saw a huge mass of trucks and tanks moving south east from Bir el Gobi down the Trig el Abd, a Bedouin track which went through Gabr Saleh and on to the border near Maddalena - where we were at LG122. There were over a thousand of them. It was Rommel making one of his daring strikes to throw our forces off balance.

We reported it after we landed but it was not believed as being enemy. Our intelligence people considered the force to be one of our supply columns returning from the battle area! We disagreed as there were too many tanks with them. A couple of forward airfields were over-run but most of their aircraft got away in time. All of their fighters came back to us at LG122, landing at dusk and in the dark. There were no radio communications and we had no flare path. With Peter Jeffrey I punched holes in 4 gallon tins of fuel and ran along the threshold of the runway and then down its right hand edge - pouring out fuel as I went. Then got out of the way as Pete lit it. It only provided about 100 yards of runway.

Aircraft were landing everywhere - some on the runway, many through our squadron dispersal area covered with aircraft and slit trenches. We had to fall flat to dodge the wheels of landing aircraft. About 60 aircraft came in which concentrated just about all our fighter force at LG122 - 175 of them! Surprisingly all the incoming aircraft landed safely. Our Wing HQ ordered a recce for first light the next morning to find the Afrika Corps (sic) force and we turned in.[15]

During the night the advancing Germans passed within ten miles of LG 122, and LG 132 at Sidi Omar had tanks pass only five miles away next morning, forcing 451 Tac. R. Squadron to evacuate its aircraft, but the opportunity was missed, and the fighter force survived.

At first light on the 25 November, with Woof Arthur as my No. 2 I flew the recce and found the enemy force only about 15 - 20 miles away to the north west. They were stationary in a big laager. It was still only half light so I went down to confirm their identity, leaving Woof as top cover, and was met with a heavy amount of rifle, machine gun and light flak. We dashed straight home and reported to Wing. They were holding our forces before turning on a big strike, awaiting confirmation. There was still some doubt in their minds so I suggested that we repeat the recce. It would take only 15 - 20 minutes and away we went. It was a bit lighter now. I sent Woof down and stayed top cover. He was heavily attacked and had no doubts. We dashed back to base and reported. We were briefed by Wing to attack as soon as possible.[16]

At 0815, 112 Squadron attacked the advancing Axis columns and although two aircraft were hit by flak, all returned safely. 3 followed them at 0825, but surprise was lost. FO Bothwell, flying alongside Rawlinson, was hit and rammed an *Afrika Korps* tank. Fl.Lt. Manford crash-landed but managed to escape with 451 Squadron as they evacuated their landing ground in the face of German armour. FO Jewell was also forced to crash-land due to damage inflicted by the accurate

Repairs to AN39? after a serious mishap. Oddly, no reference could be found to the circumstances in the ORB. (RAAF Museum)

ground fire and was quickly captured, although he attempted to hide. He was asked the way to Sidi Omar, and not surprisingly he gave his captors the wrong directions, which caused them to bump into a New Zealand patrol. In the confusion Jewell leapt out of the vehicle, the Germans drove off hastily in the other direction, (no doubt wiser for the experience) and everyone was happy, particularly FO Jewell.

The men of 3 Squadron demonstrated their resilience and determination on the afternoon of the 25th when they encountered between sixty and seventy Axis aircraft over Sidi Rezegh while on a combined sweep with 112 Squadron, led by Peter Jeffrey. Due to their losses they were able to put only seven Tomahawks into the air and 112 supplied twelve. Undeterred by the odds, the wing plunged into the fray and scored a notable victory.

The Germans were attacking New Zealand brigades from XIII Corps, who were advancing to the aid of XXX Corps, and causing dislocation of Rommel's plans in the process. Ju87s and Bf110s were bombing with a top cover of Bf109s and G-50s. Some CR42s were with the Stukas. 112 Squadron engaged the fighters, while 3 dived to attack the Bf110s, which scattered rather than forming a defensive circle. This proved to be their undoing, as they lost four of their number to Sgt. Rex Wilson (AK506), Wg. Cdr. Jeffrey (AN337), Sgt Reid (AN408) and FO Jackson (AM406). Jeffrey and Wilson also damaged Bf110s, while Sgt. Baillie (AK378) destroyed a Bf109E and damaged several more. FO Bobby Gibbes got amongst the G-50s, destroying two and damaging three more. When the wing dived on the bombers, Gibbes saw the Italian fighters above and climbed towards them. His approach was unseen, as the Italian leader was concentrating on the action below.

> One team of five aircraft came down in a gentle dive, noticed me at the last moment, and the leader tried to pull around onto me. This put me into a very favourable position as I came in at them from the opposite direction, on the inside of their turn, and I was able to have a crack at each of the five, as they swept by, in line astern. The same thing happened three or four times, and although I didn't do much noticeable damage, I did however succeed in breaking up their formation considerably. Without doubt, I prevented a few coordinated attacks on the squadrons below.

> A G50 came at me shooting madly. I returned his fire, crouching low in the cockpit behind the engine and feeling the size of a house. He made the mistake of breaking his attack too early and turned away to starboard. I pulled off a little lead, and saw bits and pieces fly from his cockpit area. The aircraft rolled onto its back and went into an uncontrolled spin, pouring black smoke. I turned my aircraft and watched it plummet down towards the sea below, and then with a jerk, realising my foolishness, I kicked on hard rudder and looked behind. I was just in time. Macchis and G50s were coming at me from all directions. I gave the old Tommy everything, weaving my way through them and climbed above. . . I saw a line of G50s below my level and dived to attack. They were doing a gentle turn to port when I joined them, making the formation six, but only for a moment. My bullets concentrated around the tail-end aircraft, and I don't think he would have known what hit him. His aircraft shuddered, hesitated in its turn, bunted outwards, pulled up into a half loop, then fell away, obviously completely out of control, leaving a spiral trail of black smoke behind it. It was probably flown by a dead pilot. I pulled around onto the next aircraft, and when I fired, it flicked onto its back and dived away, but it appeared to be under control. Maybe I didn't damage it too much, but I certainly frightened hell out of the pilot.[17]

Wilson also shot down two Fi 156s which belonged to JG 27. These were then strafed on the ground, Lt Gorny being wounded. (The Fi 156s were flown by crews on their way to attend the funeral of Lt. Scheppa, who had been admitted to an Italian hospital after the combat of 22 November. The hospital was bombed and Scheppa was one of the casualties.)

112 Squadron lost one aircraft and its pilot, and 3 lost FO Bruce Evans, who was killed. Rex Wilson's combat report tells the story of his fight graphically.

> Just as E/A were reported I could see many bombs bursting at 10 o'clock in the REZEGH Area and saw several formations of M.E.110's (sic) bearing in a westerly direction, some above and others below. As we approached I could see in the distance 6-8 A/C diving steeply below us and took them to be

J.U.87's (sic) and another formation at our own height to the left of the 110's , which I assumed were the fighter escort. We were closing in on the 110's when a formation of them turned and dived below and down sun of us and the Wing Leader peeled off after them, so I followed. I singled out 1 110 and gave him several short bursts from medium range and as I was closing on him noticed another Tommy just below and ahead attacking the same aircraft, so I turned away and engaged another 110. I fired many bursts at him and finally closed right in from astern firing many long bursts and broke away when grey smoke and what seemed to be pieces of metal blotted out my vision. My last sight of the M.E.110 was as I pulled away when I could see him going down with smoke issuing from both engines. I made similar attacks on two other M.E. 110's closing right in from astern firing many bursts and breaking off each time when I had overshot them. I then climbed as I could not see any more E/A and was at 8800 ft approx when below I could see a M.E.109F firing from astern at a Tommy. I dived on the 109 and after a few turns closed right in from astern firing many long bursts with my wing guns, both cannons having stopped. The 109 had rolled and dived. I climbed to attack again but could not see him. By this time, I was almost over TOBRUK so I climbed to 10000 approx and saw well below me 1-8 A/C flying west. I shadowed them for a while losing height and getting up sun of them but lost sight of them during a turn. I was about to return to REZEGH and when I saw another A/C well below also heading west I dived down and made sure the A/C were enemy and carried out another attack on both closing in and firing good bursts with my wing guns and 1 cannon which I had succeeded in clearing. Both A/C which I believe to be Storch crash landed and the crews ran like hell. Unfortunately my ammo was almost expended by now and I was able only to get odd bursts from the port cannon, but succeed in hitting both A/C with the one gun starting a fire of sorts with much red smoke in one of them. I set off for base and came on the wire near SIDI - OMAR where I saw an aircraft burning on the ground. I was going down to investigate but was fired on from the ground so dived away and made off. I was fired on again from another camp 1-2 miles south of the first one and here I could see another two fires burning. I then returned to base.

On 26 November at 1530, nine aircraft from 3 Squadron took part in a combined Wing Sweep with 112 Squadron over Sidi Rezegh. They lost Sgt. Geoffrey Hiller, who was shot down by Hpt. Redlich of I/JG 27 when six Bf109s of this unit attacked the Wing near Tobruk. Hiller baled out, but received some unwanted attention from a Bf109, as 'Tiny' Cameron's combat report relates.

. . . Aircraft reported in SIDI REZEGH and I saw them behind us. They came down in line astern, making individual attacks and pulling up when still well out. I saw one 109 attack a Tomahawk and set it on fire after which the pilot bailed out. I later found this was Sgt. HILLER. *Another 109 appeared to be making an attack on the parachute (author's italics)* so I went down and forced him to pull out without firing. I then circled the parachute until it landed. I could not see any place to land and pick him up but he appeared to be O.K. I climbed up-sun looking for A/C. 6 109s came down after me and made successive attacks from fairly long range. They seemed to have more difficulty following me if I turned right instead of left, so each time as I saw the leading A/C about to open fire I turned hard on to him and attacked head on. Got a good burst on several and finally hit one, drawing a cloud of white smoke. The other five kept attacking me but I was gradually getting closer to a big cumulus cloud. Eventually succeeded in beating them into it then went across to TOBRUK and landed. TOBRUK defences saw the Tomahawk pilot land in enemy territory lines and later another parachute come down. They also reported, (through W/O BLACK) that 12 A/C were seen shot down the previous afternoon. (25/11/41)

Sgt. Hiller was captured, but died of wounds on 2 December. Perhaps Cameron's gallant attempt to protect his friend failed! As no other Allied aircraft were lost in this engagement, the second parachute reported by the Tobruk garrison confirmed the success of Cameron's attack on the 109.

Their report of twelve aircraft falling on the previous day also provides good confirmation of 2 Wing's claims. 112 claimed two, and 3 Squadron claimed nine. As both squadrons lost one aircraft, which *might* have been included in Tobruk's count, at least ten of the eleven claims can be confirmed, but Rex Wilson's attack on the two Fi156s took place at low level to the west, so it is quite possible that these were unseen.

Desert dust: 3 Squadron Tomahawk during Operation *Crusader*. (RAAF Museum)

On 27 November 3 Squadron escorted Blenheims which were attacking German positions near Gasr el Arid. They did not encounter any enemy aircraft. Nor did they meet the enemy on the 28th and 29th, but Clive Caldwell claimed a Bf109 probable on 28 November while escorting bombers to Trigh Capuzzo. On 30 November, however, 2 Wing scored its second memorable success within five days.

By this stage of Operation *Crusader*, the situation on the ground had become critical. The Germans had re-taken Sidi Rezegh, and Tobruk was once again cut off. Air support for the ground forces was essential, and on a morning wing sweep, the two squadrons met approximately fifty enemy aircraft which were about to attack the New Zealand Division.

> The enemy were in several layers, 15 Ju87s at 6000 ft, 20 G-50s and MC200s from 7000 - 8000 and five Bf109Fs as top cover. The Wing Commander detailed one section of 112 to watch the Messerschmitts and the remainder of the squadron, with 3 RAAF, to concentrate on the middle and lower formations.[18]

The Stukas and escorting Italians were struck savagely, their attack being broken up before any bombs could be dropped effectively on the New Zealanders. FO Tom Trimble destroyed two MC200s and damaged three Ju87s. FO Gibbes destroyed a G-50, Sgt Mailey destroyed two MC200s and damaged three Ju87s, Sgt Scott shot down a G-50 and a Ju87 and Sqn. Ldr. Rawlinson destroyed a MC200, which was his last confirmed victory.

> I attacked a Macchi from astern at close range. He was heavily hit and pieces were flying from him. After two good bursts both . 5s stopped. I was well throttled back in order to stay behind him while I reloaded the guns, but only one was working to support the .30s in the wings which were all firing. I continued firing right in to about 50 yards when his port undercarriage leg fell down, and the aircraft was going down steeply, taking no evasive action. It looked as if the pilot was killed. When I first fired the Macchi was in a climb and after my last burst he was going down at about 1500 feet.[19]

He was the only pilot in this engagement, during which the Squadron's one hundredth enemy aircraft was destroyed, to have flown in 3 Squadron's first successful engagement on 19 November 1940.

Sgt. Wilson damaged a Macchi, a Ju87 and a Bf109 and 'Tiny' Cameron damaged a G-50 and four dive bombers, but then disaster came very close to striking, in the form of Obfw. Otto Schulz.

> Was flying Lester Blue 3 when A/C were sighted 2 o'clock below. As we approached the STUKAS dived to ground level apparently jettisoned their bombs. 3 Squadron followed them down and attacked from the rear, leaving 112 to cope with the 109's etc., above. Two other Tomahawks and myself were attacking the main force of J.U.87's (sic) (approx. 20 to 30) which were accompanied by 1 G.50. They were flying N.W. towards GAZALA at ground level. I shot at 4 J.U.87's from very short range and saw another Tomahawk set a J.U.87 on fire. Afterwards found this was Sgt. Mailey. After looking behind and seeing nothing, I went in for another 87 and had just delivered a burst when I was shot from the rear by a 109. Three of them came over as I turned away and crash landed. 2 109s and 1 G.50 circled me and one of the 109s burnt the kite with a short burst. I had previously removed rations and crystal. Two Tomahawks came over and I attracted their attention. W/Cdr JEFFREY landed and picked me up and to my great relief flew me back to L.G. 122. The best ride I ever had.

Peter Jeffrey discarded his parachute and somehow crammed Cameron, who was clearly the largest man in the squadron, into the cockpit. He was awarded a DSO on 12 December.

Otto Schulz meanwhile shot down PO Neville Duke (RAF) of 112 Squadron, who also crash-landed and survived Schulz's unwelcome attentions by hiding in some convenient nearby scrub.

Sgt. 'Tiny' Cameron and Wg. Cdr. Peter Jeffrey, after Peter Jeffrey's courageous rescue of Cameron, who was shot down by Obfw. Otto Schulz on 30 November. Jeffrey was awarded the DSO on 12 December
(Alan Rawlinson)

112 Squadron shot down one MC200 and two G-50s, one of which fell to Sgt. Rudolph Leu in AK509, for his second victory. PO Ken Sands (AK377 V) chased a G-50 at ground level for twelve miles and damaged it before giving up in frustration when his guns stopped working.

112 Squadron aircrew at LG122, 30 November 1941, after their successful combat. Standing, left to right, Sgt. Rudolph Leu RAAF, PO Neville Duke, FO Soden, FO Humphries, Sqn. Ldr. Morello (in white) Fl. Lt. Ambrose, PO Dickinson, Sgt. Henry Burney RAAF, FO Westenra. Kneeling, PO Sabourin, PO Bowker, PO Jack Bartle RAAF, Sgt. Carson RAAF. *Which* of the Carson brothers was unfortunately not recorded. (Alan Rawlinson)

The eight victories claimed by 3 Squadron took its total of enemy aircraft destroyed to 102, but this was marred by the apparent loss of Fl.Lt. Wilf Arthur, who did not return.

He had in fact shot down two Stukas, a G-50 which had interrupted his attack on the Stuka formation and was shot down for its pains, and a second G-50 from a formation of three which he saw 'heading home very low, one with the port wheel down. Got behind him and set the mainplane on fire'. His Tomahawk was now ailing, due to distributor damage from one of three bullets which had struck it during the fight, and he was eventually forced to land, which he successfully accomplished.

The final total of twelve confirmed victories for no pilot losses brought the total to 106, making them the first Desert fighter squadron to reach the century. It was duly celebrated.

A signal was received from Air Vice Marshal Coningham, AOC Western Desert Air Force. "Personal from AOC to Wg. Cdr. Jeffrey and the squadron. Congratulations on the squadron's splendid fight which has contributed so much to our present overwhelming air superiority. I regret your casualties but they have cost the enemy dearly. The Squadron has been selected for re-equipment with first Kittyhawks. Good luck".[20]

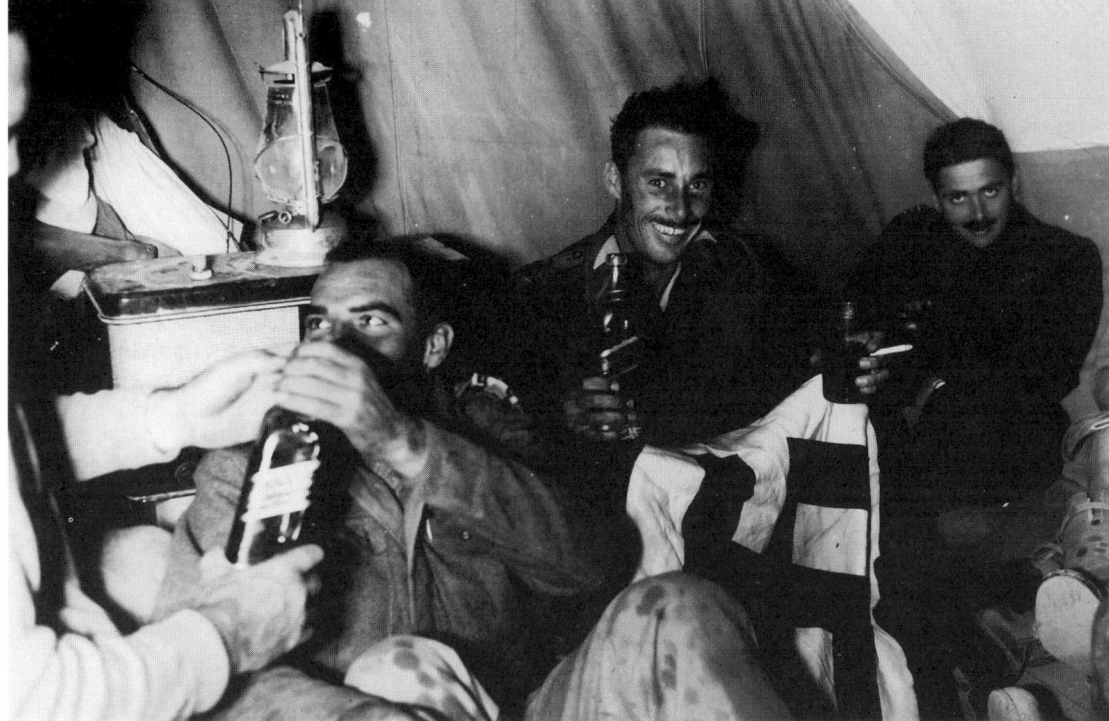

Celebrating the century 1: Sqn .Ldr. Alan Rawlinson Wg. Cdr. Peter Jeffrey and Sqn. Ldr. John Laver (MO), with trophy flag and rare bottles of Johnny Walker, after the combat on 30 November, when the squadron destroyed twelve enemy aircraft, bring its total to 106. (Alan Rawlinson)

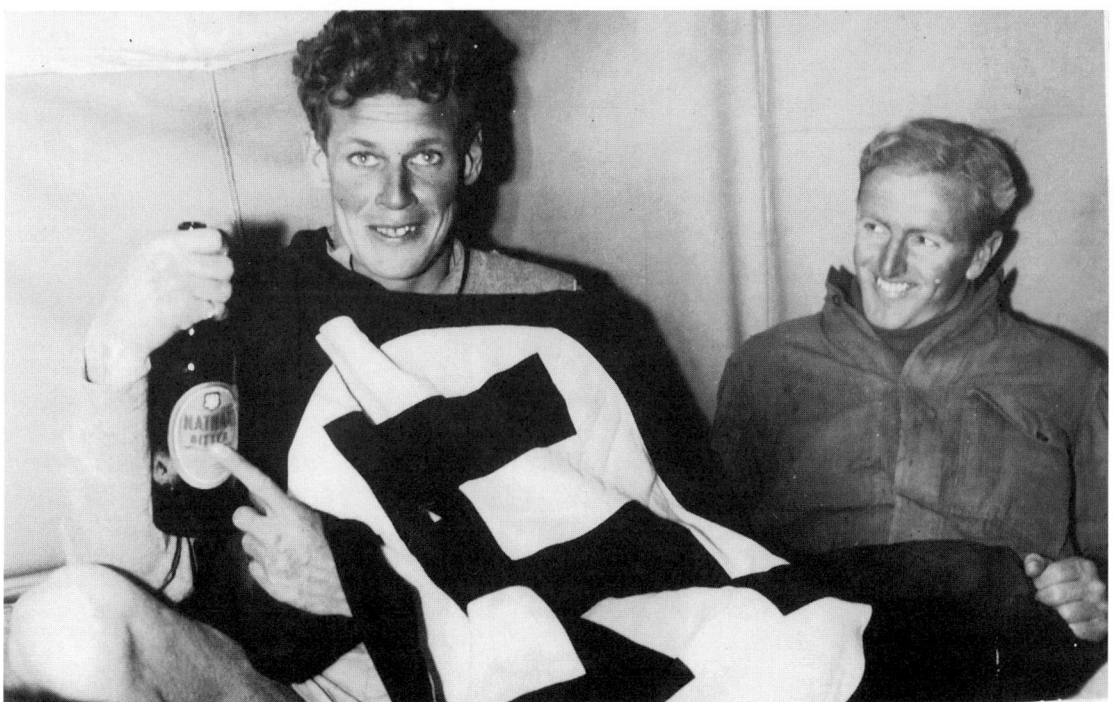

Celebrating the century 2: Fl. Lt. Wilf ('Woof') Arthur, who claimed four victories on 30 November, with Sgt. Rex Wilson, who damaged three E/A in the same combat, and destroyed a Ju88 the following day. (Alan Rawlinson)

At 1025 hours on 1 December, two Tomahawks from 3 were scrambled to intercept a reconnaissance Ju88 of 2(F)/ 123, which was shot down by Sgt. Rex Wilson in AN457. This was his fifth victory. The Squadron was then stood down for a week until replacement pilots and aircraft could be provided.

Earlier in the day PO John Waddy of 250 Squadron made his first claim, a probable Bf109. He was to make many more before his time in the Desert was over. 250 Squadron was flying as top cover to the Hurricanes of the RNFS, when at 0910 they encountered a formation of Ju88s with a close escort and a top cover of Bf109s. The Naval unit attacked the bombers and their escort, while 250 engaged the top cover. John Waddy's combat report explains his part in the action.

> In vicinity south of Sidi Rezegh and N. of Bir El Gobi, bombs were observed exploding on the ground & I observed approx. SIX E/Fighters approaching head on. They climbed and started to attack from rear quarter. I turned under the attack and while in a steep turn saw an ME.109 on the tail of a Tomahawk, both being in a turn. I fired a long burst into the E/A and observed the bullets hitting on the engine and in the cockpit. The E/A slowly rolled over on to its back and then went into a spin. When last seen, the aircraft was still spinning in a seemingly uncontrollable manner about 4,000 ft. below the combat.

Mac Twemlow damaged the tail of another Bf109, and Sgt. Murray Adams was missing, but returned safely the next day.

A group of 250 Squadron pilots, including Sgts. 'Slinger' Nitschke, second from left, Bill Cable, standing, fourth, and standing next to him, Sgt. Murray Adams. Note Sgt. Nitschke's personalised water container, a 'Jerry' can. (Bob Whittle)

PO Swinnerton RAF, of 250 Squadron, force-landed on 1 December, the manner of his return being a
novel one. He was towed home by an armoured car, returning the next day. A keen photographer,
Bob Whittle couldn't resist such an unusual scene. PO Swinnerton is at left, wearing flying boots.
(Bob Whittle)

250 Squadron pilots: from left, PO Swinnerton, FO Hart, Sgt. Bob Whittle. The seated pilot is
unidentified. (Bob Whittle)

John Waddy later recorded the circumstances of his first combat for the *ABC Weekly* after he had returned to Australia. The article, reproduced below, was found in his personal papers at the Australian War Memorial. Due to the fact that his log book had been temporarily 'misplaced' at the time of my visit, there is no means of pinpointing the exact date, but it took place between 10 November, when he flew his first operational sortie, and 1 December. It candidly reveals the confusion faced by most inexperienced pilots when first becoming involved in battle.

> On my first dogfight I didn't know much of what went on. We were flying along and I was lucky to be flying behind "Killer" Caldwell.
>
> I was a bit puzzled by some white puffs I saw - I didn't realise what they were at first, and was watching them rather interestedly instead of doing my job looking for aircraft. When one came a little close, it suddenly occurred to me that it was ack-ack.
>
> At the same time I glanced over my shoulder and saw some white noses which all seemed to be pointing at me.
>
> Now there are no white noses in our squadron and I couldn't quite make it out; but I looked in front and was in time to see "Killer" in a vertical turn. I realised then that the white noses were enemy aircraft and stuck to "Killer's" tail for all I was worth. The old aircraft went in all directions. We were upside-down, on our backs, we were on our sides. I was swearing at "Killer" because in my ignorance I thought he was doing so many fool things I'd be sure to kill myself sooner or later.
>
> There were lots of aircraft whizzing past, and I discovered that they were going round in a circle, and "Killer" and myself were inside the circle going in the opposite direction.
>
> The aircraft in the outside circle were probably doing 200 mph and we were probably doing about 200 mph so we were passing at approx. 400-odd miles an hour. All I could see was a blur going past, and I couldn't tell whether it was theirs our ours.
>
> Suddenly there were no other aircraft in the sky but "Killer's" and my own. We came home.
>
> I got on the ground and said: "Well, what was it all about?"
>
> He said "Oh, it was a pretty good dogfight up there while it lasted."
>
> 'Dogfight," I said, "all I could see was aircraft flying about. I didn't know it was a dogfight."
>
> And that's the case with most new pilots. I didn't even fire my guns.

On 5 December 112 and 250 Squadrons were paired, taking off at 1120 hours. The twelve aircraft of 250 were given top cover by ten from 112. They soon encountered between thirty and forty Ju87s in vics of three, escorted by a mixed formation of twenty to thirty G-50s and MC200s with a further twelve Bf109s as high flank cover. 250 Squadron, led by Fl.Lt Clive Caldwell, who by now had been given the grim nick-name of 'Killer', tore into the Stukas while 112 tackled the fighters.

In the resulting massacre the Australians of both squadrons made a large contribution. From 250 Squadron Sgt. Bill Cable destroyed two of the Junkers, Sgt. Bob Whittle two and a probable, which was later confirmed as having crash-landed, and PO F.M. Twemlow one and two probables. Clive Caldwell, however, was about to demonstrate that his companions' choice of nick-name was chillingly appropriate.

> I was leading the formation of two squadrons, 112 acting as top cover to 250 Squadron to patrol a line approximately 10 miles west of El Gubi and just reached this position at 1140 hours when I received R/T warning that a large enemy formation was approaching from the north-west at our own height. Both squadrons climbed immediately and within a minute the enemy formation consisting of Ju-87's with fighter escort was sighted on our starboard side....250 Squadron went into line astern behind me and as 112 Squadron engaged the escorting enemy fighters we attacked the Ju-87s from the rear quarter. ... At...300 yards I opened fire with all my guns at the leader of one of the rear sections of three, allowing too little deflection, and hit No.2 and No. 3 one of which burst into flames immediately, the other going

down smoking and went into flames after losing about 1000 feet. I then attacked the leader of the rear section ... from below and behind, opening fire with all guns at very close range. The enemy aircraft turned over and dived steeply down with the root of the starboard wing in flames. ...[at another Stuka I] opened fire again at close range, the enemy caught fire .... and crashed in flames near some dispersed mechanised transport ... I was able to pull up under the belly of the one at the rear holding the burst until very close range. The enemy aircraft diced (sic) gently straight ahead streaming smoke, caught fire and then dived into the ground.[21]

Caldwell had destroyed five Ju87s, a remarkable feat, brought about by a combination of skill, determination to get in close to his target, and superior gunnery, notwithstanding his admission that he failed to allow enough deflection in his initial attack.

'Killer' Caldwell, snapped by R. Whittle in W. Desert 1941. (Photo and caption - Bob Whittle)

Preserved combat reports from 250 Squadron are rare; those of Sgts. Frank 'Mac' Twemlow and Bill Cable have survived. Mac Twemlow:

> . . . the first attacks were delivered on the JU 87's from their starboard side, and as very little or no evasive action was taken by them, I was able to close in to very close to the formation firing all the time. The JU 87's were flying in fairly close formation and I 'hosed' the outer portion of this until forced to break away underneath to avoid fire coming from the rear gunners. F/Lt. Caldwell reported that immediately following my attack a JU 87 fell out of the formation and went straight down. I then climbed again, turning around behind the formation and came back making an attack on another JU 87 from the starboard beam and slightly above. This aircraft made a very poor attempt at turning to meet my attack. I saw my fire raking the whole length of the fuselage as I closed in to something under 50 yards. The JU 87 turned on its side and slid down under me in a dive evidently out of control. I turned steeply across to follow it but saw another JU 87 immediately in front and slightly below me, and dived down underneath it coming up directly under its belly and gave it several bursts using deflection, which [were] seen to hit the front of the fuselage. I then allowed [my a/c] to drift up into a line astern position, firing all the time and observed [smoke] coming from the JU 87 which then caught fire and began to dive towards the earth with flames coming from the front of the fuselage and the main plane. It was burning fiercely and going down in a steep dive. I was attacked by a G.50 and was forced to take avoiding action. I was unable to have a shot at the G.50.

Bill Cable:

> After observing the enemy approaching from front starboard, our formation turned into a position behind and above them and attacked from astern.

> I made my first attack from astern and above, firing a good burst and observed my bullets entering cockpit and fuselage. JU.87 spiralled down, struck the ground and exploded.

> My second attack was made from rear [port] quarter and my bullets entered aft of the cockpit, causing smoke to come out. This attack was observed by Sgt. Whittle who saw the JU.87 going down out of control with smoke streaming from it.

> My third attack was delivered from rear port quarter and astern. I fired one burst into the fuselage near the tail plane from port quarter, and a burst into starboard main plane from astern, cutting part of it away and the JU.87 went into a spin. Last seen, the JU.87 was spinning violently approx. 2,000 ft.

Sgts. 'Slinger' Nitschke (left) and Bill Cable of 250 Squadron believed in being well dug in. (Bob Whittle)

While 250 Squadron were having their 'Stuka Party' as such events were called by the Desert Air Force, 112 Squadron tangled with the escorts, destroying two G-50s, one Bf109 and a MC200. As well as this they claimed a further five Ju87s. Out of a combined claim for the two squadrons of seventeen, it seems that at least thirteen Stukas were actually destroyed.

Of the Australians with 112, Rudolph Leu in AK354 destroyed the MC200, which 'spun in' , and attacked a Bf109F which 'seemed to falter in the air' and then dive, but was not observed to crash. PO Jack Bartle(AN372) accounted for one of the Ju87s and then attacked a G-50.

'Chased 1 G.50 when about 200 yards behind enemy aircraft over El Adem enemy A/A fire shot a/c down in front of me.'

FO V.D. Fletcher, 112 Squadron's Intelligence Officer, asked Wing on Bartle's behalf 'Is this technical victory, as his action definitely caused the G.50's downfall?' Group Captain Cross confirmed Bartle's claim.[22]

JG 27 made 250 Squadron pay for their successes however, shooting down four Tomahawks, two of whose pilots did not return. One who did was Sgt. Charles McWilliam, who rejoined the squadron on 7 December with shrapnel wounds to the leg. One of the successful German pilots was Uffz. Horst Reuter, who had been shot down by 3 Squadron on 22 November.

When 3 Squadron stood down on 1 December, they had been reduced to nine serviceable aircraft, and these were flown from LG 122 to LG 102 where they could be better serviced. Peter Jeffrey and Alan Rawlinson flew to Cairo on 2 December in search of replacement pilots. The recent new arrivals had been sent to 71 OTU before becoming operational, but they were unavailable, as they had not completed their training due to illness. The Wing Leader and Commanding Officer returned on 4 December, Peter Jeffrey flying Kittyhawk AK596, the first of the Squadron's new aircraft. Due to its position as the highest scoring squadron in the Desert, 3 Squadron had been selected as the first unit to fly the Kittyhawks which were now becoming available.

A comparatively rare airborne shot of a 250 Squadron Tomahawk. (Des Cormack)

Inspirational leaders and friends for life. Alan Rawlinson, CO of 3 Squadron, and Peter Jeffrey, Leader of 2 Wing. Peter Jeffrey was the first instructor to fly with Alan Rawlinson when he began his career with the RAAF in 1939.
(RAAF Museum)

Eleven new pilots also arrived on the 4th, direct from Australia, and were taken on strength without the benefit of a course at the OTU. By mid February four of them were dead. The maintenance staff had repaired enough Tomahawks for training purposes, as well as acquiring some replacement aircraft. On 7 December the new pilots spent most of their time in the air carrying out practice flying, and during the day the unit received a signal ordering all serviceable aircraft and pilots to return to LG 122 by midday on the 8th. Accordingly, fifteen Tomahawks and the Kittyhawk left for LG 122, and at 1230 hours eleven of these flew a sweep with 112 Squadron. They were attacked by six Bf109s, which damaged an aircraft of 112 Squadron.

During this patrol, a four-engined DH86 biplane of 1 Air Ambulance Unit RAAF was en-route for LG134 to pick up casualties. As it approached LG122, it was attacked by five Bf110s of III/ZG 26 and set on fire. Its pilot, FO Ron Duffield, force-landed the blazing aircraft on the edge of LG122. Badly injured, he and his two crew members were attended by 3 Squadron's MO, Sqn. Ldr. John Laver. This reprehensible event was recorded by a war correspondent and a photographer. The Messerschmitts were subsequently attacked by 2 SAAF and 73 Squadron, who claimed one destroyed and two probables between them. Three ZG 26 aircraft were lost, the crew of one being killed and three individuals captured.

On 9 December 112 and 3 flew a combined sweep over the Tobruk-El Adem area at 1035, where they were surprised by six Bf109s from I/JG 27 led by Oblt. Gerhard Homuth. Attacking from the sun, they shot down three of the Australian Tomahawks and damaged one from 112 flown by Sgt Carson. Peter Jeffrey was forced to land at Tobruk with damage and another aircraft from 112 also force landed with engine trouble. Tiny Cameron force landed - again, returning three days later. FO David

One of 3 Squadron's new pilots was Sergeant Ian Lyons, known to all and sundry as 'Joe', because of a recent long-serving Australian Prime Minister of the same name. He is the pilot of this Tomahawk, leaving a typical trail of dust behind it just before becoming airborne on a training flight.

(Ian Lyons)

Rutter, one of the reinforcements of 4 December, was killed on his first operation, and Sgt. Wilson was shot down as well. Rex Wilson had five victories at the time of his death and had just been recommended for the DFM, which was gazetted in January 1942. He was twenty-two years old.

A variety of sources suggest that German casualties from this combat appear to be limited to one shot down and one damaged by Sgt Walter Mailey in AN374, however *Aces High* credits Mailey with two destroyed and Peter Jeffrey with one on this date,[23] which is confirmed by a letter from Mailey submitted to Wing on 26/2/42 and attached to 3 Squadron's combat reports.

Submitted to the Department of Defence (Air Force Office) for clearance.

Acknowledgment: RAAF Historical.

. . . During the sortie Sgt. Cameron of this Squadron was shot down. He saw the fight from the ground but was unable to return to the Squadron for about a week. On his return he said that on the day of the fight he saw three 109Fs definitely shot down. On further examination of both Wing Commander Jeffrey's and my own combat report, plus the fact that we were the only two to claim extensive damage to enemy aircraft, I understood that a report was put in to Wing Intelligence.

Squadron Leader Rawlinson, the CO of the Squadron later told me that the second 109F has been confirmed in my favour and Wing Commander Jeffrey's had also been confirmed. They were duly noted in the Squadron Records.

If the reader wonders how it was possible for a formation of experienced pilots to be 'jumped' with such apparent ease, the following might provide some explanation. At a range of 800 yards, the Bf109 would have an apparent wing span of 0.83cm. Such a tiny object hidden in the large area of the sky occupied by the blinding glare of the sun would be extremely difficult to see. Added to the pilot's problems were the inevitable scratches on the canopy caused by flying sand, and the resultant 'spangling'. The Tomahawk IIB cruised at a speed of 270 m.p.h. The cruising speed of the Bf109F was 310 m.p.h. at 16,500 ft. and its maximum speed was 390 m.p.h., so in a diving attack the closing speed would be in the vicinity of at least 100 m.p.h. Thus to cover a distance of 600 yards, bringing the attacker to a range of 200 yards when he would be likely to open fire, it would take 12.2 *seconds.* If the German pilot chose to hold his fire until 150 yards range, it would take 13.29 seconds. At a range of 200 yards the apparent wing span of the Messerschmitt has grown to 3.30 cm. *If* the Tomahawk pilot has observed the tiny specks in the sun, he therefore has a maximum reaction time of somewhat less than twelve seconds before he becomes a target. If he was looking somewhere *else,* other than the exact right place when the Bf109s reach a distance of 800 yards, he has a problem!

The Australians of 250 Squadron were active on 9 December. Nine Tomahawks took off at 0720 with Hurricanes of the RNFS to sweep the El Adem - El Gobi area. Here they contacted a mixed formation of Bf110s and Bf109s, and PO Waddy, flying Caldwell's AK498 LD-C, shared a Bf110 of 2(F)/14 with Fl.Lt. Bary. In the afternoon they flew another sortie, this time escorting Blenheims over Derna. Sgt. 'Slinger' Nitschke, PO Twemlow and Sgt Whittle engaged an attacking force of six Bf109s and twelve Macchi 202s, preventing them from reaching the Blenheims. Two enemy fighters were seen to crash. John Herington states that 'the credit for this does not seem to have been allocated',[24] but as Nitschke *was* credited with an MC202, and no claim is recorded for Bob Whittle on this date, it seems likely that the other aircraft to fall was shot down by Frank Twemlow. Nitschke scored again on 11 December, claiming a Bf109, while Waddy damaged a Bf109 in AN290.

A cheerful group of 250 Squadron pilots. From left, unknown, Mac Twemlow, Clive Caldwell, next two unknown. In foreground, Squadron Leader Teddy Morris, standing at rear, John Waddy, 'Slinger' Nitschke and Charlie Coward. (Bob Whittle)

3 Squadron moved its aircraft forward to a new base at El Adem at 0945 on the morning of 12 December. Australian pilots of all three Tomahawk squadrons were successful on this day, but the squadrons also suffered losses. At midday 250 Squadron provided cover for Hurricanes of 80 Squadron and the RNFS which were to strafe vehicles near Martuba. They were attacked after completing their task by Bf109s and MC202s from 1° Stormo CT,[25] which shot down four Hurricanes and a Tomahawk, but Sgt. Nitschke destroyed one of the Macchis and a Bf 109 was shot down by another pilot of 250 Squadron.

Bob Whittle destroyed a MC202 and attacked a Ju88 over Menelao Bay, between Gazala and Derna. Left with its port wheel hanging down, and black and white smoke pouring from the port engine, the Ju88 was claimed only as a probable, as he was then attacked by eight of the Macchis, and took refuge in a cloud. The Ju88 was actually confirmed on 23 December when it was found crash landed near Tmimi. His Tomahawk, AN313 *Nux Vomica,* was hit by two explosive bullets in the port wing, and one in the propeller, and classified as Cat. 1.[26]

Another *Nux Vomica* in flight. Carrying a single letter V without squadron codes, this is almost certainly AN313, which was taken on charge on 6 November. Until it was damaged in the action described above, Bob Whittle had flown it on thirty-one consecutive occasions from 21 November.
(Bob Whittle)

Eight Tomahawks from 112 and ten from 3 took off to sweep the Derna area, and at 1600 hours they found a dogfight in progress over Tmimi. The formation climbed to attack a large number of Bf109s and MC200s at all heights from 3,000 feet upwards. PO Jack Bartle(AN372) attacked a Bf109 with a long burst, which produced smoke and oil from its engine. He also attacked a MC202 which lost its canopy as a result of his fire, but he could only claim a damaged. Sgt. D.N. McQueen in AN303 hit a Bf109 near the cockpit and claimed a damaged. He lost sight of it while it was on its back after having lost 4,000 feet because he was attacked himself and was forced to take avoiding action.

112 Squadron lost three aircraft, one of them (AN413 K) flown by PO Robert 'Butch' Jeffries, who was killed. His body was not recovered, and his death is recorded on the Alamein War Memorial.

Two Tomahawks were claimed over Tmimi by Oblt. Erbo Graf von Kageneck, Staffelkapitan of 9/ JG 27. III/JG 27 and III/JG 53 had arrived in the Desert in early December, JG 53 scoring their first victories on 11 December, while Kageneck's Tomahawks, which were probably from 112 Squadron, were the first for III/JG 27. There were now four complete Gruppen of Bf109s opposing the Allied fighters. Oblt. von Kageneck was the Geschwader's leading pilot at this stage of his career, having claimed 65 victories before his arrival in Africa.

3 Squadron fared little better in the dogfight over Tmimi. Two of its aircraft collided during the initial turn into the fight, FO Fred Eggleston spinning out of control, while the other, flown by FO Robin Gray, made off for base with damage. Eggleston regained control lower down, and became embroiled in a fight with several 109s, finally being shot down and captured. FO Nicky Barr broke away to escort Gray, and while doing so, scored his first victory, a Bf110.

> While on offensive fighter sweep over Tmimi area 1300 ft (sic) E/A were reported 9 o'clock below and climbing. During the formation turn two aircraft collided. One of these turned in the direction of the base and dived for a cloud layer at 3000 ft. I turned and dive[d] to follow him.

> While catching Tomahawk to escort to base, M.E.110 was sighted above flying towards me. Cloud base was 3000 ft. and E/A was just beneath. Pulling around into his tail from beneath flames came from wing root and fuselage after two bursts. I then lost sight of the a/c.

Barr was flying AN336, which more than likely carried the letter 'N'. In the early stages of 3's Desert war, no identifying markings were carried other than serials. Individual letters were applied later in the year, although unfortunately the exact date of this is not known. The well known 'CV' codes were not used until the advent of the Kittyhawks. FO Bobby Gibbes claimed damage to a Ju87, the only other success for the unit.

FO Nicky Barr looks pleased with himself, so this photograph is likely to have been taken shortly after the events described above. (Ian Primmer, via Doug Norrie)

Later in the day 250 Squadron flew another sweep and found a formation of Ju87s with fighter escort. PO Twemlow destroyed one dive bomber and claimed two probables, Sgt. Coward claimed a Ju87 and a probable Bf109. John Waddy (AN290) was beginning to get into stride. The Bf109 he destroyed was his first individual victory after a share, a probable and a damaged. All of these were fighters.

The air war continued unabated on 13 December. Sgt. S.C. Johnson, another Australian serving with 112 Squadron, damaged a Bf109 in an inconclusive skirmish with six Bf109s flying escort for eight Ju88s. Before 112 could attack the Ju88s they were bounced by the 109s, but suffered no damage and Johnson's damaged was the only claim made by the squadron.

3 Squadron set off on a sweep at 1510 and encountered 'six unidentified bombers' escorted by approximately eight Bf109s.

FO Eric Bradbury, flying his first full operation since joining the squadron on 4 December, (he had flown a brief twenty minute scramble earlier in the day) had no difficulty recognising the bombers.

> On the 13th December 1941, 12 of us did a rhubarb from El Adem (near Tobruk) and ran into 6 Messerschmitt 110s escorted by 8 109s. It was my first contact with the enemy as a fighter pilot and (I consider) the only pilot on his first op. to (stupidly) deliberately do a head on attack on a 110 which had front firing 20 mm cannons, vividly reminding me of such. I shoved the nose of the Tomahawk down under the fast closing 110 only to be the target of an attack by an unseen 109 from the rear. The result was a great hole in my starboard wing root inside a petrol tank yet outside my cockpit. A miracle enabled me to escape further damage by kicking on starboard rudder and shoving the stick forward and to starboard all at the one time. Jock Perrin had taught me this manoeuvre just before I left Australia to go to 3 Squadron. I climbed up to 12,000 and looked around for an enemy and saw a 109. Chased it holding the stick over to the left to counteract the loss of lift in my starboard wing and managed to fire a burst of .303 machine gun fire with no result, except a strong desire for me to get out of the area quickly. I managed to get back to El Adem to be greeted by Alan Rawlinson - "Where the b. . . hell have you been?" I told him, but he ticked me off for losing contact with the others - they had landed 20 minutes before me. A decent introduction to being a fighter pilot, eh? Needless to say that first experience was a great teaching lesson.[27]

On this occasion the Messerschmitts prevented the squadron from doing any damage to the bombers, but lost three aircraft in the process. FO Gibbes (AN374) damaged two Bf109s, and a Ju87 from a formation he encountered on the way home after losing contact with the squadron. Sgt. Simes (AK291) claimed a probable and a damaged, while 'Tiny' Cameron in AN274 (back with the unit after his recent three day walk in the desert) destroyed one Bf109 and shared another with FO Briggs.

> Was flying Red 3 when aircraft were reported 11 o'clock. I saw a formation of bombers escorted by a few fighters. I looked behind and saw some fighters coming in which were then reported by someone else. As soon as they appeared to be dangerously close, I turned onto them but could not get a burst on the initial attack. After a bit of manoeuvring just below the cloud, (5,500 ft) I sneaked on a 109F and put in a long burst, which set it on fire. I looked round and could see only two A/C, a Tomahawk overhauling a 109F. I sat in behind and watched him deliver a long burst from close up. The 109 flicked over on its back and I pulled up and gave it a good burst from point blank range. It span(sic) in close to the other which was by then burning on the ground. I stayed in the area for some time and gave chase to another 109 which dived out of the cloud. I tried a burst at long range but do not think I hit him. He dived right away. As my gas was getting low, I came home.

Tom Trimble was shot down, probably by Lt. Marseille, who claimed a Hurricane over Martuba at 1600, and another ten minutes later over Tmimi. Two Hurricanes were indeed lost near Tmimi, but the second was claimed by Oblt. Homuth, so Marseille's first 'Hurricane' was probably Trimble's Tomahawk, as this was the only other Allied fighter to be lost in the Martuba - Tmimi area during the day. Mistakes in aircraft recognition were not unusual.

FO Nicky Barr (AN336) claimed his second success in as many days, another Bf109, and a lone Ju88, which he encountered on the way home, for good measure.

While on offensive fighter sweep over DERNA - MARTUBA area and flying right beneath cloud base at 5,500 ft Enemy aircraft consisting of bombers escorted by M.E. 109's were reported at 10 O'clock. M.E. 109 turned and dived on the rear left of our formation. One enemy had a sitting quarter to astern attack in(sic) a Tomahawk. I attacked this aircraft from above and 1/4 , the Tomahawk slipped down in a skidding dive to port. The 109 pulled away and headed for the cloud again. I followed it and noticed no visional(sic) effects from my fire. The 109 then half rolled and dived down. It did not pull out of the dive and hit the ground not far from where I observed another 109 burning. Three 109's were the only aircraft I observed in my vicinity then. I climbed into the clouds headed south then later east.

On coming out of the clouds I observed that I was S.W. of the GAZALA inlet and a considerable distance on my starboard enemy aircraft (J.U.88) were bombing a M/T concentration. One J.U.88 not in the formation appeared on my starboard. I gave it a short range beam attack then dived beneath and gave a burst from astern. Its port wing dropped and it dived sharply. I climbed into the cloud from this attack and on emerging, noticed black smoke and flames on the ground. This point would be north west of the bombing attack.

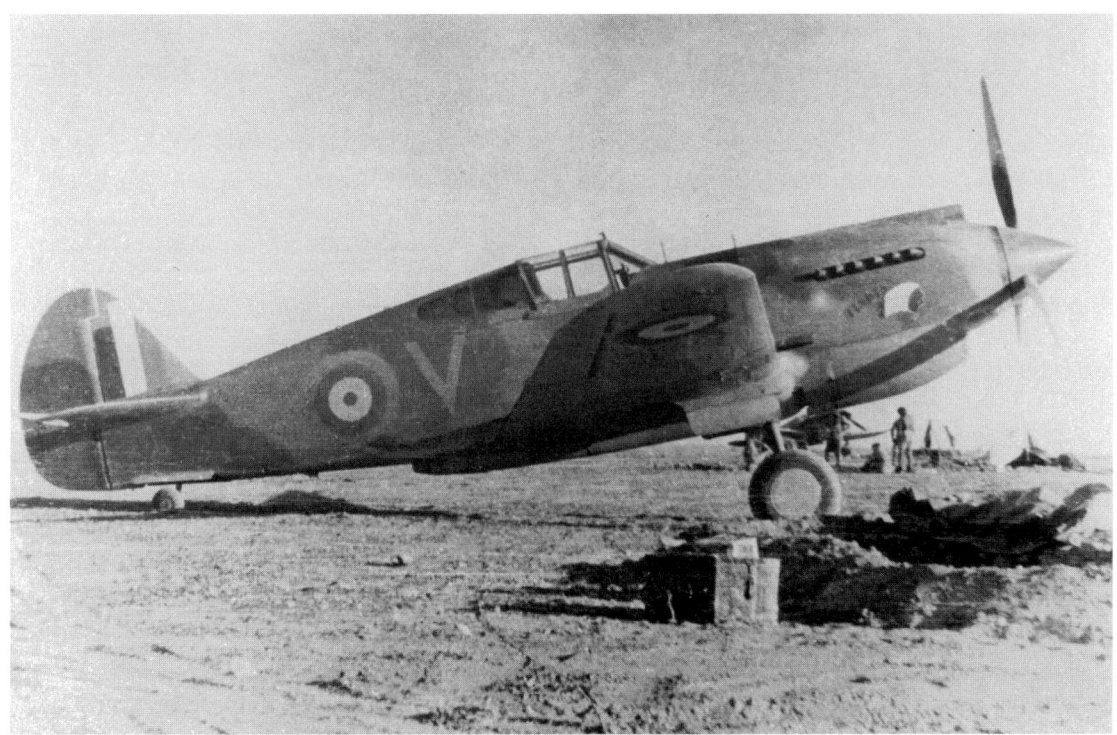

FO Tom Trimble's Tomahawk AK382 V, *'Tindian'* (RAAF Museum)

Next morning six Tomahawks of 3 Squadron flew a 'rhubarb', best described as a search for targets of opportunity. They encountered seven Ju87s escorted by eight Bf109s. One Ju87 was damaged by Sgt. Reid, but the Messerschmitts shot down Sgt. Derek Scott, who baled out of his burning aircraft at 8,000 feet to be captured, [*] and FO Donald Knight, who was killed. Knight was the second of the 4 December reinforcements to be lost. Sgt. Wal Mailey damaged one of the Bf109s south east of Martuba, scoring several definite hits before it disappeared into the clouds. FO Lou Spence also 'managed an attack on a 109, beginning from the beam and closing to 50 yards on the quarter before being forced to take evasive action'. It is likely that either Mailey or Spence attacked the aircraft of Obfw. Forster, who was shot down.

[*] *AWM 54 779/3/29 PoW debriefs.*

In the morning, Lt. Stahlschmidt and Oblt. Unterburger of I/JG 27 each claimed a Tomahawk in the Tmimi area, but Obfw. Forster bailed out and was hit and killed while on his parachute.[28]

Later in the day, Clive Caldwell damaged a Bf109 during a combat between eight of 250 Squadron's aircraft and a mixed formation of Ju88s and Bf109s.

On both 14 and 15 December 3 Squadron carried out search flights in the hope of locating Tom Trimble, who was shot down on the 13th, but without success. Happily he returned to the unit on the 20th, having been 'helped by a native'.

An uneventful wing sweep was flown on 16 December with aircraft from 3, 112 and 260 Squadrons. Fl.Lt Wilf Arthur was ordered to Head Quarters Middle East, to await arrangements for his return to Australia. He had completed 184 sorties in 316 hours of operational flying. He had seven victories, two CR42s while flying Gladiators, one Bf110 on Hurricanes, and the remainder with the Tomahawk. He was awarded a DFC in January 1942, when he returned to Australia. His association with the Curtiss fighter was not yet over.

3 Squadron's time with the Tomahawk was now coming to a close. On 17 December three Tomahawks (including Nicky Barr's AN336) were handed over to 112 Squadron, and two each to 2 and 4 SAAF. Ten pilots then left for 107 MU at Geneifa to collect new Kittyhawks, and landed back at LG 102 at 1630 hours.

When the slightly improved Allison V-1710-39 became available in early 1940, Curtiss undertook a redesign of the Tomahawk to accommodate the new engine. The power of the earlier V-1710-33 was 1,150 h.p. at sea level, which reduced to 1,040 h.p. at 15,000 ft. The new engine could maintain the same 1,150 h.p. up to 11,700 ft. Having an external airscrew reduction gear, the new engine was shorter, with a raised thrust line. This permitted a length reduction of six inches, the reduction of the fuselage cross section and a slightly shortened undercarriage. The radiator was enlarged and moved forward and extra armour was added. The fuselage guns were removed, and four .50s with improved hydraulic chargers were installed in the wings. This model was called the P-40D, only twenty two of which were built for the USAAF. The RAF took delivery of 560 P-40 Ds, but after the first 20, which carried only four guns, the remainder of this order was delivered with six guns, with total of 281 rounds per gun. It was known as the Kittyhawk I in RAF service, and serial numbers ranged from AK571 to AL230. The USAAF followed the British lead, cancelling the remaining P-40Ds on order. Their revised six gun aircraft became the P-40E, known as the Kittyhawk IA in RAF service. Serials for these aircraft were ET100-999 and EV100-699.

With the addition of extra guns, ammunition and armour and the provision of bomb racks or a drop tank, the empty weight had risen from 5,812 lb. to 6,350 lb., while loaded weight had gone up to 8,280 lb. from the Tomahawk's 7,549 lb. Consequently, the climb rate actually deteriorated compared to the Tomahawk, which could reach 15,000 ft in 5.1 minutes, while it took the Kittyhawk 4.8 minutes to reach only 10,000 ft. These figures compare most unfavourably with the Bf109F, which had an initial climb rate of some 4,200 ft. per minute, reducing to 3,300 ft at 5,000 ft. The same reference states that its time to 9,840 ft.(3,000 metres) was 2 minutes 36 seconds![29]

Nevertheless, 3 Squadron welcomed their new aircraft with enthusiasm, the ORB recording that 'first impressions were favourable. Pilots considered they would more than hold their own with 109Fs in regard to speed and climb, while the six .5 guns were considered a big improvement'.

In the five days from 15 December to 19 December the Tomahawk squadrons were not as heavily engaged as they had been, Clive Caldwell being the only Australian to record contact of any significance with the enemy, claiming a probable on 17 December, a damaged on the 18th and another probable on the 19th, all Bf109s, and all while flying AK498 'C'.

A fine shot of what is purported to be 3 Squadron's first Kittyhawk, AK596. Judging by its pristine condition and the lack of squadron markings, this may well be so. (RAAF Museum)

On 19 December a section of 250 Squadron Tomahawks took off in the early morning to strafe M/T near Mechili. Sgt. Bob Whittle, flying AN415, a replacement aircraft, was hit by AA and turned east to put distance between his target and the inevitable crash-landing which was soon to follow. His log book entry explains his predicament.

> *Dec 19. Tomahawk AN415 Ground Straf Mecheli (sic) 1.10. Bullets through cooler, spinner, sump & undercarriage. Crash landed in clouds of smoke and burning oil 15 mls east of straf. Spent afternoon dodging patrols and walked forty miles home at night.*

By daybreak he had reached friendly territory and found an advanced Polish unit, whose sentry received him at the point of a bayonet. He gave the Poles the position of the nearest Germans, was given water and chianti, and driven the last eighteen miles back to Gazala. Two days later he came close to disaster again.

On 20 December nineteen Tomahawks from 112 and 250 squadrons provided escort to a mixed force of Blenheims from 45 Squadron and the Lorraine Squadron of the Free French Air Force, to bomb an armoured column near Benghazi. The formation was attacked by Bf109s from I and II Gruppes of JG 27, numbering between twelve and twenty [30] (which suggests that their approach was not seen) and after one of the French Blenheims blew up the others jettisoned their bombs and began to scatter. PO Ken Sands (AN372) of 112 Squadron

> 'fired a long burst at enemy, noticed him wobble and lose speed. I was then forced to break off attack as my machine developed serious engine trouble. If this machine went out of control after my attack it should have been seen by my No. 1, S/Ldr. Morello. This E/A before passing me, probably attacked a Blenheim, which burst into flame on my starboard quarter.

It was indeed confirmed by Sqn. Ldr Morello, who added this note to Sands' combat report.

YEAR 1941		AIRCRAFT		Pilot, or 1st Pilot	2nd Pilot, Pupil or Passenger	DUTY (Including Results and Remarks)
Month	Date	Type	No.			
						— Totals Brought Forward
Dec.	1	Tomahawk	AN 313	Self	—	Flap for recco. F/Lt Caldwell
"	"	"	" "	"		Escort G.O.C.
"	2	"	" "	"		Patrol Sidi Rezegh – El Adem
"	4	"	" "	"		L.G. 123 to L.G. 122
"	"	"	" "	"		Patrol Gambut – Gubbi
"	5	"	" "	"		Patrol Rezegh – Gubbi
"	"	"	" "	"		L.G. 122 to L.G. 123
"	8	"	" "	"		Patrol Base
"	"	"	" "	"		Panic take-off
"	9	"	" "	"		Patrol El Gubbi
"	10	"	" "	"		" Tobruck – El Adem
"	11	"	" "	"		Test – Sollum & back.
"	12	"	" "	"		L.G. 123 to Tobrock + patrol area
"	"	"	" "	"		Escort dive-bombers.
"	13	"	" "	"		Nox Vomica Cat. I
						2 explosive bullets in port wing & one in prop.
"	13	"	452	"		Ju 88 Bombed Tobruck under
"	16	"	" "	"		Patrol South Martuba
"	17	"	" "	"		Escort 12 Blenheims
"	18	"	" "	"		" 7 Bostons
"	19	"	415	"		Ground straf Mecheli

D.3200/7.37.—C.4947.

GRAND TOTAL [Cols. (1) to (10)]
420 Hrs. **25** Mins.

Totals Carried Forward

This page from Sergeant Bob Whittle's log book reveals a very busy month in December 1941.

I was attacked from rear and lost control, just managing to avoid the Blenheim mentioned above as I dived away. Immediately afterwards I saw a 109F pass me and burst into flames. As this had presumably come from astern and just above, it must have been the machine attacked by Pilot Officer Sands.[31]

Clive Caldwell (AK498) and John Waddy (AM399) both claimed Bf109s, and Sgt Charlie Coward claimed a probable.

The Germans had somewhat the better of the engagement however, shooting down Sgt. Archie Ferguson (AK418) of 112 Squadron, who was killed, and three from 250, including Sgt. Richard Nitschke, who also lost his life. In less than a month during the *Crusader* offensive he had destroyed five enemy aircraft. The commission for which he had been recommended was confirmed after his death.

The German pilots claimed only three Tomahawks in this engagement, one to Lt. Remmer of I Gruppe, and two to Obfw. Schulz of II Gruppe.

SINGLE-ENGINE AIRCRAFT				MULTI-ENGINE AIRCRAFT						Pas-senger	INSTR/CLOUD FLYING [incl. in cols. (1) to (10)]	
DAY		NIGHT		DAY			NIGHT					
Dual	Pilot	Dual	Pilot	Dual	1st Pilot	2nd Pilot	Dual	1st Pilot	2nd Pilot		Dual	Pilot
(1)	(2)	(3)	(4)	(5)	(6)	(7)	(8)	(9)	(10)	(11)	(12)	(13)
	50											
	25			Lt.D.L got tired of waiting.								
	1·40			Port wing stalled after landing — damaged wing tip.								
	15											
	1·20											
	2·10			7a/c of 112 Sqdn. eng. 10 Me 109's. 25 Sqdn attacked 35 Ju 87's + 8 G 50's & Mc 200's								
	15			Self shot down in flames two Ju 87's & caused a third to crash-land								
	1·00			Confirmed by Wing & Army Total bag confirmed 17.								
	45			L.D.122 being straffed. 5 Me 109's above. no combat.								
	1·45			Met 5 Me 110's + 12 Me 109's — enemy made off. F/Lt. Bary shot down 1 Me 110								
	2·00			Landed in dust storm.								
	30											
	2·00											
	1·45			Gazala — Derna Rd. Led format. 9 a/c top cover. Engaged 12 Macci 202's for 20 minutes. Self shot down one Macci 202 (burnt on ground) also probable Ju 88 over Menelao Bay (black & white smoke f rom port engine + port wheel (hanging down) attacked by 8 Macci 202's escaped in cld.								
	40			over very nose. Chased him W. Gazala — Escaped in cloud.								
	2·15			6 Me 109's seen but would not engage.								
	45			Cloud covered target — no bombing.								
	125			Bombed L'irene — Derna Rd.								
	1·10			Bullets through cooler, spinner, sump & undercarriage. Crash landed in clouds of smoke & burning oil 15 mls E of straf. Spent afternoon dodging patrols & walked 40 mls home at night.								

(marginal annotations, faint:) Ju 88 found crash-landed near Tmimi by F/O Henderson on Tmr 1 F/O Harp F/Lt Harp 23/12/41 self details in C.R. submitted 13/12/41 for Wing confirmation sufficient conf. see photo.

Sands was forced to land behind enemy lines because of his engine trouble. His subsequent adventures were recounted by 112's Intelligence Officer.

Further to report of 20th December, 1941.

Sands of the Desert returns. It is with great pleasure that the return of Pilot Officer K.R. Sands is recorded. He reported back on the evening of the 23rd at Machili (sic) after adventures reminiscent of Beau Geste.

2. Forced landing at a point approx. 20 miles N.W. of Carubba, he ran for cover as there were 109's flying low. Later he joined a Bedouin camel party, who turned out to be friendly Senoussi. They disguised him as an Arab and gave him a stick to impersonate a camel driver, finally taking him to their tented encampment in a Wadi near trig point 605 near Si Saad, adjacent to the ruins of an old fort. M.E. 109's came down to investigate his party. Here he spent the night on a piece of rush mat with a threadbare blanket, and Arabs, goats, fleas etc. as bedfellows.

3. The following day he reconnoitred several areas on foot in the hopes of finding friendly forces, but without success. Late in the afternoon the Arabs spotted two armoured cars, apparently British. Pilot officer Sands watched for a long time before making his presence known, and discovered to his relief that they were the King's Dragoon Guards. He gave the Arabs two pounds, (all he had with him) and spent the night in an armoured car.

4. The following day he joined up with K.D.G. H.Q. who provided transport to their base camp, there the night was spent. Next morning a column was intercepted, who provided transport to Machili.

5. A confirmed 109F is claimed for P/Off Sands.

6. It is of interest to record that these Arabs were in possession of German propaganda depicting Arabs on the ends of British bayonets and as having been hanged by the British. . . . They were not particularly anti-German, but hated the Italians.[32]

(Ken Sands was posted to 450 Squadron on the same day as his return, 23 December 1941, to finish his first tour. On 6 December 1943 he became CO of 450 Squadron.)

112 flew another bomber escort in the afternoon of 20 December with 250 Squadron and 2 and 4 SAAF. While on the way to their target, they were passed by one bomb laden Ju88 heading in the other direction 500 feet above them. Three Tomahawks from 112 broke off to attack this aircraft, but as it was almost immediately lost in cloud, two of them returned to the formation. Sgt. Henry Burney, (who had been with the Squadron since August and was its only casualty during the battle of 22 November) persisted, and this was rewarded when he caught up to the Junkers in clear air west of Martuba. The German machine turned north, jettisoned its bombs to gain speed and turned for home. Burney (AN289) pursued it, firing long bursts all the way down to 500 feet until it suddenly blew up. The Ju88, from II/KLG 1, was Burney's first kill.

Bob Whittle was reunited with *Nux Vomica* again on 21 December, after the damage sustained on the 12th had been repaired. It was to be the last time he flew it. At 1000 a two-squadron sized

An atmospheric shot of *Nux Vomica*, undergoing servicing and gun harmonisation. In the original print the V is just discernable aft of the roundel. Note the pith helmet hanging from the pitot tube on the port wing.
(Bob Whittle)

force made up of 250, 112, and 2 and 4 SAAF took off to escort eleven Blenheims, to bomb west of Benina. A surprisingly restrained log book entry explains how the day unfolded.

> *Bombed Barce. Chased two 109Fs but could not catch. Returned to formation & was badly shot up by Hun I did not see. Hun later turned out to be a Tomahawk - an excellent shot. Blew half rudder-bar away - holed me in numerous places including sole of boot and parachute - crashed on landing at Gazala. Sustained slight superficial wounds.*

The culprit was a South African, whose identity Bob Whittle is still reluctant to reveal.

By 22 December the Germans were suffering from an acute shortage of fuel, and when 112 and 250 Squadrons attacked their airfield at Magrun, they found a busy circuit with aircraft taking off and landing, but only one Bf109 was able to get airborne. This was flown by Lt. Sinner, who had an inconclusive engagement with two Tomahawks. These were probably flown by Neville Duke and his wing man Sgt. K. Carson, who claimed a shared probable. PO Jack Bartle shared in the destruction of a Ju87 with Fl.Lt Westenra, and Sgt. Frank Twemlow of 250 shot down another Stuka which was about to land. Sgt. Coward damaged another Stuka in similar circumstances. The South Africans of 2 and 4 Squadrons were flying as top cover, and with no Bf109s about came down to join the attack on the aerodrome. As well as the two Stukas destroyed by the Australians, and a Ju52 destroyed on the ground by Sgt. Carson, the Axis lost two more Ju87s, a MC202 and a Ju88 in the air to the South Africans, who also destroyed two Ju52s and a rare Do17 on the ground. As the Tomahawks departed, sixteen Ju52s arrived, bringing barrels of fuel, and the German fighters were able to evacuate to safer landing grounds further back from the British advance.

250 Squadron pilots on standby. The two pilots standing appear to be sharing a joke with Flight Lieutenant Clive Caldwell, wearing a cap, centre. (Bob Whittle)

As a consequence of this, fighter action was much reduced over the next few days, JG 27 being able to 'muster only six aircraft in a serviceable condition between the three Gruppes due to lack of fuel and the number of ground crews lost during the retreat'.[33]

On this date Clive Caldwell's log book recorded that he strafed a retreating enemy column and shot down a Bf109E at low level. He landed beside an advance British column to pass on information, and drew their attention to smoke in the distance, which came from the 109. It was subsequently confirmed by the army.

JG27 suffered a serious loss on 24 December, when Oblt. Erbo Graf von Kageneck was wounded in action. For some time it was thought that the Hurricanes of 94 and 260 Squadrons were responsible,[34] but later research for *Aces High* suggests that a Bf109 damaged by Clive Caldwell on this date was the one flown by von Kageneck.[35] He was wounded in the abdomen, but managed to land his aircraft safely. Due to the serious nature of his wound, he was taken to a hospital in Naples, but died on 12 January 1942. (Caldwell's log book lists a claim for a damaged Bf109 during the first patrol of the day. It was his last claim with 250 Squadron.)

Dec 24 AK498   Patrol F^T Michele - Z^T Msus 1.10   DAMAGED 1 ME 109F

On 30 December, Bob Whittle flew his last sortie with 250 Squadron, an uneventful sweep over El Agheila and Jeddabia. Later in the day he boarded a Bombay and flew to Heliopolis, thence to instruct at 73 OTU. He left with 235.30 operational hours from 137 sorties, ten and one shared victories, and the following endorsement in his log book from Sqn. Ldr. Morris: *An exceptional fighter pilot. Has shown courage, determination and judgement of a high order in numerous combats.*

C hapter 5   Enter the Kittyhawk

By 8 December, Rommel had made the decision to withdraw from the *Crusader* battle, and a steady, organised retreat began. Tobruk was relieved on 10 December, and the advance continued, first to Gazala and then to Benghazi, which was evacuated by the Axis on December 23, their forces retreating to El Agheila. In the last days of December, the air war had been much reduced in its intensity, and it was into this situation that 3 Squadron returned with their new Kittyhawks.

Having overseen the introduction of the Kittyhawks, Wg. Cdr. Peter Jeffrey DSO, DFC, and Sqn. Ldr. Alan Rawlinson DFC and Bar, left by air for H.Q.M.E. to await instructions for their eventual return to Australia. Both officers had served with the Squadron from the time of its arrival in the Desert on 23 August 1940. Peter Jeffrey became its second Desert Commanding Officer, taking over from Sqn. Ldr. I.D. McLachlan DFC on 13 February 1941, a position he held until 10 November, when he was promoted to lead 2 Wing. Alan Rawlinson then led the unit during the intensive operations flown in support of Operation *Crusader* until handing over to Sqn. Ldr. D.R. 'Dixie' Chapman, who arrived on 12 December to familiarise himself with the situation, assuming command before the Squadron re-commenced operations on the Kittyhawk.

Peter Jeffrey, with four and one shared victories on Tomahawks (five and one in total), and Alan Rawlinson (with six of his eight victories on Tomahawks) had provided 3 Squadron with exemplary leadership, taking it to the position of top scoring squadron in the Desert Air Force by the end of 1941. They would be missed, but their influence on the pilots who had served with them would remain. 3 would always enjoy the benefit of strong and aggressive leadership.

The Squadron moved from El Adem to El Gazala No.2 Aerodrome on 21 December. On the same day Sgt Mailey left El Adem at 0900 to change the original Kittyhawk AK596, 'which had not proved 100%'.[1] He arrived at El Gazala on the 22nd with AK616. On 26 December the first operational flights were carried out when two aircraft provided a standing patrol over the airfield after a bombing raid carried out by a single Bf110, but no further raids eventuated.

On 28 December at 0745 thirteen Kittyhawks took off to carry out a reconnaissance sweep with the Tomahawks of 112 and 250 Squadrons over the El Ageila - Brega area, reporting enemy armoured units at a number of locations. Several more sweeps were flown over the following three days, and 3 Squadron took part in all of them, as it was, by now, the only fighter squadron at full strength.

A morning sweep on New Year's Day was uneventful, but the squadron had the opportunity to put their new Kittyhawks to good use in the afternoon. Nine Kittyhawks flying in the fluid pair formation left on a patrol over the Agedabia area, and at 1600 hours met sixteen Ju87s with six

escorting Bf109s preparing to attack British troops fifteen miles east of Agedabia. Rather than becoming directly involved, the Bf109s climbed above cloud and the dive bombers jettisoned their bombs and formed a defensive circle. While most of the Kittyhawks went for the bombers, Alan Cameron led Blue section after the Messerschmitts.

> As most of the formation appeared to be about to attack the bombers, I endeavoured to lead Blue section into the Messerschmitts and followed these with several Kittyhawks after me. When I emerged from the cloud, they were circling above and as I appeared to be alone, I decided to break off and jump them from above. I came back through the clouds, warned the Kittyhawks ... then went away and climbed to 12,000 feet. When I came back I could see nothing above or below cloud so went to Agedabia to intercept them on their way home. Here the cloud base was irregular at about 3,000 feet, and after I had done a couple of circuits, three Me-109's turned up and prepared to land on Agedabia West. I let them get settled down and then dived on one, but had to alter my attack and dive on another one head-on. I had a long burst at it and saw it flick upside down as it went under me. This was at 1,000 feet. The others by this time had their wheels down so I stalked the rear one who was only about 500 feet. After only a short burst he dropped his nose and crashed. I then attacked the other from astern, saw him waver as I fired, but immediately had to climb to avoid some Stukas that were now coming in. Icing conditions were severe in the cloud, my ring sight being thickly crusted and the motor showing signs of ice in the carburettor. I attacked a line of 5 or 6 Stukas just about to land and saw the rear one slide away as I shot at it then went for the leader. He kept ahead on a straight glide into the desert while the main group turned left and landed. I flew in and out of cloud for some time, but as two of my guns were stopped and the reflector sight useless, I thought it unwise to remain longer.[2]

'Tiny' Cameron's comment about the reflector sight is significant. Although happy with the Kittyhawk's performance, several other pilots also complained about the efficacy of the gun sight.

FO Lou Spence: 'Aircraft handled even better than Tomahawk in manoeuvrability. Reflector sight most unsatisfactory. Too weak and one had to keep ring in vision even at the commencement of a dive to attack'.

FO 'Nicky' Barr: 'Reflector sight very unsatisfactory. Not the same clearness and circle disappears upon small movement of the head. The aircraft handled beautifully and proved very manoeuvrable, particularly in tight, steep turns'.

Sqn. Ldr Chapman was also impressed. 'KITTYHAWK handled magnificently and proved extremely manoeuvrable, showing no tendency to spin out of even the most violent changes of direction'. His combat report follows.

> I was flying in the No. 3 position of the leader's section on a Squadron sweep. At 1600 hours, I heard the leader signal a turn to port and almost immediately we sighted eight or nine JU87's. Our squadron turned hard to port as the JU87's passed just underneath us and commenced individual attacks. As several Kittyhawks dived into the JU87's, I pulled up to the cloud base and looked for the enemy escort. Seeing none I attacked a straggler on the right of the enemy formation. After a couple of astern and slight deflection attacks my guns stopped. I pulled up into the cloud base and reloaded, which cleared the stoppage. As I was clearing the guns I saw at least one JU87 jettison its bombs. Visibility was extremely poor owing to dust. When I turned to resume the attack I could not see any aircraft for dust. I flew in the direction I had last seen the fight, and after about thirty seconds I came upon eight JU87's being attacked by one or possibly two, Kittyhawks. I attacked again from astern and then quickly turned round as a precaution. When I again attacked I discovered I was the only Kittyhawk in the action. This was at about 1610 hours. I followed the eight enemy aircraft S.W. until 1630 hours making repeated attacks from the rear. By this time the enemy had gone down to ground level and I could not get under them, nor could I break them up by diving on them. As I made several attacks so close that I had difficulty holding my sights on the E/A; because of their slipstream, I consider that I must have damaged at least three of the enemy. Most of my attacks were from dead astern. I broke off the attacks at 1630, as I had but one gun firing and was well into enemy territory.

NOTE :

At least three of the enemy rear gunners appeared to have lost interest in the action when I broke off.

Sqn. Ldr. Chapman's aircraft was slightly damaged by return fire, which caused him to land away from base. In the concise words of the ORB, 'S/L Chapman failed to return from this operation, but he returned the following day', obviously with AK643, which could not have been very badly damaged, as he flew it again on 3 January. Lou Spence, Nicky Barr and Frank Fischer all claimed Ju87s destroyed, and to give the first Desert combat for the Kittyhawk its due, the combat reports of the first two pilots are included.

Formation was flying south east at approximately 6,000 feet, when I observed three aircraft in a shallow dive at 11 o'clock. I called up the leader to report and then noticed approximately three more aircraft following the first three at 12 o'clock. I reported these aircraft and we turned towards them. The aircraft, ME109's went up into the clouds and I followed my number one up. I did not see any aircraft above the clouds, so I dived down out of them. I then observed approximately 12 JU87's diving towards the ground in a S.W. direction - they jettisoned their bombs as I dived on them. As I dived, I observed two other KITTYHAWKS attacking. We attacked the JU87's incessantly, for approximately ten to fifteen minutes. I made Beam, Quarter and Astern attacks in approximately twelve attacks. On one quarter attack, I made a three quarter second burst and observed flames coming from a JU87's engine and wing root. On another quarter to astern attack, on another JU87, I observed dark smoke beginning to pour from the engine. I did not observe either of these two aircraft "go in", but there were three fires burning on the ground.

I lost the 87's in the haze and as my ammunition was almost exhausted - several guns not firing I returned to base. The JU87's flew at approximately 200 feet in a pairs defensive circle.

While on a fighter sweep over the AGEDDABIA (sic) Area, and flying south below an 8/10ths. cloud layer, E/A. were reported at 11 o'clock and four ME109's flew across the front of the formation. Two half-rolled and dived away, while the other two flew up into the cloud. I then observed a defensive circle of JU87's on my port side about 1000 feet below the cloud layer. One aircraft led out and they came out of the circle into a "Vic" pairs formation. I attacked the starboard rear pair and the leader began to smoke and then dived into the ground. The JU87's then reformed the circle, but diving closer to the ground. Other KITTYHAWKS were making attacks and fire was observed from the rear gunners of the JU87's. I then made several more attacks, one of which caused a JU87 to roll over at approximately 900 feet, smoke was observed coming from beneath the tail, but further results were not observed. I exhausted my ammunition and commenced to climb away, setting course for base. I observed five fires on the ground spread over an area of approximately one square mile. Two ME109's attacked and chased me for approximately ten minutes. I headed out to sea and eventually landed at base. The airmanship of the ME109's appeared very poor to me.

Nicky Barr (left) and Lou Spence, were both successful on the occasion of the first Kittyhawk combat in the Western Desert. This photograph was taken later in the year, as they are both wearing Flight Lieutenant's insignia.
(Doug Norrie)

If Nicky Barr thought the airmanship of the Bf109 pilots was poor, one wonders what the surviving Stuka pilots thought about it. At least three were shot down in the main fight and Alan Cameron destroyed another near its base. One or more of the probables claimed by Spence and Barr may have crashed as well, considering the five fires Barr reported. 3 Squadron had made a fine start with their new fighter.

112 Squadron was the next unit to convert to Kittyhawks, twenty-one being received on 29 December. Their Tomahawks were handed over to 250 Squadron. They had lost twenty aircraft in action, while claiming the destruction of thirty six enemy aircraft.[3] Before taking their new aircraft into action, they lost two pilots, one killed in a crash on his first flight in the aircraft, and an Australian, Sgt. S.C. Johnson, who crashed in a dust storm in the Halfaya Pass on 5 January. Sqn. Ldr Tony Morello was posted, and his replacement was the newly promoted Sqn. Ldr. Clive 'Killer' Caldwell, from 250 Squadron.

Clive Caldwell was thus the first Empire Air Training Scheme pilot to be appointed to the command of a RAF fighter squadron. By the end of December, after eight months on operations, his log

YEAR 1941		AIRCRAFT		PILOT, OR	2ND PILOT, PUPIL	DUTY
MONTH	DATE	Type	No.	1ST PILOT	OR PASSENGER	(INCLUDING RESULTS AND REMA[
–	–	—	–	—	—	—— TOTALS BROUGHT FORW.
Dec	27	TOMAHAWK	AK498	SELF	–	STRAFE HASSIAT AREA
"	"	"	AK498	SELF	—	PATROL
"	"	"	AK498	"	—	TAC/RECCE AGEDABIA – AGHEILA
	28	"	AK498	"	—	SWEEP
	"	"	AK498	"	—	SWEEP
	29	"	AK498	"	—	SWEEP – STRAFFE
	30	"	AK498	"	—	STRAFFE
					HOURS FLOWN DEC 54	

GRAND TOTAL [Cols. (1) to (10)]

585 Hrs. 15 Mins.

TOTALS CARRIED FOR

Clive Caldwell's log book page for end of December.

book showed 16 and two shared victory claims, 5 probables and 17 damaged, a remarkable achievement. When he began flying Tomahawks in May 1941, he had 102 hours as a solo pilot in his log book, (total flying time 178.25). Total Tomahawk time from May to December was 330 hours, and most of this was operational. Before embarking on his first bomber escort in May, he had flown a Tomahawk on four occasions, for a total of 3 hours and 10 minutes. Sqn. Ldr. Morris, CO of 250 Squadron, endorsed his log book with the following: *An exceptional fighter pilot, whose leadership and skill in combat have been of the highest order.*

The next encounter with enemy aircraft for the Kittyhawks came on 8 January, when ten aircraft from 3 Squadron took off on a morning sweep over Agedabia - Agheila and met a mixed formation

SINGLE-ENGINE AIRCRAFT				MULTI-ENGINE AIRCRAFT						PASS-ENGER	INSTR/CLOUD FLYING [Incl. in cols. (1) to (10)]	
DAY		NIGHT		DAY			NIGHT					
DUAL	PILOT	DUAL	PILOT	DUAL	1ST PILOT	2ND PILOT	DUAL	1ST PILOT	2ND PILOT		DUAL	PILOT
(1)	(2)	(3)	(4)	(5)	(6)	(7)	(8)	(9)	(10)	(11)	(12)	(13)
59.55	508.30	2.25	1.05	4.40						11.05	10.45	6.10
	1.00			M/T & PERSONNEL. GROUND DEFENCE FIRE VERY GOOD.								
	.50			ENGAGED BY ME 109s. VERY SHORT SHOW.								
	2.15			ESCAPED FROM 6 ME 109s BY LOW FLYING.							S.D.	
	1.55			STRAFED AGEDABIA 'DROME 2 JU 87s ON FIRE.								
	1.40			Took OVER COMMAND No 112 Sqdn RAF.								
	1.10			CAUGHT M/T & TROOPS RETREATING. UNPROTECTED.						GOOD RESULTS		
	.50			M/T AND PETROL, AMMUNITION TRUCKS. BLOWN UP.						ODD PERSONNEL.		
59.55	517.10	2.25	1.05	4.40						11.05	10.45	6.10

284 Sorties   426.40 Ops...

[signature] F/Lt L.

O.C. "A" FLIGHT.

[signature] S/Ldr

C.O. 250 SQDN
R.A.F

An exceptional fighter pilot, whose leadership and skill in combat have been of the highest order.

[signature]

O.C. 250 SQDN.

of Italian and German fighters, some twenty MC200s, fifteen G-50s and CR42s and a further eight Bf109s, which were about to strafe ground forces of XIII Corps. The Italians suffered severely, and were unable to take advantage of their superior numbers. Fl.Lt. Ed Jackson, (not to be confused with John Jackson, who had returned to Australia at the end of the Syrian Campaign) destroyed a MC200 and claimed three more damaged, Sgt. Ronald Simes shot down a CR42 and two MC200s, Sgt. Pfeiffer claimed two MC200s and FO Schaeffer destroyed a CR42. FO Jones claimed Bf109s as probable and damaged and FO Hart claimed a CR42 probable. FO Alan Baster was shot down and killed in this combat. The ORB noted that the pilots considered that the MC200 was capable of out-turning the Kittyhawk.

At 0830 on 9 January, Sgt. 'Joe' Lyons (AK589) took off on what was to be his only operational flight with 3 Squadron. Twelve aircraft from 3 joined another eight from 250 Squadron for an offensive sweep over Agedabia and El Agheila. Joe Lyons recalled the formation sighting a large dust cloud which he thought might have been made by aircraft taking off. When the formation was returning, he began to experience mechanical problems.

> 'Coming back, I noticed irregularities with temperatures and pressures. I knew I was gradually losing power. I had to put this down in the desert somewhere. We came to this place called Agedabia. Rommel had just left there, and that's where I put down, on the aerodrome. It had all been heavily mined, but I didn't know that. I got down all right, had no power left at all. I landed there, pulled up at the end of the run and got out of the thing and these army blokes came along, screaming at me not to move. They had a big long low loader, for picking up tanks and things like that. They said the place was lousy with mines and not to move. Well, anyway, there's a sad story to this. Some blokes came in with mine detectors and took me out of there. We locked the aeroplane up and set off for some place that was more or less their headquarters, near Msus. It was a really hot day and I had my parachute with me. This is where you've got to be lucky. There were three blokes in the front seat, with two next to the cabin, and two more right down the back. I said to the driver, "It's a bit hot, do you mind if I sit down the back?" He said, "It'll be pretty rough for you." I got out and a bloke down the back said "You'll have a rough ride," and he took my seat. We'd gone about a quarter of a mile at most when we hit a mine. Those blokes in the front were all killed.'[4]

A lucky escape. FOs Jim McIntosh (left) and Eric Bradbury in pensive mood examining the bullet scarred windscreen of AK581, flown by FO Geoff Chinchen on 9 January, when his aircraft was damaged by Oblt. Homuth of 3/JG 27. (Eric Bradbury)

Joe Lyons suffered from concussion and ruptured ear drums. His memories of the immediate aftermath of the explosion are vague. He spent considerable time in hospital at Jerusalem, and when his hearing had still not recovered four months later, he was repatriated to Australia, much against his wishes.

In the afternoon, 112 Squadron flew again in company with 3, the two units putting up a total of nineteen Kittyhawks as escort to Marylands bombing Marsa Brega. They were surprised by a lone BF109 flown by Oblt. Gerhard Homuth, the Staffelkapitan of 3/JG27, who shot down Sgt. Simes, and severely damaged the machine flown by FO Chinchen, who crash-landed near Msus.

Twenty-two year old Ron Simes died with a victory score of five, one probable and a damaged. A DFM was gazetted three months later.

112 Squadron flew again in the afternoon, providing top cover for the Tomahawks of 250 Squadron, the whole formation escorting Blenheims on a bombing raid north of El Aghelia. They 'lost' their first Kittyhawk in action when they were attacked from above, again by a lone Bf109, which hit Sgt Ken Carson's AK672, causing him to force-land. The aircraft was later recovered, being towed twenty five miles by WO Luscombe and his determined ground crew.[5]

On 10 January 1942, Sgt. Des Cormack flew his first operation with 250 Squadron. He is seen here with a well worn Tomahawk which carries a reversed mirror camouflage pattern in Desert colours.
(Des Cormack)

In the morning on 11 January, ten Kittyhawks from 3 and ten from 112 Squadron took off to escort six Blenheims of 14 Squadron on a bombing raid. Six of the Kittyhawks from 3 acting as top cover were attacked by three Bf109s of I/JG 27, FO Jones and Sgt. Cameron (AK617) being shot down by Lt. Stahlschmidt and Lt. Korner. Other Axis aircraft then became involved in the fight, FO Nicky Barr (AK645) attacking two G-50s, one of which was destroyed. He then noticed a Bf109 harassing one of the two Kittyhawks which had been forced out of the fight by Korner and Stahlschmidt, and shot it down. Its pilot was Oblt. Hugo Schneider, a nine victory ace, who was killed. The Kittyhawk crash-landed and Barr decided to attempt a rescue. Before he could do so, he was himself attacked by two Bf109s, one flown by the dangerous Obfw. Otto Schulz of II/JG 27. With his undercarriage half down he counter attacked these aircraft and claimed one of them shot down and also apparently damaged Schulz's aircraft. He was then forced to crash-land himself due to damage inflicted by Schulz, who proceeded to strafe Barr's aircraft, wounding Barr in the process. He failed to make contact with either Jones or Cameron, and set off to walk the twenty-five miles to friendly territory, rejoining the unit on 14 January. He was awarded an immediate DFC.

Nicky Barr was assisted by a friendly family of Senussi Arabs after being shot down. He is seen here in Arab dress and flying boots, with other members of the squadron: fourth from left Vic Curtis, fifth, MO Dr. Tim Stone, sixth, Les Bradbury, and second from the extreme right of the photograph, Bob Wilson.

(Ian Primmer, via Doug Norrie)

It was a case of third time unlucky for 'Tiny' Cameron. On this occasion he was captured with FO Jones, but his adventures were not yet over. They escaped several days later, but were betrayed by unfriendly Arabs and recaptured, being sent to a prison camp in Italy. They escaped again in Italy, but Alan Cameron was again recaptured after only a day's freedom and transferred to Germany, where he remained until the end of the war. He was awarded a DFM while a prisoner, and also commissioned, being promoted to Fl. Lt. before the end of the war. Jones was eventually successful, reaching Switzerland, from where he managed to cross into France and join Free French forces in 1944.

A sweep was flown by seven of 3's Kittyhawks at 1330 hours on 13 January, and while returning one section was attacked by four Bf109s, including Lt. Korner of II/JG 27 who shot down FO Schaeffer. He force-landed near Msus. The damage to his aircraft was repairable and he returned the next day. FO Bobby Gibbes claimed a damaged Bf109 while flying AK600 CV-V, and during a sweep on 13 January Clive Caldwell (AK658) claimed a damaged Bf109. (His log book recorded that it was damaged and smoking, but he was not too optimistic, noting further that '*it may have been oil only*'.)

Both 112 and 3 Squadrons moved to Antelat, sixty miles south-south-east of Benghazi, 3 completing the move by 18 January. This was the furthest west that either squadron had ever been based, but they were not to remain there for long, as Rommel was about to commence a new offensive which would take advantage of the stretched supply lines of the Commonwealth forces. Rommel began his advance on 21 January and the fighter squadrons left Antelat hurriedly, retreating to Msus, from where the next significant contact with the enemy took place on 22 January.

At 1200 hours 3 Squadron carried out a sweep over the withdrawal of XIII Corps, where they encountered some thirty Ju87s escorted by a mixed force of twelve G-50s and MC200s, with a

further six Bf109s, attacking the Ist Armoured Division. In the sharp battle which followed, FO Hart (AK691 CV-L) and Sgt. Peter Giddy (AK604) each destroyed a MC200,* Hart also claiming a probable, while FO Bobby Gibbes (AK612) destroyed a Ju87 and claimed damage to two G-50s.

> We attacked about 30 Ju87s from down sun and absolutely surprised them as their top cover of Macchi 200s and G50s made no attempt to ward off the attack. I got a Ju87 which was later confirmed by Ed [Jackson]. We then attacked the escort. Got nice bursts into a G50 from dead astern. It flicked onto its back and dived down. Attacked it again from astern to rear quarter. It flicked again at about 500 feet and surprised me very much by pulling out. Left it looking very sick and chased the main body of enemy aircraft. Sneaked up on two G50s, and they were evidently warned by RT of my presence as they broke up rather hurriedly. Got a good burst into one. Both dived away, and last seen it was going like hell for home on the deck.[6]

On this occasion the Italians admitted to the loss of *three* aircraft,[7] an unusual occurrence, as quite often their claims and acknowledged losses seemed to be in inverse proportions to those submitted by the Commonwealth squadrons. FO Eric Bradbury (AK599) shot down a Ju87, and made another attack, but return fire from the Stukas' gunners hit an oil pipe, and he force-landed near a British column. He was picked up by an armoured car.

On the return flight the squadron was surprised by two Bf109s, Lt. Stahlschmidt shooting down FO James McIntosh, who was killed. Sgt. Giddy claimed to have damaged one of the Messerschmitts.

Damaged Fiat G-50 of 151ª Squadriglia, 20° Gruppo CT, found abandoned on an over-run Italian landing ground in December 1941. (RAAF Museum, via Lex McAulay)

* The aircraft destroyed by Peter Giddy was flown by Serg. Renato Carrari of 364ª Squadriglia, 150° Gruppo Aut CT, who was killed. (Aces High Volume 2, p.94) Given the Italian acknowledgment of three losses, it is reasonable to assume that the other two came from the same unit: the third being either Hart's probable, or one of Bobby Gibbes' damaged G-50s which was mis-identified.

Bird of prey: flying AK691 CV-L on its first sortie with 3 Squadron on 22 January 1942, FO Dick Hart shot down a MC202 and claimed another as a probable. Three days later Sgt. Victor Curtis was flying it when he shared a Bf110 with Sgt. Reid. On 14 February, Sgt. Brian Thompson shared a MC202 with FO Pace. The aircraft was lost when FO Tom Threlkeld was shot down and killed on 16 February.
(RAAF Museum, via Lex McAulay)

FO Bradbury spent the night with his British rescuers, enjoying a cup of tea in the back of a covered truck which served as the officers' mess. Gun flashes on the horizon were mis-interpreted as a night practice shoot, but the tea was hastily abandoned when a truck only a hundred yards away received a direct hit. The remaining vehicles got moving, pursued by German tanks. Bradbury's vehicle was hit and knocked onto its side, and he found himself on foot in the middle of a formation of tanks, which seemed determined to kill him. One swerved towards him and he stumbled out of its way, only to be fired on by a second. As a third tank approached, he ran *towards* it, and in desperation continued to run along beside it, using it as a shield. Inevitably, he fell to the ground, exhausted and helpless, fully expecting to be crushed by the following tank. He lost consciousness.

When he awoke, the battle had passed, and in a state of shock he walked northward, covering twenty-two miles by dawn, when he reached the Tobruk - Msus road. Retreating British transport rescued him and he spent two days in a field hospital before returning to the squadron on 25 January, still suffering from shell-shock.

At 1430 hours in the afternoon of 22 January, 250 Squadron were acting as escort for Blenheims attacking advancing German motorised transport on the coast road, and Sgt Frank Twemlow badly damaged one of three Bf109s which attempted to attack the bombers. John Waddy in AN444 claimed a probable, and the Messerschmitts were driven off with no harm done to the bombers.

By 25 January Rommel's advance had forced the fighter squadrons to retreat from Msus to Mechili. 3 flew a strafing attack and were successful in destroying four troop carriers and a petrol tanker. A Bf110 which tried to interfere was shot down by Sgt. F.B. Reid (AK612) and Sgt. Victor Curtis (AK691).

112 Squadron provided escort for Blenheims on a bombing mission to Agedabia in the afternoon, nine flying as close escort with a further five as top cover. While they were returning, they were

A 250 Squadron Tomahawk sharing facilities with two Blenheim Mk. IVs. Note the dust cloud raised by the taxying aircraft. The photograph was taken in January 1942, so the likely location is Gazala.
(Des Cormack)

attacked by five Bf109s of II/JG 27, and Sgt. Rudolph Leu, flying AK637, scored 112 Squadron's first Kittyhawk victory, shooting down one of the Messerschmitts in a head on attack, which knocked a large chunk out of its starboard wing.[8] Its crash was confirmed by another 112 Squadron pilot.

At 1045 on 26 January, eight aircraft of 3 Squadron took off to strafe targets of opportunity on the Msus - Antelat road. Visibility was poor and movement on the road very scattered. Sgt Wal Mailey was hit by AA and force-landed twenty miles north of Mechili. FO Lou Spence landed and picked Mailey up, returning to the unit at 1600.

On the same day 250 Squadron carried out two strafing attacks in the Msus area, and during the second of these, at 1400 hours, PO John Waddy in AN444 shot down a MC200 for his third individual confirmed victory.

One good turn deserves another, and on 27 January Lou Spence found himself in trouble, but was saved by the quick thinking and determination of FO Tom Threlkeld, one of the 4 December reinforcements. At 1145 four Kittyhawks took off to strafe the Msus - Antelat road, claiming eighteen M/T damaged, but Spence's engine overheated due to a loss of glycol and he force-landed. No doubt inspired by Spence's rescue of Wal Mailey the previous day, Threlkeld landed nearby. Discovering that the Kittyhawk could be made airworthy, he flew back to Mechili, collected a container of glycol and returned to FO Spence. Both pilots returned to the squadron the next day.

A further withdrawal took place on 28 January when the fighters all moved back to Gazala. Aerial combats were infrequent during this period due to heavy rain which kept the Germans grounded.

Aerial hostilities resumed with a vengeance on 8 February when Hurricanes from 73 Squadron, together with Kittyhawks from 112 and 3 Squadrons, were tasked with escorting Blenheims to

Derna. While waiting over El Adem to rendezvous with the bombers, four of the Kittyhawks from 3 were forced to return to base with engine trouble, and shortly after this the remaining aircraft were bounced by three Bf109s. FO Threlkeld was shot down by Oblt. Keller, who also attacked Sgt. Curtis's Kittyhawk, badly damaging it in the tail. Threlkeld baled out and was picked up by the army, while Curtis reached Gambut, where he crash-landed. The Messerschmitts climbed away and flew off before any response could be made, but in the confusion five more Kittyhawks lost contact with the bombers and returned to base, only FO Gibbes from 3 remaining with the formation. Over the target they were again attacked by more Bf109s and 112 Squadron lost three inexperienced pilots. Henry Burney (AK702) redressed the balance somewhat by shooting down one of the Messerschmitts and sharing another with Fl. Lt. Humphries, bringing his accumulated victories to two and one shared.

Neither 112 Squadron nor 3 Squadron made contact with the enemy on 9 and 10 February, but during a patrol led by Sgt Leu on the 11th, 112 were attacked by a mixed force of Messerschmitts and MC202s. Leu's radio was not working properly and he handed over the lead to Burney. It was during this time that the attack came, and an English pilot, Sgt Holman, was attacked twice after being separated from the main formation during the radio confusion. He avoided the first attack, but was shot down by the second. His companions could do nothing to help him as the attacks came from above using JG 27's typical dive and zoom tactics.

During February radar assistance became available for the first time, and 'an adequate controlled-interception system came into being covering the area between Gazala and Bardia'.[9] As a result of radar information, eight Kittyhawks from 3 and ten from 112, (led by FO Jack Bartle) were scrambled at 1145 hours on 14 February to meet an approaching enemy raid. The formation flew towards Tobruk at best climbing speed, and then turned west above the outer defences. Over Acroma 3 Squadron was at 8,000 ft with 112 Squadron slightly ahead and above, and just below the cloud base. Bartle spotted a mixed formation of MC200s and 202s some 2,000 ft below and warned 3, whose pilots had spotted a formation of bombers with a close cover escort flying below 2,000 ft.

The top cover Italians began to climb, either to engage the Kittyhawks or reach the cloud cover, but changed their minds at the wrong time and tried to form a defensive circle. Before this could be done effectively 112 Squadron tore into them, initiating what the squadron later called the 'St Valentine's Day Massacre'. It was thought by the pilots of 112 that everybody must have hit something in the initial attack. Sgt Burney, having dived through the top layer of fighters found himself among the bombers and attacked what he reported to be a Breda 65. It was more likely to have been a MC200, as no one else reported Bredas. Whatever the type, it hit the ground in an attempt to avoid Burney's fire, who then 'strafed him to save him a walk home. By the time he regained the formation he could see no enemy fighters up amongst the milling Kittyhawks.' This could well have been because by then they had all been shot down. 112 Squadron claimed eleven and one half destroyed, two probables and three damaged. Of the Australians, Sgt. Rudolph Leu attacked one MC200 which blew up and another which hit the ground in an attempt to avoid his attack. 112's pilots reported that the enemy evasive tactics were to 'drop down to ground level in rolls and vertical dives'.[10] This might have been the undoing of one of Leu's opponents, and the machine destroyed by Burney. Sgt. Roy Drew (AK653 GA-G) 'getting a brace of M.200s in his first real fight said "It was as easy as breakfast in bed."'[11] Jack Bartle claimed a probable MC200 after a long burst which sent it out of control and a damaged Bf109 which he chased as far as Tmimi.

Neville Duke of 112 Squadron noted that 'A dog fight followed and we used 109 tactics, diving from cloud cover and attacking and then making off for cloud again. An Australian and I finished off our particular show by chasing a Macchi at ground level and shooting it down into an army camp which it had recently been strafing'.[12] This was Sgt. F.B. Reid, flying Kittyhawk AK689 CV-W.

As 112 Squadron set about the top cover, the Australians headed for the lower formation. Before this could be attacked however, a number of fighters which were identified as Me109s dived from the cloud cover. The combat report of Sgt. Wal Mailey who was leading the squadron explains how the fight developed.

> Aircraft were reported at what I thought was 5 o'clock, but no Sqdn. code name was given. A/c were then reported at 9 o'clock below. At the same time I saw 3 109s above attacking from 9 o'clock. I turned the Sdn. up to meet them and we were attacked again from 4 o'clock. We met and broke both attacks. A series of dogfights took place. I was attacked by 2 109s but turned in under them. I then saw a 109 attacking a Kittyhawk about 1500 ft below. I dived onto him attacking from beam and near quarter. The E/A attempted to pull up but then half rolled and spun, black smoke was leaving him. I pulled up to guard my own tail , then looked down and saw a fire burning directly beneath me. I am definitely sure it was the a/c I hit. Two more E/A were to one side of me and slightly below. I dived towards them and they split. I followed one and registered very good hits, but had to pull away as the second had come around on my beam. I turned fast and climbed up to the cloud. I saw another Macchi 202 (?) delivering an attack on a Kittyhawk , and dived and broke this attack, but did not register a hit. I was attacked from the beam and dived away. I was looking for the fight when I saw a Macchi 200 heading towards the sea about 200 ft above. I tried to catch him but my engine was misbehaving and I could only get three bursts from about 300 yds. I saw my tracer entering the fuselage but he pulled up and I could not follow him. I then broke off and headed for base.
>
> NOTE - I turned onto one which was doing a beam attack on Sgt. Reid. I put a number of tracer through the cockpit and he fell away. Sgt. Reid later confirmed this plane crashing directly below me and catching fire.

The rest of 3's pilots were also successful. Sgt. B.M. Thompson (AK691) and FO H.G. Pace (AK664) shared a MC200. Sgt G.H. White(AK605) claimed one Me-109 and damage to two Ju87s. FO Peter Giddy (AK665) claimed two MC200s destroyed and another damaged. (Chris Shores in *Aces High* suggests that one of these may have been a MC202.) FO Lou Spence (AK612) claimed one Bf109, while the afore mentioned Sgt. Reid destroyed a MC200 and damaged another, as well as the aircraft he shared with Neville Duke. FO Gray (AK621) claimed damage to a Bf109.

No German losses were reported during the day, so it seems likely that the escorting fighters were MC202s. Another interesting point to consider is the type and numbers of the 'bombers' which were supposedly present. Henry Burney claimed a 'Ba 65', which was, in fact, a MC200, * the types being not dissimilar. The two units which operated the Ba 65 had replaced them with G-50s and MC200s by the end of February 1941.[13A]

There were no reports of attacks on 'bombers' other than the two Ju87s claimed as damaged by Sgt. White. It is possible that these were Italian flown Stukas. 96° Gruppo arrived in Libya in February of 1941, and the Ju87Rs of 209 Squadriglia B.a.T. were still present in small numbers up to 24 March 1942, when they were withdrawn due to losses.[13B]

Neville Duke's comment concerning the Macchi he shared with Sgt. Reid may go some way towards explaining the situation. They shot it down 'into an army camp which it had recently been strafing'. It thus seems possible that the top cover attacked by 112 Squadron, and the fighters which attacked 3 Squadron were MC202s, which were there to provide protection for ground strafing MC200s. Mis-identification of the MC202s as 'Me-109s' is not hard to understand. The wing configuration was quite similar, and the DB601 engine made the Macchi's nose profile much like the Bf109F, which was powered by a similar engine.

Neither of the Commonwealth squadrons suffered a single casualty, while claiming the destruction of twenty enemy aircraft from a force estimated at thirty two.

---

* Burney's victim was a MC200 from 363ª Squadriglia, 150° Gruppo Aut CT. The Italians admitted the loss of **three** pilots from this unit. (Aces High Volume 2, p.55)

This combat was described by John Herington as 'a text-book example of perfect interception, both top- and extra-top cover being eliminated before the bombers were attacked'.[14] As no actual claims were submitted for destroyed bombers, this description might be a trifle extravagant. What can be said without any doubt is that it was one of the very few occasions when the Kittyhawk pilots found themselves in a position to attack from above, and made the most of both their skills and the rare opportunity to initiate a combat on their terms.

A cheerful Sgt. Roy Drew of 112 Squadron, with his somewhat weather-beaten Kittyhawk I after the 'St Valentine's Day Massacre'. (Des Cormack)

On the following day two Kittyhawks were scrambled to intercept a formation of Ju88s which were approaching the aerodrome as they were returning from a raid in the Gambut area. They were escorted by 3/JG 27. Lt. Marseille had seen the aircraft taking off, and after seeing the bombers back to the lines returned with his wingman, Fw. Pottgen. They dived from 4,000 metres, and Marseille's first burst struck Sgt. Reid's Kittyhawk (AK605). Reid had not yet gained sufficient altitude to bale out, and was killed when his Kittyhawk crashed. Marseille then attacked PO Briggs (AK594), who baled out successfully, with wounds, from only 300 feet. Twenty-seven year old Frank Reid had been with the squadron for several months and was one of its few remaining veterans, having destroyed a Bf110 in November and shared another in January prior to his successes of the previous day.

Later that afternoon 112 Squadron flew in company with 94 Squadron, which had only recently converted to Kittyhawks and were flying their first operation. This was a wing sweep with the intention of strafing Martuba. As they swept over the German field, Obfw. Otto Schulz scrambled and shot down four of the attacking aircraft, including 94 Squadron's new CO, Sqn. Ldr. E.M. 'Imshi' Mason DFC, who had fifteen and two shared victories, and was the highest scoring Commonwealth fighter pilot in the desert at the time. Schulz then attacked the 112 Squadron Kittyhawk flown by Sgt. D.N. McQueen and severely damaged it, wounding McQueen, who skilfully brought his aircraft back to base. Schulz was awarded five victories, although McQueen and his aircraft survived. After recovering from his wounds, he rejoined 112 in March, then transferring to 450 Squadron in August.

On 16 February five Kittyhawks from 3 Squadron took off at 1600 hours to intercept enemy aircraft approaching El Adem. About ten miles South east of El Adem, six Bf109s were sighted 1000 feet *below,* a most unusual circumstance, but although the Kittyhawks gave chase, no contact was made. On the return three Messerschmitts were sighted behind and the formation turned for a head on attack. Sgt White fired at 100 yards and his target was seen to leave formation in a glide. It was claimed as damaged. FO Thomas Threlkeld (AK691) failed to return and the army later reported his aircraft crashing in flames twenty miles south of El Adem. His victor was Oblt. Keller of I/JG 27.

On this day 3 Squadron received reinforcements in the form of six Sergeant Pilots who were posted in from the Empire Air Training Scheme (EATS): Sgts. L.L. Boardman, R.M.H. Jennings, E.K. Kildey, T.E. Packer, K.W. Stanley and E.V. Teede. The new pilots were instructed in cockpit drill on 17 February, and the ORB reported that two of the pilots 'were put off in Kittyhawks on 18th'. Also on the 18th Bobby Gibbes, now promoted Flight Lieutenant, flew two Tac. R. missions to Martuba, but on each occasion he was unable to locate his objective due to rain and cloud. There was no operational flying on 19 February due to severe dust storms, which also interrupted the training of the new pilots.

On the 21st, Wg. Cdr. Chapman, the CO, and Fl. Lt. Ed Jackson left for Cairo, the former on duty and leave, and the latter to await return to Australia.

Later on this day 112 Squadron flew a sweep near Gazala, led on this occasion by Clive Caldwell. At midday six Bf109s of 3/JG 27 took off to patrol over Acroma. They were led by the Staffelkapitan Hpt. Gerhard Homuth. The second rotte was led by Lt. Marseille and the third by Lt. Hans-Arnold Stahlschmidt, who was not feeling pleased with life because he had been photographed by some soldiers just before he had taken off, and this was considered to be most unlucky by the German fighter pilots, no doubt dating back to the occasion when Baron von Richthofen failed to return after having his photograph taken on 21 April 1918.

> I was using the adjutant's aircraft in which I had already flown over 100 missions. It was pretty old and tired and very slow but I kept using it because it was reliable.
>
> Suddenly a flight of Curtiss P-40s approached us. Homuth pulled up, turning to the left and started to climb over the enemy aircraft. I climbed also but not as quickly. In any case I wanted to have a closer look at the Curtiss fighters. Soon I was well behind. The situation was quite clear to me. I saw the P-40s climbing behind us about 300 metres below.
>
> There did not seem to be any danger from them but my comrades were much higher so I tried to cut their curve. Keppler (Stahlschmidt's wing man) passed me easily on the outside with his faster aircraft. I now saw the Curtiss fighters directly below. I counted eleven of them. I was quite content and even hummed a little song which I sometimes still remember. I continued climbing, unsuspecting of any danger.
>
> Suddenly there was a frightful banging noise and my whole aircraft vibrated. It felt like cannon strikes! Nothing like that had ever happened before. Damn! Someone had opened up on me from behind and I hadn't even seen him. Shame on me!
>
> From then on everything happened horribly quickly. I realised I had many serious hits from heavy armament, therefore it had to be one of the new Kittyhawks. It looked as if I was finished. My Messerschmitt was turning around uncontrollably, gasolene (sic) was pouring into the cockpit, smoke was everywhere and I found myself in a crazy inverted spin. I spun down through the British fighters and heard over the radio, "Which idiot let himself get shot down?" It was Homuth calling.[15]

Clive Caldwell was the man responsible for Stahlschmidt's problems. Noticing that one of the German aircraft was lagging behind, he briefly dropped the Kittyhawk's nose to pick up extra speed, applied maximum throttle and pulled up into a vertical climb, firing as he did so. He later reported that the Messerschmitt "shuddered like a carpet being whacked with a beater" before it fell smoking and spinning to make a crash landing in no-man's land.

Looking rather sheepish about having his arm raised like a victorious boxer is Sgt. Ray Shaw, shortly after 450 Squadron's first successful combat. From left after Shaw are Sgts. Beste, Shillabeer and Kierath, all of whom pursued the Ju88 shot down by Shaw. (Gordon Steege)

Squadron Leader Gordon Steege, 450 Squadron's first CO. Hurricanes in the background suggest that the photograph was taken during the time of 450's operation as a Hurricane conversion unit. (Gordon Steege)

Stahlschmidt was rescued by a German patrol and returned to Martuba, where he presented himself to Hpt. Homuth.

> I now discovered what had happened. One of the leading Kittyhawks had suddenly pulled up into a vertical position, hung briefly on its propeller and fired just one burst. Homuth and Marseille both said it was a fabulous shot. [16]

This translation makes an interesting comparison with another from Marseille's biographer, which tells a similar story, but ends with the words 'Homuth and Marseille were of the opinion that it was only the purest chance that the Curtiss hit me at all'.[17] Perhaps this is what was meant by the use of the word 'fabulous', which is defined by the Oxford dictionary as *legendary, incredible, absurd, exaggerated*. The Germans (and the translator) may not have been given to the modern day colloquial usage of the word, which is often used incorrectly to describe something as remarkably good. Had they known the identity of the pilot who made the 'fabulous shot' their choice of word may well have been different.

Having recovered from the shock loss of Stahlschmidt, Homuth and Marseille then attacked the Kittyhawks from above and shot down three machines, all of whose pilots survived. Sgt. 'Kit' Carson of 112 Squadron also gave a Bf109 a good burst at close range without apparent result, but the squadron was told later that an enemy aircraft had crashed between Tmimi and Gazala, and this was credited to Carson.

Another Australian squadron was about to enter the arena. This was 450 Squadron RAAF, which came into existence in June 1941 when it combined with the newly arrived pilots of 260 Squadron RAF which had Hurricanes, but no ground crew, while 450 had ground crew but no aircraft or pilots! The combined unit operated during the Syrian Campaign, after which 450 operated as an

Eight of 450 Squadron's original pilots taking part in a not very military drill in January 1942. Left to right, Sergeants Bill Halliday, Frank Beste, Ivan Young, John James, Keith McBride, Jack Donald, Neil Shillabeer (without a rifle) and Max Jenkins. (Max Jenkins, via Doug Norrie)

Hec Mutch, a 450 Squadron armourer in the cockpit of one of the squadron's Kittyhawks. Certain members of the ground crew were capable of starting engines and taxying the aircraft when required, although the choice of head gear and aircraft suggests that this shot was taken for the family album.. The letter 'D' indicates that this photograph was taken early in the Squadron's career, as the original Squadron codes of 'DJ' were replaced by the more familiar 'OK' probably towards the end of April 1942. Note the swastika victory marking beneath the gun sight, and the vent for the coolant expansion tank
(Ted Lawler)

advanced Repair and Service Unit and later as a Hurricane conversion unit. Under the leadership of Sqn. Ldr. Gordon Steege DFC, it began to reform as a fighter squadron, receiving its first Kittyhawk on 18 December. Gordon Steege was one of the original pilots of 3 Squadron, recording victories over three Italian aircraft while flying Gladiators, and four German aircraft after the squadron converted to Hurricanes, including three Ju87s in one combat on 18 February 1941. The squadron moved to Gambut on 15 February and two of its pilots, Sgts. Dyson and Halliday flew scrambles with 3 Squadron on 17 February. Several interception patrols were flown between this date and 22 February, when the unit scored its first success, Sgt. Ray Shaw (AK726 O) shooting down a Ju88 of I(F)/121 from 20, 000 feet over Gazala.

450 Squadron flew a bomber escort with 3 the next day, and became embroiled in their first full scale combat. While escorting six Bostons to bomb transport between Tmimi and Martuba they

Squadron Leader Bobby Gibbes, the irrepressible leader of 3 Squadron . (Doug Norrie)

were attacked by Bf109s from I/JG 27. Lt. Sinner shot down FO C.M.T. Thompson, who was captured, * and also damaged the aircraft of Sgt. Keith McBride, who brought his smoking Kittyhawk back across the lines. He then lost control and spun while attempting to crash-land. He was thrown clear of the wreck, but was badly injured, and he died shortly after. Sgts. Ivan Young (AK732 A) and Ian Nursey (AK606 B) each claimed a Bf109 during this combat.

On 26 February Acting Squadron Leader Bobby Gibbes took command of 3 Squadron, after what must have been one of the shortest periods as a Flight Lieutenant on record. The ORB recorded him as both Flying Officer and Flight Lieutenant when he flew the Tac. R. sorties on 18 February, and eight days later he was a Squadron Leader. It proved to be a wise choice of leader. ** Up to this point, the unit had always provided its own new Squadron Leaders, Peter Jeffrey replacing McLachlan and Alan Rawlinson assuming command when Jeffrey became the Wing Leader. The one exception was Sqn. Ldr. Chapman, whose tenure lasted less than two months before he

---

* Thompson's aircraft was hit twice by the 109 and entered an uncontrollable spin. He baled out. (AWM 54 779/3/29 PoW debriefs.)

** Peter (Jeffrey) and I were walking up to the operations desk for the briefing of one of these (late November) sweeps. We stopped and looked at the assembled group of pilots putting on their flying kit and checking parachutes. Our losses over the last seven days had been very heavy. Pete said "Which of those blokes do you think could take over the squadron if either of us get the chop?" None of them had that much operational experience. "We must let the Ops chaps know of our nomination."

After a brief pause I chose Bobby Gibbes. "He has a bit of cocky self confidence. The responsibility would provide the proper harness to this and bring him out." It was necessary for him to take over command in early 1942 and he achieved a fine operational record. [18]

left to take command of 451 Squadron. Apart from a temporary break due to injuries, Bobby Gibbes led the squadron with distinction for the next fourteen months.

At 1120 hours on 27 February, six Kittyhawks from 3 Squadron and a further six from 450 were scrambled from standby to intercept enemy aircraft over Tobruk, a force consisting of Bf109s from I and III Gruppes of JG 27 and fourteen Ju87s. Before the two squadrons had joined up, 3 was attacked by the Bf109s, the attack being made initially on FO Pfeiffer and Sgt. Thompson. Pfeiffer evaded the attack and Brian Thompson (AK622) counter attacked, shooting down one Bf109 and damaging another. Lt. Marseille, who had been awarded the Knights Cross five days earlier, then attacked the Kittyhawks flown by PO Hart (AK689) and Sgt. Jennings (AK665). Hart baled out and later returned safely, but Sgt. Roger Jennings was killed when his Kittyhawk crashed near XIII Corps Headquarters. Since his arrival on the squadron on 16 February the young Sergeant had flown a scramble on 22 February, a bomber escort on the 23rd and an offensive patrol on the 25th, from which he returned early due to engine trouble. He lost his life on his fourth operational flight.

450 Squadron lost two aircraft, those of Sgt. Edward Gray, who was killed, and Sgt Crouch, who crash-landed at Tobruk. Sgt. Dyson claimed a Messerschmitt as damaged, but he may have actually shot it down, as III/JG 27 lost two aircraft, both pilots being captured. However, Bobby Gibbes' diary states that Sgt Thompson's damaged claim was confirmed, and he was subsequently credited with two victories.

Hpt. Homuth was Gray's probable victor, while Fw. Forbger of III Gruppe was the pilot likely to have shot down Sgt. Crouch.

*At 11.30 am some of our fellows left to attack some Jerries over Tobruk. On the way they ran into a bunch of 109's. Sergeant Crouch belly-landed "L" near Tobruk and was admitted to hospital with some shrapnel in his anatomy. Sergeant Gray in "C" did not return. In him I lost a wonderful friend and my faithful old kite. (Viv Herrett - War Diary) **

On 1 March the Western Desert Air Force was reorganised. 3 Squadron and 450 Squadron together with 112 and 250 Squadrons were grouped together as 239 Wing, all with Kittyhawks, while 2 and 4 SAAF and 94 and 260 Squadrons operating Tomahawks and Kittyhawks were grouped as 233 Wing.

Wg. Cdr. H.C. Mayers was appointed to lead 239 Wing. Howard Mayers was an Australian with experience from the Battle of Britain, destroying eight enemy aircraft while flying Hurricanes with 601 Squadron. He was posted to the Desert in July 1941 to command 94 Squadron on Hurricanes, sharing in the destruction of a Ju88 and damaging two Bf109s. On Christmas Day 1941 one of his pilots, Sgt. McKay, was shot down by ground fire while strafing an Axis column. Howard Mayers landed his Hurricane and in the face of approaching enemy vehicles got the pilot into the cockpit and took off successfully. This courageous rescue earned him a Bar to his DFC.

Neither of the Australian Squadrons encountered the enemy again until 8 March, when they achieved a significant victory. At 1700 hours six Kittyhawks from 3 Squadron took off on a freelance patrol over the battle area, accompanied by six aircraft from 450 acting as top cover. Enemy aircraft were sighted eighteen miles south of Tobruk and contact was made. The ORB recorded that the enemy formation consisted of two formations of Macchi 202s and 200s in echelons of five and four and approximately fifteen Ju87s flying in vic formation. 450 Squadron remained as top cover, while 3 made the initial attack. Fl.Lt Nicky Barr (AK903) claimed a MC202,

---

(his ninth victory, as his probable Ju87 from 1 January was later confirmed) while FOs Giddy, (AK876) Pace (AK712) and Curtis (AK622) each claimed one MC200. * The top cover of 450 Squadron then joined the battle, shooting down three more Italians, whose formation was almost wiped out. Sgt. Beste (AK793 W), Sgt Donald McBurnie (AK717 V) each claiming a MC200, and Sgt Shaw (AK592 P) claiming one MC200 or 202.

Giddy and Curtis were also credited with a Ju87 each, but it is possible that these did not in fact crash, as 112 Squadron encountered the Axis formation returning, and destroyed one of the two reported Macchis and one of fifteen reported Stukas, however it should be noted that 3 Squadron's count before they attacked was *approximately* fifteen Ju87s.

While 3 and 450 Squadrons were not engaged for several days after their success against the Italian fighters, the spotlight turns to 112 Squadron, where a significant event was about to take place. Prior to this however, a young Australian pilot lost his life in unexplained circumstances. During the morning of the 9th, nine Kittyhawks were scrambled to intercept four Bf109s which had strafed the airfield at Gambut Main, the Squadron's new base. Almost inevitably, no interception was made, but as the formation returned to base, Sgt Elliott was seen to roll over and enter a dive from 8,000 ft and crash. 'No reason was discovered for his death, but the opinion at the time was that he was the victim of a sneak attack out of cloud'.[19] As no German claims were submitted, his death remains a mystery. **

A group of 450 Squadron pilots with the 'battle buggy'. Standing, Sgt. Ian Nursey, then PO Kelsall, Sgt. Ivan Young, Sgt Law, Sgt. 'Rusty' Kierath with 'Timber', the squadron dog, unidentified, Sgt. Don McBurnie at the wheel and Fl. Lt. Ian Rose. Gambut Main, March 1942. The marking on the mudguard identifies this vehicle as belonging to 8 Panzer Regiment, 15 Panzer Division. (Gordon Steege)

* *The Italians acknowledged the loss of three pilots from the 150° Gruppo Aut CT during this engagement. (Aces High Volume 2, p. 69)*

** *In conversation with Tony Gaze, Lex McAulay discussed the matter of aircraft inexplicably diving into the ground or sea. Tony Gaze said that some instances could have been due to blindingly painful sinus attacks. (Correspondence from Lex McAulay)*

On 10 March an experiment was carried out which was to have a significant effect on both the outcome of the Desert war, and the future deployment of the Kittyhawk squadrons. Sqn. Ldr. Clive Caldwell made the first test drop of an inert 250-lb bomb to see whether it could be done without striking the propeller. The test was carried out over the sea with the Air-Sea Rescue organisation in attendance. The first drop proved successful, and it was repeated later in the day with a live bomb. Caldwell's log book recorded the event in some detail.

> March 10 AK900 (GA-A, author) TEST OF TYPE (as fighter bomber) .20 [time]
>
> TEST KITTYHAWK AS DIVE BOMBER.. 250 lb BOMB HUNG CENTRE. ANGLE OF DIVE 45°.
>
> H^T 3000 ^{FT} SPEED 300 MPH I. [indicated] NO THROW AWAY GEAR.. BOMB OBSERVED TO MISS AIRSCREW BY NARROW MARGIN. THIS WAS REASON FOR TEST. ALL O.K.

On the following day several of the squadron's pilots, including Jack Bartle, carried out some practice bombing, and in the evening, Caldwell

> *TOOK 250 lb BOMB AND DIVE BOMBED ENEMY FIGHTER 'DROME AT MARTUBA. BOMB LANDED SHORT OF A/C AMONG TENTS ETC; STRAFED.* [20]

Thus the Kittybomber was born, and in the following months all the Kittyhawk squadrons would be converted to the bomb carrying role, and make a significant contribution to the fortunes of the army.

> Jack Bartle, after the war, explained the technique. Initially the aircraft was made to dive at about 45°, aiming at the target. On pulling out, between about 3,000 -2,000 ft, you counted to ten, fairly rapidly (about 5 seconds) and released the bomb. The bombs were fitted with a striker extended by 2 ft. which gave the maximum blast effect. He went on to say that after releasing the bomb it was unwise to climb, so they always turned and dived again, down to ground level and 'hedge-hopped' all the way home strafing as they went. Generally one flight acted as top cover while the other bombed. The Kittyhawk became rather unmanageable when in the dive and could only be controlled by having both hands on the stick. 112 Sqn had now become the first fighter bomber squadron.'[21]

The conversions did not take place overnight however, and there was still much hard aerial combat without the encumbrance of bombs and altered tactics to come.

On 12 March 3 Squadron lost FO Peter Giddy. A panel detached itself while he was flying aerobatics, and he was killed when the aircraft crashed. He had claimed five destroyed and two damaged in just twenty-four sorties.

112 Squadron had its next encounter with the enemy on 13 March, when twelve Kittyhawks took off with five Hurricanes of 274 Squadron to intercept a raid heading for Tobruk. Fifteen minutes after they had become airborne, one Kittyhawk from Jack Bartle's flight dropped out due to engine trouble and five minutes later some unidentified aircraft emerged from cloud right on the formation's tail. During the break the two flights became separated. Over the coast near cloud, Bartle and his No.2, Sgt Rozanski, were attacked by two Bf109s which they avoided by entering cloud, but they were attacked again when they broke cloud. One of the attackers was Obfw. Otto Schulz, who shot down Sgt Rozanski, while Bartle got a burst at the second Messerschmitt. The remainder of his section, led by Sgt Burney, found themselves surrounded by four Bf109s and five MC202s, one of which attacked and overshot. Burney, in AK772 (GA-Y) promptly got onto its tail and shot it down into the sea north of Tobruk. ('The Italians claimed to have shot down eight Curtiss fighters in the Tobruk area on this mission'.[22])

On 14 March at 1215, twelve of 3 Squadron's Kittyhawks took off to provide the top cover for twelve Bostons to bomb Martuba. A further twelve aircraft of 450 Squadron acted as close cover, and 112 Squadron flew a diversionary sweep in the area. 3's ORB records that the formation was attacked by small numbers of E/A on three occasions without success to the enemy. Accurate AA was experienced E.N.E of Martuba on the run up, and the Bostons damaged three Bf109s on the ground. Two Kittyhawks from 450 Squadron flown by Sgts Quirk and Halliday, were damaged by Bf109s, one of which was shot down by FO G. Chinchen (AK891 CV-D) and Sgt T. E. Packer (AK896). Macchis were also present, and two were attacked by Fl.Lt. R. Hart,(AK849) who claimed a probable MC202, and F/Sgt Keith Kildey (AK677), who claimed a MC200 as destroyed.

112 Squadron then arrived and Sqn.Ldr. Caldwell turned his formation to assist two Kittyhawks which were being pursued by four MC202s and two Bf109s. Two of 112's aircraft were hit immediately by Bf109s, (which may in fact have been Macchis) one pilot being killed and the other baling out, But Caldwell (AK772) and his No.2, Sgt Urbanczyk, followed one of the '109s' down and both attacked it. It crashed close to a Kittyhawk which it had just shot down. Caldwell then climbed back into the fight and attacked another Macchi, which pulled up violently, shortly after which a fawn coloured parachute was seen descending. (Caldwell's log book noted that the pilot was captured.)

112 Squadron's ORB recorded the joint victory of Caldwell and Urbanczyk as a Bf109, but *Aces High* notes that both Caldwell's victories on this day were MC202s. *Fighters Over The Desert* notes that the Italians claimed four victories on this occasion and makes no mention of any German claims.

Today there was a big raid over a German 'drome at Martuba in which twelve Bostons dropped six tons of bombs whilst being escorted by 3 Squadron as well as ourselves. All arrived back safely. However Sergeant Dangar managed to put "D" on her nose on the edge of the runway, wiping off her nose.

(Viv Herrett)

(Which explains how he came by the nick-name "Pranger" He did it again on 18 March - author)

Sgt. Bill Halliday seems happily unconcerned about the damage to the leading edge of his Kittyhawk's wing. Judging from the position of the outboard gun muzzle and the open access panel, the armourers will have some work to do. (Ted Lawler)

In what appears to be an official publicity photograph, Squadron Leader Clive Caldwell of 112 Squadron is seen wearing the ribbon of the DFC and Bar. (Doug Norrie)

At 1030 on 15 March, the Bostons returned to Martuba, this time with 3 Squadron as close cover and 450 as top cover. Heavy and accurate AA was experienced as soon as the formation crossed the coast, and all the way to Martuba. FO Lou Spence led Yellow Section, with PO Victor Curtis as his No. 2. After the bombing,

> 5 - 10 miles S.W. Tmimi, we were attacked by 2 ME109s. I avoided the first two attacks without damage. Then I observed an ME109 attack Red 2. I immediately turned in on him and he did not continue his attack but dived straight through in front of me and levelled out and climbed slightly. I turned with him and fired two long bursts from about 100 ft. on rear quarter. He went down in a steep dive, (nearly vertical) I did not see him crash as there were more e/a in the vicinity. (Curtis)

Lou Spence saw the 109 attack Curtis and called a warning on the R/T which was not heard. He

> then noticed the 109 attacking the top cover to the port side. He was foiled in the attack (by Curtis - author) and I then weaved right. An a/c was reported attacking and I noticed as I continued my weave further that an ME109 was diving towards me but not with the intention of attacking me. I feel quite sure he did not see me as he was banked away from me slightly. I turned sharply right and as he passed within 50 yds. of me I gave him a 2 second burst in a quarter attack from right above as he went down and past. . . I observed my bullets hitting his canopy and fuselage. I was diving almost vertically at this time downwards on him. As I pulled out I lost sight of the enemy a/c.

Spence chased after the formation at low level and climbed back up into position. When the formation reached Sidi Rezegh they were again attacked, and Victor Curtis was once more the chosen target. Lou Spence 'reported an E a/c attacking my No.2 from 6 o'clock,' but again the warning was not heard. Curtis avoided this attack as well and

> as he dived towards the sea I turned and fired several long bursts from directly behind. I saw no damage and he continued out to sea, easily out distancing me. There were two other Kittyhawks attacking so I broke off and tried to rejoin the formation.

Lou Spence saw all this, and noted that his No. 2 joined the chase. At the same time he was looking for the 109's No.2, which

> attacked me from 5 o'clock and I was left behind the bombers, evading 4 attacks by this E a/c. His method of attack was in each case from a vertical dive, with aileron turns following me... He disappeared into the sun after these attacks. . . I flew towards Gambut and when in a weave I observed the E a/c coming up from astern in a shallow dive. I turned sharply left and when I though he had reached the position when he was about to pull up and away I whipped around right and gave him a 4 second burst as he climbed upwards from rear quarter. As I fired I noticed oil coming from his engine and covering his fuselage. The E a/c then headed for home westwards.

Spence (AK806 CV-N) claimed a probable and a damaged, Curtis (AK708) claimed a probable, later confirmed destroyed, and Fl. Lt. Hart claimed a destroyed. His combat report was not preserved, but it is likely that his was one of the three aircraft which pursued Curtis' second assailant. F/Sgt. Keith Kildey (AK677) claimed a probable.

Victor Curtis' final comments in his combat report explained why Spence's R/T warnings were not heard.

> One point which was brought home strongly was a complete disregard of R/T silence after the [bombing] attack. Several warnings vitally concerning myself were jammed by useless messages.

450 Squadron reported attacks by five Bf109s and a MC202 from Tmimi until reaching base, and obviously did a good job keeping most of these away from 3 Squadron and the bombers, all of which returned. One of 450's aircraft was slightly damaged, but the pilot's name was not recorded and it did not even warrant a damaged Cat. number. Obfw. Schulz's claim for a Kittyhawk destroyed[23] was optimistic.

Unfortunately the serial number is unknown, but CV-O, *Rima,* was a personal aircraft of FO Lou Spence. It was not generally possible for a pilot to fly the same aircraft all the time, due to rostering and maintenance requirements. From 1 January to 7 May 1942, Lou Spence flew *fifteen* different Kittyhawks. AK698 and AK612 were each used on ten occasions, so it is likely that *Rima* was one of these.
(RAAF Museum)

3 Squadron was not involved in any further aerial combats and was soon withdrawn for a well earned rest. The ORB noted that on '20 March FO Abicair (the Engineer Officer) left for RAF HQ with Mr Wickham, the Allison representative, to finalise tests on air cleaners for Tomahawk and Kittyhawk aircraft designed by FO Abicair. On 23 March all serviceable aircraft, fourteen in number, were flown to base on the Squadron's withdrawal for four weeks rest'.

The first engine change to be carried out on a 3 Squadron Kittyhawk. The presence of the crane suggests that this may well have been at Sidi Heneish, during the leave period mentioned above. Bobby Gibbes related that before the use of FO Abicair's filter, engines rarely lasted longer than forty hours: use of the new filter doubled this period. (Doug Norrie)

From 1 April to 28 April inclusive the squadron carried out no operational flying, and on 15 April took on strength PO Ritchie and Sgts. Wood, Fox, Dean and Scribner, who were newly arrived from Australia. Tom Wood describes his experiences soon after joining the squadron.

The squadron was on stand down and had sufficient pilots so the C.O. (Bobby Gibbes) organised the five of us to go to No. 71 O.T.U. in the Sudan to get some time on Tomahawks before commencing operations with the squadron.

We left base about 24/4/42, went to Alexandria, then Cairo for a few days. We left Cairo by train on 1/5/42, arrived El Shelal the next day, transferred to a river boat, down the Nile to Wadi Halfa, back on the train, arrived Atbara (a railway junction) at 2 am 5/5/42. Whilst waiting for our next train, as it was getting hot (the temperature reached 127 degrees Fahrenheit - almost 53 degrees Celsius) we were sent to the army store to get ourselves pith helmets (a vast improvement on a forage cap!), then back on the train to Summit, near Carthago and Khartoum in Anglo Egyptian Sudan where No. 71 O.T.U. (a British R.A.F. station) was situated. This was an established O.T.U., local stone buildings etc. where they were flying Harvards and Tomahawks.

We spent about a month there learning combat techniques etc. from experienced combat pilots - a vast improvement on No. 1 O.T.U. Nhill, which only had staff pilots (excluding Jock Perrin) who had never been in a theatre of war.

We then flew back to Cairo on 7/6/42 in a Bristol Bombay (took ten hours in contrast to six days to get down). The next day we were sent to No. 1 Middle East Training School at El Ballah, near Cairo to do a short conversion course on to Kittyhawks, then on 13/6/42 back to Cairo and then the next day to Wadi Natrou on the Cairo - Alexandria desert road. On 15/6/42 we flew in an Oxford from Wadi Natrou to Casferete, then by Kittyhawk to Gerawla and then on to Sidi Heneish in another Kittyhawk to rejoin No. 3 Squadron at L.G. 102.[24]

112 Squadron was also rested, all ranks departing for leave in Cairo and Alexandria on 17 March, after which a number of changes to personnel took place. PO Jack Bartle was promoted straight to Flight Lieutenant, taking over B Flight on 12 April and Clive Caldwell was soon to depart for Australia.

450 Squadron was still operational, and

on 21st March at 5.00 am we were dive bombed by eight 109F's. Several bombs landed in "B" Flight's dispersal area damaging three kites and killing Arthur Ashfield. (Viv Herrett)

Tom Wood being awarded his wings by Group Captain Roy King, DSO, DFC, the Base Commander at Point Cook, on 12 October 1941. 'Bo' King flew with 4 Squadron AFC in 1918, claiming a total of 26 enemy aircraft. He left the Air Force after the war, rejoining at the outbreak of WW II. Tragically, he died suddenly on 29 November 1941. (Tom Wood)

(A member of the squadron's ground crew - author)

94 Squadron, which flew its first operation with Kittyhawks on 15 February, losing four aircraft, including the CO, Sqn Ldr. Mason, had one Australian pilot on strength at this time, Sgt. M.M. Maxwell. After their disastrous beginning, the unit was briefly withdrawn to Gasr El Arid for further training, returning to action on 21 March, when they patrolled the Gazala-Tobruk area. During the day they were engaged with JG27, losing one aircraft, but Sgt. Maxwell managed to damage one of the attackers.

On 23 March, 94 and 260 Squadrons combined to escort Bostons raiding Martuba West. The formation was attacked by III/JG27, and again 94 Squadron lost an aircraft, but this time claimed two of the enemy, one of which was shot down by Sgt. Maxwell.

On 28 March 450 provided top cover to 94 Squadron's Kittyhawks, which in turn were providing middle cover to a close escort of 2 SAAF's Tomahawks, the whole flock offering its protection to Bostons on their almost daily trip to Martuba. Near Tmimi on the return trip, the force was engaged by Bf109s of I/JG 27, which shot down an aircraft of 94 Squadron.[*] 450 Squadron counter attacked, Sqn. Ldr. Steege (AK692 C) and Sgt Shillabeer (AK799 R) both claiming probable Bf109s. Steege's was later confirmed as destroyed. Sgt Nursey (AK668 H) claimed a probable MC202 and PO

---

[*] *After further losses in April, 94 Squadron was withdrawn, handing its remaining Kittyhawks over to 2 SAAF. It re-equipped with Hurricanes, and flew defensive patrols over Alexandria and Port Said.*

Sgt. Quirk's damaged Kittyhawk, AK706, DJ-S, after his eventful landing on 28 March.
(Max Jenkins, 450 Squadron, via Doug Norrie)

Maintenance on AK668 OK-H, one of 450 Squadron's first Kittyhawks, flown on different occasions by several of the squadron's successful pilots, Sgts. Ray Dyson, Ian Nursey, Neil Shillabeer and Don McBurnie. This aircraft served with the Squadron from 15 March until 13 May, and it is likely that it carried the original DJ codes when Nursey used it to claim a MC202 probable on 28 March. (RAAF Museum)

Kelsall (AK895 K) a damaged Bf109, but Sgt Halliday (AK659 G) was hit and force landed in no-mans-land. He was later picked up by the army, suffering from wounds. Sgt. Quirk's aircraft suffered Cat. 2 damage to the port wing, but he landed successfully without flaps at 150 mph.

> *29th March 1942: we stood to again all day, but dust storms prevented any real activity At 7.00 pm we were raided by Junkers bombers. The whole place was lit up like day by their parachute flares. Twelve bombs were dropped around the 'drome, but no great damage was done.*

> *30th March - Another raid on our 'drome by two Ju88's. Fourteen 250 lb bombs were dropped this time. One kite was damaged by shrapnel. There were many near misses in our camping area.*

> *4th April: Six rookie pilots arrived here during the arvo and got stuck into some practice flying straight up. During that brief stint they managed to put "H" over on her nose and badly damage "J's" legs. (Viv Herrett)*

The pilots referred to by Viv Herrett were POs MacPherson and Evatt, and Sgts. Davidson, Glancy, Kennedy and Lindsay. Two of these young men lost their lives the next day in tragic circumstances. On 5 April six Kittyhawks were patrolling Gambut at 6,000 ft when PO John Evatt fell out of control and entered a spin, from which his aircraft did not recover. Only moments later, the aircraft of PO Gordon MacPherson did the same thing. Both pilots were killed instantly, and the squadron could find no reason for their loss. Significantly however, the ORB recorded that they were both on their first operation, and had only about *eight hours* in the aircraft type.

On 7 April, eight aircraft of 450 Squadron provided the top cover to Bostons and lost one aircraft when Sgt. W. J. Metherall baled out due to engine trouble. Shortly afterwards the formation was attacked by Bf109s of II/JG 27 and lost FO E.T. Thompson (AK774 O) whose tail unit was shot off. He baled out successfully and both pilots returned the next day, 'and in keeping with Air Force custom, each gave one pound to the parachute section'.[25]

450 Squadron pilots at Gambut in mid April 1942. Standing left to right: Sgts. Shillabeer, Halliday, Beste and McBurnie, FO E.T. 'Mick' Thompson, unidentified, Fl. Lt. Ross, (Defence Officer) PO Mathew (Equipment Officer) unidentified, Sgt. Max Jenkins, PO Kelsall, Sgt. Ray Dyson, Sgt. Elston Quirk, Sgt. 'Rusty' Kierath. Front row; Fl. Lt. Cantrell, Sqn. Ldr. Gordon Steege, Fl. Lt. Ian Rose, unidentified. The CO seems to be well catered for. (Gordon Steege)

112 Squadron's brief rest was almost over. AVM Coningham visited the squadron at Sidi Haneish on 14 April to present the Squadron Badge and took the parade with the CO, Clive Caldwell. The squadron then moved up to Gambut No.1 Satellite and prepared for operations. Sgts Rudolph Leu, Henry Burney and 'Kit' Carson were all granted commissions. Fl.Lt Jack Bartle led the first operation on 22 April, which was uneventful.

On 23 April, the squadron was scrambled to patrol over Tobruk, encountering Ju87s and Bf109s. Clive Caldwell (AK766) made his last claim in the Desert, a Bf109 probable, which was later recorded in his log book as destroyed, confirmation no doubt coming from ground observers.

250 Squadron, withdrawn on 27 March to convert to Kittyhawks, arrived at Gambut on 23 April, and both units were joined by 3 Squadron on 26 April. 450 was withdrawn for a rest on 29 April, but the three experienced squadrons of 239 Wing were back together and ready to meet Rommel's next offensive, which would start on 26 May with a panzer attack on the Gazala line.

Sergeant William 'Bubba' Halliday, so nick-named because at nineteen, he was the youngest pilot in 450 Squadron. Gordon Steege noted that fishing was occasionally done with dynamite. This shot was probably taken during the Squadron's brief rest period, mentioned above. (Gordon Steege)

Clive Caldwell handed over command of 112 Squadron to Squadron Leader Peter Down, and made ready to leave for England with an endorsement in his log book from Sir Arthur Tedder as *'An excellent leader and a first class shot'*. His score of 19 and 3 shared made him the top scoring Desert fighter pilot and the most successful P-40 pilot of the war. He flew 94 Kittyhawk hours with 112 Squadron, making a total of 424 P-40 hours in a tour which lasted three days short of one year. In that time he flew 213 operations and engaged the enemy on some seventy-eight occasions.

For some time the Australian Government had been demanding his return to Australia, which was faced with a battle for survival. A crippling shortage of trained men in all three services, most of whom were serving in other theatres of war, was equalled by the appallingly critical supply of weapons of war. A tug-o'- war developed between the Australian Government on the one hand and Air Chief Marshal Sir

Clive Caldwell's aircraft was twice damaged in combat during his time as CO of 112 Squadron, first on 5 March and again on 3 May. These two photographs demonstrate the very fine line between survival and extinction. A 20 mm cannon strike just aft of the fuel filler cap, and hits on the windscreen need no further comment! He was flying AK766 on both occasions. The terse log book entry for 3 May said 'SWEEP MSUS - TMIMI - GAZALA. 1.35. ENGAGED ME 109Fs AND Mc 202s. OWN A/C DAMAGED E/ACTION.' (Doug Norrie)

Arthur Tedder on the other. *He had told Caldwell that he was to be given command of a new, elite Spitfire Wing consisting of two squadrons from Britain and a third to be made up of experienced desert fighter pilots whom Caldwell could hand-pick. (Author's italics)* Though Caldwell, like all Australians, was concerned for the well-being of his homeland, he could see little value in returning home to an air force devoid of equipment while the greatest prize of his short but brilliant career lay before him, leadership of a Spitfire Wing on a front that still promised plenty of action.

However, one freighter carrying the Spitfires was torpedoed by a U-boat, while others were assigned to Malta, and only one Squadron was allocated to the Middle East. Tedder now felt he could no longer resist the Australian Government's demands.

Thus Caldwell retired from the scene of Desert operations.[26]

The one Spitfire squadron to arrive was 145 Squadron RAF, which disembarked at Helwan on 30 April. It did not fly its first operation until 1 June. Writing in his autobiography *Straight and Level* Air Chief Marshal Sir Kenneth Cross, the Group Captain in charge of 258 Wing at the time of Operation *Crusader*, made the following pertinent comment.

Of course nothing made up for the inferiority in performance of all the fighters in the Middle East in comparison with the Messerschmitt 109F. Neither of our best, the Hurricane II and the American Tomahawk, could compete and the Hurricane I was quite outclassed. Even the Italian Macchi 202 was better than anything we had. Well might our Commander-in-Chief, Air Marshal Tedder have written in his journal "One Squadron of Spitfire Vs would have meant a lot."[27]

Why were adequate aircraft in the form of Spitfires unavailable? The answer lies in the offensive policy of Fighter Command, beginning in 1941 after the end of the Battle of Britain. By the end of 1941 there were some 75 fighter squadrons in Britain, and these had lost 411 pilots and over 600 aircraft from 14 June to the end of December, for a return of some 154 German fighters, not all of which were operational losses.[28]

It was for such results as these, together with the need to guard against a mass disengagement of German bombers from the east, that a force of seventy-five day-fighter squadrons were retained in this country throughout the latter part of 1941. Whether this was a wise allocation of resources at a time when there were only thirty-four fighter squadrons to sustain our cause in the whole of the Middle and Far East is, perhaps, an open question.[29]

These appalling and wasteful losses continued in 1942. Fighter Command expended 43,003 sorties on offensive operations, losing 573 aircraft in the process, for an exchange of 168 Luftwaffe fighters,[30] all of whose surviving pilots were able to return to operations, while the vast majority of RAF pilots lost over France had to be replaced.

If, at any stage between the commencement of *Crusader* in November 1941 and the Battle of El Alamein in October 1942, (when *three* Spitfire squadrons were available), Tedder had been able to make use of just one hundred of those lost airmen and their Spitfires, the Desert war might have been shortened by a considerable margin, and the lives of numerous Hurricane, Tomahawk and Kittyhawk pilots saved.

Chapter 6   Waiting for Rommel

On 27 April the four squadrons of 239 Wing were inspected by the Duke of Gloucester, and hostilities with the enemy were resumed on the 29th at 0905 hours, when Nicky Barr (AK874) damaged a Bf109 near El Adem. There was no further contact until 7 May. During the day 3 flew two uneventful patrols at 1040 and 1653, and another at 1805 when six aircraft from 3 and six from 112 Squadron scrambled from readiness to patrol Tobruk at 12,000 ft. They were vectored to Gazala, and encountered two Bf109s 20 miles south of that position, both aircraft being shot down; one by 112 Squadron and the other by Bobby Gibbes, in AK874. Aircraft recognition may have been at fault again here, as *Aces High* acknowledges the claim for a Bf109 but says that the aircraft was actually a MC202.

Twelve Kittyhawks from 3 took off at 1035 on 9 May to escort returning Bostons from a raid on Benghazi harbour. The Bostons were initially not contacted because they had changed their nominated course, but they were found, and 3 joined with them as close cover. Two enemy aircraft were reported, and a Bf110 was damaged, again by Bobby Gibbes in AK874.

For some time during May, the Germans had been flying in reinforcements for the *Afrika Korps* in Ju52 transports based on Crete. The Long Range Desert Group operating behind enemy lines had observed the arrivals of these flights and on the 12th an attempt was made to effect an interception. Six Beaufighters of 252 Squadron, with a top cover of ten Kittyhawks carrying long range tanks from 250 Squadron took off under the command of Wg. Cdr. Mayers, with Fl. Lt. John Waddy leading the top cover in AK846 LD-H. One Beaufighter and two Kittyhawks were forced to return due to mechanical trouble, but the rest of the force flew out to sea and after almost two hours of searching[1] they discovered a large formation of German aircraft, which was reported as consisting of sixteen Ju52s and three Bf110s. In fact there were thirteen of the Junkers, accompanied by only one Bf110. As with the British formation, two of the German aircraft had been forced to return, a Ju52 and a Bf110.[2] The occupants of these two machines would have good reason to count themselves as very lucky men.

The British formation tore into the Germans in a head-on attack, and it seems that six Ju52s went down in this first onslaught. The fighters then made individual attacks for the next twenty minutes, and as is often the case, over claimed enthusiastically, a number of pilots obviously having attacked the same aircraft at once. Of the thirteen Ju52s, nine were shot down and two force-landed on the beach, leaving only two unscathed. The Bf110 was shot down *twice,* in circumstances which will be explained shortly. Australian claims amounted to one Ju52 by Wg. Cdr. Mayers (AK890), one Ju52 to Sgt. G.G. Buckland of 250 Squadron and two Ju52s and two Bf110s to John Waddy. (Overall, 250 squadron claimed ten Ju52s and two Bf110s, but the

Beaufighters also claimed five more Ju52s). Obviously a large proportion of these should have been shared.

The Ju52s were carrying twenty men each, and *Fighters Over the Desert* (p110) notes that 175 German soldiers died and a further 47 were rescued from the sea. John Waddy's combat report gives an excellent account of the action, while offering no clues to the conundrum of the two Bf110 victories.

'About five to ten minutes after turning on to our patrol line I observed a number of Ju 52s approaching head-on. I gave the "Tally-ho" and immediately climbed to 1,000 ft. to look for the Me 110s, as I was leading the top cover. I did one complete circuit of the Ju 52s without seeing any enemy escort, so I made a head-on attack on a Ju 52 and my first burst of fire hit straight into the cockpit. To deliver this I dived from 1,000 ft. and pulled out of the dive and went over the top. My No. 2, Sgt. Devlin subsequently confirms this 52 as destroyed, as it went straight into the water. I then observed a Me 110 attacking a Beaufighter, so I made a right hand turn and delivered a rear quarter attack. My first burst hit the fuselage and the Me 110 pulled up into a steep climbing turn which I followed. I then put a burst into his port motor which caught fire but at the same time was hit by the fire of the Ju 52s over which the Me 110 had cleverly led me. Gave the Me 110 another burst and he dived into the sea. (*If, as German records indicated to Chris Shores, only one Bf110 was present, this was an overly optimistic evaluation of what happened to the Messerschmitt, but understandable if the aircraft was seen to dive, and then Waddy's attention was distracted elsewhere. Author*) I then made a rear quarter attack on a 52 and flew to within twenty yards before pulling away. This one was straggling a little on the starboard side of the enemy formation. It caught fire and crashed into the sea. I then observed another Me 110 about 1,000 ft. so I started to climb as it began diving. It saw me and pulled out of its dive and started a left hand climbing turn. I followed out of range and then the 110 whipped over to a right hand turn and dived. I made a rear quarter attack developing to dead astern and followed him to the sea. One burst set his port motor on fire the next hit the tail and into the rear cockpit, and the next chopped off his left tailplane. It then immediately dived into the sea. I observed a Beaufighter blow up a 52 from a rear quarter attack and I

Fl. Lt. John Waddy and his mount AK846 LD-H, probably taken after the successful action on 12 May.
(Ian Primmer, via Doug Norrie)

also saw one Beau dive into the water in flames. I, myself, counted 8 fires plus the Beaufighter. One "Red Cross" 52 was in the enemy formation. When I left the fight only three enemy aircraft were flying. all Ju 52s.'[3]

One possible explanation for the two Bf110 claims is that the 110 dived away with a burning engine, which subsequently was extinguished and gamely rejoined the battle, being the only defence available to the unfortunate Junkers. It was then attacked for the second time and finally hit the sea. (The pilot, Uffz Baumann of III/ZG 26 was rescued from the sea, and claimed one Beaufighter).[4] It is of course quite possible that German records were incomplete, and that two Bf110s *were* present. John Waddy's combat report is quite unequivocal, and it seems most unlikely that an aircraft with a dead engine would be able to climb back into the combat.

At 1025 on 13 May, twelve Kittyhawks from 3 Squadron were scrambled from readiness to patrol El Adem, but were almost immediately sent to Bir Hachiem. They were then vectored to Gazala, where they were jumped by Oblt. Marseille and his wingman Rainer Pottgen, who had scrambled to intercept them. Marseille's swift attack resulted in the loss of two Kittyhawks, FO H.G. Pace (AL172) and Sgt. MacDiarmid (AK855) both going down in flames. MacDiarmid baled out successfully and returned the next day, but Harold Pace was killed. FO Geoff Chinchen (AK854) fired at one of the Messerschmitts and claimed a damaged. He actually hit the aircraft flown by Marseille, whose biographer records that his machine was hit in both the oil tank and propeller during this combat.[5]

Geoff Chinchen's combat report (which is very difficult to decipher with certainty) gives an accurate picture of Marseille's tactics, and his use of his wingman, who (according to his biographer) was his 'abacus'[6] rarely given opportunity to make an attack, while Marseille continued to run up his score. Pottgen's first claim was made on 1 June, after more than 100 missions as wingman to Hpt. Homuth and Marseille.

Enemy attack - dive and zoom and occasionally endeavouring to follow their target in a turn. On one occasion a head on attack.

My first attack was astern to rear quarter on ME 109F attacking one of our a/c. The distance was too great to be a good attack.

A ME 109F attacked an a/c lower than my a/c and I came down and climbed with him. I was apparently unobserved as he did a stall turn while I was approx. 400 yds away. I closed to approx 200 yds. firing all the way and he seemed to be hovering in my tracer. He fell away and as I was [at] the stall I had to correct and lost sight of him.

E/A started an attack on one of our a/c and observed [me] about to make a front quarter [attack] on him, so he came in and made it a head on [attack] on me.

He flew right up my fire and at the last moment broke away. I could not observe him firing during this attack.

Beam to rear quarter attacks were made on e/a attacking our a/c. In each case the enemy broke off his attack but no result of my firing was observed.

NOTE The pair of e/a circled line astern approx 1,000 - 1,500 ft. above me and 2,000 - 2,500 ft. above the main body of our a/c. As I kept my a/c pointing in their direction I was not attacked on [any] occasion. Each attack was made on an a/c whose tail was towards the e/a, in some cases during a turn. The leading a/c always attacked and did so by starting with a wingover which gave one a little time to anticipate his target and get position. Only on one occasion were the two e/a attacking together.

16 May saw 112 Squadron fly its first Kittybomber sortie after several days of practice bombing. Fl.Lt Jack Bartle led six bomb-carrying aircraft, with a further four as top cover in an attack on some tents at Tmimi. They experienced some heavy flak, but all the aircraft returned safely, and they were well satisfied with the results of their bombing.

The two Australian squadrons had another encounter with Oblt. Marseille when they met three Bf109s over Gazala. Having the usual height advantage, Marseille dived, but found himself under attack by six of the Kittyhawks, and using his superior climb rate to avoid them, he climbed behind a further six which were higher and shot down Sgt. Teede of 3 Squadron from a climbing left turn. Teede, in AL120, crash-landed on fire twelve miles west of El Adem. The skirmish continued in a similar pattern for some time, with Marseille circling above a group of six Kittyhawks and making sharp diving attacks without further success. The Kittyhawks had now descended to about 1,000 ft. when Marseille fired at the Kittyhawk of PO Parker(AK697) of 450 Squadron, again while in a steep left bank.

The pilots of 450 Squadron did not see Parker attacked, and apparently did not see him bale out when he actually did, because they reported that 'one Kittyhawk was seen to collide with another. PO F.E. Parker baled out and made a successful parachute descent, and Sgt. William Metherall (AK604) spun in and was killed'.[7]

When Parker returned, he reported being attacked by a 109 and baling out after trimming the aircraft. He asserted that he did *not* collide with any other aircraft. His aircraft therefore must have struck Metherall's Kittyhawk after it had been abandoned. Marseille was also unaware of the collision, and returned to claim two victories.

112 Squadron took off at dawn on 18 May to bomb the Tmimi roadhouse, scoring one direct hit. The Kittyhawks then went down to strafe and encountered dense AA, losing two aircraft. In an attempt to avoid the AA, Sgt. Roy Drew flew so low that he bent the tips of his propeller. He kept AK906 in the air until he was compelled to force-land twelve miles short of base.

450 Squadron fell foul of Marseille again on 19 May, when nine Kittyhawks took off to patrol Gazala at 0715. PO Bell and Fl.Lt Rose returned with engine trouble by 0808, and the others became separated, splitting into sections of three and four. The section of four sighted nothing throughout the patrol, and landed between 0848 and 0850, but the smaller section ran into Marseille and Pottgen, again on a 'Freie Jagd' mission.

> Section of three sighted two Me 109F approaching on same level when at 16,000 ft. nine miles South of Gazala. These immediately climbed 2,000 ft. above and delivered two abortive attacks out of sun, pulling out 500 ft. above. In third attack Black 2 received several shells in wing and rudder and fired ineffective burst at attacker, avoided further action, returned and force landed at Gambut Main. Result of action disclosed several hits in wing with explosive bullets, these exploding inside wing. Rudder hit and rudder cable severed, wheel burst, A/C airframe Cat. II engine serviceable. Black 1 saw attack, turned left to attack E/A No. 2 from under, went into spin, coming out in cloud, lost sight of section and returned home. (Unfortunately the ORB does not record who Black 1 and 2 were, but it is likely that they were Sgts. Law and Oakley, as they landed at 0846 and 0840 respectively, earlier than the other group of four. This left Sgt Young (AK842 OK-A), who was Blue 1, alone.) Blue 1 witnessed E/A attack Black 2 then climb to 3-4,000 ft. above, circling about. He attempted to climb to them, got to within 1,000 ft. when they also climbed with him to 20,000 ft. Blue 1 spiral dived to cloud at 4,000 ft. followed by one ME 109. He pulled up in steep turn to go into cloud when second ME 109 came through hole in cloud and fired burst of cannon into Blue 1's engine, putting it out of action. Blue 1 attempted forced landing, doing violent weaves, levelled out approx. 10 ft. The first 109 attacked from astern, registering several hits. Blue 1 made steep left turn and stalled onto ground. Pilot got out and ran. First 109 strafed and set A/C on fire. A/C totally destroyed. Blue 1 during engagement fired an ineffective burst. Pilot unhurt. Picked up by 6th South African Armoured Cars. Cloud 6/10 1 to 5,000 ft.[8]

Kurowski noted that the first aircraft attacked by Marseille was sent 'plunging out of formation to crash land near Gambut' while, 'Wounded, Sergeant Young was able to make it back to his own troops'.[9]

At 0750 on 22 May, nine Bostons of 24 SAAF Squadron took off to attack Martuba. They were escorted by Kittyhawks from 112 and 250 Squadrons, while twelve aircraft of 3, together with 260 Squadron as close cover and 450 as top cover left on what was described as a "freelance bomber escort", which flew ahead of the bombers in an attempt to intercept and disperse the defending fighters. Four Bf109s from II/JG 27 were on a "Freie Jagd" of their own and attacked the top cover, shooting down Sgts. Elston Quirk (AK634) and Arthur Williams (AK727) of 450 Squadron, both of whom were killed. The Messerschmitts then attacked 3 Squadron, and apparently over shot without doing any further damage, as Sgt Keith Kildey attacked one from behind, which was then attacked by Fl. Lt. Nicky Barr (AL199), who fired at it briefly, but was forced to take evasive action as he in turn was attacked from behind.

> After evading another attack I was climbing up about a mile east of BOMBA and saw an ME 109 climbing up in a spiral about 1,000 ft. below. I dived on it and kept on it from beam to astern in a steep turn - it then slowly rolled over and fell over on its back. I was then attacked again and pulled away and did not observe results. Height about 1,000 ft. approx.

One of numerous Kittyhawks flown by Nicky Barr, the name suggests that it is the third one with which he had a long association. (Ian Primmer, via Doug Norrie)

Although Barr only claimed a probable in his combat report the victory was subsequently confirmed. By this time his guns had stopped working, he had sustained damage to the hydraulic line and voltage regulator and a tyre had been punctured, so he returned to base from 1,000 ft. and lowered the wheels using the auxiliary pump, making a bumpy landing which damaged the tail wheel and engine cowl.

Sqn. Ldr. Gibbes in AK874 also claimed a victory during this combat, while Fl.Lt. Rose of 450 claimed a probable, which may subsequently have been confirmed, as John Herington notes a victory for him on this date.

Shortly before this combat took place, eleven Bf109s scrambled from Martuba and attacked the close escort squadrons. They claimed a total of seven Kittyhawks, two each to Hpt. Franzisket and Lt. von Lieres and one each to Fw. Steinhausen, Lt. Stahlschmidt and Obfw. Rosenberg. The second claims of Franzisket and von Lieres were not confirmed[10] and in fact no more than three

Kittyhawks were lost, one from 112 Squadron[11] and two from 250 Squadron.[12] Fl. Lt. John Waddy, again flying AK846 LD-H, claimed a Bf109 as the bombers were withdrawing. *Aces High* identifies his victim as Uffz. Sdun of 8/JG 27 but gives the date as 21 May. Herington gives the date as 22 May during the fight over Martuba, and to confuse matters further, Lex McAulay in his book *Four Aces* states that '*Gibbes*' victory was identified as Unteroffizier Sdun, who was wounded'.[13]

It may be that Sdun was attacked by both Gibbes and Waddy, as the earlier part of Nicky Barr's combat report mentioned that the bombers were in sight of 3 Squadron when they were first attacked, and the number of Bf109s about suggests that the original four which attacked his unit had been joined by others.

John Waddy and AK846. The letters VE carried beneath the windscreen were his wife's initials.
Ian Primmer, via Doug Norrie.

20th May: Last night we were raided by four bombers. Many bombs fell in the camp area and around the 'drome proper. Two delayed action bombs are lying one hundred yards from my tent - damn them! There was no great damage or casualties although 112 Squadron had a couple of tents burnt by flares.

We paraded for the AOC who spoke quite informally and said the Jerries are about to start a push. He told us what to expect, and wished us all luck etc. (Viv Herrett)

450 Squadron's ORB recorded that AVM Sir Arthur Tedder visited the squadron on 22 May, and talked to the officers and sergeants in the mess, and his words caused the squadron diarist to write 'it seems that an enemy offensive is imminent'. The ORB further noted that '239 Wing arranged for three Army officers to visit the squadron for approximately one week, the object is to form a closer liaison between the Army and the Air Force. These officers are to be attached to the intelligence officers and arrangements have been made for them to visit the Squadron, Group and Wing operations rooms'.[14] All the squadrons of 239 Wing were soon to prove the value of the concept of inter service cooperation and support earlier propounded by Tedder and Coningham. Rommel's attack commenced on 26 May.

The battle which followed, beginning on the Gazala 'line', and ending at Alamein, nearly 220 miles inside the Egyptian frontier, marked the nadir of Britain's military fortunes during the war. All the faults of her military system, all the weaknesses of her main field army (both lying outside the scope of this volume) were relentlessly exposed; and if, at the end, the rugged fighting qualities of her Commander in Chief, General Sir Claude Auchinleck, plucked fresh hope out of disaster against all the odds, that was the very most that offered itself by way of consolation to a very roughly handled army. For the RAF, however, the story was quite different.[15]

450 Squadron was in action the day after AVM Tedder's visit, seven aircraft escorting two Tac.R. Hurricanes to Tmimi. Four Bf109s of II Gruppe scrambled to intercept and 'a general dogfight ensued. All aircraft returned safely'.[16] F/Sgt. Don McBurnie (AK998) and F/Sgt. Nursey each claimed a Bf109 during this engagement, but it is possible that they both attacked the same aircraft, as the loss of only one Messerschmitt was acknowledged, that of Uffz. Gierster, who claimed a victory before baling out. McBurnie was apparently reprimanded on his return for not having shot at the parachute.[17] It is not recorded by whom.

The pilots of 3 Squadron were convinced, rightly or wrongly, that on 12 October 1941, Sgt. Dudley Parker had been killed in his parachute, and had no doubt passed on this information to 450 when they joined the wing. It was not, however, a practice that any Australian pilot has admitted to. Bobby Gibbes' reason for refraining from such acts was pragmatic. He 'never fired on a parachute; not because he abhorred the deed but because he was never quite sure that the helpless man in the parachute was German'.[18]

The pilots of the Tac.R. Hurricanes must have been well satisfied with 450's performance of the 23rd, as the squadron received a signal the next day from No. 40 SAAF specially thanking Sgt. Young for his part in the escort.

Sergeant Ray Shaw over Sidi Barrani, May 1942. Shaw usually flew an aircraft marked 'O'. AK998 first appeared in the ORB on the 22nd of the month, and was flown by Shaw on six subsequent occasions until he was lost in it on the 29th during a patrol over Acroma, so this machine is likely to be AK998. Don McBurnie used AK998 to shoot down a Bf109 on 23 May. (Gordon Steege)

Chapter 7   Kittybombers

On 26 May Rommel launched his anticipated attack, 450 squadron had a change of commanders and Bobby Gibbes was shot down by the gunner of a Ju88.

The day began badly for 3 Squadron. They scrambled at 0655 to intercept a German raid over El Adem. When they had reached 11,000 ft. they found four Ju88s escorted by six Bf109s. Gibbes led six aircraft to attack the fighters and sent the other section of six to attack the bombers. Gibbes fired at a Bf109 which he claimed as a probable, and then turned his attention to the bombers. His first burst produced smoke from the starboard engine, but the rear gunner fired an accurate burst which set the Kittyhawk's engine on fire. He cut the petrol and dived in an attempt to blow out the fire, but it continued to blaze and at 4,000 ft. he baled out of AK874. It was not the cleanest of exits. He struck the tailplane and the parachute became entangled in an aerial wire. The landing was heavy and he broke his left ankle and fractured the leg.[1] Sgt Clabburn (AL145) damaged another of the Ju88s, but the remainder of the squadron made no claims. Interestingly, 450 Squadron's ORB for the 26th makes mention of a Ju88 attack and that 3 Squadron shot one down.

As had been done on earlier occasions when pilots went missing, Nicky Barr and Lou Spence flew a recce. at 1000 in search of the missing CO, but without success. Gibbes was later rescued by ground forces and taken to a casualty station where the leg was put in plaster, and he was back with the squadron by the next day. Nicky Barr assumed temporary command, as it was obvious that Gibbes' injuries would prevent him from flying for a considerable time.

On this date, 3 Squadron flew its first fighter-bomber sortie, when at 1900 a dive bombing raid was carried out on Tmimi landing ground by twelve aircraft, six aircraft carrying a 250 lb. bomb with the other six as top cover. The bombing was 'very accurate, three bombs bursting in the main dispersal area and two on the edge, while the other bomb burst about thirty yards from an ME 109 on the north side of the aerodrome'.[2]

In the developing battle, the Kittyhawk squadrons would be called on to spend more and more of their time on ground attack sorties in direct support of the retreating army.

260 Squadron met Bf109s over Gazala, and John Waddy, who had recently been posted to this unit, damaged the Bf109 flown by Fw. Reuter, who escaped in cloud and landed with seventeen bullet strikes in his aircraft.[3] Waddy claimed a probable.

At 450 Squadron, Sqn. Ldr. Gordon Steege, now tour expired, handed over command to Sqn. Ldr Alan Ferguson, who had previously led 451 Tac.R. Squadron. He had been with 450 since 7 May, gaining experience on Kittyhawks. He settled in quickly and soon gained the respect of his men.

Every crack air unit had a "gung-ho" leader. Ours was Squadron Leader Alan D. Ferguson ("Fergie" to us). The lean, quiet one, was the youngest commanding officer in the Desert at the time. Immensely popular and a cracking fine pilot. "Fergie" led by example.[4]

The next day Fw. Horst Reuter, who by now had amassed twenty-one victories, had his final encounter with the Australians when he was bounced by Sgt. Shillabeer (AK787) of 450 Squadron while he was returning in an already damaged aircraft from an escort mission. He baled out successfully and landed among a formation of British tanks, 'being picked up and having the dubious privilege of being taken along as a passenger into a heavy tank battle which lasted the rest of the day'.[5]

As the army was retreating, the RAF was directed to attack the pursuing German forces, and throughout the day 3 Squadron flew seven bombing and strafing operations in the Bir Hacheim area, involving twenty seven sorties, four pilots (Sgts. Thompson and Donald and FOs Chinchen and Spence) flying twice. The third operation, led by Lou Spence, took off at 1345, and met four Bf109s led by Friedrich Korner of 2/JG 27. He shot down Sgt. Thomas who crash-landed his burning aircraft south of Gambut, returning to the squadron the next day. PO Coward led the fifth op. off at 1605, but he and Sgt Donald were forced to return with engine trouble, leaving Sgt. Pfeiffer and Sgt Clabburn to proceed. Almost inevitably the two lonely Kittyhawks at low level were attacked by three Bf109s of II/JG 27. Sgt Clabburn was shot down by Lt. Jenish and crash landed south of El Adem. He too returned the following day. Not so lucky was WO Harold Norman, who was shot down during the sixth op, which took off at 1650. On only his fifth operational sortie with the squadron, he was straggling slightly when two Bf109s of II/JG 27 attacked. Ofw. Krenzke's fire stopped Norman's engine, forcing him to bale out from 1,200 ft. He was promptly captured.

The squadron had reason to believe it had lost its second CO in two days while Nicky Barr was missing for four hours. Having led the second op. of the day at 1215, he was forced to land near Sidi Rezegh fifteen minutes later with an over heating engine. He had managed to remove the engine covers when German armour appeared on the horizon. The condition of the engine now being considered of lesser importance, he took off hurriedly. The engine covers were left behind![6] The squadron dropped twenty two 250-lb bombs during the day, damaging several tanks and a gun limber and destroying a number of trucks and a petrol bowser.

On 28 May further ground attack and bomber escort operations were flown, without loss to either squadron. In the afternoon 3 Squadron's Kittyhawks led a Boston squadron with 250 and 450 as top cover to attack a concentration of some 500 enemy vehicles north west of El Adem. The fighter bombers attacked first from 4,000 ft. followed by the Bostons. The fighters then came down to strafe, and between them, the formation destroyed six Italian ammunition trucks and fifteen other vehicles.[7] This was to be the pattern of operations for several days to come.

28th May: At midnight an enemy column is reported approaching [Acroma]. Twelve "Bostons" leave here to deal with the column escorted by 250 and 112 Squadrons as well as ourselves as far as Tobruk. We peeled off there to straff (sic) motor transport columns south of El Adem. Forty vehicles were put out of action. "K" which is my kite received a few bullet holes and "G" made a slow return due to a punctured oil tank.

Like all other squadrons up here we are as busy as hell seeing our machines are doing three and four sorties a day. The big push is well and truly on.

At 9.30 pm tonight they started bombing and straffing us for one more night. There will be little sleep for us once again. (Viv Herrett)

Under this pressure from the air the German armoured divisions were unable to keep up the momentum of their attack, and after an abortive thrust towards Acroma on 28 May began to fall back towards the narrow gap in the mine field which had finally been cut by the *Trieste Division*. During the whole of 29th

Sergeants 'Junior' Davidson, John Dean and 'Pranger' Dangar (almost out of the frame) of 450 Squadron in the mess tent at Gambut Satellite East, May 1942. (Gordon Steege)

and 30th May targets were ideal for both fighters and bombers, which carried out a shuttle service devoted entirely to ground attack. On two occasions the army reported that more than fifty enemy vehicles had been left burning after attacks by fighter-bombers, which were enjoying outstanding success.[8]

450 Squadron took of at 0750 on 29 May to patrol Acroma, some twenty miles west of Tobruk, and encountered six Bf109s of III/JG 27 which were escorting Stukas. Four of these attacked the squadron without success and 450 then went after the Stukas, which withdrew in the direction of Gazala. F/Sgt. Don McBurnie (AK897) and Sgt Max Jenkins (AK789) shared one Stuka, and Sgt Nursey (AK606 OK-B) destroyed another. One of these aircraft was flown by Hpt. Drescher, the *Staffelkapitan* of 4/St.G 3, who was captured. His gunner and the pilot of the other Stuka were killed. Drescher later managed to escape and return to his unit. McBurnie then attacked the Bf109 flown by Lt. von Fritsch, who force landed his aircraft and was captured. Unfortunately for 450 Squadron, reinforcements arrived for the Germans, seven Bf109s of I Gruppe having just taken off on a "Freie Jagd". When they saw the dogfight going on four of them joined in. Hpt. Maak and Lt. Korner both shot down a Kittyhawk in flames, and Lt. Stahlschmidt destroyed one at low

To turn desert into Landing Ground required little more than grading. CV-P is on the edge of the graded strip, undisturbed desert in the foreground. (RAAF Museum)

level. 450 lost the aircraft of Sgt. John Dean, Sgt. Raymond Shaw and Sgt. Thomas Packer, all of whom were killed. Shaw had scored the squadron's first success on 22 February, and had since added one further victory to his total. The unit also lost Sgt. Henry Devlin who crashed on take off.

The relentless pressure was maintained next day. First off were 250 and 450 Squadrons at 0650, 250 providing close cover to 450 whose task was to recce and strafe in the Bir Hachiem area. They were attacked by four Bf109s of I/JG 27 and Oblt. Marseille shot down PO. Graham Buckland of 250 Squadron, who baled out, but was killed in unexplained circumstances. Buckland was two days short of his 21st birthday.

At 1445 six Kittybombers of 250, with four from 3, took off on a strafing mission, while at much the same time Kittyhawks from 260 Squadron and 2 SAAF were escorting Bostons. The Bostons and their escort were attacked by aircraft from III/ JG 53 and I/JG 27 all the way to the target and back, and it seems that they encountered the fighter-bombers of 250 and 3 as well. Seven German claims were made, and six Kittyhawks from the four squadrons were indeed lost: two from 260 Squadron, one from 2 SAAF, one from 250 and two from 3. A seventh missing aircraft was AK772 GA-Y from 112 Squadron. It was flown by PO Henry Burney, who had been with the squadron since August 1941. Twenty six years old when he died, his final score was 4 and 1 shared destroyed. His body was never found and his loss is recorded at the Alamein War Memorial. 112 Squadron's records make no mention of fighter combat that day, and it is likely that he was shot down by ground fire.

'3 Squadron had attacked its ground targets and climbed to cover 250 Squadron while they bombed in their turn'.[9] They were then attacked from above by pairs of Bf109s and Sgt Colin MacDiarmid (AL153) was shot down and killed. Nicky Barr, in AK889 fired at one of the Messerschmitts at low level, which dived but was not seen to crash. He claimed a probable. His aircraft was then hit, (he thought by flak) and almost flung inverted. He 'rolled upright - "very close to the ground indeed" - and the propeller hit the earth'.[10]

Barr survived the crash-landing and evaded German troops for an hour, finally ending up in a mine field, from which he was rescued after spending two hours in the cross fire of a battle between the 7th Hussars and Gloucestershires and German motorised units. He spent the night in a hospital in Tobruk suffering from concussion and returned to the squadron on 1 June, for the second time without his aircraft.

At 1745 elements of the four squadrons of 239 Wing flew together, 3, 250 and 450 escorting fighter bombers of 112 Squadron. They became embroiled in a battle between the Tomahawks of 4 and 5 SAAF, II/JG 27 and I/JG 27, who were escorting Stukas. The experienced trio of Lt. Karl von Lieres, Hpt. Ernst Maak, Staffel Kapitan of 2/JG 27 and Oblt. Ernst Borngen, Staffel Kapitan of 5 Staffel, shot down F/Sgt Nursey and F/Sgt. McBurnie of 450 Squadron and Lt. Saunders of 5 SAAF. Nursey and McBurnie were 450 Squadron's two most successful pilots, with three, and three and one shared victories respectively. Ian Nursey was killed, while Don McBurnie received wounds to his shoulder and leg. 'He crash landed near a British army encampment. Scrambling out before the dust settled, he crouched under the nose section as one ME 109 made a strafing run'.[11]

The last day of the month found John Waddy at the top of his form. 260 Squadron took off to escort bombers at 1315, and was attacked continuously by four Bf109s, losing one aircraft with a further two damaged. They encountered eight Ju87s during the return flight, and Waddy (AK956) claimed one destroyed, two probables and one damaged.

> As an interesting side note to this combat of 260 Squadron, when John Waddy was returning to Australia on the 'Queen Mary' some months later with the Australian 9th Division he met a captain of anti-aircraft who described the battle to him, and checked from his diary that the date, time, place and circumstances

were identical to Waddy's combat. The captain confirmed that all three Ju87s in fact crashed. However Waddy had left the area and took no further action to obtain confirmation of his two probables.[12]

At 1845 239 Wing took off to bomb and strafe targets 'in the forward area'. 3 Squadron provided four of the bombers, with an unspecified number from 112 Squadron. 250 Squadron provided the medium cover, and ten aircraft from 450 Squadron were top cover. Three of these were forced to return with engine trouble, as the pace of operations was beginning to take effect on maintenance. When the formation was about ten miles from El Adem, the leaders were ordered to 'pancake' but as 450's first aircraft was about to land the order was changed to 'orbit base, Dogsbody with four coming up'. 450's disgruntled diarist recorded 'A considerable number of a/c took off from Sat. 2 and made our leader's task of reforming more difficult'. Six of them managed to do so effectively, climbing to 6,000 ft. above the main formation, which now consisted of 'about 24 Kittyhawks and Tommys'. About ten miles west of El Adem 450's leader noticed four Kittyhawks about 1,000 ft above and well to starboard, and unidentified aircraft were reported at 11 o'clock and 3 o'clock. These then dived towards the four Kittyhawks and 450's leader pulled up with one other aircraft and attacked two of the enemy aircraft in a climb. One of the higher Kittyhawks was seen to be shot down in this initial skirmish, and then 'one other aircraft was seen to spin in'.

Three of 450's aircraft did not return. Fl. Lt. Eric Thompson (AK787) was shot down and killed, Sgt. Law (AK897) force-landed with engine trouble and Sgt. Lindsay (AL150), who shot down a Bf109, was himself set on fire, but returned safe and unhurt the next day, as did Sgt. Law.

3 Squadron's ORB also noted that 'The target was changed over the R/T after the aircraft had become airborne', however 450 kept the Messerschmitts away from the Kittybombers, whose work was carried out without interference: 'Twelve tanks and fifteen M/T. were bombed and strafed, one truck being set on fire. One a/c was hit by A.A'.

1st June: Jerry bombed and straffed very heavily in the pre-dawn hours and scored hits on our transport and some tents.

We were stood down for the day due to the lack of pilots and serviceable aircraft. News was received that Law was safe at El Adem. (Viv Herrett)

Flight Lieutenant Eric 'Mick' Thompson, OC 'A' Flight of 450 Squadron, lost in action on 31 May. The photograph was taken at Gambut in April.
(Gordon Steege)

Early morning sandstorms prevented operations until the afternoon on 1 June, when four Kittyhawks of 112 Squadron and six of 3 scrambled from readiness at 1825 to intercept enemy aircraft 17 miles SSE of Gazala. Led by Nicky Barr (AL178 CV-W), the formation found nothing at this location and in a special note in his combat report, Barr pointed out that the radar directions were not accurate, as they finally caught up with the enemy formation a further 17 miles SSE of Gazala. It consisted of four Ju88s, four Bf110s and a number of escorting Bf109s (six according 112 Squadron). 112 Squadron flying as the top cover were first engaged by the Bf109s, while Barr's section attacked the Bf110s. Barr made a front port quarter attack on one of them and saw a burst of flame from the port engine. He claimed this as damaged. He next engaged a 109 which had dived through the top cover and began to straighten out in front of him. Another Kittyhawk fired at it, and then Barr delivered a diving attack from 500 ft. above it, from port quarter astern. He saw it catch fire without having taken any evasive action.

Sgt. Garth Neill (AL148 CV-F) was flying as Yellow 2 when he was attacked from astern, taking evasive action by a steep climbing turn. His leader, PO Coward, manoeuvred to attack this aircraft, but before he could do so, saw it attacked by another Kittyhawk, (probably Barr) and it began to stream smoke. Coward (AK992 CV-V) then attacked another 109 which was below him, closing to 100 yds. He considered it to be 'hit badly and it nosed for the ground'. He was attacked by another 109, which he evaded, and then saw a Messerschmitt crash-land at high speed.

Neill saw the aircraft which attacked him set alight by another Kittyhawk, and then was attacked by another 109 which he avoided by doing two complete steep climbing turns, after which the Messerschmitt appeared directly in front of him and about 50 ft. below. He fired three short bursts and saw the enemy aircraft 'go down and hit the ground with smoke pouring from it'.

'Charlie' Coward returning from a successful sortie. This photograph was taken when he was a Sergeant with 250 Squadron. Apart from a brief break at an OTU at the beginning of 1942, he served the equivalent of almost two full tours, winning a DFC in the process. When he was finally rested, he had some 292 operational hours, and was a Flight Commander. (Bob Whittle)

Sgt. W.D. Finlason (AK745 CV-Z) and Sgt. Lloyd Boardman* (AK818 CV-R) both claimed Bf109s as damaged, and 3 Squadron's only casualty was Sgt. Alderson (AK729), who was hit and slightly wounded.

112 Squadron did not manage to get many clear shots at the enemy, claiming only two Ju88s damaged, one by Fl. Lt. Rudolph Leu in AK985. They lost one aircraft, shot down by Lt. Quaritsch, who later fell victim to one of the Australians. Two other Kittyhawks were claimed by the Germans, and one of the Bf110s claimed a Hurricane.

Heavy sandstorms limited aerial activity on 2 June, and the next day the squadrons of 239 Wing were committed to the assistance of the Free French forces at Bir Hacheim. From June 3 to 10 the Desert Air Force flew 950 fighter sorties, losing 20 aircraft in the process, but their efforts helped the fortress to hold out against intensive attacks until it was finally evacuated on the night of 10/11 June, but 'its nine-day resistance had severely disrupted Rommel's schedule - "nine days of losses in material, personnel, armour and petrol. Those nine days were irrecoverable." '13

While intensive ground support operations continued without respite, neither of the Australian squadrons encountered enemy aircraft, or suffered losses for several days. 450

---

*Lloyd Boardman was known universally as 'Danny'. He had a fine singing voice, and 'Danny Boy' was one of his favourite songs.

was stood down on 1 June, understandably, having lost nine pilots killed in May, eight of them since the 22nd.

On June 4, John Waddy of 260 Squadron scored his tenth confirmed victory when he destroyed a CR42 of 388ª Squadriglia (a ground attack unit.)[14]

On 6 June eleven aircraft of 250 Squadron took off at 0600 on a reconnaissance sweep over the Acroma - Knightsbridge area and encountered a mixed group of MC202s and Bf109s. They claimed two Macchis and one Bf109 as damaged, without loss to themselves, one each to PO Frank Twemlow and Sgt. Des Cormack. Later in the day, ten Kittyhawks of 112 Squadron took off at 1015 on a bombing and recce mission in the Bir Hacheim area, and they found a small group of Bf109s below them. They dived and claimed three destroyed and a probable, PO W.E. Carson (AL225) sharing one with Sgt. Adye (RAF). Two of these aircraft were Bf109Es from a reconnaissance unit, 4(H)/ 12.

Also on 6 June, 3 Squadron received two reinforcements when Sgts. J. Cashmore and J.H. Hooke, both E.A.T.S trained pilots, joined the unit. Five more pilots arrived on 7 June, Sgts. J. Churchill, R.N.B. Stevens, J.W. Bullwinkel, G.R. Jones and N.R. Caldwell, all coming from the recently established 239 Wing Training Flight. Considering that the level of operations was so intense and unrelenting when they joined the squadron, perhaps the most remarkable thing about these seven young men is that they all survived. They did, however have a number of close shaves, as will be seen.

On 8 June, 3 Squadron flew five operations, and five of the new pilots took part. Sgts. Cashmore (AK812) and Stevens (AL208) flew on the third operation of the day, being part of a formation of seven led off by the CO at 1315. Six aircraft of 250 Squadron flew as top cover, while the formation also contained three of 6 Squadron's recently arrived Hurricane IID 'tank busters' armed with two 40-mm Vickers "S" guns. The ORB noted that the leader saw one white St Andrews Cross on the target vehicles and did not bomb, but shortly afterwards three bombs *were* dropped on this formation by pilots who definitely identified it as enemy. (The St Andrews Cross had been used experimentally as a means of identifying friendly vehicles, but it seems that it may have caused more confusion than it prevented.) Four miles further north another concentration was identified and the remaining four bombs were dropped amongst dispersed M/T.

Sgts. Bullwinkel (AK688) and Churchill (AK992) took part in the fourth operation of the day, a bombing and recce to Bir Hachiem between 1620 and 1715.

John Hooke was keen to get some advice from the CO before his first operation.

> The night before he [Nicky Barr] bought me a beer, and he said, "Well look, there's not much I can tell you. You'll find out for yourself as you go along. But in the mean time, just make sure you keep up. Never get left behind, keep up with the bloke you're flying behind". So what happened? A few days later I failed to keep up and I was shot down.[15]

John Hooke (AK812) flew his first operation as part of an eight aircraft formation led by Geoff Chinchen at 1835. The formation bombed a group of 'much scattered' motor transport, all bombs falling in the target area. One truck was seen to 'go up' and they encountered heavy A.A. Lou Spence's aircraft receiving Cat. II damage.

450 Squadron lost another pilot on 8 June when Sgt. John James failed to return from an operation which began at 1122, the squadron escorting fighter-bombers. During the return they strafed and it was then that James was lost, most likely to ground fire.

3 Squadron scrambled six aircraft from readiness at 1925 on 9 June to patrol the Bir Hacheim area, meeting seven Bf109s, one of which was claimed as damaged by Sqn. Ldr Barr in AK745 CV-Z. All aircraft landed safely at 2045. *Only* three operations were flown on this day, and Sgt. Jones was the only new pilot to take part. On 10 June Sgt Cashmore flew on the one operation of the day.

John Hooke and Reg Stevens each flew once on 11 June, during two separate escort missions for Bostons.

On 12 June twelve aircraft of 3 Squadron took off at 0620 on a bombing and recce mission to El Adem. They were met by intense and accurate flak, and Sgt. Bray (AK786) was hit, crash landing in an Allied mine-field. 'The tail of his aircraft was blown off, but he was uninjured and rejoined the unit four hours later'. The ORB did not say how he extricated himself from the mine-field. Sgt Finlason (AL208) received Cat. II damage, and Sgt. Reg Stevens (AL187), on his third operation, had a miraculous escape from death. His aircraft was hit by flak and the undercarriage damaged. He force-landed in the dispersal area, *still carrying his bomb*, which did not explode. The aircraft was a Cat. III write off. No explanation was given as to why the bomb was still attached, but it can be safely assumed that he didn't forget it, so it must have been a mechanical 'hang up', with the aircraft having suffered sufficient damage to prevent him from climbing to a safe altitude to bale out.

Sgt. John Hooke flew AK961 CV-O on the next operation at 0915, his third sortie. * They carried bombs as well as providing escort to Hurricanes and attacked a concentration of troop carriers '6/7 miles SE of El Adem, all bombs falling in the target area'. Another concentration of vehicles was strafed as they returned and a fire was started. Sgt Ross Biden's Kittyhawk was hit by A.A. The squadron flew a further three operations before the day was over, Sgts. Bullwinkel and Cashmore taking part in the third and fourth respectively, and John Hooke flew again on the last at 1920, led by the CO. They bombed two concentrations of 400-500 M/T near El Adem, two or three trucks being seen to explode and one fire started.

Having already flown three operations, 450 Squadron took off at 1255 with five aircraft to provide top cover to a fighter sweep. Sgt. House force landed, but later returned safely. At 1855 the squadron provided two Kittyhawks to carry out a reconnaissance over Trigh Capuzzo and El Adem. The pilots, PO Young and F/Sgt Beste, reported over the R/T that they were about to be engaged by enemy aircraft and nothing more was heard from them. Neither returned. They had been attacked by three Bf109s of II/JG 27 and shot down by Obfw. Clade and Uffz. Gierster, who had himself been shot down by 450 Squadron on 23 May. PO Ivan Young, with one victory and a surviving encounter with Marseille to his credit, was killed.

260 Squadron sent eight Kittyhawks off at 1910 on a bomber escort mission and on the return flight ran into a massive dogfight involving fighters from five different Hurricane squadrons and 145 Spitfire Squadron. These aircraft had attacked a mixed formation of Ju87s and 88s escorted by eighteen Bf109s from I and II Gruppes of JG 27 and an indeterminate number of MC202s. John Waddy in ET577 destroyed a Macchi 'believed to be an aircraft of 9⁰ Gruppo, 4⁰ Stormo CT, flown by Cap. Raineri Piccolomini, who crash-landed.'[16] Losses on both sides were considerable. Two of 260 Squadrons Kittyhawks were lost as well.

The next day of the battle was to be decisive. The British armour suffered heavy losses, and a withdrawal from the Gazala position was commenced.

Due to a sand storm and dust raised by the ongoing tank battle, only one operation was flown by 3 Squadron on 13 June; a bombing and reconnaissance in the El Adem area. Six aircraft led by Geoff Chinchen, and including John Hooke, took off at 0825 and landed an hour later.

This aircraft, which was marginally 'newer' than its pilot, had been delivered on the previous day. It later carried a painting of a small white dog, ("Snifter") trotting away from the Afrika Korps palm tree symbol after leaving a puddle beneath it. This was perhaps in memory of Flight Lieutenant Lindsay Knowles, who often flew Tomahawk AN355 R, which carried a similar design in 1941. By 24 June it had flown twenty-eight sorties, including five each day on the 12th, 15th and 16th.

Nose detail of AK961, *Snifter*, a popular cartoon character of the time. Note the extensive oil leaks from the overflow hole. (RAAF Museum)

A mystery: the visible part of the serial of this aircraft suggested that it was Sgt. Stevens' AL187, which he crash landed with his bomb still attached on 12 June, however Reg Stevens states firmly that his aircraft did not turn over, and the identity and circumstances of this wreckage remains unknown. One possibility is that the aircraft was later shifted by crane and dumped in this forlorn state. (RAAF Museum)

450 Squadron provided six aircraft to cover eight from 112 Squadron on a ground attack operation in the Sidi Rezegh area. On the way to their target they encountered twelve Ju88s escorted by twelve Bf109s of I/JG 27. A further twenty fighters from 2, 4 and 5 SAAF were scrambled to intercept this raid, but the Germans shot down one 112 Squadron aircraft and three from 450 before reinforcements arrived. One of the South African aircraft was heavily damaged and crash-landed at base. Oblt. Marseille claimed four victories and Lt. Remmer one. The South Africans balanced the scale to some extent by claiming two MC202s and two Bf109s. 450's losses were Sgts. William Halliday (AL127) and R. Stone (RAF) in AK952, who were both killed. PO Osborne (AL106) crash landed and was picked up by the army.

On the ground, three British armoured brigades sustained heavy losses from a continuous attack by two *Panzer* divisions, and the British forces began to withdraw from Gazala. For the next 'two days and nights the Gazala -Tobruk road was crowded with trucks and troops heading eastward. The R.A.F. fighters at Gambut flew 286 protective sorties during this period, to such effect that only six men were killed by air attack. Though this could not reverse the verdict of the land battle, at least it enabled the Eighth Army to avoid the worst consequences of defeat'.[17]

Similar weather conditions prevailed on 14 June and only two operations were flown by 3 Squadron. Nicky Barr led twelve aircraft on an offensive sweep, with Sgts. Bullwinkel, Churchill and Hooke all taking part. Fl. Lt. Chinchen (AL215) led another offensive sweep and reconnaissance of twelve aircraft at 1940, Sgt. Caldwell this time joining the three from the earlier mission. Sgt. Ross Biden's Kittyhawk was hit by flak and he force-landed at Gambut Main with Cat. II damage. Geoff Chinchen was shot down by flak. He baled out of his burning machine at 700 ft. and 'was seen standing beside a truck with St Andrews Cross marking. Sgt Thomas received some A.A. when going down to ascertain Fl. Lt. Chinchen's position'. The vehicle carrying the supposed St Andrews Cross belonged to the *Afrika Korps*, and Chinchen was captured.

During the day 'B' Flight proceeded to LG 075 to prepare to service the squadron's aircraft while 'C' flight began to prepare for withdrawal from Gambut. LG 075 was some 100 miles south east of Gambut.

14th June: Another day of escorting and straffing. At mid afternoon we left in convoy for No. 75 LG thirty miles south of Sidi Barrani. We left behind kites and skeleton crews to continue operations.

The convoy followed the inland desert route and managed to get lost in a sand storm. We eventually made it to camp three miles south of Sidi Aziez at 8.00 pm after journeying only forty miles. (Viv Herrett)

3 Squadron carried out seven operations on 15 June, with Fl. Lt. Lou Spence flying four times. The CO led ten aircraft as top cover for 450 Squadron on a patrol to Acroma. This was followed by Spence leading five on a reconnaissance to El Adem from 1240 to 1315. Spence took off again at 1335 to lead a bombing and strafing force of Hurricanes to a target of five enemy tanks located during the previous sortie, and a concentration of motor transport dispersed behind the tanks. The task was 'successfully carried out, one tank definitely being hit', and Spence landed at 1415. Nicky Barr led six aircraft from 1600 to 1645 both to bomb and provide escort for Hurricanes. Two tanks were left burning. A further three aircraft took of at the same time to provide top cover to 112 Squadron. Spence was off again leading ten aircraft at 1900, but by 1915 the formation was back on the ground, having been recalled. The same formation took off again at 2000 to bomb and strafe stationary motor transport near Sidi Rezegh. They achieved 'excellent results'. All bombs landed in the target area and one direct hit started a fire which produced vivid red flames as if an ammunition dump had been hit.

Earlier in the afternoon 250 Squadron lost the aircraft of Sgt. Hector Hannaford, who was shot down by flak and crash landed his aircraft south west of Gambut.

86. Fl. Lt. Lou Spence and his cheerful ground crew. (RAAF Museum)

By 16 June Rommel's advance had bypassed a strong point at El Adem and struck directly at Sidi Rezegh.

> This German drive not only threatened to isolate Tobruk, but had by this time penetrated to within twenty miles of Gambut, where the whole fighter force now lay without protection. The situation was perilous but, on the 16th, when tactical headquarters of the Eighth Army retired to Sollum, not only did the fighters continue to operate from Gambut but Advanced Air Headquarters remained behind to control them. "The price of the gamble," wrote Group Captain Beamish, "was the whole of the fighter force" - but it was a gamble rightly undertaken. Morale among both air and ground crews was extremely high, and with targets at such a short distance there was a natural desire to achieve the utmost damage before retiring. A personal element had been introduced, for Gambut, desolate, barren, dusty though it was, was nevertheless the home of the fighter force. More, it was the true birthplace and testing ground of what was later to be known as the Desert Air Force, but which then existed as a proud self conscious aggressive fellowship close-knit around No. 239 Wing. At Gambut had been hammered out the problems of escort tactics, mobility and control: there had emerged the Kittyhawk-bomber and a more effective system of direct air support. [18]

3 Squadron's ORB sums up the day's activities succinctly.

> 'On this day the Squadron completed a total of 69 operational sorties totalling 40.50 hours, thus establishing a record for this Command. Great credit is due not only to the pilots who carried out their strenuous duties cheerfully and courageously, but to the ground crews who worked unceasingly during the day maintaining the necessary high standards of serviceability. Their work was particularly creditable when it is realised that the maintenance was carried out by 'C' Flight only'. [19]

Nicky Barr flew six times, Lou Spence five and Keith Kildey four. In the morning six Kittyhawks led by Lou Spence took off at 0850 on a bombing and recce to Sidi Rezegh. They were attacked four times by two persistent Bf109s, two aircraft being damaged. All returned safely at 0940.

Barr and Spence were off at 1015 to bomb and recce near Sidi Rezegh. They scored two direct hits on 'lorried troops two miles west of Sidi Rezegh drome'. They were back by 1045.

Another bombing mission led by Nicky Barr took off at 1115, being completed by 1145. Lou Spence and Sgt. Danny Boardman both scored direct hits on tanks.

Nicky Barr led the next operation at 1215, to bomb south west of Sidi Rezegh. They were back by 1245.

Having flown on the last three ops, Barr stayed behind when the fifth operation for the day took off at 1335. PO Victor Curtis led ten aircraft on another bombing and strafing mission, this time to El Adem. Sgt Boardman and Sgt Bray both had their aircraft damaged by flak and crash-landed at base.

A number of crash-landings took place during the hectic period of the retreat from Gazala. The circumstances of this one cannot be confirmed, due to the shadow covering the serial number. Perhaps the oddly reversed 'D' indicates an aircraft flown by Danny Boardman. (RAAF Museum, via Lex McAulay)

Another fighter-bomber mission was flown against motor transport and troop carriers near Sidi Rezegh by seven aircraft at 1450, again led by Nicky Barr. They were attacked ineffectually by four Bf109s, one of which was damaged by Barr at 1500. His fire struck its tail, pieces of which were seen to fly off.

A further bombing and strafing attack was flown at 1620 by nine aircraft with the tireless Barr leading, and they were attacked by four Bf109s on the way home. Sgt. Frederick Ryan (AL145) was shot down and killed and Sgt. Donald was superficially wounded by A.A. Oblt.Tangerding of III/JG 27 claimed a Kittyhawk in flames and Fw. Fink one which crash-landed. Sgt. Ross Biden (AK745) was forced to crash land at Gambut when his engine stopped. As in the case of Reg Stevens on the 12th, the bomb was still attached. On this occasion it detonated and Biden was

killed. He had been with the Squadron since 3 March, arriving with a total of 4 hours and 15 minutes experience on the Kittyhawk. Since then he had flown some 36 operational sorties.[20] Ryan and Biden were both flying their third sortie of the day.

At 1805 FO Furniss led seven aircraft to bomb dispersed motor transport near Sidi Rezegh. All aircraft had returned thirty minutes later. Between this operation and the last, which took off at 1925, Nicky Barr flew a reconnaissance in search of his missing pilots. He located the wreckage of Ross Biden's aircraft near Gambut Main. The last operation, led by PO Curtis, bombed a moving column of motor transport and returned at 1925.

The ORB became slightly erratic, perhaps due to the intensity of the day's operations. It recorded Geoff Chinchen as flying AK961 on the 6th operation, when he was shot down on the 14th. If obviously should have been Sgt Churchill, whose name did not appear on that list, but who was recorded elsewhere as having fired at a Bf109 during the sixth op. It also recorded that 69 sorties were carried out, but when the actual lists are totalled, it seems that in fact the number should be 62.

The seven new Sergeant Pilots contributed fourteen of these, with John Hooke and Reg Stevens flying three sorties each.

During this day, 450 Squadron flew twenty-five escort sorties and fifteen bombing sorties with 3 and 112 Squadrons without loss.

112 Squadron lost a long serving Australian when PO Ken Carson (AL105) failed to return from a mission which took off at 1430 hours. He had been with the squadron since October 1941 and had a score of one and one shared victories, a shared probable and a damaged. He was leading a dive bombing attack when his aircraft was hit by light flak at 150 feet. He was wounded in both legs and blacked out temporarily. He recovered to find the aircraft on fire, and crash-landed amongst the Germans he had just been attacking. He lost consciousness again and awoke to find the Germans applying first aid,[*] a remarkably altruistic act, given the circumstances of his capture.

Sgt Hannaford of 250 Squadron crash-landed on the way home for the second time in two days after being hit during a strafing mission in the Sidi Rezegh area with aircraft from 3 and 112 Squadrons. PO Cable of 250 Squadron took part in the last fighter mission of the day. While strafing south west of Acroma the squadron was attacked by four Bf109s which promptly shot down one Kittyhawk, and Cable was then involved in a fifteen minute dogfight. He damaged one of the Messerschmitts, but his Kittyhawk was in turn badly shot about and he crash landed at base. He was claimed by Lt. Korner of 2/JG 27.

Subsequent to the operations of 16 June, 'Air Marshal Sir Arthur Tedder sent a personal hand written note to Nicky, [Barr] the squadron commander:

"Congratulations on most efficient and successful fighter operations past two days. The bombers did very well because of the secure protection of 450 and 3 Sqns. The fighting by 3 Sqn was grand. You have put the Germans back a good pace and we must keep them there."[21]

Operations continued at a hectic pace on 17 June, but it was a day of mixed fortunes for the *Luftwaffe,* for although their fighters claimed fourteen kills, including six to Oblt. Marseille, which brought his score to 101, Oblt. Otto Schulz was killed in action and they lost a considerable number of aircraft to ground strafing later in the day.

274 Squadron's Hurricanes took off at 1055 to escort Bostons to El Duda. They engaged a number of MC202s, shooting down two, but were then attacked by four Bf109s of II/JG 27.

---

[*] *AWM 54 779/3/29 PoW debriefs.*

Schulz shot down the Hurricane flown by Canadian Fl.Lt. Wally Conrad, who crash landed with slight wounds to one hand. His life was almost certainly saved by another Canadian; Sgt James 'Eddie' Edwards of 260 Squadron. Schulz, having just recorded his fifty-first victory, made the elementary mistake of starting his usual strafing run without looking behind. Edwards, then a young Sergeant with three victories to his name, claimed Schulz's aircraft as a probable. 'Edwards was flying alone; he believes he actually shot down 2 Bf109s. As he was still quite new to the Squadron, he only claimed one probable, as he thought he would not be believed'.[22] He ended the war as a Wing Commander with 15 and three shared victories. Not included in this official total are his victories over Schulz and Lt. Wolf Schaller of III/JG 53, whom he shot down shortly after Schulz.

Earlier in the day at 1000, 450 Squadron escorted 3 Squadron to El Duda and El Adem. The formation was attacked by four Bf109s of I/JG 27, forcing 3 to jettison their bombs, and two Kittyhawks were shot down without loss to the Germans. Sgt Alexander Glancy (AK934) of 450 Squadron was killed, and Sgt. Hooke (AK813) on his 10th sortie since 8 June, returned later, after an unpleasant adventure. The successful German pilots were Lt. von Lieres and Lt. Korner.

John Hooke related what happened after the combat.

' I just belly landed it, but what I didn't realise at the time was that I elected to do this in a mine field. I got out and I took the things that I needed and I started walking. Then it occurred to me that the cracks in the ground made a curious pattern. It had rained since the mines were put in you see, so there were cracks in the ground which showed exactly where the mines were laid. It occurred to me that this was a bad place to be, so I turned around and very carefully picked my way back to the aircraft, using my own footsteps. Ultimately I got on to a piece of ground where there were no cracks. I'd been told to take the IFF and I couldn't find out how to get it out, so I took the whole bloody wireless out. I had a wireless on one hip and my parachute on the other one. By and by I was rescued by a Pommy officer in a Bren gun carrier. He rode up in this thing you see, and indicated that I ought to put my hands up. I said in good round English that he should have been able to understand, that I was the same side as the aircraft that was just over there, and I didn't feel like putting my hands up just because he told me to. He said, "That's all right about that, just put your bloody hands up!" So ultimately I agreed with him and put them up. It seemed better than being shot.

He took me back to our lines, and when we got there they had to clear a path through the mine field that we had to go through. There were these Pommy sappers with bloody great skewers, pushing them down into the soil to see whether they could feel a mine or not. One of them looked at me. I was absolutely soaked with engine oil, and probably looking a bit tired by this stage, and "Ooh," he said, "you've been shot down." I said, "Yes, that's exactly right." "I wouldn't have your job for *some*thing," says he. I thought, everyone to his own trade. I didn't particularly want *his*.

John Hooke, known to his squadron mates as 'Hobson', which they used as a nick-name, (although it *is* actually his second given name). This photograph was taken in May 1943, shortly after his promotion to Pilot Officer.
(John Hooke)

We were operating from one of the Gambut scrapes, and we could see the Hun tanks driving along the top of the escarpment over there, three quarters of a mile away, I suppose. . . That night I spent in the back of a shooting-brake, soaked with oil in my wet shirt, no singlet, no pullover. That was the coldest night I ever spent.'[23]

At 1120 112 Squadron set out on a fighter-bomber operation, and lost F/Sgt. Roy Drew (AK586) in unexplained circumstances. He was shot down between Sidi Rezegh and Gambut, and it is considered possible that he was Marseille's one hundredth victim. If so, his aircraft was mis-identified as a Hurricane.

The German fighter force by this stage had advanced to Gazala, and when this was confirmed by reconnaissance, 239 Wing mounted an attack. Fifteen fighter-bombers and a further sixteen Kittyhawks as top cover took off for Gazala at 1345 led by Wg. Cdr. Mayers. To avoid detection they flew out to sea, turning west and climbing to 17,000 ft. before turning south towards their target. Surprise was complete. They found thirty Bf109s and fifteen of them were destroyed or damaged by the Wing's low level attack. A.A. was light and the only enemy aircraft seen in the air was a lone Bf109 which attempted to take off. It was promptly shot down by a pilot of 250 Squadron. The wing suffered no losses, and noticed a reduction in enemy fighter activity for several days afterwards.

Refuelling and maintenance, 3 Squadron, mid 1942. (RAAF Museum)

In spite of this success, the Germans held sway in the land battle. El Adem fell and by dusk the spearheads of Rommel's armour were within twelve miles of Gambut. The fighter squadrons withdrew to Sidi Azeiz, a small salvage and demolition party remaining at Gambut until midnight. 'By 4 a.m. the next morning the headquarters of the *21st Panzer Division* was established on the airfield'.[24]

Tom Wood and his companions had arrived from 71 OTU to rejoin 3 Squadron on 15 June, and two days later, his youthful enthusiasm got the better of him.

On arrival at 3 Squadron base camp at Sidi Heneish we learnt that the squadron was operating from Gambut, but things were far from clear, as Rommel was making a concerted push. We were advised that no further aircraft were to be flown to the Advanced Landing Ground. At this time Rex Bayly arrived from the front and said they needed more aircraft. I didn't need much urging and the two of us literally "stole" an aircraft each and flew to Gambut, to find on arrival our lot had evacuated and the Germans were coming in the other side! We flew back to Behira, then on to Sidi Azeiz and as Bayly was running short of fuel, landed near a British tank Corps. They used 90 octane fuel (we used 120). We both took on about 40 gallons each and flew back to the Squadron at L.G. 075 at Mischeifa. Miraculously nothing was ever said, even though Bayly had bent his prop through a bad landing.[25]

With the Kittyhawk squadrons hastily re-established at Sidi Aziez, operations resumed on 18 June at a considerably reduced pitch. 3 Squadron put up five aircraft led by the CO for a recce patrol from 1210 to 1345 while 450 flew two operations. The first of these was a two aircraft recce which left at 0755. Fl. Lt. J. Williams and PO K. Murdoch were in the Gambut area when they were attacked by a lone Bf109, which Williams (AK636) shot down.

One hour later PO Shillabeer led five aircraft back to the Gambut area where they had a skirmish with two Bf109s. Three Kittyhawks were slightly damaged, but Sgt. Dyson (AL195) destroyed one of the Messerschmitts. The formation experienced 'intense Breda and small arms fire in the Gambut area'.

Due the speed of the German advance, the 239 Wing squadrons were compelled to pull out of Sidi Aziez and left for LG75 south of Sidi Barrani. Within a few days they would be bombing Sidi Aziez.

18th June: Jerry is now in possession of our old 'drome. We remained at Sidi Aziez and Flight Lts. Williams and Dyson each bagged a 109F on an early morning patrol. "D" and "N" were badly holed by ack-ack near Gambut.

Streams of transport and troops are passing this 'drome and heading east. A heavy pall of smoke can be seen coming from burning dumps.

We are ordered out of Sidi Aziez at noon and are the last squadron to leave, being escorted by armoured cars for some twenty miles to prevent being cut off. We are turned east through gap D in the wire and head once again for No.75LG. The desert is full of moving vehicles all going east. We arrived at our destination dirty, tired and hungry. Our first meal for two days tasted good. (Viv Herrett)

There were few sorties flown on 19 June, with 3 providing six and 450 eight. None made contact with the enemy.

On 20 June Rommel directed his forces to attack Tobruk, garrisoned by a mixed South African and British force under Major-General H.B. Klopper, and it fell the next day.

After the epic four month defence of the port by the Australian 9th Division in 1941 and a further four months by a mixed force of Australian, British, Polish, Czech and New Zealand troops, its loss within two days shocked and dismayed the Allied forces in the Desert, and Churchill called it a disgrace. Rommel's forces captured almost 33,000 prisoners, '5,000 tons of supplies, 2,000 vehicles and most importantly, 1,400 tons of fuel'.[26] The Desert Air Force was unable to help. Because of the army's sudden retreat, the fighters were forced into bases which were so far to the east that they were unable to reach Tobruk. Apart from a small number of light bomber sorties which had no effect on the attackers, no air support was possible.

Fl.Lt. Rudolph Leu became a PoW on 21 June. At 0825 112 Squadron sent eight Kittyhawks on a bombing and reconnaissance to the Bardia area. They dropped their bombs on Sidi Aziez airfield, but Leu's aircraft (AL225) was hit by A.A. and set alight. He crash-landed, suffering burns to his arms and legs and injuries to his head and back. PO Johnson attempted a rescue landing, but rough terrain and enemy fire prevented him from doing so and Leu was captured, spending the next two months in hospital. He had been with 112 Squadron since June 1941, flying Gladiators

before the unit converted to Tomahawks. His final score was 6 and 1 shared destroyed, 1 probable and 1 damaged.

While the German fighters were moving into the Gambut airfields on 22 June, 3 and 450 Squadrons withdrew further to LG 102 at Sidi Heneish.

23rd June: "A" Flight has been preparing to move out again. "S" burst a tyre on take off. This subsequently held up our departure while it was being repaired.

During the morning a Ju88 raided an ammunition dump nearby. We all ran frantically for cover with fireworks all around us.

We finally moved out at 8.00 pm and travelled until the moon gave out. We bunked down by the roadside. Jerry bombed and straffed us all night. There were bullets flying around me on five occasions during the night. Our trucks sustained plenty of holes, but fortunately no one was wounded. (Viv Herrett)

There was no contact with the enemy for the Kittyhawks on 23 June, but on the following day, 3 Squadron had the better of an uneven encounter with Bf109s and G-50s.

Four Kittyhawks led by Nicky Barr took off at 1105 on a reconnaissance of the forward areas and were attacked by a reported six Bf109s and four G-50s. Sgt Fox (AK806 CV-N) was shot down by a G-50, which was promptly destroyed by Nicky Barr (AK756), who stayed with it in a steep turn and saw it hit the ground inverted. Sgt Danny Boardman (AK961) scored his first victory.

> Whilst on recce sweep to identify enemy M.T. moving East approx. 15 miles N.E. MADELENA I was flying No. 2 to Instep leader in a formation of 4 Kittyhawks of 3 Squadron. We flew over large concentration and received a certain amount of A.A. We were then attacked by 6 109s at 6 o'clock. Time of attack 1200 hours and height 3,500 ft. Kittyhawk formation took avoiding action and the 109s made repeated attacks for approx. 10 mins. 2 109s made attack from rear quarter on my machine. I took avoiding action by turning into the attack when E.A. passed over me I swung round and got 2 short bursts into one machine from astern. The plane continued climbing for a short while then flicked to the left on its back and I observed it drop almost vertically and hit the ground and burst into flames.
>
> I also observed 2 G 50s in an (sic) area but made no attacks on them.
>
> I made three attacks on different 109s with no results. Medium barrage of A.A. was put up by the concentration whilst the dog fight was going on.
>
> One enemy aircraft (unidentified) was seen to momentarily spin and a fire was seen to start on the ground.
>
> On leaving area 3 aircraft fires were seen in the area. I proceeded in South Easterly direction, saw a Kittyhawk (S/L Barr) force landed with engine trouble on clearing. Went down and landed to check up - all O.K. Flew back and landed at 1300 hours.

Keith Kildey (AL101) managed to make an attack on a 109, closing to 'twenty yards astern and above', which produced smoke from its engine and it continued to dive steeply from below 2,000 ft. He was not able to follow it as he was attacked by another 109 and hit before getting away from it. Two 109s followed him for five miles before making off in a westerly direction. He also reported three fires on the ground.

It is possible to identify the victors and casualties of this combat fairly conclusively. Two Hurricanes of 33 Squadron were in the area and 'PO Inglesby dived from 17,000 ft, failing to return. Oblt Sinner claimed a Hurricane south of Tolata (Inglesby), but crash-landed himself after this combat'.[27] The three fires observed by all three pilots of 3 Squadron may then have been Inglesby's Hurricane, the G-50 shot down by Nicky Barr and the Bf109 shot down by Danny Boardman. Sgt Fox landed on his wheels and his aircraft did not burn. Sinner's crash-landing was most likely the result of Keith Kildey's attack .

3 Squadron and 112 Squadron frequently flew together. A 112 Squadron aircraft is in the foreground, showing the unit's distinctive shark's mouth marking, while AK961 CV-O, *Snifter,* stands beside it. Sgt Danny Boardman claimed his first victory in this aircraft on 24 June 1942. (RAAF Museum)

On 25 June 3 Squadron flew forty-two fighter-bomber sorties against motor transport advancing along the coast road towards Matruh, and against tanks of the *21st Panzer Division*. 450 flew forty-one sorties, all as escort to Bostons, but they also carried bombs on fifteen of them. Neither squadron suffered any losses.

Unfortunately this was not to be the case on 26 June, which was a day of intensive and continuous air combat. 3 flew sixty-two sorties and 450 forty-five, often carrying bombs as well as providing escort to Bostons in an attempt to hinder the rapid advance of the *Afrika Korps.*

3 Squadron's third operation of the day began at 0910 when three bomb carrying Kittyhawks provided medium cover to Bostons, with others of 250 Squadron as top cover. As they were approaching the target from south of the El Alimat area, the third aircraft in the formation was attacked by a G-50. This was immediately followed by six Bf109s and a MC200. PO Victor Curtis (AL101) jettisoned his bomb and chased an aircraft which was attacking the bombers. Having driven this Axis fighter off, he then saw a 250 Squadron Kittyhawk flying straight and level and being fired on by a Bf109. He attacked this machine, which broke away. He opened fire on another Bf109 from the front quarter and 'saw tracer bouncing from engine cowling'. Curtis was unable to see what happened to his target, as he was then attacked by three Bf109s. He fired at the second of these aircraft on the stall and at that moment his guns stopped working. He spun off the stall and as he pulled out he was hit by explosive shells in the rudder and fuselage.

Curtis brought his damaged aircraft back safely and was later awarded a half share in a Bf109 by 239 Wing Headquarters with Fl. Lt. Marshall, a very successful pilot with 250 Squadron.

450 Squadron's fourth operation of the day was a bomber escort at 1105. They were attacked by three Bf109s and PO Thomas Jones was seen to dive and flatten out close to the ground. He did not return and lost his life in unexplained circumstances, possibly the result of a high speed stall. He had only been with the squadron since 15 June, when he arrived from the Wing Training Flight.

3 Squadron's sixth operation of the day left five minutes either side of midday. PO Pfeiffer took off at 1155 to lead a formation of Bostons to their target and five more Kittyhawks led by Nicky Barr took off at 1205 to act as close cover. They were accompanied by 112 Squadron. This was Nicky Barr's 90th operational flight and his third of the day. The Bostons would not follow PO Pfeiffer and unloaded their bombs on a line of 100-plus motor transport near Mingar El Amar. Shortly after the bombing the formation was attacked by two Bf109s, both of which fired at Barr's aircraft, (ET873 CV-N). One pulled away and was attacked by Sgt. Bray, but the other got a good burst into Barr's aircraft from 100 yds. behind. Other pilots of 3 saw a big flash from the Kittyhawk, which then went down in a very steep dive. The aircraft was hit in the engine, wings and tail. Barr was hit in the leg and the cockpit filled with flames. The speed of the dive was so great that he had difficulty opening the cockpit canopy.

> I've no idea of my dive speed, but suddenly, in a flash, the canopy shot back to the armour-plate and I was sucked out of the cockpit with such force that the flames on my arm, hand, trouser leg and parachute harness were extinguished. My vision was now impaired and I had no idea where the ground was. [28]

He had baled out at 4,000 ft. and opened the parachute at 2,000. The Bostons pinpointed the spot and Sqn. Ldr. Barr was reported as 'missing believed PoW'.

Barr's likely victor was Lt. Werner Schroer, who claimed a Kittyhawk at 1240, from a formation of ten Bostons and twelve Kittyhawks encountered near Mersa Matruh. However, 112 Squadron also lost the aircraft of PO Cuddon near Charing Cross and two other JG 27 pilots made claims: Ofw. Rosenberg and Fw. Kabisch.[29] The three locations mentioned are along the line of withdrawal of the bombers and are some forty miles apart.

Squadron Leader Nicky Barr was 3 Squadron's top scoring pilot, with twelve destroyed, two probables and seven damaged in only seven months of operations. Badly wounded, he spent more than five months in Italian hospitals, first in Tobruk and then Italy. His subsequent adventures are covered briefly in Appendix 11.

450 Squadron took off on its fifth operation at 1310 as top cover to Bostons attacking a target west of Matruh, with three more aircraft from 250 Squadron. 250 was attacked by MC202s, losing one aircraft, with two more badly damaged, one flown by Sgt. Roy Wallis. PO M.J. Jones (AK750) of 450 Squadron was hit and other pilots saw him going down in a steep dive. He baled out safely but was captured. * Several more of the squadron's aircraft received varying degrees of damage. Jones could have been shot down by any of three JG 27 pilots, but his likely victor is Lt. Stahlschmidt, who made claims at 1320, 1327 and 1330 hours, the last of which was for a Kittyhawk.

Two more operations were flown by 3 Squadron at 1305 and 1355. Then at 1505 six aircraft led by PO Pfeiffer left on 'an armed recce to locate S/L Barr'. They found a smouldering fire and another Kittyhawk on its wheels marked CV-N. This was the aircraft of Sgt. Fox who went missing on 24 June. They bombed a concentration of motor transport near Mingar El Amar and were then attacked by two Bf109s which broke off after a brief exchange of fire, but not before they had inflicted light damage to ET911 flown by Sgt. G.R. Jones.

---

*Jones reported being attacked by two 109s. He turned to protect his No.2 and was hit by cannon fire from the second 109. With the controls dead and his aircraft on fire, he baled out at 8,000 feet. (AWM 54 /779/3/29)

450 Squadron were off again on their sixth mission at 1519, again as top cover to Bostons. The formation was attacked by three Bf109s west of Charing Cross. PO K.A. Murdoch was shot down in AK990 and was later confirmed as a PoW. * Sgt Dyson (AL195) fired a burst at one of the Messerschmitts, which stalled, but he did not see what happened to it.

3 Squadron's seven E.A.T.S. Sergeants contributed fourteen of the day's sorties, Cashmore, Hooke and Stevens flying three each.

By the end of the day it was clear that Rommel's advance was going to continue and at 1030 the squadrons at Sidi Haneish were ordered back to El Daba.

> For the next four days fighter operations declined; partly in order to rest the squadrons and build up serviceability for the next great battle which all knew would come when the Eighth Army made its projected stand at El Alamein; and partly because ground parties became inextricably mixed in the great mass of army vehicles scrambling back from Matruh. [30]

El Daba was evacuated on 28 June, but all the serviceable aircraft of 239 Wing stayed until the next morning to provide cover for X Corps which had become encircled at Matruh. In the event X Corps managed to fall back from Matruh on the night of the 28th, and the aircraft and their reduced maintenance staff left at midday. *Panzer* forces occupied the landing ground soon afterwards and had reached a point twenty miles further east by nightfall - Sidi Abd el Rahman. The four squadrons of 239 Wing were now based at LG 91 near Amiriya, some sixty miles east of El Alamein. There would be no retreat beyond this point.

Most of the Landing Ground evacuations took place at night, for day-time movements could sometimes prove to be hazardous, as George James, an armourer with 450 Squadron relates.

> The retreating vehicles, of course, were more or less nose to tail on the one and only road. They were a mixed bag, as trucks of different units were joining in wherever a gap was created, and there were many deserted trucks along the side of the road. Some may have broken down or been damaged possibly by enemy strafing. Most of this road was through soft, stony sand where it was not possible to drive off the road. My mates and I cruised along with all the others, taking it in turns to watch front and rear for enemy kites.
>
> At one point I was in the truck and had just removed my boots and socks (for whatever reason I don't remember) when the truck stopped and someone shouted 'RUN!' Along with the others I went over the back and on to the surrounding desert for a hundred yards or so before stopping. Three 109s were strafing the vehicles on the road but luckily our vehicle wasn't hit. It was then I discovered I was barefoot and couldn't walk back across the stony desert to the truck! One of the boys had to get my boots for me. Fortunately for me, the convoy couldn't move as some trucks ahead had been immobilised and had to be pushed off the road. I put my boots on and while walking back to the truck I wondered how the Hell I had got so far over such a stony terrain without touching down! I still can't walk barefoot outdoors![31]

Bobby Gibbes had rejoined 3 Squadron on 23 June, and assumed command again after the loss of Nicky Barr. He was unable to fly immediately however, and the squadron was often led in the air by the experienced Sergeants, Keith Kildey and Danny Boardman in particular. On 30 June the Squadron received news that Sgt Fox, shot down on 24 June, was safe in hospital, and 450 Squadron's F/Sgt Beste, missing on 12 June, had also returned earlier, flying a sortie on 20 June.

Murdoch observed five 109s attacking the formation. He stated that he had no time to report it. He dropped his bomb and climbed to engage the enemy. He claimed to have shot one down, but as the rest of the flight was initially unaware of the action he received no help. Four of his guns stopped working, and were soon joined by the other two. His aircraft was hit and he lost height to avoid the enemy attacks, but to no avail. The aircraft caught fire and he crash-landed at 260 mph in the enemy lines. He received a broken ankle and nose in the crash, and was wounded in both legs, the left elbow and arm, the scalp and forehead when he struck the gunsight, and had a piece of metal lodged in the bone underneath an eye. (AWM 54 779/3/29)

Since Rommel's attack on the Gazala Line on 26 May, the pace of operations for the Desert Air Force had been hectic. The Kittyhawk units in particular were called upon to act as fighter-bombers and to carry out strafing as well as defending themselves and providing escorts for the Bostons, frequently carrying bombs at the same time. As a result, their losses were severe, but without their efforts, the damage done to the Eighth Army might have been catastrophic.

From 26 May to 30 June, 3 Squadron lost 12 aircraft, with three pilots killed and three captured.

450 Squadron paid the highest price, with 17 aircraft lost, eleven pilots killed, and one captured. They lost another aircraft and its pilot in a take off accident.

112 Squadron lost 18 aircraft, with six pilots killed, two of whom were Australian, and three captured.

250 Squadron lost 13 aircraft in action, with six pilots killed, including one Australian.

260 Squadron lost 11 aircraft, with four pilots killed.

There was to be no respite for the weary fighter pilots. On 1 July came the opening phase of what was to become the first Battle of Alamein, and they would once again find themselves flying numerous daily operations in support of the army, but with one significant difference: their base was permanent and the army would not retreat again.

Chapter 8   The Stand at El Alamein

On 25 June the Commander in Chief of Middle East Forces, General Sir Claude Auchinleck, took over direct command of the 8th Army from its confused and demoralised commander General Ritchie, and his troops began occupying previously prepared defensive positions at El Alamein. On 29 June Benito Mussolini left for North Africa to be ready for a triumphant entry into Cairo. On the same day President Roosevelt was warned by his Chief of Staff that Rommel might be in Suez within a fortnight, and Churchill sent a telegram which ended with the words 'Egypt must be held at all costs'. On 1 July, Rommel ordered his forces to advance on El Alamein.

The defensive position had been well chosen.

> The line was unique in the desert; no other line had a top and a bottom. Every other line, British or Axis, had been turned because its southern end lay in the open desert. The Alamein line was based at its northern end on salt lakes by the sea and at its southern end on the Qattara quicksands. It was only forty miles in length. The Qattara Depression is a geological freak in the desert. It is a long, lozenge shaped hollow, some of it below sea level. The desert here breaks up into steep cliffs and little plateaux, and the flats below will not support armoured vehicles. ... To run round the depression and make the long trek across the open desert to the south was out of the question for Rommel at this stage. He was simply not equipped for it and would have been exposed to the R.A.F. and raiding columns every mile of the way.

> So the enemy was forced to come along the coast. The next important thing about the Qattara Depression is that it approaches the coast as one draws near to Alexandria, and Alamein is its narrowest point. It is, in fact, a bottle neck and therefore excellent for defence. Months before its importance had been realized. Alamein, which is on a ridge, had been formed into a box with a number of concrete underground dugouts and earthworks surrounded by barbed wire and minefields. A number of other positions had been prepared inland. [1]

Rommel's offensive began with a two pronged advance on Alamein itself and Deir el Shein to the south, and 239 Wing's Kittyhawks responded with vigour. At 0905 on 1 July, six bomb carrying aircraft from each of the Australian squadrons took off to escort nine Bostons to Deir el Shein. The *Luftwaffe* was also producing a maximum effort, and the formation was harried by four Bf109s of III/JG 53. Sgt George O'Neil (AK729) of 450 Squadron was shot down and baled out over the sea. Sgt R.C. Davidson had his aircraft badly holed, but F/Sgt. Don McBurnie (AK634) balanced the scale by destroying one Bf109 which went down in a steep dive 'emitting much black smoke' after he fired four bursts at it. It was confirmed by Sgt. Gleeson, who saw an aircraft crash-land.

The aircraft were back on the ground by 1020, but Sqn.Ldr. Ferguson and PO Osborne took off again at 1106 to fly a sweep at 500 ft. in search of Sgt. O'Neil. They landed again at 1330, having

An imminent change of engine for 450 Squadron's OK-V. CO Alan Ferguson regularly flew ET918, V, and it is possible that this was his aircraft. Of necessity, such maintenance was invariably carried out in the open. (Ted Lawler, 450 Squadron)

spent almost two and a half fruitless hours in the air. They saw three Bf109s flying at 6,000 ft. but were not attacked. George O'Neil disposed of most of his equipment during his descent, and the remainder of his clothing once he was in the water. He reached the shore an hour later, wearing nothing but his wrist watch. He was quickly rescued by South African troops who provided him with clothing and food and he was returned to the squadron by the end of the day, the first of three occasions he would return without his aircraft.

3 Squadron sent out eight aircraft to escort nine Bostons and two Baltimores at 1300, four of them carrying bombs. 450 sent three more as low cover. This operation concluded at 1430, unlike the desperate half hour sorties carried out in the early stages of the Gazala break-through.

Another combined bombing and escort mission took off at 1910, eleven Kittyhawks from 3 escorting Bostons south of Daba. PO Ritchie (AK598) was shot down, but parachuted safely and was back with the unit the next day. 450 provided six bomb carrying aircraft for the close escort on this mission and noted a dogfight involving the top cover. Thanks to 3 Squadron, neither the Bostons nor 450 were attacked and the pilots reported accurate bombing of large masses of M/T and armour: 'several new fires added to those already blazing, probably 50-plus'.

The two squadrons flew together on three operations, totalling forty sorties, while 450 Squadron flew four more sorties in two separate operations.

On 2 July the battle continued, the two Australian squadrons flying forty-six sorties between them, escorting bombers while carrying bombs themselves, or bombing combined with reconnaissance and 'delousing' Bostons, which basically meant meeting the bombers as they were withdrawing from their target and adding to their escort.

92. When a mobile crane was unavailable, a tripod device known as a sheer legs was used to lift a new engine into place. 450 Squadron ground crew at work, mid 1942. (Ted Lawler)

The next day was a turning point in the battle as the various German thrusts were held, and at the end of the day Rommel was forced on to the defensive, due partly to the increasing difficulties with supplies brought about by continuous bombing, and the fact that his units were physically and mentally exhausted, having been on the offensive since 26 May. On occasions men were literally falling asleep while under artillery fire.

'The RAF flew 900 sorties against the Axis troops, about four times more than the *Luftwaffe* managed to undertake against the 8th Army'. [2] Of these, the Australian squadrons contributed seventy-one sorties flown over five operations. 450 Squadron passed the day unscathed, while for 3, Sgt. Cashmore (ET837) damaged a Bf109 which attacked the squadron on its second operation of the morning at 1110. After the bombs were dropped the squadron went down to strafe and PO Pfeiffer's AL128 was hit by A.A., which caused him to crash-land three miles north of the landing ground. The aircraft received Cat. II damage.

On 4 July, XIII Corps counter-attacked in the south while the 9th Australian Division began to move forward to strengthen the northern sector. At 0705 the first operation took off; six Kittyhawks from each squadron to bomb and provide escort for eighteen Bostons to the Deir el Shein area. 450 Squadron were the top cover and they were attacked by a solitary Bf109 from 6 o'clock out of the sun. Four of the Kittyhawks jettisoned their bombs and one received Cat. II damage from the 109's attack. 3 noted that the 109 climbed back into the sun and the bombing was carried out without interference.

The day's fourth operation left at 1402, with six 3 Squadron aircraft acting as top cover to 450. They bombed two landing grounds west of Daba where twelve twin-engined E/A were reported, and on the way back 450 went down to strafe a long column of motorised troops near Daba. A lone Bf110 of 4(H)/ 12 failed to take avoiding action in time and was attacked by Don McBurnie (AK886) whose fire shot off its tail. It crashed into the sea, killing Oblt. Schult and his gunner. This was the last of McBurnie's victories, bringing his total to five and one shared destroyed.

The two squadrons flew a total of fifty-nine sorties over five operations for the day.

During the day 450 Squadron received two new pilots, PO T.J. Forsyth and Sgt. R.C. Hughes.

On 5 July both squadrons took off at 0806, but obviously went their separate ways after that, because 450 had a very successful time, while 3's ORB had nothing significant to report.

Led by FO Shillabeer on what was termed 'an armed recce', 450's seven Kittyhawks climbed to 8,000 ft. and flew out to sea, following the coast to Daba. Cloud cover was 10/10ths on the way and cleared to 5/10ths close to Daba, giving enough visibility to reveal a Ju88 of I/LG 1 flying along the road. The Squadron followed him in to LG 21 where Fl.Lt. Williams (AK634) shot him down. They sighted 8-plus Ju88s dispersed on the northern and southern sides of the drome, 12 Ju87s at the western end and 4-plus Bf109s dispersed throughout. Five bombs were dropped from 5,000 ft. producing 'very near misses'. The squadron then went down to strafe from 500 - 300 ft. with the following results:

FO Shillabeer one Ju88 damaged, F/Sgt. McBurnie one Ju88 and one Ju87 damaged, Sgt Taylor two Ju88s damaged, Sgt. O'Neil one Bf109 destroyed, Sgt. Jenkins one Ju88 damaged. Pilots reported that some of the Ju88s were painted black. Not satisfied with this performance, they then paid a visit to LG 20 where two further bombs were dropped, one 20 yards from a twin engined aircraft on the south side and one close to another. They went on to LG 106 where PO Schaaf strafed a Bf109. A tent and nearby personnel were then strafed and the squadron turned for home. On the way back they sighted six M/T through a break in the clouds and strafed these as well, obtaining two direct hits. A covered truck travelling north was also hit. The formation was

A group of 250 Squadron pilots known as 'the fighting six': PO Whitside, PO Rogerson, (missing on 10 October), PO MacLeod (missing on 10 July) and three Australians: Sgt. Des Cormack, Sgt. Hec Hannaford and Sgt. Roy Wallis, who baled out into the sea on 10 July and was not rescued. (Des Cormack)

attacked ineffectively by two Bf109s over Ghazal, and the only damage recorded was a shrapnel hit to the starboard wing of one aircraft, in spite of light and heavy A.A which came up after bombing LG 21. They reported 660 trucks on their return flight.

At approximately 1000, eleven aircraft from 112 and 250 Squadrons attacked LG106, and caught two Bf109Es taking off. One was shot down by Fl. Lt. Marshall (RAF) and the other was claimed as a probable by Sgt. Roy Wallis.

450 Squadron's second operation at 1053 was also successful, with great damage done to trucks, personnel and aircraft at LG 106, but two aircraft failed to return, victims of intense A.A. fire. F/Sgt. Frank Beste (AL164) was shot down for the second time. His aircraft was hit by flak and the engine stopped, forcing him to crash-land half a mile east of the target. Dazed and bleeding, he retrieved the first aid kit and went into a depression in the ground to use it, but was captured when two Germans arrived in a car.* Sgt. Stanley Simpson (AL144) was also shot down and killed in action.

PO Forsyth flew his first sortie with 450 as part of a six aircraft formation acting as top cover to 3 Squadron. His introduction to operational flying was eventful. Just as 3 dived to bomb, five Bf109s attacked 450 from 2,000 ft above and up sun. In spite of this favourable tactical position they did no harm and all aircraft had returned safely by 1745. Sgt. Rex Bayly of 3 Squadron damaged one of the Messerschmitts. The two squadrons flew a total of forty three sorties in four combined operations during the day.

During this day, 260 Squadron escorted Bostons to El Daba, and Ron Cundy, (ET908) a twenty year old Australian, made his first claim, a damaged Bf109, the pilot of which was a lucky man, as Cundy's log book explains.

> We were jumped by 6 ME109's. Sgt. England shot up - I got head on quarter at one - did stern attack on another & damaged him - all my guns jammed.

He had been with the squadron since November of the previous year when they were flying Hurricanes. Although he had taken a considerable time to get into his stride, his successes were now to mount steadily, and by September he was in command of 'B' Flight.

Both Australian squadrons doubled their efforts on 6 July, 3 flying forty sorties in five operations, while 450 flew thirty-nine from five ops. On the first op. of the day, 3 took off at 0600 as top cover to 450, which took off at 0603. They set off for the landing grounds near Daba, and were attacked by four Bf109s on the way, which caused one of 3's pilots to jettison his bomb. 450 dropped seven bombs on LG 20 and 3 contributed a further six, which fell amongst two Ju88s, motor transport and a tent. Six aircraft followed up with a strafing attack which silenced a gun post, but not before 450's leader, F/Sgt. Dangar (AK916) was hit by A.A. causing him to force-land at Dekheila for running repairs. Danny Boardman, leading 3 Squadron, carried out a recce on the way home. All aircraft returned safely. This was the first sortie for Sgt. Hughes.

Apart from marauding 109s, the danger from anti-aircraft fire was great. Des Cormack of 250 Squadron summed it up this way.

> We were on the defensive a fair bit, and getting knocked around a lot too, because we were strafing aerodromes which were well protected, and not only just dive-bombing, but coming down and strafing them, and you could see the ack-ack blokes firing straight across the aerodrome, and as far as we could, we had to keep going straight ahead, which took us over the aerodrome, and get away that way, but we lost six out of twelve one day doing that. . .

Keith Kildey of 3 Squadron also had a healthy respect for the flak.

> That used to be the dangerous bit, because the buggers would see you coming, and by the time you'd get there, you could have walked on the flak that came up, but you had to go through it. . .

---

* AWM 54 779/3/29

Difficult to identify with certainty, this aircraft might be AK778, which was first on line on 16 July, and flown by Sgts. Rex Bayly and John Hooke on this date. Tom Wood and John Hooke regularly flew CV-J during July. (RAAF Museum)

At 1220 450 Squadron were off on their third op. as escort to Hurricane tank busters, again led by F/Sgt. Dangar, with 250 and 112 Squadrons as top cover. As the tanks the formation was searching for proved to be elusive, Dangar went down to 2,000 ft. for closer observation but when he rejoined the formation, the Hurricanes had disappeared. He was then jumped by two Bf109s and spent the next fifteen minutes taking evasive action while making his way home. PO Forsyth and Sgt. Hughes both flew on this operation.

3 Squadron sent eight aircraft to bomb LG 106 at 1255. Seven bombs were dropped, two among ten Bf109s dispersed on either side of a narrow runway. A further two fell amongst motor transport in the dispersal area and another amongst Ju88s and two other unidentified aircraft. No enemy aircraft were sighted and there was only slight A.A.

A further seventy-one bombing sorties were flown by the two squadrons the following day (7 July) without loss or significant damage, PO Forsyth and Sgt. Hughes of 450 Squadron both flying twice.

On 8 July the 239 Wing squadrons combined for a bombing attack on LGs 21 and 22 near Daba. At 1200 Wg. Cdr. Mayers led eleven aircraft of 250 Squadron, 112 Squadron supplied ten and the two RAAF units a further ten each, with 3 acting as top cover. Their timing was fortuitous, as they caught four Bf109s of I/JG 27 taking off with an indeterminate number of Stukas. Two more Bf109s from III/JG 27 were already in the air to cover the take off of the Stukas, and these attacked 3 Squadron. Sgt. Donald (ET871 CV-E) claimed one as a probable, and Fw. Maraun from this unit was hit and force-landed near Daba. The lower squadrons meanwhile fell upon the Bf109s and Stukas which had just become airborne. Wg.Cdr. Mayers (ET826) shot down a Bf109. Pilots from 112 and 250 Squadrons claimed two more Bf109s, and another 250 pilot claimed a probable. Three German fighters (including Fw. Maraun) were shot down, and it is likely that Donald's probable was one of them. 250 Squadron also claimed two Stukas, and a number of aircraft on the ground were destroyed or damaged by the bombing and strafing which followed. Sgt. Des Cormack (LD-E) of 250 claimed two Ju87s as damaged on the ground, and the pilots of 3 Squadron strafed Ju88s on each of the landing grounds, as well as damaging six or seven vehicles and a gun emplacement. 450 Squadron also fired at a number of Bf109s in the air, but claimed nothing more than a damaged to Sgt. Vince McFarlane (ET789), who attacked a 109 which climbed, and then fell away in a stall turn after McFarlane had fired a one and a half second burst at it. The only damage to a 239 Wing aircraft occurred on the way home when the trouble-prone Sgt. Hec Hannaford (AK844) of 250 Squadron was shot up by two Bf109s and wounded in the leg and hand, crash-landing his aircraft. On this occasion, he was hospitalised, and did not return to the squadron until late August.

PO Forsyth flew on this operation, his sixth since 5 July, and PO Alf Glendinning flew his first sortie with 3 Squadron.

450 flew another bombing operation at 1845, dropping four 500 pounders and five 250 pounders, claiming five trucks destroyed. 3 followed them five minutes later, their bombs causing an explosion followed by a fire amongst motor transport.

On the next day 3 flew a further thirty-seven bombing sorties while 450 contributed forty, all without loss. Sgt. Rex Bayly of 3 saw four Bf109s on the first op. and three of them attacked him without result.

Early in the morning of 10 July eleven Kittyhawks of 3 Squadron attacked gun emplacements in front of the 9th Division as they moved forward to attack Tel el Eisa. Four Bf109s made a desultory attempt to interfere, and fire was exchanged, both sides withdrawing without inflicting damage on each other.

3 and 450 flew a combined bombing and reconnaissance operation south of Bir Mukheisin at 0925 and were back on the ground without loss sixty-five minutes later.

239 Wing mounted more raids on the landing grounds at Daba, the two Australian squadrons despatching twenty one aircraft at 1200. Thirty-plus Ju87s and Ju88s were bombed and strafed to good effect. On the way home, pilots of 3 Squadron strafed troops carriers heading east, while three aircraft of 450 Squadron lost the formation and were attacked by Bf109s, resulting in damage to two aircraft.

LGs 20 and 21 were revisited in the afternoon by six Kittyhawks from 450 Squadron, together with aircraft from 112 and 250 Squadrons. Two Bf109s were in the air and Lt. Schofbock of III/JG 27 shot down PO Osborne (ET868) of 450 Squadron, who was captured. * 450 Squadron dropped a mixture of 500 and 250 pounders from 3,000 ft. through dense heavy AA. None of 450's pilots saw what happened to Osborne.

Three more Bf109s scrambled and joined Schofbock, shooting down two aircraft from 250 Squadron. One was flown by Sgt. John Power, who had only been with the unit since 19 June. His body was not found, and his name is recorded on the Alamein Memorial.

---

* The constant speed unit in Osborne's engine failed, the engine over-revved and the glycol was about to flame. He was at 10,000 feet over the sea with no Mae West or dinghy, so he had to glide to land. He crash-landed in enemy lines and was captured at once. (AWM 54 779/3/29)

The same three squadrons departed yet again for LG 21 at 1807, 450 providing ten aircraft, but were intercepted over the sea by Bf109Es and MC202s, which caused all but three of 450's pilots to jettison their bombs. The raid was abandoned and as the Kittyhawks turned for home, Sgt. A.W. Taylor (AL142) damaged a Bf109, firing from a head on to front quarter position. He saw pieces drop off his target, which entered a steep dive. Sgt. Des Cormack of 250 damaged one of the Macchis.

450's pilots reported a burning Kittyhawk at 8,000 ft, and a parachute which opened at 7,000. The unfortunate pilot was Sgt. Roy Wallis from 250 Squadron. He landed in the sea and was not rescued. The Air/Sea rescue flight was requested to pick him up, but was unable to do so due to the presence of enemy aircraft.

3 Squadron was released from operations at 1330, and their aircraft were made available to 112, 250 and 450 Squadrons for the remainder of the day. Sgt. Wallis was flying one of these aircraft, ET837, and it may be due to this that he is incorrectly commemorated on 3 Squadron's Roll of Honour at the AWM.

By the end of the day, 250 Squadron had lost five aircraft: four of the pilots were killed, two of them Australians. These losses were redressed to some extent by Canadian Sgt. Gordon Troke, who destroyed a Bf109E and a MC202 during the last combat.

Neither Australian unit flew operations on 11 July, but they were called on again the next day as Rommel counter-attacked against El Alamein.

3 Squadron sent six aircraft off at 0610 on an armed recce. south of the battle area, bombing and strafing dispersed motor transport and starting one fire. 450 took off at 0619 to fly an armed recce over the Qattara Depression and bombed 500-plus well dispersed motor transport, but

By July the 239 Wing Squadrons were more or less established on a permanent basis at LG 91 near Amiriya, and living conditions became more acceptable. Tom Wood's caption of this photograph sent home to his family in 1942 says: 'In the tent - inspecting some of our "yaffle", more under the bed. Note the "mozzy net". All comforts for us'. (Tom Wood)

they reported that their bombs were ineffective. At 1220 Sgt. Keith Kildey led eight of 3's Kittyhawks to bomb an enemy position south of Ras el Shaqiq. As they went in to bomb they saw a Fieseler Storch about to land right in the target area. Kildey led his aircraft down through heavy anti-aircraft fire and they dropped six bombs, all of which landed within thirty yards of the unfortunate Storch. After this attack there was nothing to be seen but a small fire. The last operation of the day was flown at 1840, and another brief encounter with Bf109s took place with no result.

On 13 July, 3 Squadron flew forty-four bombing sorties from six operations, and 450 flew twenty-four from three, bombing motor transport, tanks, gun emplacements and mobile columns. By the end of the day the enemy thrust had been repulsed and General Auchinleck launched his own counter-attack against two Italian divisions along Ruweisat Ridge in the centre, and against the German *90th Light Division* in the south between Bab el Qattara and the El Taqa plateau.

Although engagements on the ground were continuing, signs that the war was about to become static were starting to appear. On 14 July, Fl. Lt. Williams led eight 450 Squadron aircraft off at 0738, and they found two different concentrations of 1000-plus and 2000-plus stationary motor transport, and what they described as workshops and *permanent buildings.* Rommel was by now short of fuel, ammunition and spare parts for tanks and vehicles and his supply line was stretched to its greatest length. The *Afrika Korps* was now lacking both the energy and resources to advance any further.

> The Axis were now paying the penalty for their failure to subdue Malta, for this thorn in their side was the base from which the Royal Navy and Royal Air Force were crippling their efforts to convoy Rommel's supplies from Sicily to Benghazi and Tripoli. Hitler had shrunk from the Malta operation that had been planned (*Operation Herkules, an airborne invasion scheduled for July, and finally postponed, against all common sense, until the conquest of Egypt was completed - Author*) and Rommel, against the advice of his staff and the Italian Comando Supremo, had agreed with Hitler's decision, preferring to stake everything on the headlong dash for Egypt in the summer. It was a notable case of the gambler in Rommel, so attractive to his more romantic admirers, fatally swaying his military judgement.[3]*

Fl. Lt. Charlie Coward led nine 3 Squadron Kittybombers off at 1030 to bomb in the Bir Makhkad area. They dropped their bombs on 2,000-plus well dispersed motor transport, which was well protected by anti-aircraft fire. Ironically, the German A.A. helped bring about the destruction of a Bf109, as Sgt. Garth Neill (AL102 CV-R) related in his combat report.

> After bombing I headed E. As my aircraft was not performing well, I was left about two miles behind our formation.
>
> A concentrated burst of a/a was fired at me, and, on turning away from it, I saw a 109 F on my tail about 150 yards away. The E/A fired at me with cannon and machine guns. I did a steep turn to the left in which the 109 tried to follow me. When I saw the E/A well out to my right, I turned into it. The 109 immediately turned to the right and climbed. I pulled around on to its tail and climbed also, firing three short bursts into it. A large piece flew off the tail section and the E/A went into a spin and crashed in an enemy concentration. The pilot did not bail out, and I did not see it burn.

This was the squadron's only confirmed victory in July, due mainly to their low level fighter bombing role, but also to the fact that the Bf109s did not seem inclined to press home their attacks with their usual vigour in the few encounters which occurred during the month. The persistent attacks on the landing grounds at Daba no doubt contributed to the reduced *Luftwaffe* effort as well.

The two Australian squadrons flew sixty-four sorties from nine operations on the 14th.

---

* *Over thirty Australians lost their lives while serving on Malta: fifteen fighter pilots from a total of forty-nine, and nineteen bomber, reconnaissance and torpedo squadron aircrew. Australian fighter pilots claimed 102 enemy aircraft destroyed.*[4]

Fewer sorties from six operations were flown on 15 July, but 3 Squadron lost another pilot on the first of these. F/Sgt. Danny Boardman led four aircraft, with another eight from 450 Squadron led by F/Sgt. Dyson on a bombing and reconnaissance west of Alamein at 0915. They found an estimated 150-plus well dispersed motor transport: (450 Squadron's estimate was 300-plus M/T and tanks). This variation of numbers gives a good indication of the difficulties involved when trying to accurately count large numbers of vehicles from a fast moving aircraft which is being subjected to vigorous anti-aircraft fire.

3 Squadron reported the concentration as a poor target because of the skilful dispersal, but they attacked anyway, and the Kittyhawk of PO George Dougall (ET911) was hit by intense A.A. over the target. He was reported as missing, and later confirmed as killed in action.

The last operation of the day commenced at 1740 when Boardman and Dyson again led nineteen aircraft from the two squadrons to bomb ten tanks and 500-plus motor transport south of Ras el Shaqiq. Before the attack had begun, a voice was heard over the R/T which said, "They're not Jerries, they're British. Don't bomb!" It was quickly established that neither squadron had made this transmission, and the voice was believed to be German. 450 reported direct hits on two tanks and a truck; 3 reported near misses close to two tanks and the remainder of their eleven bombs fell amongst the motor transport.

The two squadrons flew eighty-seven sorties from five operations each on 16 July, in the Mireir - Mukheisin area, attacking tanks, motor transport, gun emplacements and mobile workshops.

A photograph which is proof of the Kittyhawk's ability to withstand battle damage. ET916 was a regular mount of Fl. Lt. Alfred Marshall RAF, of 250 Squadron. He used it to shoot down a Ju87 on 8 July. By 19 July he was flying a new 'A', ET853, so the damage visible in this photograph is likely to have occurred between these two dates. Other photos reveal a large hole in the port aileron, and a badly bent starboard tail plane. As the fuselage fuel tank is situated directly below the rear cockpit glazing, the cannon strike must have gone perilously close to igniting it. PO Collier was shot up in the combat of 16 July. It is possible that he was the pilot of ET916 when it was damaged. (Des Cormack)

Danny Boardman, Keith Kildey and Don McBurnie led two operations each. From the fifth sortie on 13 July, until the end of the month, 3 Squadron flew forty-eight operations. Of these, Boardman led fifteen, Kildey fourteen, and Fl. Lt. Charlie Coward nine.

At 1145 0n 16 July, eight 250 Squadron took off to dive bomb enemy tanks, but were intercepted by enemy aircraft. Des Cormack (LD-G) was one of the pilots involved. His log book explains what took place.

> Dog fight with ME 109's & Macchi 202's. F/Lt Marshall and myself chased a Macchi and fired hundreds of rounds at it but it got away. Flew over raging tank battle at 20 ft! - terrific ack ack. Then [we] were attacked by two more Macchis but shook them off.

By 17 July the ground fighting had reduced in intensity, and the squadrons also reduced their efforts, flying thirty-seven sorties between them from five operations. On the first of these at 1130, 3 Squadron found a worthwhile target consisting of fifty-plus motor transport and two tanks, and their bombing started two fires. Two Bf109s intercepted the formation between Alamein and El Amayid and were engaged by Sgt. Reg. Stevens, (ET1017) whose aircraft was severely damaged. These aircraft were part of a formation of eight from III/ JG 53, who broke through the top cover of four Spitfires from 145 Squadron to attack the Kittybombers.

18 July was a comparatively quiet day, thirty-nine sorties being flown between the two squadrons. Sqn. Ldr. Ferguson (ET918) damaged a Bf 109 when 450 Squadron was attacked by four Messerschmitts after bombing on their second operation, which had begun at 1856. The skirmish lasted almost fifteen minutes, Ferguson's 'damaged' claim being the only result for either side.

Attention was turned back to the *Luftwaffe's* landing grounds on 19 July, 250 Squadron attacking LG 21 with Bostons at 0625. A Ju52 was shot down and others strafed on the ground. These aircraft were being seen more frequently as attempts were made to alleviate the *Afrika Korps'* supply problems.

Des Cormack of 250 Squadron flew his last op. in July on the 16th, after which he had a brief leave. He returned to discover that another pilot had crash-landed his favourite aircraft, *Mary*, which was named after his wife. The name is visible in white under the port side wind screen. (Des Cormack)

The rest of 239 Wing visited LG 21 again: eight Kittyhawks from 112 Squadron, ten from 3 and eleven from 450 taking off between 1035 and 1040, again with Bostons.

As 450 swept in to bomb, they found four Ju52s and a Ju87 about to land, and attacked them with their bombs still attached. Sqn. Ldr Ferguson (ET918 OK-V) shared one transport with Fl.Lt. Parker (ET864) and went on to shoot down the Ju87. Parker then destroyed another Ju52, the third being shared by F/Sgt Dyson (AK634) and Sgt. Brown (ET869). The last Ju52 was destroyed by Sgt Lindsay in AK886.

The formation's bombs were then unloaded on LG 21 and both LG 21 and LG 22 were thoroughly strafed, 450 attacking five Ju87s, three Bf109s and a Ju88. 112 Squadron strafed and damaged four Ju88s and 3 reported attacking one Ju52, five Ju87s, five Ju88s, two Bf109s, four Bf110s and one Fi 156. Apart from the five luckless Junkers, no enemy aircraft were seen in the air and surprisingly no A.A. was reported. This was the only operation for the day.

The pressure was maintained on the landing grounds the following day, with a big raid mounted on LGs 17 and 18 at Fuka at 0930. 233 Wing escorted eighteen Bostons, while 239 Wing sent Kittybombers from all four squadrons, including eleven from 3, led by Danny Boardman and eight from 450, led by PO Shillabeer. 3 Squadron's bombs were well aimed, one landing near a Bf110, two near three Ju52s and one between eight 'badly dispersed aircraft'. After bombing they strafed both landing grounds, claiming damage to a Ju52, five Ju88s, three Bf109s and a Bf110, as well as setting a petrol bowser on fire. The A.A. from light, medium and heavy guns was intense.

This time enemy fighters *were* in the air. Wg. Cdr. Mayers was seen to shoot down an MC202, and was then hit himself, probably by one of four Bf109s of III/JG 53 which were scrambled to intercept the raid. Also shot down and captured was Sgt. R.G. Brown (AK872), a Canadian pilot flying with 450 Squadron.

Mayers crash-landed some distance away from the target in the Qattara Depression. A search was carried out by Spitfires of 601 Squadron, who found his Kittyhawk with the cockpit open, but no sign of the Wing Commander. It appears that he was captured, but what happened to him after that is unclear. Chris Shores and Clive Williams in *Aces High* suggest that he may have lost his life when a ship used to transfer prisoners to Italy was sunk. He had been recommended for a DSO just prior to his loss and this was gazetted on 28 July. With eleven victories and one shared, he had also been awarded the DFC and Bar. He was thirty-two years old at the time of his loss.

His replacement as leader of 239 Wing was Wg. Cdr. David Haysom, a Battle of Britain veteran with 79 Squadron. Haysom was later responsible for the development of the 'Cab-Rank' system of close air support with the call sign 'Rover David', used with devastating effect in Italy by the squadrons of 239 Wing.

The two Australian squadrons flew together twice on 21 July. At 1100 Sgt. Lindsay led six aircraft of 450 Squadron as top cover to seven from 3. They attacked 150 M/T and troop carriers east of Ghazal Station. The roles were reversed at 1845, when Keith Kildey led five aircraft as top cover to another six from 450 to bomb M/T either side of a road near Qaret el Khadin. After the bombing all aircraft strafed with good effect.

In the evening 4 SAAF Squadron was escorting Bostons when they were attacked by Bf109s. Two of their aircraft were damaged, and FO John Waddy, who had been posted to the unit after a short period of leave, claimed a probable Bf109.

At 0700 on 22 July six aircraft led by Danny Boardman took off on an armed recce over the central battle area. They dropped their bombs on 'badly dispersed M/T' and claimed five trucks totally destroyed.

450 Squadron were off at 0923, led by F/Sgt. Law, and bombed in the same area as some Bostons. They saw two enemy aircraft attack the Bostons after bombing and swung back to help, but the 'E/A retired' before they could be attacked. 3 Squadron were with 450 on this operation, and dropped their six bombs on an enemy held ridge prior to an attack by the army. One pilot then strafed, and two Bf109s were sighted, Sgt Thomas (ET875) managing to get in a good burst, although no results were seen. (Perhaps this was why the E/A 'retired'.)

On 19 July the *Afrika Korps* had received special orders to dig in the armour as protection against air attack, as they were now down to only twenty-eight serviceable tanks. [5] That these orders were carried out quickly and thoroughly became obvious, when both RAAF squadrons attacked 70-plus well dispersed and *dug in* M/T in the Deir el Abyad area after taking off at 1535. The German vehicles were also being shelled by the army as the bombs fell.

3 Squadron's ORB recorded that 'prior to taking off on this sortie, the pilots drew lots to see who should drop the 1000th bomb since the Squadron became a fighter-bomber unit. The honour fell to Sgt Kildey, who dropped his bomb with excellent results'. This seems appropriate, as he was also leading the squadron on this occasion.

One more operation was carried out when both squadrons took off at 1725 to bomb north west of El Mirier. Sgt Hughes of 450 was hit by A.A. and his aircraft (AK804) spun in. He baled out over the target and was captured. He was lost on his eighteenth sortie since flying his first operation on 6 July.

By now both armies had almost reached the point of exhaustion and as the battle 'stuttered to a close',[6] both sides began to dig in and erect defences which ran from Alamein to the Qattara depression. Nevertheless, on 23 July the two squadrons flew forty-three sorties between them, bombing and strafing motor transport and starting several fires.

That the Air Force played a significant role in the outcome of the first Battle of El Alamein is indisputable. The concept of army-air cooperation first elucidated by Tedder and Coningham before the commencement of *Crusader*' in November 1941, had evolved to the extent that a request for air support from Eighth Army Headquarters could now be met within thirty-five minutes. Losses amongst the Kittyhawk units were fewer than those incurred during the retreat from Gazala, and their ability to carry out a variety of roles was invaluable. Whether escorting bombers, (while frequently carrying bombs themselves), dive bombing and strafing enemy vehicles and troops, attacking *Luftwaffe* landing grounds, or carrying out protective fighter sweeps and occasional reconnaissance sorties, they gave their all. In contrast, the *Luftwaffe* fighter force had no effect on the outcome of the battle, and their bomber force was impotent.

> What emerges from these two months of costly fighting, with all their humiliations, is an even greater emphasis than ever before on Army/Air cooperation - this time as a means, indeed, the *only* means, of staving off absolute disaster. If one tries to imagine subtracting the Desert Air Force effort from the crucial fighting of July one finds oneself at once in the realm of the unimaginable. And, indeed, throughout the whole battle . . . the air support system worked well - in fact better and better.[7]

On 24 July only one operation was carried out by the Australian squadrons. This was at 0935 when Fl. Lt. Coward led seven Kittyhawks from 3 as top cover to a formation of twelve Baltimores to bomb LG 20. They also carried bombs, as did the eight 450 Squadron aircraft led by Don McBurnie. The other two squadrons from 239 Wing were also present, as were 260 Squadron and the three South African squadrons of 233 Wing, escorting eighteen Bostons. Although there was some aerial combat, neither of the Australian squadrons were involved, and after bombing they strafed, claiming a Ju87, a Ju88 and a twin engined aircraft damaged on LG 20, and a Ju88 and a Bf109 destroyed on LG 21.

At 0616 on the 25th, Sgt. Jenkins led eight 450 Squadron aircraft off on an armed recce, Sgt. George O'Neil failing to bring back his aircraft for the second time. AK912 suffered engine failure over Axis territory, but he managed to reach forward British troops, where he carried out a successful belly landing.

3 took off four minutes later for an armed recce north of the battle area and dropped six bombs on well dispersed motor transport with 'fair results'. John Waddy claimed a damaged MC202 with 4 SAAF during the day.

A group of 450 Squadron pilots at LG91, during mid 1942. Left to right rear: Rod Hughes, (Canadian) George O'Neil, Max Jenkins, F.E. Parker. Front, left to right, Don McBurnie, Frank Schaaf, Gordon Lindsay.
(Max Jenkins, 450 Squadron, via Doug Norrie)

Neither squadron flew operationally the next day, but 27 July saw intense activity, which began when both squadrons took off at 0957-1000, with 450 acting as top cover to 3 on an armed recce north west of Mukheisin. Nine bombs were dropped by 3 Squadron on motor transport dispersed along both sides of a road and 450 dropped a further nine, estimating the number of M/T at fifty-plus. After the bombing, Sgt. Cashmore(AK651) became detached from the squadron and was attacked by two Bf109s, one of which he claimed as a probable. A 450 Squadron pilot reported sighting two Bf109s attacking a lone Kittyhawk, obviously Cashmore, who returned safely.

The next operation took off at 1550 with 3 providing the top cover to 450, eight aircraft from each squadron making up the formation. They dropped their bombs on the west side of a road in the Deir el Dhib area and while no definite results were observed by the pilots, the army reported that the bombing was excellent.

PO Schaaf led ten 450 aircraft off on the last operation of the day at 1818 to act as top cover for 3, Keith Kildey leading six Kittyhawks off seven minutes later. The formation returned to the Deir el Dhib area and bombed 100-plus motor transport and gun posts accurately. Several Bf109s from I/JG 27, which had previously been involved in a confused dogfight with the Hurricanes of No.1 SAAF and 80 Squadron and the Spitfires of 92 Squadron, then came on the scene.

450 Squadron reported being attacked by two Bf109s and losing one Kittyhawk which fell in flames. 3 Squadron's pilots counted three Bf109s and claimed damage to two of them. The successful pilots were Keith Kildey (ET840 CV-P) and Sgt. Churchill, (AK862 CV-B).

Lt. Stahlschmidt and Oblt. Unterberger both claimed a Kittyhawk: probably they were jointly responsible for the loss of PO Thomas Forsyth (AK805), whose aircraft spun and hit the ground without the pilot attempting to bale out. Forsyth was flying his twenty-fifth sortie in the twenty-one days since he had joined the squadron.

28 July was a generally quiet day and neither Australian squadron flew operations, although 450 took the opportunity to carry out practice bombing and strafing. One combined operation was flown on the 29th, twenty-two aircraft led by PO Schaaf taking off at 0955 to bomb and strafe motor transport and gun emplacements. One 450 Squadron machine was carrying incendiaries for the first time, but brought its load back due to a faulty electrical system. The bombing was accurate, and four aircraft from 3 then followed up with a strafing attack, damaging a further five M/T, but Sgt Donald's ET576 was hit by the intense heavy A.A. and he crash-landed, returning to the unit the following day.

The Wing did not fly operationally on 30 July, but once again 450 practised; Sgts. Taylor, Oakley O'Neil and Dyson flying from 1746 until 1900.

The month closed with one combined operation, Keith Kildey leading twenty aircraft on an armed recce of the southern battle area from 0810 to 0920. 3 Squadron dropped eleven of their bombs on fifty 'badly dispersed' M/T achieving good results and starting two fires. Both squadrons reported sighting Bf109s over the target, but they were not contacted and no fire was exchanged. If the *Afrika Korps* soldiers on the receiving end of the bombs saw the Bf109s as well, they could be excused for wondering why they had bothered to take off.

The squadrons of 239 Wing were soon to be withdrawn for rest and training, but before this welcome and necessary respite, the two Australian squadrons flew a further sixty-one sorties between them in three operations spread over the first two days of the month. The second of these, again led by Keith Kildey at 1230 on 1 August, was to the south west of El Mirier, and bombs were dropped on a group of M/T and tents which was thought to be a headquarters. All

3 Squadron pilots in Cairo 10/08/42, on the occasion of Sgt. Tom Wood's 21st birthday. Left to right, Ian Roediger, Tom Wood, unknown, Gordon Jones, unknown. (Tom Wood)

aircraft then strafed and a 'terrific explosion' caused a further three tents and three vehicles to be destroyed or damaged.

On 3 August, the squadrons of 239 Wing were released from operations for three weeks, including seven days' leave.

Danny Boardman, Garth Neill, Gordon Scribner and Jack Donald of 3 Squadron at Aboukir beach camp, probably during the squadron's leave period, August 1942. (Tom Russell)

233 Wing was still active however, and on the afternoon of 4 August, Kittyhawks of 260 Squadron were escorting Bostons south west of Alamein, where they were attacked by three Bf109s of III/JG27. Fw. Stegmann shot down one Kittyhawk, and was then shot down himself, probably by Sgt. Ron Cundy, (ET861 HS-V) who claimed his first confirmed victory on this date. (This was his one hundredth operational flight, making a total of 125 ops. hours. By the end of the month, his ops. hours had reached 142.55.)

John Waddy claimed a probable Bf109 with 4 SAAF Squadron south of Derna on 4 August.

260 Squadron was actively engaged for the next ten days, and on 14 August, twelve of their aircraft, with another six from the 57th US Fighter Group* , escorted Bostons to bomb Fuka station. The formation was consistently harried by Bf109s of II/JG 27 and III/JG 53, losing two aircraft from the top cover. Ron Cundy (ET1016, HS-D) claimed one Bf109 probable, and the CO, Sqn. Ldr Devenish, force-landed.

The 57th Fighter Group of the USAAF arrived in Egypt at the beginning of August and joined the DAF Kittyhawk Wings to gain combat experience. The 64th and 65th Squadrons flew with 233 Wing, and the 66th Squadron joined 239 Wing, remaining with it until 17 November. Their introduction to DAF operational procedures did not go smoothly at first, as Bobby Gibbes relates. 'When the 57th Fighter Group arrived in the desert, 66 Squadron under the command of Major Buck Bilby was attached to our wing. Shortly afterwards our operations control rostered them to fly on a wing sweep which I was leading. I asked Buck what formation they were flying, and learning that it was quite different to ours, I refused to take the squadron. There was quite a fuss about it, but I was completely correct as it would have endangered our squadrons to have a number of aircraft flying a completely different formation. I told Buck to take his pilots out and practice the same formation as ours. He did this and later joined us for a period while they got operational experience'. (Correspondence with Bobby Gibbes)

Danny Boardman, Garth Clabburn, Andy Taylor, unknown member of ground crew, 'Donk' Bray and Garth Neill (front) skylarking at the beach camp. (Tom Russell)

John Upward, Norm Caldwell and Tom Wood of 3 Squadron at the Stanley Bay Baths, Alexandria - on leave. (Tom Wood)

Meanwhile, significant changes in the army command were about to take place. In spite of Auchinleck's success in holding the *Afrika Korps* at Alamein, Churchill became convinced that another commander must be chosen for the Middle East. His intention was to replace Auchinleck with General Harold Alexander, while General W.H.E. Gott would take over the 8th Army. Before these changes could be put into place, Gott was killed on 7 August when a Bristol Bombay of 216 Squadron in which he was a passenger was shot down by Uffz. Schneider of II/JG 27. His replacement was General Bernard Montgomery. Alexander took over from Auchinleck on 9 August, and Montgomery left for the Middle East the following day.

While 450 Squadron did no flying until 10 August, 3 were busy training and assimilating seventeen new pilots. Sgt. I.H. Roediger landed heavily on 5 August after a practice flight, causing Cat. II damage to his aircraft, and another new pilot, Sgt. J.J. Manderson, was killed while practice flying in a 250 Squadron aircraft on 6 August. 112 Squadron also lost a new pilot on 15 August when Canadian Sgt. H.V.Schofield crashed, and Sgt. P.O. McTaggart of 3 Squadron lost his life on 18 August when he spun in after losing control while practice bombing. An inquiry followed, and the new pilots were sent to 21 P.T.C. prior to attachment to an O.T.U. for further training.

The other squadrons resumed training on 12 August, carrying out practice sorties in formation flying, bombing, strafing, aerobatics, dogfighting, shadow shooting and 'bounces'. Operations resumed on 20 August.

450 Squadron pilots outside their mess tent at LG 91, Amiriya, Egypt, late July or early August 1942. Back row, left to right: Jack Phelps, Rod Hughes, George O'Neil, Max Jenkins, Frank Parker, Ray Dyson, 'Frank' Shillabeer, 'Junior' Davidson. Front row, left to right: 'Willy' Williams, Don McBurnie, Frank Schaaf, 'Blondie' Gordon Lindsay, Andy Taylor, Dick Winn (face only), 'Mouse' House, Vince McFarlane, Al Markle, Alan Ferguson, CO. (Caption and photograph, Al Markle, via George James - 450 Squadron Association)

A number of armed recces and bombing operations were carried out over the next three days, the two Australian squadrons flying fifty-nine sorties. Then on 23 August, 3 Squadron encountered the enemy in the air again; the first time in almost a month.

Eight aircraft led by Bobby Gibbes took off at 0815 as top cover to 450 Squadron, on an armed recce to the Deir El Qattara area. They dropped their bombs on 200-plus dispersed M/T and were attacked by three Bf109s and an MC202 as they were returning. Lt. Stahlschmidt attacked ET875, flown by F/Sgt. Reg Stevens. It burst into flames and Stevens baled out with slight burns, returning to the unit by 1700 on the same day. As the Germans attacked, Gibbes called for a turnabout and both he and Sgt. H.J. (Donk) Bray got in quick bursts, without result. Bray (AK939 CV-Z) then noticed another enemy fighter well above the formation enter a steep dive and pull up to attack one 3 Squadron aircraft from below. He

.... turned and met this in a head on attack, firing a short burst as I closed in. The enemy aircraft then turned away downwards and I had no difficulty in turning on to his tail. When at a range of approximately 100 yards dead astern I fired a longish burst at the aircraft. Black smoke commenced to pour from it almost immediately and he continued in a shallow dive in a north westerly direction.

Bray broke off due to other enemy aircraft attacking the formation, and claimed a damaged, which was later upgraded to a probable. Gibbes, flying a new aircraft (ET953) for the first time, got in another burst which resulted in another damaged claim. One of the Messerschmitts followed the squadron back to their landing ground, and made an ineffective attack on Sgt. Rex Bayly at 4,500 ft.

Eleven further armed recces were flown by the two squadrons over the next five days and then on 29 August there was another clash with JG 27. At 0905, four aircraft of 450 Squadron led by PO Neil Shillabeer, took off as top cover for a further eight from 3 Squadron, led by Danny

Tom Wood, 'Donk' Bray, Reg Stevens (at rear), Gordon Scribner, John Upward and Danny Boardman of 3 Squadron on the ops truck outside the mess, on the way to the ops tent. (Tom Wood)

Boardman. The top cover was attacked by two Bf109s from II Gruppe, and PO Shillabeer (ET1029) went down immediately, shot down by Uffz. Schneider. Sgt. Garth Neill (ET953 CV-V) saw the attack on Shillabeer, who was killed when his aircraft crashed in an inverted spin. Neill fired four bursts at the Messerschmitt and claimed it as damaged.

Four more 109s from I Gruppe had scrambled, and moments later reached the Kittyhawks' altitude. Hpt. Homuth shot down another Kittyhawk, flown by Canadian Sgt. Al Markle (ET918).

On August 29th I almost met my maker. By the Grace of God and the intervention of two armoured cars of the 11th Hussars (British) I was spared to fight another day. The laconic "log" entry:

Kittyhawk OK-W (self), dive bombing - armed "recco" T(top) cover, op #28, time 40 minutes. Skull and crossbones. Shot down supposedly by ack ack fire over El Alamein line. P.O. Shillabeer missing, F.O. Marting, Sgt. Harrison and myself top cover to #3 Squadron. Had dropped 250 pounder. Almost direct hit in cockpit at 5000'. Went through all preliminaries prior to "bailing" out. Changed my mind - crash landed west and south of Lake Maghra, southern most side of Kattara (sic) Depression. Flying glass splinters in scalp, left knee, right hand, also back (right shoulder). Cut forehead on gunsight. Picked up 1 1/2 hrs. later by two armoured cars (11th Hussars). Rushed to Burg El Arab, thence to No. 1 General Hospital by ambulance train.

But there was much, much more. Every day's tumult of war reinforced an abiding faith. Catastrophe couldn't happen to you. When it did, the shock of reality turned seconds into a lifetime.

With a great thud and roar the canopy perspex shattered. Blood speckles dotted the "stick" hand. A light headed feeling as blood streamed from the scalp. Coolant gauge flickering red. Glycol could "blow" any time. Elevation near 3,000'. Bail out or "prang" wheels up? Too low for the former. Just maybe scrape over the tail end of the escarpment. What will Mom say? Big black mushroom, right on the Depression. Must be "Shill" - went straight in. Shoulder harness OK. Stretch the glide. Nose up. Just made it. Stall. Whump. Out, out. She could go up. For a moment a wave of helplessness. Could scarcely move. Weak and giddy. The only exit - grip the side of the cockpit, pull up with all you've got. Flop on the wing and out. Shade! Shade! Crawl under the tail. Where in the blinkin' Desert am I? First aid. Blasted flies swarming. Medical supplies and rations they said, in panel at rear. What side? Gotcha. A tube of ugly purple ointment. A roll of bandages. Squirt over the head and wrap around. It's got to be No-Man's-Land. Which side are the Jerries"? Have my "Smith and Wesson" but it won't do any good. Can't stand the heat. Back to the shade. This place is deserted. Wonder if anybody saw me "pancake"?

Away off. Two puffs of dust heading my way. No use checking the side arm. This is it. OK - friend or foe? Looked like two tanks with pennants fluttering. Can't see with the desert shimmering. Could be a mirage. Closer now, one heads out to the left (the "Jerry" side)' the other straight at me. Chap with a "berri" standing in the turret. Not tanks but armoured cars. His first words "Are you badly hurt?"

Thank God for the "Brits".

No time for pleasantries. This was hostile country. Jerry could intervene at any time. Quick like Flynn a primus stove had boiling water. Bandages rudely off. Quick head scrub. Up and in with the 11th Hussars. Off to "advance" hospital.

No nonsense place this. First a shot of anti-tetanus. Possible "lock-jaw" from the flies, old chap. In a light headed state I recall a strenuous verbal battle with the Doc (British Major). Suddenly a consuming passion to hang on to my pistol. Of course, it had to be surrendered. Finally they said yes, in writing, they'd return it.

It was the injection that really did it. We'd had lots of needles in training. A piece of cake. Invited to lie on a stretcher. Thank you, I'll stand. Suddenly everything blank. The stretcher it was. Have had an aversion to needles ever since.

Poor devils. They'd just come out of the "line". Many of them badly busted up. My discomforts seemed minuscule to theirs. Within a day a Red Cross convoy had been whistled up. Stretcher cases were stacked along the side walls. Able to move about in the gangway. I could help those who weren't going anywhere on their own. Our destination - No. 1 Military Hospital, Cairo. Dug in sand we were within birdshot of the Suez Canal. Quite a sight and quite a spot. Seemed anytime, day or night, great ships, like huge "Colossi" moved serenely across the desert dunes. The effect was mesmerising.

The minor perspex wounds to hand, head and knee were healing nicely. Began feeling more like oneself. The service and food was excellent.

Ushered into surgery the British "Doc" took an X-ray of the shoulder. Confirmed, a fair chunk of foreign substance there. Also a nasty bit of something at the base of the skull. The shoulder bit wasn't bothering. Surgery would only hack up the area. Decided to leave well enough alone. The "skull" job was something else. First a "local" then the "Doc" got busy with "pliers" (forceps). It had to be a chunk of perspex. Great grating going on. Forceps slipped. "Doc" suggested some firm leverage. When he pulled one way I'd go another. That did it. Dangling a small blood drenched object, I remember his exact words.

"Markle, does this look like perspex to you?"

Unbelievable. The head of an armour piercing bullet. So much for the "ack ack" theory. "Shill" and I were swastika statistics for one or more of Hitler's desert "aces". No question. The "nasty business" had enough gumption to penetrate the cockpit's armour plating. Just a bit more get up and go and it would have been "curtains". [8]

Canadian Sgt. Al Markle of 450 Squadron, who was shot down on 29 August by Hpt. Homuth of 3/JG 27, and later had a piece of armour piercing bullet removed from the base of his skull.
(Al Markle, via George James - 450 Squadron Association)

On 30 August six aircraft of 3 Squadron flew a fighter sweep over the forward area at 0915. They were attacked by four Bf109s north west of Deir El Abyad, the CO's machine being hit in the tail. Sgts. Bray and Thomas both fired, without visible results.

On the same day, Sgt. Hec Hannaford (AK907 LD-F) finished his eventful time with 250 Squadron by flying a long fighter sweep, which lasted 2 hours and 25 minutes. True to form, he found himself engaged with six Bf109s, but on this occasion, he returned intact, with 65 very eventful operational hours behind him. On 1 September, he was posted to 450 Squadron, where two days later, he once again found himself the focus of attention of numerous Axis pilots.

While Montgomery settled in as commander of the 8th Army, Rommel was planning a last desperate attack which would break through to Cairo and the Suez Canal. Although short of all the necessary resources, and only able to add to them slowly, due to the constant threat to his convoys by the rejuvenated forces in Malta, his only alternative was to wait while the British built up their strength. Consequently, he decided to attack on the night of 30 August, penetrate the British minefields in the south, and then turn north to outflank his enemy. It was a desperate gamble, and was doomed to failure.

In the Battle of Alam El Halfa which followed, 239 Wing's squadrons were not called upon to act as fighter-bombers, instead devoting most of their efforts to escorting Bostons and Baltimores and carrying out fighter sweeps. Each of the Australian squadrons flew one uneventful escort operation on 31 August but the tempo of operations increased markedly the next day.

Six Kittyhawks of 450 Squadron led by the CO took off at 0738 as top cover for eighteen Bostons. 3 Squadron followed seven minutes later as medium cover. As the bombers were commencing their attack from 13,000 ft., four Bf109s were seen at the same level, two coming in to attack. Sqn. Ldr. Alan Ferguson (EV169) made a beam attack on one, which was seen to go down on its back, black smoke being observed on the ground afterwards. 3 Squadron were not close enough to join the fight, but made the interesting observation that the formation was attacked by 'two E/A thought to be Heinkel 113s, but probably MC202s'.

Another combined escort was carried out from 1020 to 1125 without contacting enemy aircraft, but at 1400 the Wing was scrambled to intercept enemy aircraft east of El Alamein. At 1500 they had reached 13,000 ft and 3 Squadron, acting as top cover, was attacked ineffectively by two Bf109s. Fifteen minutes later thirty-plus Ju87s escorted by thirty-plus Bf109s were seen lower down. 3 and 450 Squadrons attacked the 109s, while 112 Squadron went after the Stukas, claiming four and one damaged.

Bobby Gibbes (ET953 CV-V) fired at five different 109s, one of which dived away with glycol and smoke pouring from it after an attack which began from the port beam, ending from dead astern. He claimed it as a probable, but it was later confirmed as destroyed by 239 Wing. Sgt. Wood's aircraft (AK776) had developed an oil leak which spread over the port side of his cockpit, and with his vision obscured he was badly shot up, probably by Fw. Fink of III/JG 53, who claimed a victory.

Fl. Lt. Williams (EV367) of 450 Squadron attacked a Bf109 from quarter to fine quarter and saw his De Wilde ammunition hit the fuselage near the cockpit. He claimed a damaged.

Sgt. Lindsay (EV158) attacked a 109E from astern, getting in several good long bursts. The E/A rolled onto its back, followed by Lindsay, who lost sight of it when pulling out close to the ground. He later saw an aircraft fire, but as he was uncertain whether it was the machine he had attacked, he claimed only a probable.

F/Sgt. McFarlane (AK907) attacked a 109 from above with 80 to 90 degrees of deflection. The E/A turned into him, so McFarlane climbed and resumed his attack with another burst at 30 degrees deflection, closing to 100 yards. White smoke began to stream from the 109, which headed west. He continued his attack and the E/A was last seen issuing black smoke in a 45 degree dive. Sgt. McFarlane also claimed a probable.

Sgt Ewing (AK615) saw a 109 break away from three Kittyhawks and gave it a three second burst from beam to aft, but broke off his attack without making a claim when he saw another Kittyhawk attacking from dead astern and black smoke issuing from the E/A.

The aircraft attacked by 450 Squadron were all Bf109Es, and it seems likely that one of them was flown by Major Roland Bohrt, the *Kommandeur* of III/ZG 1, who was shot down on 1 September, dying from his wounds on the 9th. 450 was the only squadron to report contact with Bf109Es, and as ZG 1 was a ground attack unit, it is likely that they would have been with the Stukas.

239 Wing did not lose an aircraft, and owing to the large number of German fighters present, Gibbes later felt that they 'were lucky to get away with it so completely'.[9]

When the aircraft returned, the pilots found a 'Sun' war correspondent in the mess, who sent this colourful report back to Australia, under the following headline.

FLEW "BLIND" INTO 70 NAZI AIRCRAFT
From the Sun's special correspondent with the A.I.F.

WESTERN DESERT, Wednesday. Sgt. Tom Wood of Lane Cove, Sydney, flew into 30 Messerschmitts and more than 40 Stukas with his cockpit screen smothered in oil, preventing him from seeing. The oil pipe burst as the fleet of enemy planes was sighted by R.A.A.F. and R.A.F. fighters which had gone out to intercept them.

"I didn't want to miss the fun," Wood told me.

His horrified colleagues saw two Messerschmitts dive on the blinded pilot. German bullets tore through his Kittyhawk from propeller blades to tail and then Squadron Leader Gibbes, of Manly, and Sergeant Caldwell of S.A. swooped down on the attackers.

Alternately dipping the nose of his fighter to peer through the reflector sight and straightening up to fire his guns, Wood continued in the battle until seven enemy planes had been destroyed and some badly damaged. The rest fled.[10]

The correspondent (William Munday) has obviously included the probable claims of 450 Squadron in his report, but nevertheless it makes fascinating reading, and appeared in four different publications back in Australia.

One more escort was flown at 1820 before the day ended, six aircraft from each squadron escorting twelve Baltimores. 450 Squadron, providing the medium cover, saw twenty-plus E/A emerge from out of the sun, but were not attacked, while 3 Squadron acting as close cover were attacked by four Bf109s just before the Baltimores bombed, but no one was hit. One of the Baltimores was hit by flak and spun in.

One of Sqn. Ldr. Bobby Gibbes' distinctively marked Kittyhawks. A Mark IA, it is probably ET953, CV-V, in which he shot down a Bf109 on 1 September. (RAAF Museum)

On 2 September there were three combined escorts to Baltimores, and 450 Squadron also escorted Bostons, but only on one occasion were enemy aircraft seen. This was on the last operation of the day, at 1705, when four Bf109s were sighted 4,000 ft higher and half a mile behind. These aircraft stayed with the formation for the rest of its outward journey and followed it back to within twenty miles of base without making any effort to mount an attack.

On the following day twelve aircraft from the two squadrons escorted twelve Baltimores from 0725 to 0825, sighting seven Bf109s 3,000 ft. above. Two of these came down to within 1,500 ft and pulled back up without attacking. There was a similar occurrence during the next operation at 1045, when two Bf109s were sighted 3-4,000 ft. above, but made no move to attack.

The Germans finally made an attempt during the third operation of the day, when an estimated sixteen Bf109s and MC202s attacked the two Australian squadrons after the Baltimores had bombed. Five 450 aircraft led by Sgt. Hannaford, (formerly of 250 Squadron) were top cover, and were attacked by four of the 109s during a left turn. One succeeded in getting through the top cover and was promptly attacked by PO Alf Glendinning (ET322 CV-S) of 3 Squadron, which was flying medium cover on this occasion. He got in several good bursts from close range and followed the E/A down, but was forced to break off due to his cockpit canopy opening. Sgts. Scribner and Caldwell fired at the same aircraft. Glendinning claimed a probable and Scribner was awarded a damaged. More of the German fighters came down, and attacks continued all the way back to Burg El Arab. Sgt W.W. Thomas (EV167) was severely wounded but managed to bring his aircraft back for a successful belly landing. His aircraft was Cat. II. He may have been the victim of Oblt. Sinner, who claimed one victory in this combat.

F/Sgt. Dyson of 450 fired at two different 109s, the first of which received three long bursts from quarter astern, 'went up, then fell on back and went down, apparently out of control'. Dyson claimed a probable. Sgt Hannaford (EV367), who was posted in from 250 Squadron on 1 September, saw a 109E attacking Dyson and drove it off, attacking from the starboard quarter and seeing tracer hit the engine and cockpit. He was forced to break off when he was attacked by two MC202s. Hannaford was wounded and crash-landed at base with Cat. II damage to his aircraft. Dyson saw the aircraft which Hannaford attacked 'pull out to the right, turn on its back and dive vertically to earth'. This observation was the basis for Hannaford's probable claim.

The German fighters seem to have been reluctant to attack escorted bombers, even when having the advantage of superior numbers, as they did on this occasion, while their comrades on the ground had 'nothing to do but wait and endure the air attacks'.[11]

3rd September: Jerry is still falling back in the Central sector after losing ninety tanks, scores of trucks and two thousand men. He has been using smoke screens to try and cover his movements. According to our pilots the battle-field is a scene of charred desolation defying any description. The Allied Air Force has command of the skies and [is] making good use of it. Hannaford and Dyson each shot down a 109E whilst on a late sortie this evening. Hannaford was then attacked by several Macchis and ME109's, but proved too good for them. He belly-landed here suffering from shrapnel wounds and loss of blood, but still smiling. (Viv Herrett)

During the day Rommel's frustrated and battered forces began to withdraw as a result of the relentless bombing attacks, and 'Air observers, on September 3, had the satisfaction of seeing the Axis forces in full retreat'.[12]

The *Luftwaffe* failed entirely to carry out its directed tasks, and was completely incapable of interfering with the light bombers. On 4 September, the squadrons of 239 Wing were called on to fly only one bomber escort, which did not meet enemy aircraft.

In a confused and badly controlled engagement on 5 September, 450 Squadron claimed three damaged Bf109s, while suffering Cat. II to one of their own aircraft. Five Kittyhawks from 450 were scrambled with others from 3, 112, 250, and Spitfires of 145 Squadron at 1130, to intercept reported enemy aircraft. When the formation was at 10,500 ft. Control informed them that the bandits had bombed and were twenty-four miles south west of Alamein at angels four, heading west. They were then told that the bandits were south of El Daba and going north west. This provided a consistent enough track, but at this stage

> top cover were attacked by E/A and top cover leader gave a 'turn about', whereupon our A/C also turned. Control then instructed leader to 'pancake'. A/C then turned east, but were informed group of 'schnappers' (sic) at 17,000 ft. E along railway. Saw three 109Fs dive out of sun to cloud level. We turned to attack E/A. They climbed and we followed, gaining on them. Four 109s came down from 11 o'clock to join others. An engagement followed. Four of our A/C fired.

Sgt Oakley (EV158), Sgt. Lindsay (EV160) and F/Sgt. McQueen (AL157) all claimed a damaged, and Oakley's aircraft received Cat. II damage, without injury to the pilot. 112 lost an aircraft and the Spitfires lost two, while 250 was unscathed, and 3 Squadron was not engaged.

A 450 Squadron aircraft about to undergo gun harmonisation. Ted Lawler is on the left, supporting the tail plane. Note the lifting rod which passes through the rear fuselage. The attitude of the aircraft will be set by an adjustable stand, held ready by the man in the foreground. (Ted Lawler)

Twenty-four more sorties were flown in the afternoon without contacting the enemy, and both squadrons flew only one uneventful operation each on 6 and 7 September, but on 8 September they were involved in a lively and successful action in the afternoon.

At 1320, 3 and 450 Squadrons were scrambled from readiness with 145's Spitfires to intercept enemy aircraft near El Alamein. On this occasion the controller put the Kittyhawks in a good position to make their attack, and F/Sgt Danny Boardman, leading eight 3 Squadron aircraft as top cover to eight more from 450, saw eighteen-plus Stukas and only six Bf109s at 9 o'clock almost at ground level. The Kittyhawks were at 7,000 ft. and cloud base was 6,000. The pilots reported 3/10 cloud cover, so the remaining *twenty-two* Bf109s were obviously not acting as close cover. Sgt. G.G. Scribner later recorded that there were twenty 109s and 202s as escort, but he didn't know that when Boardman, with his transmitter U/S, waggled his wings and dived head on at the Stukas. Sgt. Garth Neill, (AL167 CV-F) flying as Blue 1 carried out a vertical attack on a Stuka with no visible result, then 'turned right and did a head on attack on one Stuka which struck the ground and turned over'. The Stukas got off lightly. Scribner (AK778 CV-J) got a good burst at one, and then pulled up steeply to rejoin the formation. So did the other pilots, who became suddenly aware that there were rather more 109s about than they had first anticipated. After the first attack Boardman (EV322 CV-I)

> climbed up and saw in all 20+ 109Fs, 109Es and 202s, which were circling at 3/5,000. A dogfight ensued for approx. 25 mins. I made 6 attacks on different e/a and on one attack on two 109Fs (with yellow noses) I hit No. 1 a/c from engine to rear of cockpit. A piece flew off hood and e/a went into a gentle glide to deck level with engine smoking.

Sgt Neill reported that

> the 6 109s had turned away to attack other Kittyhawks. I climbed up to 3,000 ft. and dived on one 109 which I chased to ground level, fired five bursts into it and the E/A crashed among enemy tents. It did not burn. After being attacked several times by 109s I climbed up again to 2,000 ft. and attacked a 109F which had just broken off an attack on a Kittyhawk and gave it three bursts as it went climbing away. The E/A went into a spin and I last saw it still spinning below 1,000 ft.

Sgt. Scribner recorded his first and only victory in this combat. As he was climbing to rejoin the formation

> a 109 made an attack on 2 Kittyhawks which were slightly above me. As I turned now slightly above the Kittys, another 109 made a similar attack, breaking away into a climbing turn. As he did this he gave me a perfect quarter attack. I saw my bullets hitting the cowl and back to the cabin. Whitish smoke started to pour from the engine ports, and he rolled over and dived away towards the S.W. with whitish smoke nearly hiding him from view. F/Sgt Boardman also saw an a/c diving towards the S.W.

> As I was watching this e/a I was hit by cannon fire from another 109. I did a steep turn as he broke away upwards and noticed the hole where I was hit in the tail. I then observed a fire in the S.W. where I had last seen the 109 heading. I was then attacked by three light chocolate coloured 202s. I managed to get a good burst into one as he broke downwards. I chased him and was able to give him a quarter attack from 300 yards and saw tracers striking wings and fuselage. He then dived away steeply.

Sgt. Scribner was then involved with four more 109s which gave him 'a very busy time', hitting his aircraft three times, but he fired bursts at two of them, one of which he hit, causing it to break off and dive away to the west. Danny Boardman also found '109s everywhere and on my tail'. He fired two good bursts into a mottled 109E which flicked and dived away.

Sgt. Taylor (EV169) of 450 had also attacked the Stukas without result, but then climbed to attack (optimistically) *eight* 109s, and claimed a probable, when a 109 which had attacked him from head on 'broke off attack at 500 yards and continued straight on in dive with white smoke coming from him'.

Above all this mayhem the Spitfires of 145 Squadron claimed another Messerschmitt and lost one of their own aircraft. The sole Australian casualty was Sgt. Freer (AK625) of 3 Squadron who crash landed with minor wounds in a minefield.

German claims were for one damaged smoking fighter, (Uffz. Jurgens, II/ JG 27), two Spitfires, (Lt. Schroer, III JG/27), and one fighter, (Ofw. Stumpf, III/JG 53),[13] while no losses were reported. It can only be assumed that the pilots of the fighters attacked by Neill and Scribner were unwounded, and therefore the loss of the aircraft was not sufficient cause to record a loss to the unit, which only reported KIA or KIFA as actual losses.

The Australians claimed one Ju87 destroyed, (Neill) two Bf109s destroyed, (Neill and Scribner) three Bf109s probable (Neill, Boardman and Taylor) and one MC202 damaged (Scribner).

After this day's exciting events, both squadrons were released from operations for the next two days. They each flew two scrambles on 11 September, but the controller could not bring them into contact with enemy aircraft on either occasion.

450 Squadron enjoyed a successful day on 12 September. At 1004, Fl. Lt. Williams (EV363), led ten of 450's aircraft, in company with six from 112 and several more from 250 to carry out a fighter patrol over the line, perhaps because of the recent increased activity from the Ju87s and the difficulties the controllers were having in effecting interceptions before the Stukas could bomb. The formation found twenty five Ju87s and fourteen Bf109s, 450 reporting only five Stukas and ten 109s through the broken cloud cover below them. Flying at the bottom of the formation, 450 attacked the 109s and then plunged through them to get to the Stukas, which were heading west, so it would appear that this formation had also dropped their bombs. Sgt Ted Oakley

3 Squadron Kittyhawks about to take off in September 1942. The second aircraft, CV-I, is a late model Mark IA, in spite of its extended fin. In the original print, the letter E is visible as the first part of its serial number, identifying it as such.(Mark IIIs carried FR serial prefixes.) The dark tone of the squadron codes indicates that they were Azure Blue rather than white, and the older style of fin flash on the first aircraft suggests that it is a survivor from earlier in the year. It is almost certainly AK778, which carried CV-J on 8 September, when Sgt. Gordon Scribner used it to shoot down a Bf109, as well as damaging another 109 and a MC202. CV-I on the same date was EV322, a newer aircraft from the last serial block of Kittyhawk Mark IAs, and therefore likely to have had a modified fin. It first flew with the squadron on 4 September. Danny Boardman was flying it when he damaged a Bf109 on 8 September, also claiming a probable in it on the 13th. Sgt. Gordon Scribner lost his life when EV322 was shot down on 15 September. John Hooke and Tom Wood both flew AK778 on many occasions.
(RAAF Museum)

(ET869) claimed a Bf109E. (This obsolescent type was being reported with increasing frequency, serving with I/SG 2 as fighter bombers and 4(H)/12 for tactical reconnaissance duties. Either some had been pressed into service with the fighter units as replacements, or these two units were on occasion carrying out fighter missions in addition to their normal functions.)

The Stukas were attacked from above, astern and from the fine quarter, and 450 quickly made up for any missed opportunities on 8 September when Fl. Lt. Williams destroyed two of the dive bombers and damaged a third. 112 Squadron also hit the Stukas, claiming one destroyed, two probable and five damaged, as well as a damaged 109.

One of 112 Squadron's aircraft received Cat. II damage and three from 450 returned with Cat.I damage, probably inflicted by Ofw. Stumpf and Uffz Nairz. of III/JG 53, both of whom claimed Kittyhawks. Two aircraft, flown by Oakley and Sgt. Reg Watt, landed away due to petrol shortage, but both returned later.

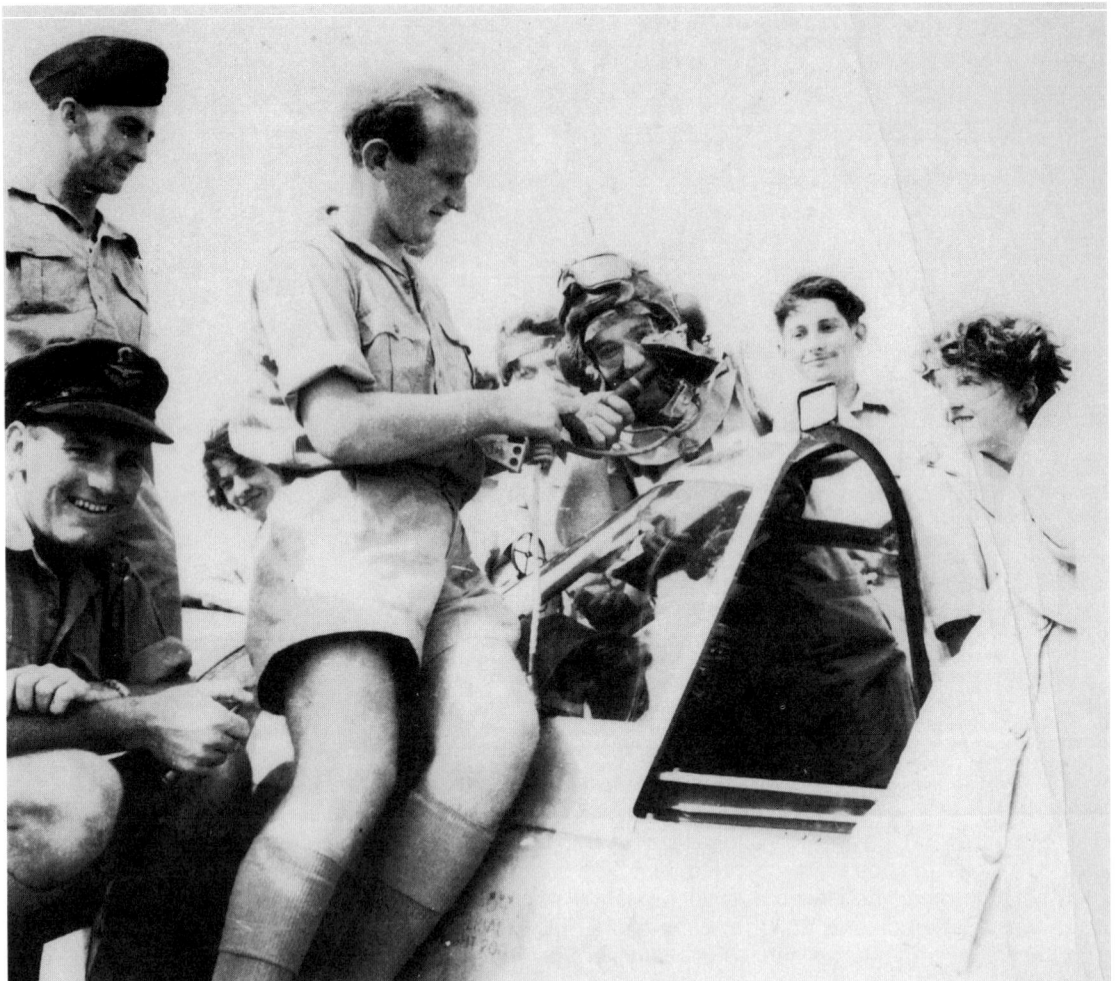

On 12 September, 3 Squadron received a visit from a party of sisters and V.A.D.s from the 7th Australian General Hospital. They were royally received, and shown over the Squadron's aircraft. Sgt. Keith Kildey, the effective leader of 'C' Flight, is assisting one of the ladies as she dons a flying helmet and oxygen mask. Danny Boardman is kneeling, at left. (Keith Kildey)

It was 3 Squadron's turn in the early morning of 13 September. At 0800 Danny Boardman, again flying EV322, led sixteen aircraft from 3 and 450 Squadrons with 250 Squadron as top cover in a scramble. Six enemy aircraft were reported twenty miles south west of El Alamein, and 450 Squadron, at the bottom of the formation, was initially attacked by two Bf109s, (four, according to 450 Squadron pilots, who reported being attacked ineffectively for ten minutes). Boardman fired two long bursts into the belly of the trailing aircraft, which produced a stream of glycol, and it broke off downwards, turning west. It was claimed as a probable. Bf109s from III/JG 27 were escorting Stukas at this time, and reported meeting eight Hurricanes, ten Kittyhawks and some Spitfires near El Alamein. Lt. Herfried Korner's aircraft was hit in the cooling system and force landed in Axis territory.[14] He might have been Boardman's target.

An early afternoon scramble produced no results, but at 1730 a full wing scramble led by Sqn. Ldr. Billy Drake, the aggressive CO of 112 Squadron, made contact with thirty-seven Bf109s from JG 27 and JG 53 escorting Stukas. Drake shot down a 109 and other members of his squadron claimed a probable and a damaged. 450 were the middle squadron on this occasion

and although they dived with 112 they did not score, and climbed away again to resume their task of medium cover. 3 Squadron were top cover, and stayed there, as other enemy fighters were seen higher up.

At 1035 on 14 September, 3 and 450 Squadrons were scrambled to intercept an enemy formation near Alamein. Fl. Lt. Charlie Coward (EV361 CV-C), who was nearing the end of his tour, led the formation with 450 as top cover. When they were almost due south of Alamein, just as the controller informed them that six E/A were in the vicinity *above* the formation, Coward saw six 109Es 4 to 5,000 ft below, and ordered the formation to attack.

> I made a rear quarter attack on one of the 109s and observed De Wilde bursts on wings and fuselage. The E/A immediately dived to ground level and myself and Sgt. Jones followed him down. I made two more stern attacks on him closing up to 20-30 yds., and observed more bursts on his A/C.

As Coward broke away to avoid overshooting, Jones (EV323 CV-X) delivered 'two long bursts from 300 yds. closing to 25 yds. range' but he too was forced to pull out due to his greater speed.

The 109 was claimed by both pilots as a shared probable, but was subsequently confirmed as destroyed.

Unidentified armourer, Rex Bayly, Tom Wood, Jack Donald and Kevin Springbett on Kittyhawk wing receiving instructions on rearming. (Tom Wood)

On 15 September, there was good news for Sgts. Alderson, Boardman, Bray, Clabburn, Donald, Finlason, Kildey and Thomas of 3 Squadron, who were all commissioned. In the afternoon, PO Kildey led eight aircraft, accompanied by ten more from 450 Squadron as top cover on a scramble to intercept a Stuka raid escorted by almost the entire strength of JG 27, forty-three Bf109s from all three Gruppen. 112 and 250 Squadrons also scrambled with eighteen aircraft to provide the top cover.

South west of Alamein at 12,000 ft. the two Australian squadrons sighted eleven Bf109s above them in two layers at 13-14,000 ft. The 109s attacked and 'in general engagement our formation broke up, individual pairs doing figure of eight turns into the sun'.[15] PO Clabburn (ET824 CV-K), who made 3 Squadron's only claim, submitted the following combat report.

> I was flying No. 2 in Blue section in a formation of eight Kittyhawks, and was in a right hand turn when I saw one ME109F coming down to attack Blue 1 (Sgt Donald) and I continued in the turn and got in a 2 second burst from 50 yds. full deflection attack. I saw my explosive ammo. strike E/A from nose to tail. It went into a long shallow dive due west, leaving a trail of white smoke.
>
> I was then attacked by another ME109F, and was unable to observe what subsequently became of the E/A
>
> I had fired on.

Clabburn's report was supported by Sgts. Bee and MacKenzie, and his probable claim was later upgraded to a destroyed.

In spite of Clabburn's efforts, Jacky Donald's Kittyhawk (EV345) had the port aileron shot away and the engine set on fire.* He baled out, landing by parachute on an Italian mess tent. Sgt. Gordon Scribner (EV322 CV-I) was shot down and killed.

More 109s joined the fight, which went on for almost fifteen minutes, gradually losing height to 4,000 ft. 450 Squadron's FO 'Tex' Marting, (EV160) an American who had enlisted with the RCAF, claimed a Bf109 destroyed, which was confirmed by Sgts Davidson and Watt, and another 109 damaged, also seen by Sgt. Davidson. Sgt. Gleeson (EV324) fired at a 109 which lost its canopy as it dived away. It was claimed as a probable, and later confirmed. (See Appendix 3) 450 Squadron lost one aircraft; Sgt P.A. Ewing (ET869) received cannon hits in the wing which severed his control cables. He baled out and landed among panzers.**

Keith Kildey (EV346 CV-U) claimed a damaged 109 and in turn had the tail of his aircraft badly damaged. Sgt. Ken Bee in AK867 was wounded, but managed to bring his aircraft back to base.

As the embattled Australians were fighting for their lives, 112 and 250 Squadrons joined the unequal battle with a height advantage, which relieved the pressure. However, 250 Squadron lost two aircraft, one of which had a wing shot away. This may have been the Kittyhawk reported by 450 Squadron to have been involved in a collision with a Messerschmitt. In fact, the collision was between Lt. Hoffmann (I Gruppe) and Uffz Prien (II Gruppe). Hoffmann baled out; Prien was killed.

Sgt. Des Cormack, (ET977 LD-C) who was leading the top section of 250 Squadron, claimed a probable, the unit's only success.

> Sgt. Cormack leading top section of 250 Squadron acting as top cover to 112 Squadron going south saw 4 ME 109s at 3 o'clock in sun. 112 Sqdn turned left away. Sgt. Cormack ordered his section turn about left into sun flew north and were dived on from behind by two 109's. Sgt Cormack turned into enemy aircraft foiling their attack and on completion of 360° turn saw two a/c above and to left app 300 yds away fired 1 to 2 sec burst at leading a/c and saw thin trail of dense white smoke from behind. F/Sgt. Chap flying little behind Sgt. Cormack confirmed seeing white smoke. Sgt. Cormack was not able to maintain attack as he was attacked from behind by further e/a.

(His log book notes that it was confirmed by the Army on 17 September.) 112 fared little better, losing one Kittyhawk and making no claims.

---

* (AWM 54 779/3/29)

** (AWM 54 779/3/29)

As the battle drew to a close, the desert was littered with aircraft fires, three parachutes hung in the sky and a smoking 109 dived away to the west, while a Kittyhawk and a 109 continued to spin downwards.

The Australians claimed two destroyed, (Clabburn and Marting) two probables, (Gleeson and Cormack) and three damaged (Marting, Kildey and Sgt. Alderson). Six Kittyhawks in total were lost. German claims were considerably more imaginative.

> At 1715 hours 18 Bf109s of I Gruppe, 15 of II and 10 of III Gruppe finally took to the air on the second mission. 36 Kittyhawks intercepted them. There ensued a series of aerial battles of such proportions not hitherto seen in the skies over the African desert. I Gruppe accounted for eleven kills during several engagements lasting well into the evening. II Gruppe scored one, and III Gruppe brought home seven claims, four of which were scored by Uffz. Krainik alone and another three by Lt. Schroer.

> *During the engagements fought by I Gruppe, which lasted a total of only six minutes, Marseille was able to score against seven of the enemy. Hpt. Homuth and Oblt. Borngen shot down one plane apiece. After this outstanding victory Marseille had brought his account up to 151 kills, meaning that he had reached third place in the absolute record list, - behind Hermann Graf and Gordon Gollob.* [16]

This remarkable list of claims deserves some consideration. Given that in a close combat involving large numbers of aircraft, more than one pilot would often fire at the same aircraft at the same time, it is stretching credibility to the limit to accept that the six aircraft actually shot down each suffered from at least three assailants, none of whom knew anything about the others. It is a wonder that there were not more collisions.

While *most* of the claims submitted by *experten* such as Marseille, Homuth, von Lieres (who claimed two victories in this combat) and Schroer can be substantiated, the exaggerations of 15 September, (which are apparently accepted by Marseille's biographer without question) are difficult to explain. In some cases, such as Marseille's, it might have been due to over confidence brought about by his past successes, leading to the belief that any aircraft he attacked would be destroyed.

Fourteen of the claims on 15 September were made by recognised 'aces'; JG 27's operations book recorded 'eleven victories over our own territory' for I Gruppe.[17] All they had to do was count the crashes.

Werner Schroer made another claim for a 3 Squadron aircraft the following day, but he might have been surprised to discover that the pilot concerned managed to bring his Kittyhawk back to base, albeit slightly the worse for wear. At 0945 PO Danny Boardman led six aircraft of 3 Squadron on a scramble as top cover to 450, with a further eight from 112 as high cover. Two of these were forced to return early, Boardman and Keith Kildey suffering from engine trouble, and PO Dave Ritchie returned when he was unable to catch the rest of the formation. The three remaining aircraft of 3 Squadron were attacked by several of the numerous 109s which were escorting the Stukas that 239 Wing had been sent to intercept. Sgt. Tom Wood was one of pilots involved.

> It was an interception job. We climbed to about 10,000 feet, going through light cloud at approx 2,000 ft. We found six plus ME 109s SSW of El Alamein. A dogfight ensued, during which my aircraft was hit in the wing root with a 20mm. cannon shell which exploded, shooting bits of metal all around, including into my ribs and legs. Reflex action - jammed left rudder on - violently spun. Seemed to be blissfully drifting - suddenly cloud - S___ ! I had better do something ! ! Got out of the spin and headed for home. I was slightly stunned and groggy but managed to get back to L.G. 91 and land after a fashion - overshot the strip and stopped among the oil drums, the propeller stopping just before hitting [one]. I was carted off to a casualty clearing station for X-rays and sulphur drugs, back to the squadron and then off to the beach camp at Dakheila for three or four days with Charlie Coward, who had just finished two tours straight. . . . I was back flying again on the 24th September and on operations by the 27th.[18]

Sgt. Tom Wood relaxing at the Dakheila beach camp, after being shot up and wounded by Lt. Schroer on 16 September. The building in the background was the living quarters. (Tom Wood)

Garth Neill and Charlie Coward had a hectic time before they could break off the engagement. Both returned uninjured and without damage. Lt. Schroer and Lt. Schofbock each claimed a Kittyhawk, but Tom Wood's AK867 was the only aircraft to be hit, neither 112 or 450 Squadrons reporting any damage.

Charlie Coward's first tour commenced with 250 Squadron on 5 May 1941. By December he had joined 3 Squadron, initially helping to convert new pilots on to Tomahawks at OTU. Bobby Gibbes explained the manner of his leaving.

> 17th October. Nothing of importance in the way of ops. Managed to get Charlie Coward posted back home to Australia. Started something of a precedent, as Charles is EATS (Empire Training Scheme). He did 292 ops hours all told. We gave him a farewell party in the mess the night before he left. Hell, what a party. About the wettest in 3 Squadron's history. Doc ended without a stitch on with a blanket wrapped around him. A sorry lot next day.[19]

For the remainder of September, 239 Wing had little further contact with the enemy, and the intensity of operations decreased, 3 Squadron flying only six operations from 16 to 29 September, and 450 seven. On 23 September ten aircraft from 450 led by Sgt. Taylor were flying a practice interception, having taken off at 1030, but after 45 minutes the controller took over and instructed the formation to gain height to 20,000 ft. and vectored them towards Burg El Arab. Enemy fighter-bombers and 'schnappers' (sic) had been reported at 15,000 ft. so 450's formation began descending again to 16,000 ft, when the controller reported E/A going west. 450's pilots then saw the enemy; two 2,000 ft. below and five more at the same level, and an engagement followed. Four Kittyhawks fired, but Sgt. R.J. Prowse (EV339) was the only pilot to make a claim, a damaged Bf109, which he attacked from above the stern quarter. Sgt. Taylor, after avoiding a head on attack from three E/A, 'saw the white bursts from Prowse's shots strike all along the fuselage, and E/A with white smoke coming from it'. The engagement was broken off at 13,000 ft. six miles west of Burg El Arab. None of 450's aircraft were hit.

At much the same time, (1100) six Bf109s of III/JG 27 reported a combat with eight Spitfires over El Hammam while they were escorting 'Jabos' (fighter-bombers) . 'One Spitfire was seen to crash-land south-west of the airfield'.[20] El Hammam and Burg El Arab are some fifteen miles apart, and it would seem likely that these two combats were one and the same. It was much more fashionable to fight Spitfires; indeed, one of Lt. Schroer's claims on the afternoon of 15 September was for a Spitfire. Perhaps the crash-landing 'Spitfire' was Dick Prowse's target, one of the 'Jabos'.

On 27 September, 450 Squadron received new aircraft, which pleased Sgt. Gus Officer, a new arrival on the Squadron. He had been flying

> 'an old clapped out Mark I kite, which was the slowest one in the Squadron. The practice of giving new arrivals the worst kite was widespread throughout the service and had to be accepted ..... 28/9/42 Said good bloody riddance to OK-P. We were re-equipped with brand new Mark III Kittyhawks. Much more pleasant and easier flying, and a cruising speed of 210 m.p.h., but no better at 15,000 feet than the older models'.[21]

Equivalent to the P-40K, the early models had an extended fin with a fillet to reduce the take off swing brought about by the 200 extra horse power available from the new engine, and to improve directional stability. It was supposed to have a marginally improved climb rate compared to the Mark I, but when tested by Sqn. Ldr. Ferguson and Sgt. Taylor on 6 October, it took them sixteen minutes to reach 21,000 ft. using 36 inches of boost. The manufacturer's claimed time was 11.2 minutes to 20,000 ft. compared to 11.5 for the Mark I.

3, 112 and 250 Squadrons were the ungrateful recipients of 450's old aircraft.

A bombed up Kittyhawk Mk III of 450 Squadron, carrying a 500 pounder and six 40 lb wing bombs. 450 received their first Mk IIIs on 27 September. (George James - 450 Squadron Association)

Both Australian squadrons flew together four times on 30 September, escorting Baltimores on the first occasion, and then carrying out three scrambles. Enemy aircraft were sighted on two of these, but were not inclined to fight, as they 'made off at top speed' and the Kittyhawks could not catch them.

On 30 September, Hans-Joachim Marseille, promoted to the rank of Hauptmann on 16 September, lost his life when the engine of a new Bf109G caught fire due to escaping lubricant caused by a failure in the reduction gear. The cockpit filled with smoke and Marseille baled out after crossing the German lines. It seems that he struck the tail unit when he left the aircraft, the resulting injury rendering him incapable of opening his parachute. He claimed a total of 158 Allied aircraft, (151 of them in Africa), many of these being pilots of 239 Wing. His death, following the loss of Obfw. Steinhausen (forty victory claims) and Lt. Stahlschmidt (fifty-nine claims) earlier in the month, caused a severe drop in the morale of I Gruppe, and they were withdrawn to Sicily until late October.

For the Australian squadrons of 239 Wing, October began quietly, 3 and 450 carrying out one patrol at 1627, and although many enemy aircraft were reported by control, no interceptions were made. However, 112 and 250 Squadrons farewelled their old Mark IA Kittyhawks in style.

PO Des Cormack's day began with an early morning air test, followed by an uneventful fighter sweep between 0820 and 0935. From 1325 to 1400 he flew a Mark III Kittyhawk for the first time, and was pleased with the new aircraft, recording in his log book, *A NOTICEABLE IMPROVEMENT MORE SPEED BETTER CLIMB.*

At 1730, 250 and 112 Squadrons were scrambled to intercept enemy aircraft, and were vectored on to a formation of some twenty Stukas of III/St.G 3, escorted by numerous Bf109s. Flying ET977, LD-C, Des Cormack was one of several successful pilots, as his log book relates.

> *AT LONG LAST WE MEET THE STUKAS. WE MET 20 STUKAS ESCORTED BY 20+ FIGHTERS. I SHOT DOWN A STUKA IN FLAMES. FL/LT BARBER SHOT DOWN THREE. F/O CALVER 1 PROBABLE, F/O MILLUCK 1 DAMAGED.*

112 Squadron was flying top cover, and successfully kept the 109s from interfering with 250 Squadron, claiming two Stukas themselves.

112. Fl. Lt. Maurice Barber, left, and PO Des Cormack, after their successful interception of a Stuka formation on 1 October. Barber was appointed CO of 450 Squadron in November when Sqn. Ldr. Williams was shot down and captured. (Des Cormack)

On 2 October, the wing was scrambled from readiness at 0850, twelve aircraft from 3 Squadron providing top cover to a further six from 112. At 0950 Fl. Lt. George Plinston RAF (EV346 CV-O) saw a Bf109 approaching the rear of the formation, pulled around sharply and attacked it from the beam, which immediately produced a trail of glycol. The 109 continued its dive into the ground.

3 and 112 Squadrons, with six Merlin-powered P-40Fs of the 66th Squadron USAAF as top cover, were scrambled again at 1620 to intercept a large formation of Ju87s escorted by Bf109s and probably several Macchi 202s. Keith Kildey, now a Flight Lieutenant, after being commissioned only seventeen days earlier, was leading the unit. 239 Wing ran into the Axis formation over Deir

El Dhib, where 112 Squadron claimed one destroyed and one damaged, and Sgt Garth Neill (ET1016 CV-B) claimed a probable. This, or the damaged claim by 112 Squadron, might in fact have been destroyed, as two Italian fighters flown by Capt. Livio Ceccotti and Ten. Ezio Bevilacque of 4⁰ Stormo were lost during the day.[22] 3 Squadron reported that 'Enemy pilots made very timid attacks, and were thought to be Italian pilots flying 109F'. Aircraft recognition might once again have been faulty.

Sgt Neill's combat report reinforces the possibility that the aircraft engaged were Macchis, as he noted that he was attacked from astern and hit by four small calibre bullets, his attacker then overshooting him and going into a steep turn, which gave Neill the opportunity to 'fire five long bursts into it. A large part of the fuselage fell off the A/C and it rolled onto its back and dived vertically through the clouds emitting a large amount of glycol and black smoke'. Most MC 202s were equipped with two 12.7 mm and two 7.7 mm machine guns. Had his attacker been a Messerschmitt, it is likely that he would have been hit by cannon shells as well as machine gun bullets, as the Bf109's armament was concentrated in the nose. The 'large part of the fuselage' Neill mentioned might have been the pilot baling out, as both Italian pilots were reported to have abandoned their aircraft.

On the same day, 450 Squadron was withdrawn to LG 124 at Mena, officially as part of the air defence of the Delta, but effectively for a rest. 3 Squadron flew a number of sweeps, scrambles and armed recces over the next five days without making contact with the enemy but they recorded an interesting observation on 7 October.

At 1115, PO Danny Boardman led eleven aircraft on an armed recce, with six P-40Fs of the US 66th Squadron as top cover. They bombed dug in M/T and tents, starting one large fire, and then the top cover was attacked by enemy aircraft which did not succeed in doing any harm. The squadron's pilots noted that one of these E/A had a yellow cowling and wing tips, and was thought to be a Focke-Wulf 190. If so, it might have been mis-identified by the Germans, as Uffz. Rohrlack of III/JG 27 claimed an unidentified radial-engined aircraft[23] at much the same time as 3 Squadron observed their "Focke-Wulf". *

At 1610, Keith Kildey led ten aircraft on a bombing mission west of Deir El Qattara. He was flying a new Kittyhawk III, FR305, which at this stage, appears to have been the only example of its type used by 3 Squadron. (Several others were on strength briefly in 1943). Bobby Gibbes later appropriated it as his personal machine, but it was often used by the formation leaders when Gibbes was not flying. On this mission, Sgt MacKenzie force landed AK819 with engine trouble fifteen minutes after taking off; he was uninjured.

The Mark III Kittyhawk must have been acquired by somewhat devious means, as Bobby Gibbes relates.

John Beaman, a well known historian and author on Luftwaffe subjects, confirmed the likelihood of the mysterious aircraft being a Focke-Wulf. 'Erprobungskommando 19 was organised at Flugplatz Castel Benito near Tripoli for a duration of two months. Mission of E-Kdo. 19 was trials with Bf 109G and Fw 190 types for suitability as fighter and Schlachtflugzeug under tropical conditions'. (Correspondence with John Beaman)

Bobby Gibbes had no doubts. He chased after it, thinking it was a G-50. 'I was closing on it when suddenly its pilot saw me and he powered away and left me standing, despite the fact that I was flying a Kitty III'.

Bobby provided a copy of his diary entry for 30 November, which recorded 'Helped the Saafs (South African Air Force) to get the Macchi serviceable and had a look at a Fock Wolf (sic)190 on northern drome.' He went on to explain that the Fw190 was on a graveyard of wrecked Italian and German aircraft near the main aerodrome of Benghazi.(Correspondence with Bobby Gibbes)

450 and 250 are now equipped with Kitty IIIs. I have got hold of one, but am having a hell of a job to stick to it. Ordered to hand it over to 250. Told them where to go. Don't know what the outcome will be. [They] are a slightly better aircraft than the Kitty I. A little faster and a better rate of climb. Has a 1350 H.P. motor against the 1150 in the Kitty I.[24]

FR305 remained on strength until 4 November, by which time the squadron had begun to re-equip with the superior Mark II.

PO Des Cormack of 250 Squadron in a new Kittyhawk Mk III, named *Mary,* after his wife. It is almost certainly FR294 LD-C, which he flew exclusively from the middle of October. (Des Cormack)

There were no operations on 8 October, but plans were afoot to attack the Axis aerodromes at Daba and Fuka the following day. Recent heavy rains had made Fuka barely useable, and Daba was under water. 450 Squadron was recalled from leave, and on 9 October the Desert Air Force flew some 500 sorties, of which the two Australian units contributed fifty.

Both Australian squadrons took off at 0940, 450 led by Fl. Lt. Williams to provide escort to Bostons heading for LG 104 at Daba, with Keith Kildey leading 3 Squadron as their top cover. Both squadrons had instructions to strafe LGs 21 and 104 after the bombing. A number of Bf109s had managed to get airborne, and five of these attacked PO Clabburn of 3 Squadron, but he avoided them and none of the squadron's other aircraft were hit. After strafing, PO Ritchie (EV346 CV-O)

> was doing a climbing turn to the east over the coast, when I saw a ME109E flying north on my right hand side and just behind me and about 300 ft. below. I pulled down onto him, and fired only a short burst from about 200 yds. I saw the strikes on the enemy a/c near the marking on the side of the fuselage. The tail unit came completely off and the balance of the a/c rolled over and went straight into the sea.

Lt. W.J. Mount of the 66th Squadron also claimed a 109 in similar circumstances, and it is possible that both pilots attacked the same aircraft.[25] 3 Squadron was unaware of Mount's presence, and Ritchie's claim was accepted.

The mystery solved. Fw190 A4/U8 of E-Kdo 19 discovered at Benghazi in November 1942 by the SAAF and 3 Squadron. Its performance in the air impressed 3 Squadron's CO Bobby Gibbes, and the photograph indicates that it aroused quite a bit of interest, although in an un-airworthy state. (Doug Norrie)

450 Squadron strafed both landing grounds, experiencing intense light AA over the targets. They estimated that there were 20-plus enemy aircraft dispersed on each LG. Fl. Lt. Clarke claimed damage to a Ju52 and three Bf109s, PO Schaaf claimed damage to a 109, as did Sgt. Cummins. PO Law damaged two 109s and Sgt Oakley strafed a Ju88 and an AA post. A number of vehicles and tents also received the squadron's attention. PO Schaaf observed an aircraft hit the sea west of El Rahman. This might have been Sgt. Holloway's FR239, as he did not return, probably the victim of AA. He became a PoW.

The Australian squadrons were off again at 1300, providing twenty Kittyhawks as close, medium and high cover to twelve Baltimores and six B-25s of the 12th Bomb Group USAAF to attack LGs 21 and 104. Although enemy aircraft became involved with the top cover of Spitfires and the 66th Squadron's P-40s, neither of the Australian squadrons were engaged.

3 Squadron flew again at 1630, providing six aircraft as part of the escort to Baltimores attacking LG104. This series of raids was recorded in Desert Air Force history as 'The Daba Prang'. Inevitably, both sides over claimed, the RAF considering that it had destroyed fifty aircraft on the ground and a further ten in the air. The Luftwaffe acknowledged thirty aircraft destroyed or damaged on the ground, and claimed rather more fighters shot down than were in fact lost, (twenty-six and ten by Italians, for the actual figure of sixteen, three of which fell to A.A.) as well as two bombers. It seems that only one Baltimore was lost during the day, a testimony to the effectiveness of the escorting fighters.

Flight Lieutenant Keith Kildey awaiting the return of 3 Squadron aircraft. (Keith Kildey)

450 Squadron had the next three days off, probably because of their sudden recall from leave, but 3 Squadron were operational, albeit at a reduced scale of intensity. PO Boardman in FR305 carried out a recce over Daba with one other aircraft from 1130 to 1240, and Keith Kildey used it again in the afternoon when he led six aircraft on a 'rhubarb' of the Daba area at 1530. Visibility below a 10/10ths cloud cover at 15,000 ft. was fair, and slight AA came up on occasions. The 'patrol consisted of sneaking back and forth in the clouds and popping out occasionally in the hope of interception'. After some time 'F/L Kildey and Sgt. Neill jumped two 109s, and dove after them with guns firing from 13,000 ft., but although F/L Kildey in a Mark III Kittyhawk reached *500 m.p.h.* (author's italics) the e/a escaped'. The pull-out must have been interesting! Sgt. Cashmore had a lucky escape when 'his perspex was split by an AA shell which exploded in front of him at 13,500 ft. *Otherwise* (author's italics) the operation was without incident'.[26]

Sqn. Ldr. Gibbes flew FR305 for the first time the next day when he led a patrol over the Lake Maghra area at 1440. They spotted three Bf109s 4,000 ft. below the formation, but they made off hurriedly and no interception was made.

3 Squadron returned to the Maghra area at 0935 on 12 October, and twenty enemy aircraft were reported above, but they maintained height, and no combat between the Luftwaffe and the RAAF took place. After the Kittyhawks had turned for home they were attacked by four or five Spitfires, one of which received two or three good bursts from Sgt Cashmore, as it was firing on one of the Kittyhawks. The ORB recorded that 'no one was injured. Sgt. Jones A.N. (AL169) crashed on landing at LG 91. A/C Cat. II. pilot unhurt'. It did not go on to say whether the crash was a result of the encounter with the Spitfires, which were not identified.

In the late afternoon of 13 October, six aircraft from 3 Squadron led by PO Clabburn scrambled at 1725 to intercept enemy aircraft over Alamein. Ten Bf109s attacked and a general dogfight took place. PO Finlason (FR305 CV-V) fired four 'good bursts' but no claim was made. PO Taylor's AL103 was holed four times in one wing and the tyre was punctured, but he landed successfully.

From 14 to 20 October 239 Wing operated on a much reduced scale, 3 Squadron flying no operations at all from 16 to 19 October, while 450 flew twice in the same period. In preparation for the coming battle, AVM Coningham visited both Australian squadrons and 'spoke about the forthcoming offensive and the increasingly important part being played by the air forces'. This was followed by a visit from Marshal of the RAF Lord Trenchard on 16 October, who 'addressed personnel from 3, 250 and 450 Squadrons, and 66 USAAF on the growing striking power of the UN air forces and complimented all members of the Wing on their performance throughout. The visit was well timed, and an inspiring prelude to the offensive which should drive the Axis from the shores of North Africa for good'.[27]

On 18 October Sqn. Ldr. Alan Ferguson of 450 Squadron was posted to the UK and Fl. Lt. John (Willy) Williams was promoted to command the unit, Fl. Lts. Schaaf and Law now commanding A and B Flights respectively.

18th October: The CO Sqn. Ldr. Ferguson, Flt Lts. Sheppard and Matthews have been posted. Fergie made a touching farewell speech. He was a marvellous CO and the fellows loved him. It is rotten to see him go now. (Viv Herrett)

On the same day PO Danny Boardman was granted the rank of Acting Flight Lieutenant and 'appointed to command B Flight vide F/L Springbett, who was to proceed to H.Q. RAF M.E. for disposal'. The next day 3 Squadron moved to LG175, which offered a bitumen runway and dispersal bays. It was considered to be a 'vast improvement [which would] result in the prolongation of the operational life of the aircraft'.

Operations resumed with vigour on 20 October. At 0831 twelve aircraft of 450 took off as top cover to Baltimores and Mitchells to bomb the 'dromes at Fuka. 66 USAAF and 3 Squadron with twelve aircraft each provided the close and medium cover. The bombing from 8,000 ft. was accurate, two large and three small fires being started. Over Fuka one MC202 attacked 450 Squadron. This was promptly engaged by FO 'Tex' Marting (FR251) and shot down, being confirmed by six pilots. It burst into flames when it struck the ground. The squadron was then attacked from astern by three more Macchis, which broke off when the formation turned 180 degrees to counter attack. Another group of three Macchis then appeared and engaged the Kittyhawks of Fl. Lt. Clarke and Sgt. Gregory, each Australian pilot ending up with three Macchis to himself, the first three having rejoined the fray. The fight went on for fifteen minutes, descending from 8,000 ft. to ground level. Fl. Lt. Clarke saw his shots hit three different enemy aircraft, one of which broke off the fight by climbing away vertically, followed by Clarke, who lost sight of it when his own aircraft spun. All the 239 Wing aircraft returned, Clarke (FR250) and Gregory (FR300) having Cat. II and I damage respectively.

3 Squadron was off again at 1135, PO Neill leading in ET1016 CV-B, an aircraft with an interesting history. The unusual serial might have been a mistake by the manufacturers, as the intended serial block ranged from ET100 to ET999. 112 Squadron had similar examples, ET1017 and ET1024. It is possible that several more aircraft were delivered before the serial block was changed, and were numbered consecutively by the factory. ET1016 had originally been issued to 260 Squadron, and was used by Sgt. Ron Cundy when he claimed a probable Bf109 on 14 August. 260 Squadron was re-equipped with the Merlin engined Kittyhawk II in early September, and ET1016 was passed on to 450 Squadron, until they in turn re-equipped with Mark III Kittyhawks. It was then passed on to 3 Squadron, where Garth Neill used it to claim a probable Bf109 on 2 October.

3 Squadron flew as medium cover to a mixed formation of twenty-four Baltimores and B-25s attacking Fuka, 112 flying top cover, with several more aircraft from 250 as medium cover. The leading section of 3 Squadron was ordered to attack four enemy aircraft seen directly beneath them. They were unable to manoeuvre into an attacking position, but then saw an unidentified twin engined Italian bomber flying at 500 ft. POs Neill, Taylor and Ritchie fired eight bursts at this machine, which was hit many times, but it put its wheels down and succeeded in landing near Abu Haggag. While this was happening, the formation was attacked by a mixed formation of Bf109s and MC202s, and a sharp action followed, 112 Squadron claiming a probable and a damaged, while the Messerschmitt pilots claimed three destroyed, a claim which was conservative, as five Kittyhawks did not return, one each from 112 and 250 Squadrons and three from 3 Squadron. PO Edward Alderson (EV361) was killed and Sgt. T.G. Wood (ET954) was missing. Fl. Lt. Plinston (EV315) force landed in the sea due to engine trouble on the way back and swam ashore, returning to the unit with slight head injuries. Tom Wood provided the following description of his experience on this day.

On 20/10/42 I was scheduled to go on an 8 am sortie. I got in my plane [but] it wouldn't start. It had a flat battery. I was re-scheduled for an 11 am sortie - a bombing raid with us as medium cover. Had a skirmish with two ME 109s which I managed to outmanoeuvre, but unfortunately I was attacked by two more who outmanoeuvred [me] and eventually shot my rudder control wire. I was losing height to go faster, as with no rudder I couldn't weave. I was a 'sitting duck' - the desert looked reasonably clear so I switched the petrol off, waited until the engine stopped and did a belly landing at about 250 mph !

I got out of the aircraft, opened up the hatch to get water bottle and survival kit, but the 109s started to strafe. (*in spite of the crash being well behind their own lines - author*) I ducked from side to side of the aircraft, then dashed off into the desert and curled up under a small saltbush. Some minutes later a German jeep arrived, the occupants of which spread out and started a ground search. It wasn't long before they found me, their first words to me being "For you the 'var' is over". They relieved me of my Smith and Wesson and emptied my pockets, (wallet, gooley chit, cash.) Whilst he was going through the wallet he asked what rank I was. At that very moment a set of PO tapes fell out. (If we went to Cairo I often wore them even though my commission wasn't finalised.) So as I picked them up I naturally told them I was a Pilot Officer.

I was taken back to the German air strip where I was placed in the custody of several pilots in their dugout, offered food and some attempts at conversation.

During the afternoon of my capture I was flown by Fieseler Storch (a small communications plane) to an interrogation centre about 30 minutes' flying time from where I had been captured. As I was a "desperate character", apart from the pilot and I, there was a big German guard crouched behind me. He insisted on shoving his Luger, fully cocked, finger on the trigger, in the middle of my back. As we were only several feet off the ground the light aircraft bounced and I was prodded in the back at each bounce. [28]

In the later part of the combat Lt. Kientsch and Uffz. Vavra of II/JG 27 each claimed a Kittyhawk, as did a pilot from JG 53. It is likely that these pilots were responsible for 3 Squadron's losses.

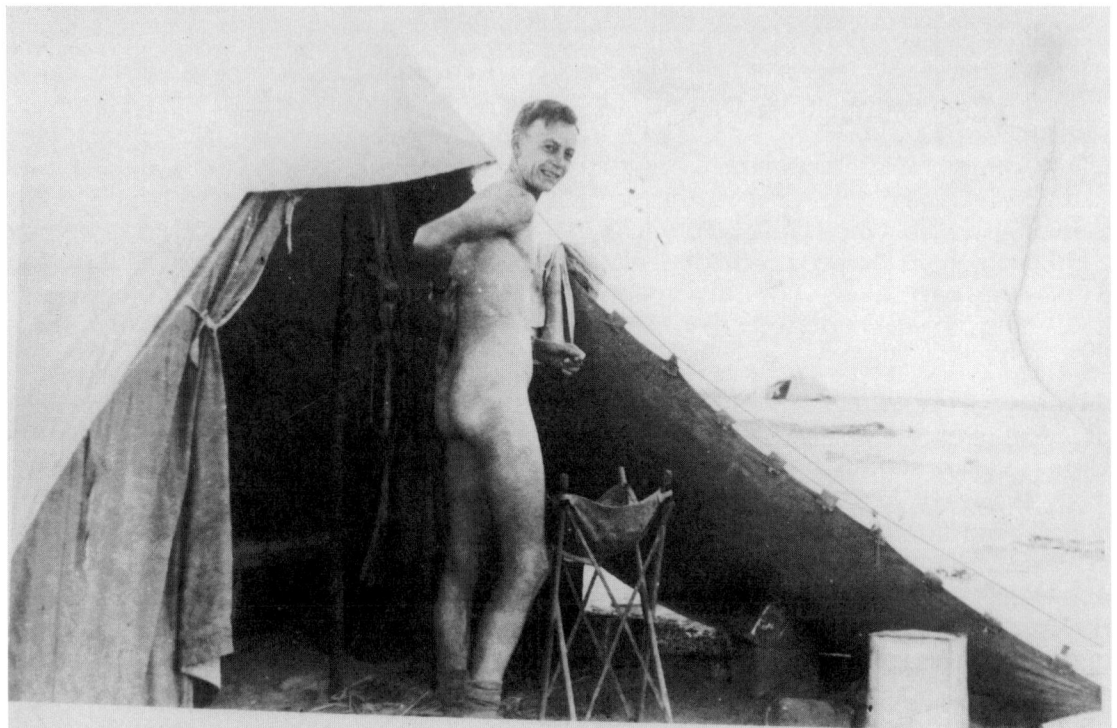

Last bath? Tom Wood reminded his family to 'note the boots and socks'. (Tom Wood)

Later in the day, fifteen aircraft of 450 Squadron spent half an hour testing new long range belly tanks, which would be put to extensive use in the coming battle.

On 21 October the two Australian units flew together, twenty-four aircraft escorting eighteen Baltimores to LG21 at 1205. 3 Squadron gave top cover, while six 450 aircraft also carried bombs as part of the close cover. shortly after arriving at the target Sqn. Ldr. Gibbes (FR305 CV-V) saw eight Bf109Es climbing in line astern from below. Gibbes took his section down and attacked the tail end aircraft, 'getting in two good bursts, and each time observing strikes right along the fuselage to the cockpit. What appeared to be an explosion occurred at the port wing root.' Sgt Churchill also followed this aircraft down with the CO and fired two bursts which he saw strike near the tail. The 'E/A was last seen going down in a steep dive,' disappearing into cloud at 3 to 4,000 ft. Gibbes claimed only a damaged.

Sgt. A.J. Richardson (EV306 CV-O) was part of Gibbes' section and after their dive he had pulled up into a climbing left hand turn when he 'saw an ME109 about 500 feet above and approx. 200 yds. in front'. He pulled up the nose and 'gave the E/A two half second bursts, seeing tracer round the A/C'. His own machine stalled and he lost sight of his target while recovering. Both Gibbes and Sgt Rex Bayly saw Richardson's attack, which caused the 109 to stall and then dive away vertically streaming both glycol and dark smoke. It disappeared into the cloud and although it seems obvious that Richardson's fire affected its behaviour, his combat report did not actually record a claim for a damaged. Richardson became detached from the rest of the squadron and was attacked by four MC202s, but although his aircraft was holed, he took successful avoiding action and returned safely.

At 1045 on 22 October eighteen B-25s were escorted to LG104 by 3, 250 and 450 Squadrons. 450 provided the close cover, with six of their twelve Kittyhawks also carrying bombs. Twelve aircraft from 3 Squadron were the medium cover and 250 flew as top cover. The Germans reacted with as much strength as they could muster; thirteen Bf109s from II and III/ JG 27 and four more from III/JG 53. The flak was very heavy, almost all of the Mitchells being hit. One which dropped out of formation due to flak damage was shot down by Hpt. Rodel of II Gruppe.

Immediately after the bombing, two Bf109s made a head-on attack on Sqn. Ldr. Gibbes, who took evasive action. One of these aircraft then went on to attack F/Sgt. Vince McFarlane of 450, but it broke off and disappeared into cloud when 450's aircraft turned to engage. 3 Squadron pilots reported a Kittyhawk receiving a direct hit from flak and the pilot baling out. This was probably Sgt. J.D. 'Curly' Evans (FR298) of 450 Squadron, who was captured. * Sgt. K. Marrows of 450 reported two aircraft colliding, one of them (unidentified) going down in flames while the other appeared to go down under control with a wing tip chopped off. He also reported seeing Sgt Lindsay going over to investigate this occurrence. Other pilots of 3 Squadron saw PO Garth Neill (ET1016) going down under control in a steady glide, leaking glycol and heading east. Four more enemy aircraft then attacked and the pilots of both squadrons had their hands full, PO Harris of 3 Squadron being attacked by three 109s. Sgt. Jones engaged two of these, firing several bursts without observing results. Sgt MacKenzie also fired without result. Sgts. Jones and Bayly then attached themselves to a Mitchell with a dead engine and escorted it home.

Spitfires of 145 Squadron accompanied by Kittyhawks from 112 and P-40Fs of the 66th Squadron on a 'delousing' sweep then joined the fight, but when the Australian squadrons landed, Sgt Lindsay and PO Neill were missing. Lindsay was also captured, but Garth Neill was killed, the two Australians being the likely victims of three claiming Bf109 pilots. (see appendix) A long

---

* Evans' aircraft was hit in the rear by flak and entered a spin. The pilot tried unsuccessfully to correct it three times, and then baled out at 5,000 feet. He landed in the middle of the airfield, fifty yards from his wrecked Kittyhawk. (AWM 54 779/3/29)

serving member of 3 Squadron, PO Neill had made four victory claims; three Bf109s and a Ju87. The DFM awarded to him as a Sergeant was gazetted on 13 October.

On 23 October, the eve of the opening of the Battle of Alamein, 239 Wing took off at 0710 to attack the landing grounds at Daba yet again. 112, 250 and 450 Squadrons carried bombs and 3 Squadron provided the top cover. 450's bombs fell amongst tents and M/T, and eight dispersed aircraft. One aircraft was seen to take off from LG104. A Kittyhawk was seen to engage an enemy aircraft and follow it down just after the bombing. The squadron lost sight of this machine, but assumed that it must have been FO 'Tex' Marting (FR309) who did not return, probably the victim of ground fire.* 3 Squadron had a brief and inconclusive engagement with ten enemy aircraft over the target, which apparently did not attract the attention of the other 239 Wing pilots below. Sgt. Dick Prowse (FR254) force landed with his wheels up due to engine trouble on the return. He was back with the squadron by 1130. Sgt. Caldwell of 3 Squadron experienced similar trouble on the way home and he force landed ET953 at LG28 without injury.

Both Squadrons flew twice more during the day, but engaged the enemy on only one more occasion, during 450 Squadron's second operation at 1100, F/Sgt. McFarlane leading six aircraft on a fighter patrol to Daba. Sgt Gregory returned early with engine trouble, and the remaining five aircraft climbed to 18,500 ft. Over Daba they sighted five Bf109Fs approaching from the north at the same level, with another some 2,000 ft. below. Yellow Section was detached to attack the lower E/A and the others took on the five 109s. Neither side succeeded in doing any harm to the other in this preliminary skirmish, the lower E/A also escaping. Shortly afterwards Fl. Lt. Schaaf (FR270) and Sgt Gleeson (FR212) sighted and engaged four more 109s at 16,500 ft. The aircraft attacked by Schaaf was confirmed by Gleeson, who also shot down his opponent, watching it hit the ground. Both Australians sustained Cat. I damage to their aircraft.

The heavy and continuous raids on the Axis landing grounds in the days leading up to the commencement of the land battle achieved their aim. The two armoured divisions and four infantry divisions with which General Montgomery intended to open his attack moved into their positions unobserved by the enemy.

> ...the Germans knew that an offensive was more than probable and the extent of air attack probably meant that it would come soon, but the war diary records only on 23 October: "Air reconnaissance observed small scale movements in a westerly direction ..... Owing to strong fighter defence observation could be made over only part of the southern area. No changes were identified." [29]

There were other reasons for the Germans' uncertainty. Rommel's wireless intelligence company, under the command of Haupt. Alfred Seebohm, had been able to provide 'an extremely accurate portrait of British plans and the order of battle on the front lines and, frequently, far to the rear'.[30] At first unaware of its efficiency, or indeed its existence, British radio security had been careless, to say the least, but Seebohm's unit finally came to the attention of its British equivalent, the Y service. The German unit was located on a hill called 'Trig 33' at Tel el Eisa.

At 0340 on July 10, an assault was mounted, as part of a larger attack, with the intention of clearing the enemy from the high ground of the Tel el Eisa area. 'The task fell to the 2/48th Battalion of the Australian 9th Infantry Division, commanded by Lieutenant Colonel H.H. Hammer, a sheep farmer from Victoria, who was known as "Hard-as-nails Hammer".'[31] By dawn, the Australians had worked their way into position and attacked with bayonets from the cover of a smoke screen laid down by the artillery. Seebohm's company was wiped out; one hundred men were killed and the rest captured, including Seebohm, who died of wounds without revealing any of his secrets. But the Germans had no time to destroy their equipment, and much valuable material was captured, revealing the extent of the harm which was being done to the British

---

FO Marting was captured, but later escaped, and returned to the squadron briefly in February 1943, when he recounted some of his adventures. He was awarded the Military Cross for his escape.

cause by their poor radio security. It also revealed that the Germans were regularly reading the messages sent to America by Colonel Frank Bonner Fellers, the US military attache in Cairo, as Italian intelligence had stolen and photographed the 'Black Code' book from the American military attache's safe in Rome as far back as August 1941. 'The loss was bound to hamper Rommel in the months to come, and the captured materials were certain to show the enemy how lax their radio security was. Now the Panzer army would be fighting blind'.[32]

Denied their usually excellent sources of intelligence, the Germans were deliberately lulled into the assumption that the British would not be able to mount an offensive until several weeks after its intended beginning, and that when it did begin, it would most likely be in the southern sector. This impression was created by means of elaborate and skilful camouflage, which concealed Montgomery's true build up in the north, and created the false impression that his southern sector was being reinforced in preparation for a major attack.

Suffering from low blood pressure and stomach disorders, Rommel left for Germany, and an intended rest cure, on 23 September, confident that the British would not attack. His replacement was General Georg Stumme, 56 years old, and, ironically, a sufferer of high blood pressure. So well concealed were Montgomery's plans, that on 20 October,

> Stumme could issue a directive no more specific than to be prepared for an attack at any time from any direction: and in the event it was not until D plus 3 (according to the Alexander despatch) that opposition developed its full strength to the main Eighth Army attack. On the other hand, it is well established that the un-Rommel like dispersion of the Axis armour between north and south, ordered by Rommel before he went away, was in fact not due to the British deception plan, but to the Axis need to conserve its petrol. It could not initially allow its armoured divisions the luxury of unlimited mobility. [33]

The *Panzerarmee Afrika* was about to fight a defensive battle against a General who was determined that it would be fought on *his* terms, with the Axis reacting to Montgomery's moves, as they had been forced to do at Alam Halfa, and not the other way round, as had been the case since April 1941. The tide was about to turn irrevocably in favour of the Allies.

C hapter 9   The Battle of El Alamein

At 1740 on 23 October the battle began with an immense artillery barrage which lasted for fifteen minutes. 'The earth from the Qattara Depression to the Mediterranean quaked. Far back from the front line men were jarred to their teeth'.[1] Twenty minutes later the main infantry advance began between Tel el Eisa and Miteiriya. 'Subsidiary attacks were launched simultaneously in the central and southern sectors, while above the battle Wellingtons bombed gun positions and troop concentrations, and night-flying Hurricanes harassed traffic in the immediate rear of the enemy lines'.[2] The infantry opened three gaps in the enemy minefield and consolidated their gains throughout the day on 24 October. The armour had not yet made a move to advance, and would not do so until after night-fall.

The *Panzerarmee Afrika* suffered an unexpected setback when its commander, General Georg Stumme disappeared after driving forward to the front line to survey the situation. His vehicle came under fire, and he died of a heart attack, which brought about the immediate recall of Rommel from his rest cure. He resumed command on the evening of 25 October.

At 0703 Sqn. Ldr. Williams led eleven aircraft of 450 Squadron on an armed recce to determine whether there was any movement from the *21st Panzer* and *Ariete Divisions* in the southern sector. Neither division showed any sign of movement, and the squadron bombed tents. 3 Squadron, led by Bobby Gibbes, took off at the same time on an armed recce to Deir El Abyad, where they bombed 300 to 400 badly dispersed M/T with excellent results.

An uneventful bomber escort was flown by both squadrons at 0930, followed by another at 1225, when six 450 machines carried bombs, 3 Squadron providing the top cover. Six MC202s in line astern emerged from cloud as the bombing commenced. They were turned away by 3 Squadron, several of whose pilots put in bursts and saw strikes without making any claims, 'however the engagement was successful in that it prevented the e/a from attacking the bombers'. Three of these made another attempt to approach the bombers, but climbed away when they were attacked by PO Crouch, F/Sgt. McQueen and Sgt. Officer of 450 Squadron.

450 Squadron flew their third operation of the day at 1525 as top cover to Baltimores and Mitchells with the US 66th Squadron as close cover. Four enemy aircraft were sighted and one of these made a head-on attack on Sgt. Jenkins (FR252) who responded by placing a good burst into his assailant.

3 Squadron flew two uneventful bomber escort operations during the morning on 25 October against enemy troop concentrations, and then joined with 450 and 66 to escort fifteen Baltimores and six B-25s to a German airfield near Fuka at 1330. The Axis reaction was more determined on

this occasion, as four enemy aircraft attacked the formation, one of which, identified as a MC202, was hit by PO Harris, leaving the action in a steep dive while streaming glycol. POs Ritchie and Caldwell also fired, Ritchie noting strikes around the cockpit of his target. Sgt. Richardson (EV219) did not rejoin the formation after the combat and was posted as 'missing'. He had attacked a Macchi at 10,000 feet, but was hit by another and chased almost to ground level, where his engine stopped. He crash-landed and counted seven bullet holes in his aircraft. Two of them were in the engine. *

In the land battle, progress had been slower than expected, although the armour had begun its advance through the minefields during the night of 24/25 October. This attempt was abandoned after some twenty-four tanks were destroyed by German anti-tank guns. The Australian 9th Division attacked in the north, making a small advance, but suffered heavy losses as they did so.

25th October: We are on stand by all morning but not called upon. In the afternoon we escorted "Baltimores" which raided a landing ground near Fuka. . . No bombs have been dropped on our troops since our push began. That is good news. (Viv Herrett)

At 0700 on 26 October the CO led twelve 3 Squadron aircraft as top cover for twelve Kittybombers of 450 Squadron on an armed recce. 450 bombed static and dispersed M/T and tents from 8000 ft. Just after arriving over Alamein the top cover was attacked by eight or nine Bf109s from II/JG 27. Three of these aircraft concentrated on Sgt. John Bullwinkel's aircraft (EV317) and he was shot down by Lt. Kientsch.[3] Bullwinkel baled out, breaking his leg on landing. Sgt. Cashmore

One of numerous photographs and pieces of abandoned German equipment found by the pilots of 250 Squadron after the German retreat began, this one shows the grave of Lt. Werner Boden, III/JG 27, who was shot down in the morning on 25 October, probably by 260 Squadron Kittyhawks. (Des Cormack)

(AK653 W) fired two bursts at a Bf109E which dived away with glycol pouring from it. It was claimed as a probable.

AK653 was a replacement aircraft, issued to the squadron on 25 October, being one of the original Kittyhawks used by 112 Squadron when they re-equipped in January 1942. The Maintenance and Repair Units of the DAF salvaged and reconditioned hundreds of damaged or war weary aircraft which were beyond the scope of the squadrons' ground crews. It was recorded as carrying the letter 'W' on 26 October, and when it was used again the next day by F/Sgt. Reg Stevens, it was recorded as 'X'. This apparent anomaly may have been caused by the squadron already possessing a machine marked 'W'.

3 Squadron flew two more uneventful operations for the day, escorting bombers, but 450 carried out three successful long range strafing operations, living up fully to their self chosen title of 'Desert Harassers'. At some stage during the Desert Campaign, William Joyce, the propagandist better known as Lord Haw Haw, referred to 450 as "Australian mercenaries whose harassing tactics were easily beaten off by the *Luftwaffe*". This led to the Squadron adopting the title of 'The Desert Harassers'.

Six aircraft, carrying long range belly tanks operationally for the first time, took off at 1017 and flew to the west of Sidi Heneish, eighty miles behind the lines. Here they strafed a small convoy travelling east on the escarpment road, destroying or damaging sixteen vehicles, including two petrol lorries which were 'flamers'. As the Axis forces were already desperately short of fuel, raids such as this were a significant contribution to their eventual defeat.

On the return, they encountered a lone Ju88 which was attacked by all six pilots, F/Sgt. Phelps (FR273), Sgt. Cameron (FR212), Sqn. Ldr. Williams (FR270), Sgt. Borthwick (FR295) Sgt. Prowse (FR237) and Fl. Lt. Schaaf (FR196). They 'had to desist due to lack of ammunition' and the aircraft was credited as a 'damaged' to the squadron as a whole. In fact it force-landed.[4] They landed at 1256, the operation taking over two and a half hours.

The squadron flew twice more in the afternoon, destroying a further seven vehicles, three of which were petrol lorry 'flamers'.

Fl. Lt. Ron Cundy of 260 Squadron had already flown a dive-bombing sortie in the southern sector when the squadron took off at 1615 as top cover to a mixed formation of Bostons and Baltimores attacking LG21. Four Bf109s attacked 260 Squadron; two were shot down, one by Ron Cundy (FL287). Other squadron pilots claimed two probables and a damaged. Since 21 October 260 Squadron had claimed four confirmed, four probables and four damaged, for the loss of two aircraft and one pilot, during the seven operations flown by the young Australian Flight Commander.

On 27 October, Rommel ordered the *21st Panzer Division* northward and ten mixed bomber and fighter-bomber formations were sent against it.

> The counter-attack, which Rommel directed in person, was smashed up by our old enemies, the medium bombers and the 25-pounders. He tried again the next day, but was beaten off once more. He lost Panzers that he could ill afford - Panzers that would not now be replaced. The 9th Australian Division hammered him farther back.[5]

Not all the bombing raids were in direct support of the army. At 0846 Wg. Cdr. Haysom led twelve 450 Squadron aircraft with long-range tanks as close escort to six Baltimores and twelve B-25s to attack Mersa Matruh., more than one hundred miles behind the lines: no enemy aircraft were seen.

Slightly earlier than this, at 0830, 3 Squadron sent twelve aircraft, led by the CO, as top cover to eighteen Baltimores bombing LG17 at Fuka. The performance of the old Mk I Kittyhawks was found wanting. The ORB recorded : 'As top cover we were forced to fly at 19,000 ft. and some pilots had difficulty keeping up with formation'. By the time the bombing was finished, the formation was down to 11,000 ft. and F/Sgt. Reg Stevens (AK653 CV-X)

> saw a MC202 diving from N.E. to S.W. behind the formation, and gave it a good burst from 200 yards, beam to rear quarter. I followed the e/a down and as it pulled up I got another good burst into it from dead astern closing from 300 to 50 yards, observing strikes along the whole of the top of the fuselage. The e/a flicked over onto its back and went into a spin.

Stevens followed it down to 3,000 ft. but then pulled up in case of an attack from other enemy aircraft and did not see what happened to it.

This machine had also been attacked from astern by Sgt. Alan Righetti, who opened fire from 800 yards, closing in to 500, when he saw Stevens commence his beam attack from much closer. He wisely ceased fire 'in case he moved into line astern position'. The last he saw of the Macchi was when it began to pull out of its dive 'with the Kitty following up very close'. Stevens' initial claim was for a probable, but PO Dave Ritchie saw 'an e/a go in and burn' and Stevens was credited with a victory.

Sgt. Churchill (EV168) was 'last seen diving down towards the bombers, evidently with engine trouble',[6] and was reported as missing. In fact he was attacked by a MC202 which put a burst through the port side of the cockpit, severing the throttle, mixture and pitch controls. He crash-landed twenty miles away from the combat and evaded the enemy for two days, but was finally captured by Italian troops.*

At 1215 3 Squadron provided eleven aircraft (six carrying bombs) as close escort to bombers, but the intensity of operations and the age of some of the Kittyhawks was beginning to take its toll. PO Tom Russell force-landed AK811 at LG81 with an over-heating engine, while Sgt Howie crash-landed two miles south of Amriya with engine failure. The pilot sustained slight injuries and the aircraft was burnt out. 450 Squadron with their newer Mk IIIs were on the same operation, but also had two aircraft drop out, F/Sgt McQueen suffering engine trouble with FR246 and F/Sgt McFarlane returning with an unserviceable radio. One more combined bomber escort operation was carried out before the end of the day, without making contact with enemy aircraft. The two Australian squadrons despatched 69 sorties for the day.

At 0945 on 28 October Kittyhawks from three 239 Wing squadrons took off to escort another bombing raid on LG20. The formation consisted of twelve Baltimores and six B-25s, the close escort coming from twelve 450 Squadron Kittyhawks (six bomb carriers) led by Fl. Lt. Law. The US 66th Squadron flew as medium cover, and six 3 Squadron aircraft led by Bobby Gibbes were top cover. Four Spitfires of 92 Squadron patrolled above the formation as high cover.

At 1010 six Bf109s of II/JG 27 took off to cover their airfield and some of these attacked the high cover Spitfires, shooting one down. Another Spitfire was damaged, crash-landing in the Allied lines on the way back. One Spitfire pilot claimed a damaged Bf109.[7] The Kittyhawk escorts were apparently unaware of this higher action, concentrating their attention on the bombers, which made an accurate attack, their 'bombs straddling the 'drome with what appeared to be good results'. 450 Squadron reported a large fire, and considered that it might have been a bomber going in, but no bombers were lost, and the fire must therefore have been the Spitfire shot down earlier, or one of a number of German aircraft damaged by the bombing.

Either at the same time as the bombing, or very shortly after, three Bf109s were observed by Sqn. Ldr. Gibbes, climbing in line astern at 11 o'clock at the same level as 3 Squadron. These were probably the same three aircraft reported by 450 Squadron which were sighted above the target. One came down, firing ineffectually from long range at the port section of bombers, which became detached from the main body, no doubt due to their evasive action.

Bobby Gibbes, flying FR305, which had a noticeably better performance than the rest of the squadron's aircraft, was able to pull away into a good attacking position. He 'attacked from the port beam at about 100 yards. Observed glycol stream from No. 3 a/c and it dived away vertically'.

His diary told a slightly more colourful tale.

> Managed to get a squirt at one as it climbed up. I hit the bugger behind the one which I aimed at and he went down streaming glycol. Later confirmed by the Yanks, 66 Squadron.[8]

Slightly underneath Gibbes, who had climbed to deliver his attack, PO Bray saw 'the third a/c fall out of formation into a vertical dive streaming glycol. Being slightly below I followed the e/a down firing a short burst, but did not hit it. I broke off at approx. 6,000 ft. having dived from 16,000. I last saw the e/a in a vertical dive at approx 4,000 ft. and apparently out of control'. PO Harris and PO Austin saw the Messerschmitt go down, and later both reported seeing an aircraft fire on the ground.

Gibbes' original claim was for a probable, but it was up-graded when the 66th Squadron confirmed the crash: their evidence, combined with reports from Harris and Austin, being clear indication of a victory.

---

* AWM 54 779/3/29

And the fight was not yet over. Gibbes' combat report went on.

> At approx. 1025 hours (when returning to base) when north of Ras El Shaqiq, a single ME109F dived across in front of formation, turned W. and passed over our formation. I pulled up steeply and firing, very nearly ramming the e/a. It continued ahead in a shallow dive. It is unlikely that I hit it.

Other evidence suggests that his fire was more accurate than he gave himself credit for. This comment from PO John Upward was appended to Gibbes' combat report.

> At approx. the same place and time, 1025 hours N. of Ras El Shaqiq, I saw an aircraft diving vertically downwards and spinning slowly. I watched this aircraft which finally hit the sea some 5 miles out from the coast off the point Ras Gibeisa. The a/c was too far behind me to identify it, but it could have been the a/c referred to by S/L Gibbes.

Sgts. House and Officer of 450 were escorting a Baltimore with a sick engine, having successfully driven off three Bf109s which remained above them for some time without making any further attacks. After things had settled down, Sgt. House reported an unidentified aircraft going into the sea at map reference 840325.

Squadron records credit Sqn. Ldr. Gibbes with one confirmed and one probable for 28 October. Chris Shores, in *Fighters Over The Desert* noted 'Sqn. Ldr. Gibbes of 3 RAAF Squadron attacked three Bf109s and hit one, claiming a probable. He then sighted a lone Bf109 north of Ras el Shaqiq and shot it down into the sea, almost ramming it, so close did he press his attack; this was the squadron's 200th confirmed victory'.[9]

In *Aces High,* published twenty-five years later, the first of Gibbes' two engagements on this date is recorded as the victory and the *second* a probable, conforming to Squadron records. Given the available evidence, it does not seem unreasonable for *both* of Bobby Gibbes' combats on 28 October to be recorded as confirmed victories: flimsier evidence sufficed in countless other cases throughout the war.

However, only one victory was needed to bring the squadron's score to an *apparent* total of 200,* and congratulatory messages flowed in to the unit. The celebration did not take place until

---

* Since the end of the war there has been a long held belief that 3 Squadron shot down a total of 217.5 aircraft, and these figures have been published in a variety of sources without question. In 1992, two former Commanding Officers of the unit, Alan Rawlinson and Peter Jeffrey, felt that these figures were not accurate, and with the assistance of researcher and author Russell Guest, they examined the squadron's records in considerable detail. They found that the figure of 217.5 was based on statistics in a document entitled 'The Book of Original Entry', started in August 1942 by Flight Lieutenant G.H. Barnes. The original document has not been found, but a claims list based on its entries was kept by the Squadron.

*It became obvious that there were a number of mistakes in 'The Book of Original Entry' list for the period 1940/41, which gave a total for that period, (ie. the end of 1941) of **25 too many**. Fl. Lt. Barnes did not join the squadron until May 1942, and he clearly made a number of clerical errors when he compiled his list. Very few other personnel in the squadron at that time would have had first hand knowledge of its earlier period, and obviously accepted the inaccurate figures without question.*

Thus when Sqn. Ldr. Gibbes scored his victory on 28 October, the actual total was still well short of 200. Gibbes' victory was the squadron's 62nd since 1 January '1942: this, when added to the correct total of 115 at the end of 1941 makes 177.

The 'Book of Original Entry' gave the incorrect total of 140 at the end of 1941, and two claims, (made by FO Bradbury, 22 January, and PO Curtis, 8 March) before Barnes joined the unit, were not recorded. So, when Bobby Gibbes claimed what seemed to be the squadron's 60th victory for the year, 140 plus 60 equalled 200, which was cause for celebration.

It is worth recording that by the end of 1942, the Squadron's total had reached 182. Only ten more claims were made for the remainder of the war, six in 1943, two in 1944 and two in 1945. Due to a marked decline in Luftwaffe activity in North Africa and the Mediterranean, and the Squadron's role as a fighter-bomber unit, targets became very hard to find.

Similar problems befell 112 Squadron, as they considered that 200 aircraft had been destroyed by the end of the Tunisian campaign. Their historian, Robin Brown, gives an end of war total of 194.5, remarkably similar to 3 Squadron's eventual total.

30 October, but it was a memorable occasion. Extra supplies of beer and food had been specially acquired from Alexandria by the Adjutant, and perhaps influenced by the former, Bobby Gibbes admitted that he had aimed at the second Messerschmitt and not the one which he hit. No one would believe him! As part of the celebrations, half of Sgt. John Hooke's imposing walrus moustache was ceremoniously removed.

But before the celebrations could take place, there was work to be done. At 0930 on 29 October, twelve 3 Squadron aircraft flew as top cover to twelve Kittybombers of 450, tasked to bomb landing grounds at Fuka. Owing to the presence of enemy aircraft, they were instructed by 'Blackbird' (the controller) to bomb the first suitable target, which happened to be a Ju52, destroyed by a direct hit, the only bomb to land within 50 yards of a target, owing to the hurried nature of the bombing. Then instructed to climb to 10,000 ft. on a vector of 300^0, the formation sighted twelve Bf109s 3,000 ft. above them, which did not immediately attack. Reports from 'Blackbird' indicated that enemy aircraft were present all around the clock. Soon a formation of thirty CR42s and Ju87s with a strong escort was encountered, but could not be attacked, because the 109s above came down and the Kittyhawks were forced on the defensive. Sgt Keith Marrows' aircraft (FR295) was hit in the magazine, suffering Cat. II damage. Sgt. Caldwell of 3 Squadron was the only pilot to open fire, but this was without result, and F/Sgt. Reg Stevens was attacked simultaneously by two Messerschmitts, but he took effective avoiding action and rejoined the formation.

3 Squadron flew an uneventful bomber escort at 1400, some of their aircraft also carrying bombs. Keith Kildey's bomb landed between three trucks.

450 had another clash with enemy fighters later in the afternoon, when twelve of their aircraft as top cover to the 66th Squadron were ordered 'Buster' to Alamein. 109s were encountered and a

Celebrating the 'double century'. Standing, left to right: Alex 'Huc' Finlason, Andy Taylor, 'Doc' Tim Stone (MO), Garth Clabburn, Joe Holder, (face in shadow) Ken Bee, (head only) Alex MacKenzie, Reg Stevens, (head only) Rex Bayly, (face in shadow, holding board) three unidentified mess stewards, 'Pat' Henning, unidentified mess steward, Gordon Jones. Front row, left to right: Ron Matthews, Nev Austin, Danny Boardman, (partly obscured) Keith Kildey, Bobby Gibbes, Gordon 'Donk' Bray, George Barton, Ops Officer. (3 Squadron Association)

general engagement followed. Fl. Lts. Schaaf and Clarke, and Sgt. McFarlane all fired, but made no claims. The 66th Squadron lost contact and missed the fight. All the Squadron's aircraft were safely on the ground by 1817.

On 30 October, 450 Squadron flew five separate operations with smaller formations of aircraft, totalling 24 sorties, while 3 Squadron flew 23 sorties on two bomber escort operations. Not all were eventful, but 450 Squadron flew three of their ops. with long range tanks, and wrought considerable havoc behind the German lines.

At 1340 Sqn. Ldr. Williams led four aircraft on a ground level strafe which lasted for two and a half hours. They returned claiming nine trucks, an armoured car, and numerous personnel.

Four more aircraft under Fl. Lt. Schaaf left at 1349, flying to Maghra on the edge of the Qattara Depression and thence to the coast road. From there they flew east, approaching the enemy from his rear with the sun at their backs. Significantly, the movement which they reported was heading *west*. They strafed LG14, where they found twenty-plus Bf109s in pens, a Ju52 and twelve gliders. They returned with the following claims.

Fl. Lt. Schaaf: 8 trucks and a Bf109 damaged
Sgt. Gregory: 7 trucks and a Bf109 damaged
Sgt. McFarlane: 6 trucks - 1 flamer and one turned over
Sgt Borthwick: 1 Bf109 flamer, 1 truck flamer, 1 Ju52, and the twelve gliders damaged.

The Squadron's last op. of the day left at 1358, four aircraft with long range tanks led by PO Crouch, at deck level to Maghra, from where they set course for the Sidi Barrani road. Near Charing Cross they sighted a lone Ju52, and all four pilots attacked, the unfortunate Junkers crash-landing in flames. The successful pilots were PO Crouch (FL879), Sgt. A.G. Markle (FR273), Sgt M.A. Jenkins (FR252) and Sgt. H.B. Reid (FR274). Markle's Kittyhawk received a hole from the rear gunner. Al Markle recorded the combat in his log book.

Duty - long range straffing, road between Sidi Barrani and Mersa Matruh. Time - 2 hours and 40 minutes. P/O Crouch, Sgts. Jenkins, Reid and myself took off at 2 pm. (long range tanks) to strafe all and sundry between Sidi Barrani and Matruh. Went out via Quattara Depression. At nought feet and with "vis" cut to 200 yards (dust storm) unsuspecting Junkers '52 at 150' stooging along east loomed up on our left. P/O Crouch and I immediately made quarter attacks. Rear gunner (plenty plucky till end) nicked me in left leg slightly below knee. Followed through with a short second burst, but P/O Crouch fired the Ju just ahead of me. Big orange flame. Occupants (4). Claimed fearless rear gunner for my own satisfaction. Hun aircraft must have been ferrying petrol judging by explosion. Near road at time. Super effort.[10]

On the last day of the month, two Australians flying with RAF squadrons were successful, but 450 Squadron had a bad day. At 1025, twelve Kittyhawks of 260 Squadron took off as top cover to 5 SAAF's Tomahawks on an offensive sweep over Fuka. II and III/JG 27 had a number of aircraft in the air, intended as escort for Stukas, but they first engaged 250 Squadron, who were escorting B-25s attacking LG 17. 260 Squadron and the South Africans arrived, and Fl. Lt. Ron Cundy (FL229) shot down one and shared another with Sgt. Thomas. Fw. Steiss of II Gruppe force landed and Uffz. Moycis of III Gruppe was shot down, but returned later.[11] This was the tenth of eleven operations flown by Ron Cundy since the beginning of the battle. He flew 23 hours and 40 minutes on operations for the month, fifteen of these in the last eight days.

450 Squadron was part of the escort for this raid, also carrying bombs, which they dropped with the B-25s. The formation was attacked by two Messerschmitts, but they were driven off by 450 without doing any harm.

At 1340 Sqn. Ldr. Williams (FR270) led four of 450's aircraft on a strafing patrol with long range tanks. PO Winn returned early with engine trouble, but the others continued to the Sidi Barrani road and strafed it for five miles in an easterly direction. 'Willy' Williams set a petrol dump alight,

Fl. Lt. Ron Cundy of 260 Squadron with his father, Captain George Cundy, who received the MC and Bar during the 1914-18 war, when he served with the 1st Australian Light Horse Regiment. He volunteered for service again in the Second World War, and served as both a training officer and voyage officer. This photograph was taken when he visited the desert with reinforcements for the 9th Division. The aircraft is a Merlin-engined Kittyhawk IIA, referred to by 260 squadron as a Warhawk. (Ron Cundy)

the second pilot damaged a truck and also claimed two petrol bowsers as flamers, and Sgt. Max Jenkins hit three trucks. Then disaster struck. The second pilot had somehow become separated, and while flying at 200 feet, slightly to the left, and above Williams, Max Jenkins saw the missing aircraft approaching from almost head on. It opened fire, and some of the bullets struck Williams' aircraft. He force-landed, and was captured shortly afterwards. Max Jenkins' log book recorded the tragic event thus:

> *LONG RANGE STRAFE. 3.30. BAD DAY. LOST REID AND POOR BLOODY . . . . . ACCIDENTALLY SHOT THE C.O. DOWN 10 MILES WEST OF BUG BUG. NO CHANCE OF ESCAPE.*

John Williams was a New Zealander who joined the RAAF in 1938 while living in Sydney. He served with 94 and 260 Squadrons before joining 450 as a Flight Commander in June, taking command on 18 October. He claimed four aircraft destroyed and two damaged with 450 Squadron, and was awarded a DFC in March 1943. His story ended tragically. He took part in the 'Great Escape' from *Stalag Luft III* and was one of the fifty officers shot by the Gestapo on Hitler's orders, after his recapture on 29 March 1944.[12]

Shortly after Sqn. Ldr. Williams' group had departed, four more aircraft led by Fl. Lt. Law took off with long range tanks on a similar operation. They strafed the Sidi Barrani road in a westerly direction for a few minutes, claiming fourteen trucks damaged and one petrol lorry in flames. Looking behind, Law sighted two Bf109s with long range tanks and yellow noses weaving behind the formation. He was far enough in front of the formation to turn through 180 degrees, flying over Sgt Reid to attack the 109 following him at the same time as it opened fired on Reid's aircraft. When Law turned again, he saw a cloud of dust and fire on the ground. This was the Kittyhawk of Sgt. Harold Reid (FL879) who was killed in the crash. Sgt. David Borthwick (FR300) fired at another 109 which was attacking Fl. Lt. Law, and saw it break away with glycol streaming from it. He claimed a probable. F/Sgt McQueen (FR246) attacked another 109 without result. There were actually four Bf109s from I/JG 77 involved in this combat. They had been escorting Stukas when they saw the Kittyhawks strafing below them and broke downwards in what would have been a perfect bounce, if Law had not taken a timely look over his shoulder.

During 3 Squadron's second operation of the day, bombing Ghazal station, they encountered several Bf109s, one of which Sgt. Rex Bayly (AL217) claimed as a probable at 1442. Then at 1630 twelve Kittybombers of 112 Squadron, with 3 Squadron as top cover, took off to bomb and strafe between El Daba and Fuka. At 1710 Sgt. N.R. Caldwell, leading the top section of aircraft of 3 Squadron, saw twenty-plus Ju87s at the same altitude flying east.

Both squadrons attacked aggressively, 112 claiming three Stukas and two Bf109s destroyed, as well as several probables and a damaged. Australian Sgt. Reg Wild, (FR215 GA-V) who had been with 112 since August, made his first claims: a Ju87 destroyed and a damaged Bf109. 3 Squadron made no victory claims, but Sgt. Caldwell (ET899 CV-Y) damaged two Stukas, as did Sgt Cashmore (EV346 CV-O). PO Ritchie (AL154) claimed a probable Stuka, and the CO damaged a Bf109.

This successful combat prevented the Stukas from carrying out their mission and cost 239 Wing one Kittyhawk from 112 Squadron, the pilot being safe.

On the ground, General Montgomery, having decided to turn the southern flank over to the defensive, was now in the process of re-grouping his forces in preparation for another major attack in the northern sector, to be called Operation *Supercharge*. Rommel had anticipated this move, sending his best remaining armour north to relieve the *90th Light Division,* 'that was penned with its back to the sea by the 9th Australian Division'.[13]

Another 250 Squadron trophy, this photograph of Field Marshal Rommel was obviously taken during happier times, perhaps after the fall of Tobruk in June. (Des Cormack)

Montgomery....now proceeded to alter the direction of 'Supercharge' : the Australians should make a third attempt to strike towards the sea on the night of the 30th to keep Rommel committed, but the main attack would come further south just above the lower corridor. By shifting northwards, Rommel had separated his German formations from the Italian: Montgomery would strike at the hinge of the two enemy armies, with the greatest weight falling on the Italians.[14]

At 1 am on 2 November, the attack commenced on a front of four thousand yards, the first stage of a breakthrough which began on 4 November, as the Germans had already begun to withdraw. The Squadrons of 239 Wing would soon be on the move westward. By 11 November, British units had reached the border of Libya.

C hapter 10   Break-Through

3 Squadron took delivery of six Packard Merlin powered Mark II Kittyhawks on 1 November, and the pilots received them with enthusiasm. Sqn. Ldr. Maurice Barber, a South African with 250 Squadron, arrived to take command of 450 on 2 November, and operations continued with unabated intensity.

112 Squadron had begun re-equipping with Mark III Kittyhawks in October, and at dawn on 1 November twelve of these new aircraft flew an armed reconnaissance with the US 66th Squadron. They bombed tents and shortly afterwards encountered thirty Ju87s of StG 3, escorted by a considerable number of Bf109s, from JG 27 and JG 77. The German dive-bombers had been unable to provide any effective support to their embattled army. 'Even the *Staffelkapitan* of 5/StG 3, Oberleutnant Hans Drescher, admitted that 'the position of the English at El Alamein could no longer be penetrated'.'[1]

And so it proved on this occasion. 112 Squadron tore into the Stukas, claiming six destroyed, three probable and two damaged. Sgt. Reg Wild (FR789) destroyed one in flames and damaged another, and PO G.F. Allison (FR215 GA-V) an Australian who had been with the squadron since May, claimed one of the probables. The Stukas jettisoned their bombs over their own troops.

112 Squadron's only loss was an aircraft which force-landed behind British lines. The Messerschmitts claimed four Kittyhawks, but it seems that only one American aircraft was lost during the day, over Gambut airfield.[2]

The two Australian squadrons flew ninety sorties in four operations during the day, sharing the top cover and bombing tasks. The only contact with enemy aircraft was on the second operation at 0945, when 450 sighted four Bf109s 3,000 ft. above. One of these attempted to dive through the formation to attack 3 Squadron's Kittybombers, but it was driven off by Sgt. Gleeson (FR212) who got in one good burst.

In contrast with the previous day, 450 flew only twenty sorties from three operations on 2 November, two armed recces in the early morning, and a bomber escort to Baltimores and Mitchells with the US 66th Squadron in the afternoon. 450's aircraft carried bombs and dropped them with the bombers. 3 Squadron escorted bombers on three occasions, encountering numerous enemy aircraft on their third trip at 1455.

Bobby Gibbes led ten Kittyhawks with bombs as close escort to eighteen Baltimores and B-25s tasked to bomb M/T on the road south of Rahman. The result of the bombing was enthusiastically recorded as 'very excellent'. After the bombing 3 Squadron was vectored onto enemy aircraft. Six Bf109s were reported ahead of the formation and four attacked, Sgt. Holder's AK643 being hit, but PO Clabburn drove the attacker off with a well aimed burst. Seven Kittyhawks led by Gibbes then attacked a formation of Stukas, but were thwarted by six more Bf109s which engaged the Kittyhawks, who were trying to keep a wary eye on five more 109s 3,000 ft. above and up sun, with another twelve above these. Fortunately they did not come down to join the fight. Although Sgt. Alan Righetti fired and hit one Messerschmitt, and PO Clabburn damaged a Stuka which was last seen going down trailing smoke, no positive claims were made, in spite of the fact that almost all the squadron's pilots fired at and saw strikes on enemy aircraft.

Considering themselves fortunate to have avoided losses, the Kittyhawks broke off the action, but while returning home, Sqn. Ldr. Gibbes and PO Ritchie were attacked by a Hurricane. They evaded its unwelcome attention, but the incident disturbed Gibbes, who recorded in his diary 'The mad bastard, he frightened hell out of me.'[3]

PO Taylor was attacked by two Bf109s while returning low over the sea, but several long range bursts from Gibbes, and friendly AA fire scared his attackers away. Sgt Holder, who force-landed with cannon strikes to the engine, fin and rudder, * was reported as missing. His capture was later confirmed.

Each squadron flew three operations on 3 November, 3 Squadron making the first use of their precious new Merlin Kittyhawks. At 0550, the CO, still flying FR305, led seven aircraft on an armed recce of the battle area and thence to Daba, where they bombed eighty-plus M/T with excellent results. Sgt Caldwell (FL291) and FO Harris (FL294) were the first squadron pilots to fly the new Kittyhawks in action. At 1455 Fl. Lt. Keith Kildey led all six MK IIs to escort eighteen Mitchells bombing west of Ghazal. The Kittyhawks started a fire of their own at Daba station, in addition to one caused by the Mitchells.

Fl. Lt. Clarke led twelve 450 aircraft on their first op. of the day at 0859, providing the top cover to a mixed formation of Baltimores and B-25s, with the US 66th Squadron as close escort. After the bombing 450 was attacked by two Bf109s, Oblt. Fritz Geisshard of I/JG 77 shooting down Sgt. Gus Officer (FR218), who baled out successfully. * Sgt. Gregory (FL881) was flying with Officer when they were attacked, and made a steep turn to avoid the Messerschmitts, but he lost control and spun to 4,000 ft. where he found himself under attack by three more 109s. He fired 200 rounds at his assailants without effect, finally managing to evade them and return at ground level with Cat. I damage.

Up with the main formation, ten more Bf109s engaged, one being fired at by Sgt. George O'Neil, who saw strikes before it fell away trailing white smoke. O'Neil fired at another which rolled slowly onto its back and fell away. Still with plenty to do, O'Neil had no time to note further details or effects. Fl. Lt Schaaf and Sgt. Minchin also got in bursts, but made no claims.

At 1540 six 3 Squadron Kittyhawks, led by the CO, flew top cover to eighteen B-25s, with eleven from 450 as close escort. Twelve Bf109s attacked 3 Squadron and Sgt. A.N.Jones' EV355 was hit in the engine and fuel tank. It burst into flames and the pilot baled out immediately, falling into the sea. * 3 Squadron kept the 109s occupied, 450 reporting an attack by only six enemy aircraft when over the target, which had no effect on either their aircraft or the bombers. The dogged determination with which the Kittyhawk pilots successfully defended their charges was admirable.

AWM 54 779/3/29

* Gus Officer was attacked from behind at 10,000 feet. He was wounded in the right thigh and elbow, the engine was hit by cannon fire and his radio was shot out. He half rolled to avoid the attack, but, blinded by escaping glycol, he was forced to bale out at 3,000 feet. His aircraft exploded on the ground directly below him and he was captured by two Germans in a staff car as soon as he landed. (AWM 54 779/3/29)

* Although the report did not mention it, he must have been picked up by enemy ASR, as he was captured. (AWM 54 779/3/29)

Fl. Lt. Ron Cundy of 260 Squadron flew his second operation of the day in FL274 as part of close cover to eighteen Bostons bombing Fuka. His log book recorded that he *had a squirt at an ME 110 but did not get it.* However, a Bf110 of III/ZG 26 force-landed in a mine field during the day, killing the crew, and as no other claims for a Bf110 were made on 3 November, this might well have been the aircraft he attacked.[4]

At the end of the day, 3 Squadron's ORB recorded 'Today marked the first use by the squadron of Mark II Kittyhawks in operations and all pilots who flew them were more than satisfied with them. They have, according to pilots' reports, a greater ceiling and faster rate of climb, at the same time retaining all the manoeuvrability of the Mark I Kittyhawk.'

On 4 November the break-through on the ground began in earnest, and Rommel ordered a withdrawal to Fuka, which continued in spite of a personal signal from Hitler, demanding that the position at El Alamein be held to the last man.[5] Throughout the day the Desert Air Force attacked without respite, 450 Squadron alone flying thirty-five sorties in six operations, either escorting bombers, usually while carrying bombs themselves, or dive-bombing in conjunction with 112 Squadron.

3 Squadron flew three bomber escort operations totalling twenty-two sorties. On the first of these, led by Bobby Gibbes at 0655, two Bf109s attacked over the target and two Kittyhawks were hit, PO Finlason (FL294) and PO Harris (FL345), but both returned to base safely. Sgt. John Hooke fired several bursts at the attackers without results. On their third op, at 1315, they carried bombs while acting as top cover to eighteen bombers, which attacked the landing grounds and road at Quatafiya. Significantly, they reported a scarcity of M/T in the area and no activity in the central sector. The retreat was well under way.

At 1415 hours, twelve Kittyhawks of 260 Squadron escorted twelve Kittybombers of 2 SAAF to attack M/T west of Daba. While the South Africans were busy at ground level, 260 Squadron encountered a Ju88 at 10,000 ft. and this was shot down into the sea by Fl. Lt. Cundy (FL274), his fourth victory within the space of ten days, including the Bf110 mentioned above, plus a half share in another.

3 Squadron were off early on 5 November, six aircraft led by the CO carrying out an armed recce of the Daba - Fuka areas at 0620, where they were attacked by twelve-plus Bf109s and MC200s. Outnumbered by more than two to one, all the pilots were engaged, but were 'unable to make claims owing to confusion'. Two Kittyhawks were damaged, and F/Sgt. Reg Stevens (ET957 CV-K) claimed a damaged when he saw white smoke coming from the Bf109 he had fired at. This was the squadron's last claim while flying MK I Kittyhawks.

No ground observations were possible, so four aircraft repeated the recce at 1540, landing at LG106 to determine its condition, which was found to be fair. There was no sign of the enemy, who appeared to have left the area in a hurry.

450 Squadron also had an inconclusive brush with Bf109s on this day, when providing fighter cover for a New Zealand long range army patrol. When the controller reported bandits, they climbed to 13,000 ft. and sighted three Bf109s approaching from the north 2,000 ft. above. The 109s would dive and take long range shots at the Kittyhawks and then climb back up out of range. This went on for twenty-two minutes with no damage to either side, and no claims being made.

5th November: "B" Flight left for No.106 LG near El Daba. "A" Flight continued operating all our aircraft. We were unable to bomb though, as the armour of both sides is locked in a death struggle. Instead we carried out three straffing runs on motorised stuff heading west. No opposition was encountered. (Viv Herrett)

At 0610 on 6 November Fl. Lt. Danny Boardman flew a lone recce of the Daba area. He landed at LG106 and reported it to be serviceable. 450 Squadron carried out two uneventful operations during the day, before flying their seventeen Kittyhawks to LG106 at 1650. 3 Squadron followed ten minutes later with thirteen aircraft. The westward advance was in full swing, and the hard working ground crews came into their own, demonstrating their ingenuity by scrounging whatever was necessary to keep the squadrons' transport functioning. They often worked through the night to change truck engines, which were sometimes acquired by unconventional means.

> Several of the old Chevrolet trucks used by the Squadron (450) had seen better days, and requests for replacements through the "proper channels" proving fruitless, the Senior NCO "old boy line" was brought into play. Six crated new engines were acquired from Helwan Transport Pool with the strict injunction that the crates containing some sort of engines had to be back within 48 hours. As Roy Denny recollects "all hands and the cooks, and indeed anyone who could handle a spanner, worked through the night to change the clapped out engines. They were cleaned up, crated and back in Helwan in time and the old Chevvys served faithfully throughout the campaign." [6]

Now established at LG106, both Australian squadrons flew two operations on 7 November, Fl.Lt. Keith Kildey in FL306 obtaining strikes on one of three Bf109s which engaged 3 Squadron during their afternoon armed recce at 1540. 450 Squadron flew a fighter patrol with long range tanks along the Charing Cross, Barrani, Sollum road, where they reported 'roads literally packed with vehicles 3 to 4 abreast, bonnet to tail, all moving west'.

A typical scene in the desert as a 3 Squadron convoy pauses for a rest during a move between bases.
(Tom Russell)

7th November: At 6.30 am we moved out in convoy. "A" Flight proceeded to Sidi Haneish and we in the Maintenance Flight pulled in at No.106 LG to join "B" Flight. On the way we saw plenty of evidence of the recent fighting between El Alamein and No.106 LG. There were wrecked tanks and guns by the hundreds. There are thousands of prisoners and pathetic little lone graves all over the place. Many bodies of the Jerries still lay un-buried as they have been placing mines under the bodies of some troops - making them dangerous to move. There are thousands of trucks on the road - all heading west. Owing to traffic jams etc, we did not arrive at No.106 LG until just after dark. (Viv Herrett)

On 8 November, 3 Squadron flew only one brief operation, but 450's two operations were eventful. The first of these, led by Fl. Lt. Law at 0927 consisted of twelve aircraft with long range tanks and wing bombs, and attacked a convoy of 100-plus M/T. Many of the bombs hung up, only four being seen to burst. Two Bf109s attacked the squadron as they were re-forming after bombing, only one opening fire without effect. Four of the Kittyhawk pilots returned fire and the enemy aircraft broke away, apparently unharmed.

Then at 1415 eleven aircraft took off to strafe the Barrani - Sollum road. The traffic was less dense than the day before, being spaced some twenty yards apart, but it provided a rewarding target, the squadron claiming six flamers and another thirty-one vehicles damaged. Light AA of moderate intensity, and much small arms fire was reported, and Sgt Al. Markle was hit, force landing FR273.

> Our flight was the last to "peel off" over target. No trouble locating the "rolling stock". Full throttle into the main road melee. Poor devils were huddled in ditches and taking a royal pounding. My turn to get in a quick "poop" and straight out to sea. Lots of forward momentum. Enough for one more burst. Fatal. OK-N quivered. Oil spattered the left canopy. A hit in the front nacelle. Forward visibility suddenly nil. Got to get down and quick. Telephone poles and wire whizzing left. Camel thorn and blurred bodies gesticulating right. This is it. End of the road. Check straps. No time to ditch long-range tank. Throttle down. Nose up - stall. Whump. Great bags of dust. Everything intact. The "auxiliary" should have gone miles high. Forget the sidearm. Liability.
>
> They were on me like locusts. Wild eyes, threatening, screaming a foreign language. Scary. Probably "game over". An Italian "tenente" (lieutenant) clambered aboard.
>
> "Basta, basta" (enough) to the rest. Then in impeccable English: "If you'd join me Sir? As you appreciate we're in retreat".
>
> Decision time. Nobody flew with insignia. Just "dog tags" (name and serial number). Handy for burial purposes. Top "gen". If captured an officer's rank "assumed". To avoid reprisal, London would "recognise" but not pay you for it. Fair enough. A "slip" of the lip and Sergeant became "Pilot Officer" Markle. And so it was for 17 months. Surviving secretly. With occasionally a niggling pang of conscience.[7]

Far to the west, the Allies landed in French Algeria and Morocco. Operation *Torch* meant that the Axis forces now faced a war on two fronts, which would hasten their eventual expulsion from the continent.

Both Australian squadrons were on the move again on 9 November, 3 taking off for LG101 at 0625, followed twenty minutes later by 450. Only two hours after they had landed, 450 left on their first operation of the day, a bomber escort as close cover to twelve Bostons attacking the road between Buq Buq and Sollum. The US 66th Squadron provided top cover, and the bombing, through 'heavy, intense and accurate' AA was effective, three fires being seen. Two Bf109s made an attack without result.

Thirteen Kittybombers of 3 Squadron (including all seven MK IIs on strength) took off at 1400 to bomb convoys in the Halfaya Pass. They were accompanied by several more from 250 Squadron, with six from 112 Squadron as top cover. The bombing was spectacularly successful, two 500 lb. bombs landing 'right on the road amongst the M/T several of which, including a troop carrier, became airborne and went over the side of the pass.'

After bombing they encountered a number of Bf109s, Keith Kildey (FL323 CV-V) at first sighting two below at 10 o'clock.

I turned the squadron round to attack as our A/C were climbing too fast to attack head on. Apparently two more E/A were in a shallow dive behind us at the same time. (*112 Squadron had fought three at a higher level while 3 Squadron was bombing*) I observed PO Clabburn firing at a 109F which he climbed up after, the 109 throwing some glycol and spinning off the top of a loop.

The [other] 109F dived underneath, and I engaged it in a front quarter from above observing strikes on fuselage. I then closed to a head on, the 109 broke upwards and I raked him along the belly of his A/C observing several small explosions. The E/A smoked momentarily and disappeared over my head. I last observed him going to earth in a shallow dive.

The 109 was seen by the pilots of 112 Squadron to hit the escarpment and explode. PO Clabburn's attack (FL291 CV-A) resulted in a claim for a probable.

Keith Kildey in the cockpit of a 3 Squadron Kittyhawk IIA, after his promotion to Flight Lieutenant. (Keith Kildey)

450 Flew their second operation, a bomber escort, at 1445, twelve aircraft with long range tanks as top cover to Bostons and Baltimores bombing the Barrani - Sollum road. 250 Squadron provided the close cover. The bombing was accurate, and only a few shots of heavy AA were seen; the squadron considering that these may have been indicators to draw the attention of 109s. If this was the case, it worked, as the squadron was attacked by eight aircraft from JG 77 as they were turning south after bombing. In a willing engagement, four of the squadron's Kittyhawks received Cat. I damage, and two pilots made claims, Sgt Oakley (FL881) a probable, and Fl. Lt. Clarke (FR237) a probable and a damaged. JG 77 made a total of five claims, including a Spitfire of 92 Squadron, which was shot down by Maj. Muncheburg, the *Kommodore*.[8]

Sgt. Dave Borthwick (FR210) was shot down by Obfw. Hackler, and this extract from an article written by him in 1988 describes the circumstances of the combat and his subsequent ordeal in great detail, as well as providing an excellent picture of the way the squadrons dealt with the constant forward moves to keep up with the advancing army.

After the breakthrough of Alamein, 450 Squadron moved forward by being divided into an advance party, which went on ahead to the next landing ground, and a rear party, which serviced, refuelled and rearmed the aircraft until the advance party was established. The aircraft continued to operate from the old landing ground until things were ready at the next place and then landed there after a sortie, instead of returning to their point of departure. The pilots of the aircraft on the last sortie had to do all the ops. until the others travelling with the rear party arrived a day or two later.

On the first move I travelled by road. It was a two day journey (to Daba from the Cairo - Alexandria road) and at night we pulled over to the side of the road and slept under the trucks. A Ju88 came along the road with its machine gun in the rear going, but never hit anything. He was so low you could not have missed him with a rifle but nobody had one, and he flew on unimpeded. Next morning I found I'd been sleeping in a heap of Italian stick grenades, so I was lucky nothing was hit.

We arrived at the new landing ground and took over the aircraft while the other pilots had a rest, operating as before, shooting up ground transport, escorting light bombers, and dive bombing, with Rommel's retreating army getting more concentrated as they closed in on Halfaya Pass.

On the next move, I was one of the pilots of the aircraft moved further on to Fuka and we were to do all the ops. until the others caught up. We were escorting Bostons on the third outing I did that day, Nov. 9th, 1942. We were supposed to have one squadron of 12 aircraft as close cover - three each side of the bombers and six up behind them about a thousand feet. The middle cover was two lots of six aircraft - three pairs in line abreast - stepped up and down to one side of the close cover, with the top cover stepped up again in two sixes on the other side. Unfortunately for me, the squadron that should have been top cover did not rendezvous, and six other aircraft returned unserviceable, leaving 18 aircraft as escort instead of 36. At the top of this not very high stack of fighters, and as number two on the extreme outside was I.

The American squadron that did not rendezvous was doing a lot of chattering on the wireless, and whether it was this, or some other cause, that caused the ME109s to attack I don't know. There were eight of them and the six of us in the top stack had one each on our tails and I and a F/Lt Nobby Clarke each had two. I found out afterwards that he got rid of his by flying out to sea. He had been in the Fleet Air Arm and did not mind flying over the sea, unlike the majority of single engined pilots. I was on the south side of the formation before it broke up, on the corner where the attack came.

The ME109 could out-climb, out-dive and out-speed the P-40s we flew. The one thing it could not do was out turn us. When I got the 109s on my tail I went into a steep turn with the 109s following me. After several turns - I don't know how many as I had other things to think about - I found myself gaining on one of the ones previously on my tail. Eventually I got far enough around to have a shot at him. He pulled down and away and I made the irresistible but fatal mistake of following him. At this point, the other 109, which I later discovered was flown by Oberfeldwebel Hackler, got what must have been an easy shot at me. Three 20mm cannon shells hit the left side of my aircraft, starting back near the tail and coming forward. They sounded like kicking a kerosene tin, and the last one went off under my legs, cutting the control cables, paralysing my left leg, and hamstringing my right achilles tendon. The cockpit filled with smoke and there seemed little future in staying there. I jettisoned the hood, which flew off and hit me in the right eye as it went. When I recovered from this blow the necessity of an urgent departure was even more apparent, so I did not stop to undo the oxygen and microphone leads as I went out.

I next found myself dragging by the ears beside the fuselage of the aircraft. I thought if I pulled the parachute ripcord it would probably tangle with the tailplane, but that if I did not I was a goner for certain, so I tried, unsuccessfully, to find the rip cord handle. I thought "I've read somewhere what to do now - Tee Emm (an RAF training manual) and it said to look down for it". It would not have occurred to me to do this, so I owe my continued survival to Tee Emm. When I looked down the earphones pulled out of my helmet, the face mask pulled off, the tail went past and I pulled the string.

The Sydney Bulletin once had an article about suicides jumping from high places having no sensation of falling. In my case, the rate at which the scenery was enlarging conveyed an entirely adequate sensation of falling, and I felt the jerk of the parachute and thump of landing on my backside almost simultaneously.

When I took stock of the situation the first thing I did was to jam my handkerchief behind my left knee, which was bleeding like a stuck pig, and bend it so that the foot was next to my buttock. I cut a cord off the parachute and wound it round the bent knee. This stopped the bleeding all right, but when I got into hospital a week or so later, it took an anaesthetic and three or four more days to straighten it out again.

After fixing my leg I felt a wet patch spreading on my back and thought I'd been hit there too. However it was only coming from my water bottle which had been punctured. I drank what was left in it and that was the last decent drink I had for nearly a week.

It was stinking hot during the day, and as I soon found out, bitterly cold at night. I was 50 or 60 miles ahead of the Eighth Army, and, I thought, about fifteen or twenty miles inland from the coast road. I could hear the artillery a long way to the east, and later at night, follow the progress of the advance by the flashes as well. I had visions of the Eighth Army advancing in a wall, but it wasn't like that - all the advance was along the coast roads - the main road and a desert road, parallel and a few hundred yards inland from it.

I decided that my best chance was to make my way north as best I could. By using my two hands, my bent left leg and my right leg I could progress sitting down. I don't suppose I went very far, but it must have been a considerable distance. By the second day I could see a pimple on the horizon, and I thought, "If I can make that I'm right". About the third day the artillery passed me by and disappeared (at night) into the west. There were very heavy dews at night, and although there had recently been a very rare rain, and the ground was damp, there was no water at all on the surface, or as far down as I could dig by hand. On the fourth day I reached the pimple, which had grown slowly into a cairn of loose rocks, about a foot by six inches, roughly hewn and piled up to a height of about eight feet. By this time I had worn a lot of skin off my hands and backside, and had a thirst which I have been trying to quench ever since. By pulling out a few of the key stones at the bottom, I brought the whole lot down, and laid them out with the concave side upwards. The next morning about a tablespoon of dew was waiting for me in each concavity. It was too cold to sleep at night but in the morning when the sun first rose it was just right. Later it got too hot and I spent the rest of the day trying to find shade in the camel thorn which grew about three feet high all around. I thought my best chance was to stick to my water supply such as it was, and it turned out I'd done the right thing but for the wrong reason. I'd altered the scenery in an otherwise featureless landscape, and this attracted the attention of two Bedouin. I awoke after my sleep on the sixth morning to find these two standing over me. They carried two or three rifles each, picked up from the passing armies over the years, and several water bottles of different patterns from the same sources. They gave me one of the water bottles, which contained a pea soup like mixture of water and mud, with, in all probability, a bit of camel shit thrown in. However, in the years since, I have never tasted a better drink.

We carried a goolie chit, which, written in Arabic and English, explained that if returned in good condition, there was a reward payable. I was a little concerned to see them 'reading' this upside down, but had enough Arabic to explain the situation and ask them to get the *Inglisi Askaris* which were "hennak" - over there.

These chaps were a patrol of the KRRC who put me in a stretcher in the back of a utility truck and drove me into Sidi Barani. It was a nightmare ride. Every bump, and there were plenty, went through me like a knife. I'd ruptured a disc when I landed and worn the skin off my backside, which had become, it turned out later, infected. About half way, when they were going east along the desert road in the dark, they hit a tank going west. Fortunately my head was on the other side of the truck, and I heard it hit the front mud guard. I pulled up my right leg and saw the end of the stretcher disintegrate. The rest of the journey I did on the knobbly contents of the utility tray.

Eventually we arrived at a camp occupied by a Radar Unit, whose fresh faced P/Os were celebrating their advance with a party. The drivers of the truck inquired the way to the first field dressing station, explaining about me in the back. They all gathered around the rear of the truck, in the dark, and I could hear them saying "Get a torch, get a torch" into the distance. When they shone it on me I could hear "Christ", "Jesus!" etc. as they saw me. I wasn't looking my best, with a week's whiskers caked with blood from my eye and sand, and I was, as the hospital report says, emaciated. However, I said, "What about a drink for me" and they gave me a full half pint mug of rum. From then on the journey was much more comfortable, and it wasn't far to the dressing station. There I was asked what I would like. I expected the usual Bully Beef, with or without dog biscuits, but said "What have you got?" "Anything you like" was the reply. I thought I'd try them out, and requested a glass of water with mist on the outside, and tomato soup with a lump of cream in the middle.

They came right back with these too, and also a Mickey Finn, which on top of the rum put me right out until next morning, when I was flown back to Cairo in the air ambulance, one of whose pilots was a former member of our squadron, Bill Carson. Although I had no money on me, and never saw him again to pay him back, he sent my parents a cable. This, to say I was all O.K., was the first notification they got after the local postmaster had told my sixteen year old sister, the only one home at the time, that I had had it. *

---

* The severity of Dave Borthwick's injuries prevented him from resuming his tour with 450 Squadron, and he returned to Australia in a hospital ship. For details of his subsequent career, and a note about Obfw. Hackler, refer to Appendix 11.

الى كل عربى كريم

السلام عليكم ورحمة الله وبركاته وبعد فحامــل هذا الكتاب ضابط بالجيش
البريطانى وهو صديق وفىّ لكافة الشعوب العربية فنرجو أن تعـاملونه بالعطف والاكرام .
وأن تحافظوا على حيـاته من كل طارى. ونأمل عند الاضطرار أن تقـدموا له ما يحتاج
اليه من طعام وشراب .
وأن ترشـدونه الى أقرب معسكر بريطانى
وسنكافئـكم ماليا بسخاء على ما تسدونه اليه من خدمات .
والســـلام عليكم ورحمة الله وبركاته ؟

القيادة البريطانية العامة فى الشرق

To All Arab Peoples - Greetings and Peace be upon you. The bearer of
this letter is an Officer of the English Government and a friend of all Arabs.
Treat him well, guard him from harm, give him food and drink, help him
to return to the nearest English soldiers and you will be rewarded. Peace
and the Mercy of God upon you.

The British High Command in the East.

Useful Words

English	Arabic	English	Arabic
English	Ingleezi.		
English Flying Officer	Za-bit Ingleezi Tye-yar.	Water	Moya.
Friend	Sa-hib, Sa-deek.	Food	A'-kl.

Take me to the English and you will be rewarded.
Hud-nee eind el Ingleez wa ta-hud mu-ka-fa.

PME/1554-9/41

An example of a 'goolie chit', as mentioned in Dave Borthwick's account of his harrowing
experience. This one was never used. (Des Cormack)

During the day, B Flight of 3 Squadron left LG101 to make preparations to receive aircraft at LG76. 'Near Sidi Barrani, the convoy was stopped by members of an armoured column and advised to delay the journey until the enemy had been driven out of Barrani!' They reached LG76 the following day, having been 'ineffectively strafed by low flying ME109s en route.'

Both squadrons flew one uneventful patrol on 10 November and transferred their aircraft to LG76 in the morning on 11 November, being available to fly on operations by 1130, both sweeps which did not contact the enemy.

260 Squadron, which had moved from LG97 to LG75 near Mischeifa on 10 November, took off at 0915 on the 11th as part of a Wing formation to attack LG2 at Gambut. The Wing was attacked by ten Bf109s en route, 2 SAAF losing two aircraft, with two more damaged. After the bombing, 260 lost one pilot, and another of their aircraft was damaged. Fl. Lt. Ron Cundy (FL316) then saw an Fi 156 close to the ground and shot it down. As they were leaving the Gambut area, 260 Squadron found a Ju88, which was attacked by six pilots, including Fl. Lt. Cundy, and shot down.

On 12 November twelve 450 aircraft took off at 0926 to provide top cover to eight more from 3 Squadron, intending to strafe M/T on the Tobruk - Gazala road. (Readers who have been following the narrative on the map will appreciate both the extent and rapidity of the westward movement.) Over El Adem four Bf109s were engaged by 450 Squadron, Fl.Lt. Schaaf (FR212) claiming a probable, which broke off the fight, climbed, and then fell away on its back. 450's pilots saw a fire on the ground which was not there before the engagement. Three other pilots also fired bursts without making any claims. Undisturbed by the skirmish above them, 3 Squadron found the road almost deserted, so turned back east and found moving M/T which was strafed effectively, five pilots each claiming one truck destroyed.

At 1315 3 Squadron were off again, with the US 66th Squadron, to strafe the Tobruk - Gazala road and to search for barges being used to evacuate stores and troops from Tobruk. The barges were easily located. The Americans set one alight, and Fl. Lt. Keith Kildey, leading 3 Squadron, set fire to the other, 'which was obviously carrying fuel, as packing cases were seen with drums on the deck.' The squadron then turned south and strafed M/T, Keith Kildey destroying a troop carrier (full of troops) while Sgts. Caldwell and Righetti damaged four more trucks.

450 Squadron maintained the pressure on the retreating enemy, twelve aircraft strafing near Tobruk between 1435 and 1650, claiming three flamers and fifteen damaged.

Later in the day 260 Squadron also went after the barges, and one which was full of troops was destroyed by Ron Cundy, whose aircraft was hit by AA fire, causing a large hole in the wing. The following day while ground strafing at Gazala, his aircraft (FL272 HS-W) was hit again, this time by a machine gun bullet which struck the perspex in front of him.

There was no operational flying for either squadron on 13 November, both units flying their aircraft to Gambut between 1315 and 1430. At Gambut Main, Fl.Lt. Ken McRae, the Engineer Officer of 3 Squadron found a lightly damaged Bf109G, which was returned to an airworthy state by the replacement of the tailplane, tail wheel and canopy. Bobby Gibbes estimated that it had a low number of hours, and this was indeed the case.

It had belonged to 8/JG 77, and its pilot, Lt. Heinz Ludemann, was slightly wounded by American P-40s on 4 November. Being only superficially damaged, it had been ferried to Gambut for repair, and then left behind as the Germans retreated. 3 Squadron knew none of this when they found their prize. It was repaired and repainted on 14 November, the ground crews working until after dark. The spinner was painted red, the yellow lower cowling covered with a neutral colour, and the codes CV-V, (Gibbes' personal marking) were applied. The national insignia were of course painted out and replaced with roundels. The squadron hoped to use it for instructional purposes before sending it home to Australia as a war trophy.

One might not expect so much attention to be paid to a captured aircraft as this. The squadron had already acquired a Bf109F which had been flown by Gibbes, who enthusiastically approved of its performance. However, this second Bf109 became famous, and was destined never to reach Australia. It was, in fact, the well known 'Black 6', restored to flying condition in England over a period of eighteen and a half years by a dedicated team of enthusiasts led by Russ Snadden. It made its maiden flight on 17 March 1991. From that time until its unfortunate crash on 12 October 1997, it entertained thousands of aviation enthusiasts at air shows in the UK. It is currently under restoration for static display.[*]

Coincidentally, 450 Squadron acquired an enemy machine of their own on 14 November, when two fitters, Allan Sherwood and Eddie Meakins, with PO Gough and Fl. Lt. Clarke, salvaged a Henschel 126 from the desert and quickly put it into going order.[9] On 15 November, when the squadrons moved to Gazala No2, Clarke flew the Henschel.

While the extracurricular activity was taking place with captured aircraft, both squadrons found time to fly two operations during their brief stay at Gambut. In the afternoon 450 gave top cover to 3 Squadron on an armed recce of the Gazala - Derna area. They bombed and strafed a concentration of 300-plus M/T moving west, starting three fires and claiming thirteen more trucks damaged between them, one by Sgt. Frederick Silk, who was flying his first operation with 450 Squadron.

450 flew its aircraft to Gazala Satellite No.2 at 0800 on 15 November, followed by 3 Squadron at 0915. Bobby Gibbes took off in the Bf109 at 0930, escorted by F/Sgt. Reg Stevens and Sgt. John Hooke. Both squadrons flew recce and strafing operations in the afternoon.

Change of ownership 1: 450 Squadron's captured Henschel 126. (RAAF Museum)

---

[*] *Bobby Gibbes next saw Black 6 while it was under restoration in England, and given that it was his unit that captured it, he suggested that it should be returned to Australia, as was the original intention. This was a request which Russ Snadden denied! Gibbes was also present as an official guest on the day of its first public viewing, 2 May 1991.*

During the rapid advance by the 8th Army after the break out at El Alamein, the squadrons of 239 Wing found numerous abandoned enemy aircraft as they occupied the former *Luftwaffe* landing grounds. These photographs show, top left: personnel of 250 Squadron examining a Bf109E, probably from the reconnaissance unit 4(H)/12, top right: PO Des Cormack beside a Bf109E *Jabo,* bottom left: PO Cormack with a Ju87 of 4/St.G 3, and bottom right, S9+OS, the Bf109 in the photograph above. This aircraft originally belonged to 8/ZG 1, the third Gruppe of which was reformed as I/SG 2 at the beginning of October. Note the unidentified Bf109F in the background, and the Hurricane and Kittyhawk partially concealed by tents on the horizon line.

(Des Cormack)

On 16 November, 3 Squadron was saddened to learn that Acting Sqn. Ldr. Terry RAAF, formerly the Adjutant of 3 Squadron, and Sqn. Ldr. Strawson DFC, RAF, the Sqn. Ldr. Flying at 239 Wing HQ, were both killed when their vehicle struck a land mine while travelling to Martuba Satellite No.4 with C Flight. Sqn Ldr. Strawson had flown on a number of operations with both 3 and 450 Squadrons.

450 Squadron flew two uneventful operations on this day, and 3 attacked M/T, damaging four trucks and a tanker.

The following day 450 flew four operations totalling twenty-three sorties, while 3 Squadron flew twenty-three sorties from two operations. The first of these was fruitless, but on the second, at 1240, carried out in poor weather with a cloud base of only 2,000 ft. there was a sharp exchange with II/JG 27.

Accompanied by twelve aircraft of 112 Squadron, 3 Squadron set out to strafe the Benghazi - Magrun road, and encountered three Bf109s. Sqn. Ldr. Gibbes (FL323 CV-V) attacked one which went into a dive with one wheel down. PO Dave Ritchie followed it down, firing without effect and saw it strike the ground. Fl.Lt. Smith (RAF) of 112 Squadron had also attacked this aircraft, and the victory was shared between he and Gibbes.

One of the other 109s became involved in a fight with PO John Upward (FL306) and Sgt. John Hooke, both of whom had become separated from the rest of the squadron because of cloud. It was first sighted by Hooke as it was making a rear quarter attack on Upward. Hooke fired from the front quarter, thwarting its first attack, and then followed a series of turnabouts until the Messerschmitt pilot positioned himself for a front quarter attack on Hooke's machine; his avoiding action causing him to spin. He recovered close to the ground, and as he was climbing back he saw the Messerschmitt carry out a front quarter attack on PO Upward, without appearing to fire its guns. Seconds later the two aircraft collided, each losing part of a wing. They spun into the ground and blew up. The collision occurred at 1,500 ft. and neither pilot had time to bale out. Fw. Buter and John Upward both lost their lives.

Five aircraft of 450 took off at 1429 to strafe Magrun LG. No aircraft were present, so they strafed roads in the vicinity, claiming two flamers, (one a tanker) and eleven damaged M/T: two of the pilots reported five and three personnel, who were seen firing small arms, as 'damaged' !

Six more aircraft of 450 Squadron returned to the area at 1506, strafing aircraft on Barce aerodrome, destroying a Ju52, a Heinkel 111 and a Bf110. Sgt. Keith Marrows (FR330) was hit by AA and crash-landed. He avoided capture and eventually returned to the squadron.

On 18 November the two Australian squadrons were employed on widely differing tasks, 450 flying no fewer than six convoy escort operations, their formations replacing one another in relays. On 16 November a twenty-five ship convoy had left Alexandria for Malta, which was in need of re-supply, and under almost constant air cover by fighters from Africa, and Malta, it reached its destination unscathed.

During 450's second operation, between 1011 and 1230, four Ju88s attacked the convoy at 1125 without success. PO Crouch (FR267) attacked a Ju88, seeing an explosion and a piece of the tail break off. Even though wreckage, oil and a light green substance were seen in the water, it seems that a definite claim was not made, as Crouch did not see the aircraft go in, owing to an attack on him by one of the other Junkers. Sgt Silk (FR345) also attacked a Ju88, observing black smoke coming away, but it was acknowledged that this may have been the result of boost. The Kittyhawks chased the Ju88s for fifteen miles, gaining only slowly, and left the convoy when their relief arrived. Sgt. Gleeson failed to return from the operation, and the squadron feared the worst, mounting a search of four aircraft led by the CO at 1459. They found nothing, but it turned out that he had force-landed safely at Derna.

Pilot Officer T.E. Crouch of 450 Squadron. The photograph was taken at Gambut in April 1942.
(Gordon Steege)

Six aircraft of 3 Squadron took off at 1015 to locate 7 Armoured Division, thence to patrol Magrun, Benina and Barce. The armoured division was not located, but when the formation reached Magrun, they found considerable activity on the 'drome. PO Dave Ritchie (FL345) attacked a Ju52 which was just taking off and saw it start to burn. PO Dent (FL358) followed Ritchie in and also fired at the Junkers, which burst into flames. Bobby Gibbes (FL323 CV-V) waited for a Bf109 to lift off, and shot it down inside the aerodrome boundary. Wing disallowed his claim because of the fact that it crashed on its own aerodrome! PO 'Donk' Bray attacked a He111 which was being towed by a tractor and also saw strikes. Not yet content with their work, the formation strafed the road between Agedabia and Magrun, destroying four M/T and damaging twelve more.

The Ju52 attacked by Ritchie and Dent is not included in 3 Squadron's final list of air to air claims, apparently considered to have been a ground strafing victory. However, Chris Shores, in *Fighters Over the Desert* states that: 'The Luftwaffe reported that one Ju52 of III/ KGzbV I and one Savoia transport of the Regia Aeronautica were *shot down* (author's italics) on Magrun, so either 260 or 3 RAAF's victim was in fact a three engined Savoia, and not a Ju52. From conversations with an Italian pilot present, it seems more likely that the SM82 was shot down by the Australian squadron'. [10]

A road strafing operation by four aircraft at 1053, during which one M/T was destroyed and three or four damaged, was followed by another visit to Magrun, led by Fl. Lt. Danny Boardman at 1515. Four Ju52s were present, and Boardman set one on fire, then strafing a Bf109. PO Taylor attacked another Ju52, which also blazed, and another unidentified aircraft which also caught fire. PO Rex Bayly and F/Sgt. Reg Stevens strafed two more Bf109s and one truck. Sgt Alan Righetti crash-landed at Tmimi 'drome, his rudder controls having been damaged by AA.

Next morning the westward advance continued. British armour reached Benghazi, and Bobby Gibbes flew to Martuba at 1025, landing to inspect the surface. It was found to be serviceable, and nine MK II Kittyhawks left at 1325, landing there at 1655 after carrying out a recce of Barce and Benina. At 1510 Gibbes ferried the Bf109 to Martuba with the remaining four Kittyhawks as close escort, John Hooke flying the CO's FL323, the other CV-V.

450 transferred their sixteen aircraft at 1500, PO Crouch arriving 15 minutes after the main formation in the Henschel, apparently without escort.

19th November: At 7.30 pm we moved out in a terrific sand storm to proceed the sixty miles to Martuba. We passed through rugged country for some miles and then over the wind-swept Gazala Plain. We reached our destination at 10.30 pm, had a can of baked beans and went to bed. I could not get warm all night long and sleep was almost an impossibility. Food is very light on. I haven't had a full stomach for over two weeks. (Viv Herrett)

The receiving end. Taken from a German PoW, this photograph shows the aftermath of a successful low level strafing attack by 239 Wing. (RAAF Museum)

Squadron Leader Bobby Gibbes with a Kittyhawk IIA, probably FL323 CV-V, which he flew regularly from 6 November, until he was shot down in it on 14 January 1943. The kangaroo and dachshund motif was designed by his mother, and appeared on all of the aircraft which he flew regularly. (Bobby Gibbes)

20 November saw forty sorties carried out in five operations between the two squadrons, but no contact was made with the enemy. 3 Squadron was then rested for the next six days, while 450 flew two more convoy escorts on 22 November, the first of which met with mixed success, destroying a Ju88, but losing a pilot due to difficult weather conditions. Six aircraft with long range tanks took off at 0858, identifying themselves by Verey signal, and establishing radio contact with the directing ship. Thereafter, several vectors were received until a single Ju88 was sighted and attacked by the top cover, Fl. Lt. Schaaf (FR242) and PO Winn (FR274) getting in several good bursts. The Junkers was obviously hit hard, as its port wheel dropped and the port engine stopped. It went into a vertical dive into a 10/10ths rain storm five miles north east of the convoy. The Kittyhawks waited outside the rain storm for the E/A to appear, but it did not do so. The weather was appalling, 7/10 cloud from 1,000 to 13,000 ft. and 10/10 to sea level in rain storms. Flying through one such storm on the way home, Sgt. R. Payne, a New Zealander, disappeared and was not seen again.

Sgts. Gleeson and Oakley took off at 1355 to search for Sgt. Payne, but found nothing, being hampered by constant low cloud and rain. 450 were then also rested for three days, resuming operations briefly on 26 November, before going on leave in Cairo and Alexandria. 3 Squadron flew six sorties on 27 November, and then enjoyed a break until 8 December. 450 did not operate again until 10 December.

Fl.Lt. Ron Cundy of 260 Squadron flew his last operation in November on the 18th. His operational hours for the month totalled 23.25 and his total time on operations to that point were 202 hours

and 20 minutes. In December his tour ended, and he returned to Australia with a DFM (gazetted on 22 January 1943), a DFC, (gazetted on 9 February) and was Mentioned in Despatches. Apparently promoted from Sergeant to Flight Lieutenant within the space of six days, he had in fact been an officer for five and a half months without knowing it !

Promotion was slow coming through - at least notification of it was. I remained a Sergeant until 15th September 1942 when I was promoted to Pilot Officer. Six days later (21st) I was again promoted, this time to Flight Lieutenant. I had been running "B" Flight for some time and had led the squadron on a number of occasions and the wing on several. You may wonder how this could be. Our losses were fairly high, (33 while I was with the squadron) so that I became one of the most experienced desert pilots there. From memory I was one of only two who were with the squadron in November 1941. Subsequent examination of my records reveals that I had been commissioned on 30th April 1942. Communications between headquarters and active desert squadrons left a lot to be desired. [11]

130. A youthful Fl. Lt. Ron Cundy wearing the ribbons of the DFM and DFC. At the completion of his long desert tour, he was still not twenty-one years of age. (Ron Cundy)

While the squadrons of 239 Wing were resting, Bobby Gibbes took the opportunity to try out 'his' Bf109. He had already remarked upon its performance in his diary. 'The 109 is a hell of a nice kite with a terrific performance. On lowest

Year 1942 Month	Date	Aircraft Type	No.	Pilot, or 1st Pilot	2nd Pilot, Pupil or Passenger	Duty (Including Results and Remarks)	SE Day Dual (1)	SE Day Pilot (2)	SE Night Dual (3)	SE Night Pilot (4)
						Totals Brought Forward	46·10	376·50	3·05	6·55
Nov.	1	Warhawk	FL224	Self	—	Dive Bombing German H/A.		1·10		
	1	"	FL224	"	—	" " Again		1·10		
	2	"	FL274	"	—	Top Cover to 18 Bostons. N. Sector.		1·15		
	3	"	FL299	"	—	Top Cover to 18 Bostons - Sidi Abdel Rahman		1·20		
	3	"	FL274	"	—	Close Cover to 18 Bostons - Fuka. I had a squirt at an Me110 but did not get it		1·40		
	4	"	FL274	"	—	Top Cover to Kitty-Bombers - W. of Daba. I destroyed a JU88 N. of Daba the 1 JU88 Destroyed		1·25		
	5	"	FL316	"	—	Top Cover to Bostons - Sidi Haneish. Chased 2 Me109s. No real Engagement. Me109s missing		1·50		
	6	"	FL274	"	—	Engine Test		·30		
	10	"	FL316	"	—	L.G.97 to L.G.75		1·25		
	11	"	FL316	"	—	Bombed L.G.2 Gambut. 1 JU88 Destroyed, Hull missing, destroyed & Perspex store		1·25		
	12	"	FL316	"	—	Top Cover to Kitts Bombers. I destroyed a barge full of troops off Tobruk. Got shot up - large		2·10		
	12	"	FL273	"	—	L.G.75 to L.G.148 Sidi Azeiz. hole in wing		·40		
	13	"	FL273	"	—	Ground Straffing at Gazala. Got shot up again. Machine Gun Bullet in Perspex in front of me		3·35		
	13	"	FL273	"	—	Sidi Azeiz to Gambut Main.		·20		
	15	"	FL341	"	—	Mecle. to Maroua - Derna - Martoba.		2·30		
	17	"	FL341	"	—	Gambut Main to Gazala No.2		·30		
	17	"	FL341	"	—	Interception Patrol for JU52s. Nothing Seen.		3·05		
	17	"	FL341	"	—	Gazala No.2 to Gambut Main.		·30		
	19	"	FL341	"	—	Ground Straff Aerodrome at El Magrun		2·30		
						27·20				
						Totals Carried Forward	46·10	404·10	3·05	6·55

Summary for November 1942
Unit 260 Squadron
Date 30th Nov. 1942
Signature ...

Ops. Hrs. for Month: 23 hrs. 25 mins.
Ops. Hrs. to Date: 202 hrs. 20 mins.
Total Warhawk Hrs.: 6 hrs 35 mins

Grand Total [Cols. (1) to (10)] ...... Hrs. ...... Mins.

D.3206/7.37.—C.4947.

Ron Cundy's log book entries for November show a very successful and strenuous month's work.

possible boost and revs was clocking 220-230 mph'.[12] On the afternoon of 21 November he flew it briefly for an RAF film unit, but landed after ten minutes with a flat battery and pitch mechanism problems. It was flown several more times, on 26 November and again on 1 December, once by Gibbes for thirty-five minutes, and then by Fl. Lt. Ron Watt, (an experienced pilot who had joined the squadron on 21 November, directly from Australia) for twenty minutes. Then officialdom intervened. A signal from HQ Middle East was received, stating that the 109 had to be flown back to Heliopolis. As it was the first Bf109G to be captured in serviceable condition, it was required for testing and evaluation. Gibbes took off early on 2 December, later recording in his diary 'On the way down I was mean enough to fly alongside several unarmed American Dakotas and enjoyed watching the reaction of their startled crews'.[13] When he took off from Amiriya the replacement cockpit canopy blew off, hitting the starboard wing. Bobby Gibbes returned from Heliopolis on 4 December, ferrying back a new Kittyhawk for 250 Squadron.

112 Squadron left 239 Wing on a temporary basis, on attachment to the USAAF 57th Fighter Group, to operate together and give them the benefit of 112's desert experience. The other two American squadrons, (the 64th and 65th) had previously been operating with 233 Wing. In spite of this, the Wing's squadrons stayed close together, 112 moving to Belandah No.2 on 6 December, while 3, 250 and 450 moved to Belandah on 8 December. 450's Henschel force landed on the way, its pilot, PO Crouch arranging for guard to be placed over it until it could be recovered. He and his passenger, PO Gough, the engineering officer, walked to the main road and met 450's road convoy.

3 Squadron spent the next two days escorting Tac. R. Hurricanes to Agheila. On the first of these trips (1345 on 8 December) heavy AA was encountered, but there was no enemy reaction to the

Change of ownership 2: Bobby Gibbes' Bf109G, formerly 'Black 6' of 8/JG 77, in the hands of 451 Squadron ground crew after it had been flown to Lydda for evaluation. (RAAF Museum)

two ops. on the following day. On 10 and 11 December they carried bombs, attacking the 'drome at Nofilia, which was well behind the Germans' defensive line at Agheila. On 12 December they bombed the southern sector of the Agheila line, and carried out three armed recces on 13 December, the day Rommel's forces began to withdraw from Agheila. The first two were uneventful, but enemy aircraft attacked the formation from behind near Marble Arch during the third operation.

At 1615 ten aircraft led by the CO had taken off on an armed recce of the road between Marble Arch and Nofilia. They bombed tents and M/T between these two locations and then turned for home. The formation was attacked by eight Bf109s and a MC202. Sgt Cashmore (FL348) was wounded in the arm and crash landed his aircraft at base, causing Cat. II damage. Three Kittyhawks managed to return fire, but observed no results.

From 10 December to 13 December, 450 Squadron carried out eight operations, a mixture of strafing, bombing and fighter sweeps. Three of these resulted in claims for a variety of M/T destroyed and damaged. There was more of the same during the next four days, the squadrons flying twelve operations independently of one another, and combining to escort Bostons at 1100 on 16 December.

Since resuming operations on 8 December, 3 Squadron had been flying MK II Kittyhawks exclusively, but four MK IIIs were taken on charge, and at least three of them, FR112, FR335 and another, simply recorded as 'Kitty3', flew briefly on operations. These were exchanged with 260 Squadron, who handed over four MK IIs on 16 December. Although 260 began converting to the MK III in December, It seems that they were still operating a few MK IIs as late as May 1943. Keeping engine spares for two different types would have been unnecessarily complicated, but while the two squadrons were operating from the same base, this would have been alleviated to some extent.

Kittyhawk Mark IIA FL341. Originally with 260 squadron, it was flown on only seven widely spread occasions by 3 Squadron: first in the hands of Wg. Cdr. Burton on 28 December 1942, and again by Acting Sqn. Ldr. Ron Watt, 20 January 1943. It then disappeared from the line until 8 May, when it was used by Sgts. Laver and McLeod (twice), FO Harris, and PO Dawkins, between 8 and 10 May. This photograph is likely to have been taken at Kairouan in May. (RAAF Museum)

On 18 December extensive use was made of transport aircraft for the first time when 3, 450 and 250 Squadrons moved to Marble Arch, and 'the excellent results brought appreciating [sic] remarks from responsible officers'. Essential oil, petrol, ammunition and a maintenance party were all moved by air, enabling the fighters to resume operations within two hours of arriving. 3 Squadron took off from Belandah at 0900, carried out a recce of the Sirte area and landed at Marble Arch at 1140. They had carried out two more bombing operations from their new base before the day was over. 450 flew a morning recce, twelve aircraft landing at Marble Arch at 1333. The remaining aircraft were ferried from Belandah No.1 between 1224 and 1314.

> As soon as the Kittyhawks landed, they were re-armed and re-fuelled and set off to attack enemy motor transport east of Sultan. All hands worked on making the site habitable, and the aircraft serviceable. To quote from the Squadron's unofficial diary . . .

> "Pilots helped re-fuel and re-arm, rolled oil drums, struck tents, etc; and tonight they sit under the moon yarning around a bottle of whisky, while the erks, not far off, do likewise around their issue rum. It's a bombers moon but we're all too tired to care much. To the south-west, Mussolini's Marble Arch straddles the road, a gaunt silhouette to remind us that no other Wing has ever been this far west".[14]

This successful day was not without its tragedy, however. The departing Germans had thoroughly mined the airfield, and one member of a 3 Squadron refuelling party jumped off a truck, landing on a German 'S' mine. LACs Maurice Thompson, Tom Waugh and Les Horne were killed instantly, and LAC Gates died in an aircraft taking him to hospital. LAC George Bartsch died later in hospital and LACs Guerney and Kelly were badly wounded.

On 19 December the squadrons' road convoys arrived during the day, and the remaining 3 Squadron aircraft were ferried to their new base, but the squadron still managed to fly five operations, four bombing and one recce, destroying a gun post consisting of four 88mm guns as well as damaging several M/T.

450 flew two productive operations, the first, at 0750, resulting in claims for five trucks as flamers with fifteen more damaged. Twelve aircraft took off at 1305 with long range tanks and strafed 50-plus M/T. Sqn. Ldr. Barber attacked and silenced an AA post, Fl. Lt. Glendinning destroyed a truck and Sgt Keith Marrows destroyed a staff car. On the return journey over the sea the top cover were attacked by two Bf109Fs, which made three separate attacks, damaging the aircraft of Sgt. Marrows (FL888). Fl. Lt. Alf Glendinning, Sgt Gleeson and FO Norton (FR237) all got in good bursts in response, Norton damaging one, which shed pieces, and both enemy aircraft then broke off the engagement.

Alf Glendinning had recently joined 450 after serving first with 3 Squadron, followed by a spell flying Spitfires on 92 Squadron, with whom he destroyed a Bf109 on 27 October. He enjoyed further successes with 450 in early 1943.

450 did not operate on 20 December, and 3 Squadron flew three operations which made no contact with the enemy, but they were heavily engaged the next day.

At 0750 on 21 December, Fl. Lt. Keith Kildey led twelve aircraft to escort two Tac. R. Hurricanes to Sirte. Ten miles SE of their objective, the top cover was attacked by four or five Bf109s. Sgt. Roediger (FL346 CV-Z) became detached and 'was tied up for 15 minutes with a resultant claim of one ME109F damaged'. PO Finlason (FL273) disappeared, shot down by Hpt. Anton 'Toni' Hackl of JG 77. He was captured. *

The next operation was at 1305, when the CO led six aircraft on a long range recce and strafing attack on the enemy landing ground at Hun. It was occupied by a number of aircraft, and when

---

* Finlason and (he thought) two other aircraft (one was Roediger - author) were separated from the squadron. Finlason's port aileron was shot away and he baled out as the aircraft was uncontrollable. (AWM 54 779/3/29)

the Kittyhawks swept in on their first strafing run, not a shot was fired at them, so Gibbes decided to make a second attack. This time they were met by intense light AA, but they all survived the barrage, and Gibbes felt well content with the results: two SM79s destroyed, (Gibbes) one Ju88 destroyed, (Fl. Lt. Watt) one Ju52 destroyed and another damaged, (PO Bayly) one Bf110 destroyed, (PO Taylor) one Ju87 destroyed and one Hs126 damaged, (PO Austin) and one glider and a CR42 damaged, (F/Sgt. Bee). Gibbes called for the flight to re-form, but

> To my horror and annoyance a RAAF officer who had very recently arrived in the Middle East, and who was to take over from me, not realising the danger, led his number two in for a third attack. I urgently called for him to abort his attack, but he continued, and unfortunately two of my other pilots followed him in. The result was inevitable. The second two aircraft were both shot down.[15]

F/Sgt. Kenneth Bee was killed instantly when his aircraft (FL286) struck the ground and rolled end over end, bursting into flames. In spite of the danger, an enemy ambulance crew was seen to drive up to the wreckage.

PO Rex Bayly's machine (FL327) was hit in the engine, but he managed to belly-land about a mile away from the aerodrome, and called up to say he was OK. Gibbes called back to ask whether the area was suitable for a landing. Bayly replied that it was impossible, and asked Gibbes to leave him. Gibbes, however, had other ideas, and flew down to inspect the area. He found a marginally acceptable space and landed two miles further on, after telling Bayly to 'get weaving'. While waiting for Bayly to appear, he removed the half full drop tank, and marked out a rudimentary take-off run by tying his handkerchief to a camel thorn bush. With the remaining Kittyhawks circling overhead, Gibbes waited impatiently for Bayly to reach him, and when he did, they climbed aboard after discarding Gibbes' parachute. The take-off run was not long enough, and when the overloaded Kittyhawk reached the wadi marked by the handkerchief, it careered down the slope. Gibbes applied enough back pressure on the stick to coax it into the air. It struck the other side of the wadi, tearing off the port wheel, but now there was enough air speed, and to Gibbes' 'great relief, we cleared the ridge and were flying'.[16] He carried out a skilful cross-wind landing at Marble Arch to compensate for the missing wheel, causing slight damage to the port flap and wing tip.

After 3 Squadron's intensive action on 21 December, both RAAF units spent the time until Christmas comparatively quietly. A number of uneventful sweeps, scrambles and Tac. R. escorts were carried out, none of which made contact with the enemy, and the two squadrons were able to celebrate Christmas in some style.

> The squadron (450) spent their second Christmas Day overseas at Marble Arch. . . Christmas dinner was soup - roast pork with baked potatoes, green peas and beans - followed by plum pudding, tart and custard, with a double issue of rum, plus a packet of cigarettes (from King Farouk), and a tin of tobacco from the canteen. Nor was the advance party forgotten - "Xmas Day 1942, and who will forget what was being a very lonely Xmas being vitalised in the afternoon when two of the cooks arrived, up from Marble Arch, with a spread of specialties they had created with the nothing they had to work with". [17]

3 Squadron's members also enjoyed a 'very excellent Xmas Dinner' and Fl. Lt Keith Kildey DFM received news 'that he had been relieved from operations after an excellent tour of duty'. He left the squadron with a score of three confirmed, one probable and two damaged, and had 'earned a reputation as the squadron's ground strafing expert'.[18] In addition to his aerial victories, he considers that the Fieseler Storch he destroyed by bombing should be included in his total. He flew 200.25 operational hours in 146 sorties, dropping 94 bombs. PO Garth Clabburn assumed command of C Flight.

The next four days were occupied with uneventful patrols, sweeps, Tac. R. escorts and training flights, but on 30 December, the war for both squadrons resumed with vigour. First off at 0921 were 450 Squadron, eight aircraft led by Fl. Lt. Schaaf on a patrol over Bir El Ziden and further west. On the return, when the formation was at 4,000 ft. east of El Ziden, four Bf109s attacked the

A Christmas card from 3 Squadron, perhaps influenced by the American method of designating their fighter squadrons, but certainly indicating the squadron's changing role as a fighter bomber unit, and its personnel's preferred leisure activities. (RAAF Museum)

formation from behind. The outnumbered Germans were uncharacteristically persistent, the dog fight going on for twenty minutes, before PO Winn (FR123) damaged one of the Messerschmitts, which then broke off. The Squadron landed as planned at El Gzina LG to refuel, before returning to Marble Arch.

3 Squadron's day began with all pilots carrying out practice bombing. At 0950 PO Bayly and Sgt. Roediger took off, and shortly afterwards were instructed to gain angels over base. Bayly had to return with oxygen trouble, but Roediger (FL295 CV-B) climbed to 26,000 ft. and followed the vector given, finally contacting a HeIII three miles ahead and 1,000 ft. above. When he was within 500 yards the E/A sighted him, and it

> made a long shallow dive to ground level. I followed him down, closing to 400 yards and opened fire with two short bursts. I chased him for ten minutes at this range without being able to gain on him, and in his endeavours to evade me, E/A touched the ground with his starboard propeller, as a trail of dust trailed behind the starboard motor. His speed from then on decreased, and I closed to 150 yards after throttling back violently to avoid over-shooting. From this range I fired bursts until my ammunition was exhausted. Unfortunately my reflector sight had fused before I commenced firing and my aim was inaccurate. Nevertheless, many strikes were observed at wing roots and fuselage, whilst I am convinced that E/A was damaged as a result of touching the ground.

Photographs reveal that not all MK II Kittyhawks carried a ring and bead sight; perhaps FL295 was one of these. Sgt Roediger claimed a damaged.

At 1300 the CO led six aircraft to Alem El Gzina where they landed to refuel before carrying out a patrol over the forward troops at Bir El Ziden. They saw fifteen Bf109s and a further ten specks in

the distance, but no engagement took place. They continued the patrol and reported on various ground movements.

Fl. Lt. Danny Boardman led off seven aircraft at 1350 on the same task as the previous sortie, and again saw fifteen Bf109s from II/JG 77, which stayed to fight. 3 Squadron ended the year triumphantly. Three Messerschmitts were destroyed and another claimed as a probable, for no losses. Danny Boardman claimed his second victory.

> I was leading formation of 6 Kittyhawks. (*FO Dave Ritchie landed 45 minutes before the rest of the formation, and although the ORB made no comment, it would seem that he had been forced to return early with a mechanical defect. Author*) Proceeded to Gzina, refuelled and flew to Wadi Cherir at 10,000 ft. Noticing bomb bursts S.W. of my position, turned in that direction and I reported 12 a/c at 2 o'clock on the same level. Expecting e/a I ordered formation to climb. The e/a then climbed and manoeuvred to all positions. I ordered turnabout left, but half way round saw 4 109s coming down out of the sun, so ordered "turning right". The formation of Kittys then split up due to 109s attacking from all directions.

> In the melee I noticed 2 109s (F or G) about to make a long dive onto a Kittyhawk. I climbed into sun and made an attack on second 109 from starboard, rear quarter. Closing in to 200 yards I fired two medium bursts. As my strikes hit e/a in engine and near cockpit, black smoke and flame came from engine. E/a rolled to the left and was heading N.W. losing height.

> 4 109s then attacked me, and; whilst taking evasive action, I kept looking N.W. for signs of burning a/c. Noticed a fire at approx. X 1880, which was 10 to 15 miles from where I hit it. Several other attacks were made on me, but working E. I joined up with another Kitty and returned to base. Whilst circling scene of fight I noticed two more fires in our lines.

Fl. Lt. Ron Watt (FL334 CV-L) fired at three different aircraft, hitting the first, destroying the second, which prevented an attack on a Kittyhawk in a vulnerable position, and claimed the third as a very likely probable, as his combat report reveals.

> . . . A/C attacked and I fired a short burst full deflection at one e/a. A piece flew off and he climbed quickly into the sun. I then saw FO Russell with a 109 above him. I flew over and closing to about 200 yards fired a 15⁰ deflection and shot him down. Tail fell off e/a which burst into flames and hit the ground.

> I lost the formation so flew W. and found four more e/a. I climbed up under them after diving from slightly above and dead behind. I allowed them to attack from the beam and throttled back. I let the first three pass and closed on the fourth, firing a short burst at very short range (about 50 yards.) I did not observe strikes, but e/a stayed on its side and commenced going down with much white smoke and a bit of black smoke coming from what appeared to be the front of the a/c. His nose was almost vertical when I lost sight of him when he was at 1,000 ft.

Sgt. Alan Righetti (FL277 CV-I) was the third successful pilot, and this extract from his war diary explains how the fight developed from his point of view.

> There were 2 gaggles of 6 sent out in the afternoon. The 'boss' (Bobby Gibbes) led the first, and Danny (Boardman) led the second, with Watty as my No 1 in Black section. The job was a patrol over our forward troops in the ZIDAN area. We stooged out along the coast at 10,000 feet, when we saw bomb bursts inland, so we flew that way to investigate. Immediately sighted 10+ Me109s (later reported as 15+) which went around into the sun. They sent in a stooge below us as a decoy which we let go, and then they all attacked. They did not have much height on us and for the first time in my limited experience, did not employ their 'dive and zoom' tactics, but came in with the intention of 'mixing it'. This suited us perfectly, for although they had greater numbers, we had the manoeuvrability in steep turns.

> We 'turned-about' on their first attack, they dived through us, then climbed and circled above us. They dived again and Danny called "Turnabout". I turned the wrong way! To avoid the others I had to do a climbing steep turn, and this brought me right amongst the enemy! I managed to get one 109 in my sights, and immediately the reflector sight went out, which did not help matters. I began to gain deflection and every time I looked behind to clear my tail there seemed to be 109s everywhere. I gained what I thought to be about right for deflection (I did not find it difficult to turn inside the 109) and gave him a short burst. The tracer seemed to go just underneath his airscrew, so I applied a little top-rudder and

fired again. Immediately glycol began to stream from his port side - a very lucky fluke shot. He came out of the turn and went down in a long dive towards enemy lines. I flattened everything in the cockpit and began to gain on him, at first slowly and then quickly. The range decreased from 500 yards to 250 and I gave him a quick burst. White smoke was now pouring out, and it began to turn black. I thought he must have 'pulled the tit' (the supercharger) and I was expecting him at any moment to zoom upwards in a terrific climb under the added power - as I have seen them do (just when you think they are done) time and time again.

I was gaining very quickly now, and he was not taking avoiding action, just going down and down. At about 390 mph on the clock I closed in to about 30 yards and held the button down, until I had to break to the right. As I passed him I could see flame in his engine and knew that he'd 'had it'. As I did a wing-over to make a last attack I saw something fly from his cockpit (probably the canopy) and then papers, (probably maps) before the 109 turned down vertically towards the ground, a long arc of black smoke following, then a tremendous explosion as it crashed. Then I saw a parachute open. He must have got out at about 1500 feet. Although a most unpleasant task, I briefly considered strafing him (they had been doing that to our chaps), but I might have been 'jumped'. It was just as well, because I found later that we were over our own lines still. (The pilot was picked up by our army). I looked around for the rest of our flight but could not see an aircraft in the sky! It is amazing how quickly they disappear! I called up Danny to tell him my luck.

He said "Good show, boy, I saw it!" The risk in going down after the 109 had been worth it because it meant positive confirmation. I flew to the coast at Beurat and climbed to 9000 feet, and found a sole Kitty, but not the rest of the 'gaggle' and we returned to Marble Arch together.

Did not feel very excited about my first victory until we got down and began the de-briefing. Danny had got one, and Watty one destroyed and a probable.

As 260 Squad. had got 5 109s and 2 probables in the morning, 239 Wing collected 8 confirmed and 3 probables for the day, without suffering any casualties, a real smack in the eye for Jerry. Rex Bayly and Mackenzie were holed but got back OK. The boss was delighted, we reported to Wing, had to give our names and home-towns to an RAF reporter, (posed for official photographs) and went to the mess very pleased with ourselves!

This was an 'amateur' photograph, taken at the same time as the official RAF photograph. Left to right. Fl. Lt. Ron Watt, Sgt. Alan Righetti and Fl. Lt. Danny Boardman. The Kittyhawk IIA was the aircraft flown by Alan Righetti in the combat described above. (Alan Righetti)

Ted Oakley, 'Jenks' and Jack Gleeson, all of 450 Squad. came over to see us to tell us the good news that they are going off operational flying. They have done great jobs, and have thoroughly earned a rest. Had a beer with them, and to a great day.

My day was spoiled by one thing - the news that Jock Steele (260 Squadron) was killed at dive-bombing practice this morning. He tore the wing off a Kitty in the pull-out and went straight down into the sea without a chance. He was a fine pilot and an extra fine chap. Another very good friend gone. His close mate Peter Carver will be really cut-up. I would not have thought it possible to tear the wing off a Kitty. It just proves - if your luck is out, you've had it.

Oblt. Burchard Boker was killed[19] and Uffz. Gunter Mielenz was captured as a result of this combat. As Fl. Lt. Boardman reported two fires within British lines, it would seem likely that Boker was Watt's victim. Mielenz was the pilot who baled out of the machine attacked by Alan Righetti. (Boardman's 109 crashed ten to fifteen miles N.W., behind the German lines.)

The last day of the year was something of an anti-climax, considering the furious action of the previous day. 450 Squadron ferried eighteen aircraft from Marble Arch to Ghel 2 between 0820 and 0855, and 3 Squadron flew eleven of their aircraft from Marble Arch to the advanced LG at Alem El Gzina at much the same time, five more following at 1010. Immediately after take off they were ordered to gain height and vectored onto unidentified aircraft, but disappointingly they turned out to be Hurricanes, and the Kittyhawks landed at their new base at 1115. The ORB summed up the year with an optimistic note.

> The end of a most eventful year, finds the unit, like the rest of the Allied Forces, confidently awaiting the next move in the campaign which will clear Africa for all time of the forces of aggression. All personnel are confident that the New Year will bring fresh victories and lessen the distance to final victory.

New Year's Day found both squadrons ready for action, 450 carrying out a patrol over the forward troops at 0707, encountering AA near Buerat. Twelve 3 Squadron aircraft took off at 1040 to escort two Tac. R. Hurricanes to the Tauroga - Churgia road area. Two Bf109s were seen taking off from Tauroga, and shortly after this four more were reported taking off from another LG nearby. The awesome climbing ability of the Bf109 was clearly demonstrated when a little later at 9,000 ft. the top cover was attacked by five 109s, and Sgt. Roediger (FL283 CV-D) was cut off from the rest of the formation, and found himself under attack by a large number of enemy aircraft. (He counted *eight*.) He managed to fire a burst which he was certain hit one of his attackers, but was

"De-briefing" - 30/12/42. L. to R. 'The Boss' - Bob Gibbes (looking dubious!) Sgt. Ulrich, R.Y. Sgt. Mackenzie, R.J. Sgt Righetti, A. (with mug of tea, trying to convince the 'boss'.) Partly obscured, L. to R. P/O Russell, T. F/O Ritchie, D. P/O Bayly, R. F/O Taylor, A.B. (caption and photo, Alan Righetti)

POW German With Broken Leg
British Evacuation Tent — 168th 2FA
Libyan Desert 1/2/43

POW GERMAN

Corporal Mieleng, Gunther — German Luftwaffer pilot — twenty years old — from Bromberg, Germany. He spent two and half years in the Luftwaffe and was in the Russian campaign. In the German air force, all ranks were pilots. After ten days in the Libyan campaign, he was shot down by a Britisher flying a Kitty Hawk on December 30, 1942.

A week or so after I completed this sketch, a British colonel watching me paint in the field asked to look at the book. When he came across this picture, he went into a dignified but vehement tirade. He informed me that this chap was the one he had witnessed shot down after strafing a red-cross-marked main dressing station. His verification was that he had interrogated the downed POW when this Jerry was brought before him.

Although the colonel enjoyed and complimented me on the painting, his personal remarks concerning this POW left me ready to remove the picture from the book — but reporting and art can't be personal — so here it is.

An interesting sequel to 3 Squadron's combat on 30 December is provided by this sketch, which was done by Clifford Saber, a war artist attached to the American Field Service Ambulance in North Africa, and comes from his book *Desert Rat Sketchbook*. The Artist's hand-written comments about the subject are significant. *Note that the American method of recording dates means that this was done on 2 January, **not** 1 February.* (Via Alan Righetti)

then hit in the rudder and suffered shrapnel wounds in the right leg. He baled out, and after walking east for five miles was picked up by an armoured car of the King's Dragoon Guards. Its crew told him that they had witnessed the engagement and seen two aircraft crash. This was the likely basis of his probable claim, * which was made when he returned from hospital. However, it is possible that the other aircraft they saw go down was FO Dave Ritchie's FL297, as he was also shot down, returning to the unit after a two day walk. Two German pilots submitted claims after this combat, Ofw. Neiderhagen and Hpt. Heinz Bar of I/JG 77.[20]

Dave Ritchie had been searching for Ian Roediger when he too was attacked by five Bf109s, which emerged from cloud behind him. He saw them coming and turned into them, getting off a burst at the leader, which at once began to lose height in a steep dive. He was attacked continuously by alternate pairs of the 109s, as he tried to work his way eastwards, turning into each attack as he did so, and losing valuable altitude in the process. After his last turn, with the airspeed indicator showing 360 m.p.h.

> one wing tip and the propeller hit the ground. In this critical situation, Ritchie noticed bullets and explosive shells hitting the ground a few feet from his port wing tip in the split second before he crash-landed the Kittyhawk at a speed of about 350 m.p.h.-probably the fastest landing ever made in the Desert in which the pilot survived. . . Dave stated that there was no problem about getting out of the aircraft-he found himself looking at an empty space-as the whole engine section had parted company with the fuselage. "All I had to do," said Dave, "was to undo my straps and step out. I then ran about fifty yards where I took some cover behind the airscrew and spinner which had been torn off in the landing." The four 109's which had attacked him flew over the area, one coming down to 300 feet, but evidently thought Ritchie hadn't survived and as the aircraft was so badly damaged they didn't bother to strafe the wreckage.[21]

He had covered about forty miles on foot, when he met some friendly Arabs who gave him food and hired him a donkey and two guides on credit. These good Samaritans were rewarded when they reached the 11th Hussars.

Neither squadron encountered the enemy during the next four days, several fruitless scrambles being flown, as well as a number of training flights. The advancing army had paused: 'a signal from Alexander on 5 January warned that "administrative situation of 8th Army makes it impossible for its main body to move forward before night 14/15 January" '.[22]

Sqn. Ldr. Gibbes had an eventful day on 5 January. In the morning he flew to Benghazi in an endeavour to locate Sgt. Roediger's whereabouts, but was unsuccessful. Since his rescue, all the squadron knew was that he was safe with the army. On the return flight he force-landed south of Nofilia with an airlock in a petrol pipe, returning by road. When he arrived, he was greeted with the news that he had been awarded the DSO for 'courage, determination and devotion to duty'.

450 Squadron flew only one scramble over the next three days, being mainly occupied with bombing practice and shadow shooting, while 3 Squadron also flew a scramble, and escorted a Fieseler Storch to Hamraiet and back on 7 January. This would appear to have been a recce of suitable new landing grounds, as both squadrons were soon to move to Hamraiet.

3 Squadron flew a patrol over Hamraiet at 0755 the next day, finding fifteen Bf109s bombing five miles west of the landing ground. The squadron attempted to attack these aircraft, but due to the unexpected appearance of some Spitfires, the fight became confused and congested and no claims were made. Bobby Gibbes saw an enemy aircraft on the ground three miles west of the LG, so he 'landed and warned RAF personnel that the pilot was at large'.

---

* The location and time frame of the two crashes needs to be considered here. It would seem that Dave Ritchie went down some time after Roediger, and if Roediger was rescued by an armoured car, it is odd that Ritchie was not, if they crashed in the same locality. It is therefore quite likely that Ian Roediger's probable did, in fact crash, and that Ritchie's crash-landing was both later, and further away from Roediger's rescuers.

The first combined bombing operation of the new year took place on 9 January, when the two squadrons put up twenty-three aircraft between them at 0820 to bomb dug in M/T and tanks north of Bir Ziden. 450 were satisfied with their efforts, while 3 acknowledged that their bombing was only 'fair, most bombs falling short of the target'. Perhaps this was because 450 had spent three of the previous six days carrying out bombing practice!

450 provided the top cover to 250 Squadron for another bombing operation on 10 January, while 3 scrambled only three aircraft, one of which returned early with engine trouble. The other two followed several vectors, but found nothing. The next day both Squadrons moved to Hamraiet where they found 112 Squadron already in residence. The Army was showing signs of stirring to continue its advance, evidenced by the sudden increase in the number of sorties flown in the following days.

On 12 January 450 scrambled eleven aircraft at 0813 as top cover to 260 Squadron. They were vectored to Tamet, thence to Buerat. Four Bf109s were seen 3,000 ft. above the formation, which turned right to foil an attack out of the sun, but the 109s made no effort to attack, and all aircraft were back on the ground by 0923.

At 1302 the squadron was called on for another scramble, five aircraft being told by the controller (Commander) to gain height over base. When they had reached 5,000 ft. they were told to vector 330 and that three-plus E/A were in front of the formation, heading S.E. They were then informed to Buster on same vector and gain Angels near the coast, then to orbit at their current position. They patrolled for fifteen minutes, until another controller (Blackbird) ordered them to pancake. A considerable number of scrambles ended in this frustrating manner.

450 carried out a more rewarding task when they took off at 1455 to 'delouse' Kittybombers returning from a raid at Churgia. They engaged five Bf109s, F/Sgt McFarlane expending 1,000 rounds without making a claim, but keeping the E/A away from their prospective targets.

The following day, 260, 450 and 3 Squadrons combined in a strafing raid on what *should* have been Tauorga LG. 3 Squadron as top cover noted that the 'formation swung left south of Tauorga and continued south down the road, swung east of Churgia drome along the coast to Wadi Tamet and landed at base at 0915, without seeing any E/A. It was later learned that 450 Squadron strafed Churgia instead of Tauorga LG'. 450 would probably not have accepted the blame for this mistake, as *their* ORB noted that 260 Squadron was leading. As they flew south down the Tauorga - Churgia road, they found worthwhile targets, strafing the road and both sides, claiming two flamers and several vehicles damaged. When they reached the LG at Churgia, several things happened. Fl. Lt. Schaaf damaged a Bf109, F/Sgt. McFarlane damaged a Fieseler Storch, and Sgt. George O'Neil damaged his propeller. He had gone down *very* low to strafe, which caused him to glance a small rise in front of him, which he had not noticed. The rapidly overheating engine caused him to force-land behind enemy lines, and for the third time, he returned to the squadron without his aircraft. On this occasion it took him somewhat longer than usual, working his way eastwards through the enemy lines and returning to the squadron on 15 January. He was awarded an MM for this successful evasion, and had his name engraved on the squadron's 'Boomerang Club' shield for the second time. This was the squadron's record of pilots who had 'walked back'. The DAF maintained a similar institution, returning aircrew being presented with a 'Winged Boot' after returning from no-man's land or behind the enemy lines. After the disaster which was to befall both Australian squadrons the next day, two more names would be added.

On 14 January things began to go wrong for 3 Squadron on their first operation, a strafing attack against Tauroga LG at 0755. The top cover leader lost contact with the rest of the formation and returned early, while the leader of 260 Squadron, who was leading the operation, failed to locate the target, all aircraft returning by 0905 without incident.

At 0825 twelve aircraft of 450 Squadron took off to patrol the forward area. They sighted two Bf109s at 13,000 ft. which dived to deck level, pursued by the whole squadron. Six pilots managed to get into a firing position and all reported strikes, but the Messerschmitts escaped, and no individual claims were made.

Between 1130 and 1135 twelve Kittyhawks each from, 3, 250, 260 and 450 Squadrons took off to escort a raid by eighteen Bostons on Bir Dufan airfield. The formation, with 3 as close escort, 450 the medium cover, 250 top cover and 260 as a fluid unit, flew out over the sea and came back in over the coast north of Bir Dufan. Before reaching the target six aircraft of 260 Squadron were forced to return with mechanical problems, and two other aircraft left the formation to escort these. From 3 Squadron, PO Bayly landed again at 1140 and FO Ritchie left the formation, landing at 1210. Two from 450 squadron also returned early, FO Norton at 1155 and Sgt Taylor at 1207.

After crossing the coast the formation was continuously attacked by approximately twenty Bf109s of I/JG 77, led by Maj. Muncheberg and Hpt. Bar, and a smaller number of MC202s. The enemy aircraft employed dive and zoom tactics before, during and after the bombing, which nevertheless was uninterrupted and accurate, 3 Squadron reporting bombs straddling the dispersal area. Tied to the bombers, and determined to defend them at all costs, the Kittyhawk squadrons suffered dreadful losses, most of which occurred before and during the bombing. The first went down in flames immediately the attacks began, and Sqn. Ldr. Gibbes saw another which was straggling attacked by three 109s. He turned to help this aircraft, firing at one of the Messerschmitts, but then was hit by the other two, and their fire caused his engine to cut out. Too low to bale out, he belly landed at high speed, and scrambled out of the cockpit. Both 109s circled him, but made no attempt to strafe.

3 Squadron lost five aircraft and three pilots: Gibbes (FL323), PO L.J. Weatherburn (FL330), who was captured,* Sgt. N.R. Caldwell (FL363) who was missing until 23 January, FO William Diehm (FL346) killed in action, and PO Alan Tonkin (FL345) killed in action.

450 lost Sgt. Gilbert Cameron (FR279 OK-P) killed in action, Sgt. Max Harrison (FR415 OK-K) killed in action, Sgt. L.A. Frost (FR329 OK-W) and F/Sgt. A.D. Nicholson (FR345 OK-D), both of whom returned to have their names engraved on the Boomerang Club shield.

250 Squadron lost two aircraft, and had another badly damaged, while claiming one probable and a damaged Bf109. The four aircraft of 260 Squadron returned intact, but without making a claim.

F/Sgt. Vince McFarlane (FR125) of 450 Squadron claimed one German fighter destroyed, and four other 450 pilots submitted claims for damaged aircraft: Fl. Lt. Glendinning a 109 and a Macchi, PO Winn a 109 and a Macchi, and Sgts. House and Cummins each damaged a 109.

Two of 3 Squadron's pilots took what little opportunity there was to inflict some damage on the Germans after the bombing. Sgt. John Hooke (FL294 CV-H) was flying on the starboard side of the bombers and found himself out of position as they turned left after coming off the target.

> When regaining position still slightly behind, an ME109 attacked bombers from 11 o'clock, passing above them. I turned into the attack, opening fire in a front quarter attack and closing from 300 yds. until we almost collided. The E/A appeared to be right in my cone of tracer for some moments as I turned in, and I am satisfied he was hit. I watched for a moment after we had almost collided and observed E/A to climb slightly whilst rolling to starboard, whereupon his nose fell. I had to weave to the right and so lost sight of E/A. Upon weaving back again, I observed a pall of dense black smoke on the

*A flak hit damaged PO Weatherburn's port aileron. He was then attacked by three Bf109s and his fuselage tank burst into flames. He baled out at 2,000 feet, landing close to where his aircraft crashed and burned, fifteen miles SSE of Dufan airfield. He was captured minutes after landing. (AWM 54 779/3/29)

ground which rapidly grew in size in the position I expected to see E/A hit. I did not see any other aircraft attacked in such a position as to cause it to go in that area, which was approximately 15 to 20 miles from the target in the direction taken by the returning bombers. A very short time after the E/A went in I observed another A/C flying in a westerly direction losing height and giving off a dense plume of black smoke. I did not see what happened to it.

This might well have been the Bf109 which was attacked by F/Sgt. Reg Stevens at 1245. (The time recorded on John Hooke's combat report is 1200, which is clearly inaccurate, as this is less than half the elapsed time after take off. Maj. Muncheberg's first victory was recorded at 1212, with the next at 1217. The bombing would presumably have taken place around 1235, by which time most, if not all of the lost Kittyhawks had gone down, thus any ground fires observed would have been well beyond the location of the crashed Kittyhawks.)

[Reg Stevens] was flying "black one" as close escort to the Bostons and [after] they had bombed, and were flying N. from the target, 2 Me-109's (F or G) made an attack from rear quarter on another Kittyhawk which was behind me at the time. I turned left and made a rear quarter attack on the second 109, closing from 400 yds. to 250 yds. Observed strikes on the fuselage near the cockpit, and on the elevator, a part of which flew off. Then E/A streamed black smoke rolled to the left and fell away. I then did a weave to the right, when I finally weaved back the E/A was not in evidence, but I saw from 7,000 ft. a large cloud of dust mingled with smoke on the ground in a position I estimated the E/A would be. During its dive and whilst I was watching it, the stream of black smoke was very much in evidence.

The grave marker of FO William Diehm, shot down on 14 January 1943. (Tom Russell)

John Hooke and Reg Stevens both claimed probables, while the Germans claimed a total of fourteen Kittyhawks for the day. This was close to the mark, as twelve Kittyhawks were lost; another aircraft from 3 Squadron being shot down later in the afternoon. JG 77 acknowledged four losses for the day. As Spitfires of 1 SAAF Squadron and P-40s of the 57th Fighter Group claimed at least three victories in a morning combat, it may be that only one was lost in the midday fight, but it should be reiterated that loss returns from the *Jagdgeschwadern* frequently recorded only pilots killed, wounded or captured. One certain loss was Ofw. Walter Brandt, who claimed a Kittyhawk in the midday battle, and was shot down himself by Kittyhawks south of Buerat, losing a leg as a result.[23]

A little over three hours after 239 Wing's squadrons returned from the midday battle, 3 and 450 Squadrons were airborne again, flying an armed recce of the forward areas. 450 returned with their bombs, finding no worthwhile targets, but 3 Squadron, acting as top cover, once again clashed with enemy fighters. Fl. Lt. Clabburn returned early with pitch mechanism problems and PO Bayly took over the lead. The formation received some AA, and noted Bostons bombing, and then was attacked by several Bf109s, and a dogfight followed. Rex Bayly was the first pilot to see the approaching 109s.

> Whilst flying N.W. I reported 2 109s at 6 o'clock. When they attacked I gave a turnabout. E/A went to 6 o'clock and attacked white section. There were now 5 E/A in the area. I followed E/A which had attacked white section up in its climb and gave it a 1 1/2 second burst from 200 yds. from front quarter observing strikes on fuselage from nose to tail. My No. 2 F/O Russell observed the attack, but as we were attacked by other 109s, he did not observe any results. I last saw E/A heading S.W. in a shallow dive.

> Two minutes after I had attacked E/A I saw an A/C fire at X3255, but believe this may have been P/O Austin's A/C as he is the only pilot missing from this operation. I formed this opinion because I saw a 109 dive steeply and deliver an attack on a Kittyhawk which was flying straight and level well below me.

> A fire at X1375 was reported by 450 Sqn. whom we were escorting, and it seems possible that this might have been the A/C which I attacked.

PO Arthur Austin lost his life, and the squadron at first thought that they had suffered another loss when F/Sgt. Hankey also failed to return, but it was soon discovered that he had landed safely at Ghel.

At the end of this grim day 3 Squadron had six aircraft and pilots missing, including the CO. Regardless of their losses, both squadrons flew a combined patrol over advancing New Zealand troops on 15 January. Fl. Lt. Ron Watt assumed command of the Squadron with the acting rank of Squadron Leader on 16 January.

However, the irrepressible CO was alive, and determined to make his way back. When he scrambled out of his machine, he was unable to open the emergency hatch to get at the water and ration pack, for the simple and annoying reason that he did not have a coin with which to open it, and it would have been unwise to remain near the aircraft trying to improvise a means to do so when he knew that the Germans would soon come looking for him. He got as far away from the aircraft as he could, before going to ground to hide from a Fieseler Storch which appeared and circled around the wreck without finding him. He walked all night, and slept briefly towards dawn, before resuming his march southward towards the approaching army. Sometime during the morning he heard nearby rifle fire, and went to ground again. It turned out to be a small patrol of German soldiers shooting at gazelles. He was not seen, and trudged onwards after the Germans drove away. At midday, he made a helpful and surprising discovery, a British Army greatcoat, which he thankfully took with him as protection against the bitter night cold. In the late afternoon, suffering from thirst, he lay down in the shade of a small bush in a shallow wadi, and slept.

He awoke to the sound of engines, and saw a convoy of German trucks towing anti-tank guns crossing the wadi three hundred yards from where he was concealed. Again he was lucky. After the convoy had passed he slept again, until woken once more by the sound of approaching vehicles.

This time the first vehicle passed within twenty yards of where he lay, partially concealed by a camel thorn bush at the top of a sand bank. One vehicle stopped fifty yards away due to a blown tyre, and it seemed that every truck which passed it would stop to have a chat. The convoy finally passed his hiding place and he continued his journey, covering several miles before sunset, when he scraped out a hollow and slept beneath the greatcoat. Again he was awoken by the sound of engines, and found that a convoy of tanks was crossing a wadi only a few hundred yards away. He felt certain that they must be British, as he could hear laughter and the sounds of voices, but as he crept closer, he could hear that they were speaking German.

When the sun rose, he could see a continuous flow of vehicles, all heading west. The Axis forces were in full retreat. Shortly after the last German vehicle had passed, he saw another armoured car, which was heading straight towards him. He tried to hide, but to no avail. It drove right up to where he was lying. To his great relief, it was British. He was taken to the 7th Armoured Division HQ where he was given food and more importantly, as much water as he could drink.[24] The squadron was notified of his rescue on 17 January, and he flew operationally again on the 21st.

Bobby Gibbes, still wearing his prized army greatcoat, tucks into his first meal for three days after meeting up with the advancing 7th Armoured Division. (RAAF Museum)

The vehicles observed by Bobby Gibbes were part of the German retreat, which began on 15 January.

> Rommel made a show of standing again on the Wadi Zem Zem, just west of Beurat. The enemy at the time wondered why, and so did some of our officers. It seemed more logical for us not to defend this position, which was about twenty-five miles in length and could fairly easily be outflanked, but to stand on the naturally strong line between Homs and Tarhuna. . .

> We were not strong enough to put up great resistance. The New Zealanders swiftly crept around our flank. On the front he got troops across the Wadi Zem Zem on the first day. . . By the night of January 17 we had given up Homs.

> The rearguard fought sharp actions west of Homs, but although the defences prepared here were sound, our numbers were small, and Rommel already had his eyes firmly on the back country in Tunisia. We scrapped a bit at Corradini and Castelverde, and then the 90th Light put up a last showing by night, a dozen miles outside Tripoli. And there was rearguard resistance at Castel Benito, Azizia and Garian. Then we were finished, and leap-frogging away again.

> Montgomery entered Tripoli on the 23rd, just three months after the Battle of El Alamein had opened.[25]

At 0945 on 16 January twelve Kittybombers of 450 bombed and strafed in the Sedada area, claiming one direct hit by Sgt. Minchin, one flamer to F/Sgt. McFarlane and a number of vehicles damaged. In the afternoon they escorted twelve 3 Squadron Kittybombers sent to bomb Tauorga 'drome, but no aircraft were present, and the bombs were brought back. PO Knox of 3 Squadron changed tanks in the circuit area before landing. His engine cut out and he belly landed FL296, causing Cat. III damage, but fortunately he was not injured.

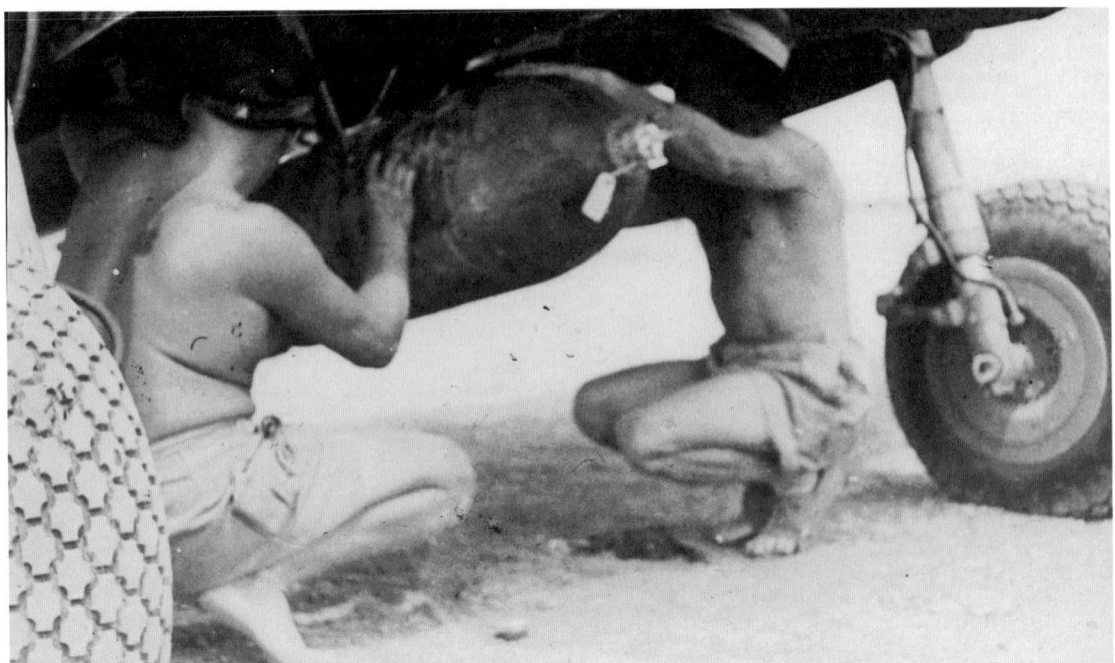

450 Squadron armourers at work: Hughie Halcrow and 'Shorty' Harwood loading a 500 lb bomb, Western Desert 1943. (George James - 450 Squadron Association)

Another combined op. was flown between 1020 and 1215 on 17 January, 450 bombing M/T in the Tauorga area. On this occasion, the Kittyhawks were carrying drop tanks, with 40lb. bombs under the wings. In the afternoon, both squadrons visited Bir Dufan 'drome, and finding no worthwhile targets, bombed and strafed M/T on nearby roads. This operation was another example of the efficiency of the forward movement the 239 Wing squadrons had developed. All of 3 Squadron's aircraft landed at Sedada Forward LG at 1710, joined by six 450 aircraft at 1810. Their remaining aircraft arrived at 0840 on 18 January, by which time the 3 Squadron aircraft had already left on their first op, escorting 250 and 260 Squadrons' Kittybombers to Tarhuna. The Squadron was led by Wg. Cdr. 'Billy' Burton (FL347), relieving Ron Watt, who had led on the previous three operations. Just before reaching the target area, the top six aircraft lost sight of the formation, and shortly afterwards, twenty-plus Bf109s were reported. Five or six of these attacked the remaining aircraft of the top cover, and Wg. Cdr. Burton 'got a good burst into a 109 which was last seen diving very steeply and pouring glycol by Sgt MacKenzie, who also fired, but without result'. 250 Squadron reported seeing a parachute descending, and the Wing Commander was credited with one E/A destroyed.

At 1120 eight aircraft from 3 Squadron carrying 40lb wing bombs attacked M/T west of Tarhuna, and followed up with strafing runs on 'scattered M/T, causing at least four fires'.

At 1430, twelve Kittybombers of 450 took off with 250 Squadron leading and 260 as top cover. Closely packed M/T south of Tarhuna were bombed and strafed, and accurate Breda and small arms fire came up. Sgt. Frederick Silk's bomb scored a direct hit on one vehicle and started a fire. Sgt A.H. Gregory (FR129 OK-F) failed to return, the victim of ground fire. He rejoined the Squadron on foot on 22 January.

The last operation of the day was at 1700, when twenty-one Kittybombers from the two Australian squadrons took off with 250 as top cover on an armed recce of the Tarhuna area. M/T was bombed and strafed to good effect and the leading vehicles of the advancing 8th Army were contacted. The ORBs of both the Australian squadrons recorded that enemy aircraft were not met, and the loss of Sgt. Dick Prowse's aircraft (FL894 OK-D) was presumed to be from ground fire. Prowse's right arm had been almost severed by a cannon shell. In spite of such a traumatic wound, he succeeded in crash-landing his aircraft near an army dressing station close to Bir Dufan. Here his arm was amputated, and he was later evacuated by air to a base area hospital.

Enemy aircraft *were* actually present during this operation, as a 250 Squadron aircraft was badly damaged by Bf109s and Hpt. Bar of I/JG 77 submitted two claims for Kittyhawks during the day, (which were not confirmed) as well as another by Uffz. Weidlich.[26] 450 Squadron noted that the visibility was hazy, and it would seem that Sgt. Prowse was attacked by fighters without the squadron being aware of it.

On 19 January both squadrons were busy, twelve aircraft from each unit taking off for an armed recce at 0745, with 3 Squadron as top cover. Owing to dense cloud it was impossible to find a target, and Fl. Lt. Schaaf ordered a return, but four of 450's aircraft which had not been able to join up initially, did not hear this order, and found a gap in the cloud, then flying down the main road at 50 to 100 ft. They found nothing, but after turning left they flew over several strong points and defiles which threw up intense AA, damaging PO Winn's aircraft (FR123) in the tail unit, and shooting down Sgt. A.W. Taylor (FR114), who kept his machine flying long enough to reach No Man's Land, where he belly landed; another name soon to be added to the Boomerang Club shield.

The Wing was frustrated by cloud for the rest of the day, two more attempts to mount four-squadron bombing operations being forced to return due to 10/10ths cloud close to the ground. Later in the day 450 Squadron ferried sixteen aircraft from Sedada to Bir Dufan. The landing Ground at Bir Dufan was unserviceable due to being heavily mined, and a new LG had been prepared close by at map reference R6054. 3 Squadron referred to its new base as "Sirru Main"; it would seem that the two locations were actually the same place, as Stan Davidson's diary* has him at Bir Dufan from 19 to 23 January, and mentions that Bostons were using the same LG, while 450's ORB noted that Bostons were operating from their LG on 21 January, and that 450's ground crews were assisting in refuelling and re-arming them.

The weather cleared sufficiently for several operations to be carried out on 20 January, armed recces being flown in the Tripoli - Castel Benito area. The two squadrons flew fifty-six sorties between them, bombing M/T on roads near Castel Benito. 3 Squadron carried out a final recce of enemy landing grounds later in the day, destroying one vehicle by strafing as they went.

21 January: Did not move today after all. Modified wing racks and releases. Had to bomb up 20 A/C with 40lb bombs. Finished 2130 hrs. Had first wash for 3 weeks. 'J' shot down today. (Davidson) *

'J' was Sgt. Goulder's FL262, hit by ground fire during the first operation of the day, a strafing attack on the road between Zuara and Tripoli. Although he went down in enemy territory he avoided capture and walked back to the squadron by 25 January. 3 and 450 Squadrons flew forty-six sorties from two combined bombing and strafing operations, claiming nine flamers, which were thought to be vehicles 'attempting to take out petrol' as the enemy was retreating. The number of vehicles damaged was impossible to estimate, so densely packed were the roads.

On 22 January 450 had their best day in aerial combat since July 1942, destroying four enemy aircraft for the loss of one of their own, the pilot of which returned. 3 Squadron was also in the thick of the action, destroying two enemy aircraft, but losing two aircraft and pilots in the process.

---

* One of 3 Squadron's armourers, Stan Davidson, kept a diary which meticulously recorded his activities while he was with the squadron. This document, beginning in late January 1943, was made available by the RAAF Museum, and from this point onwards, excerpts will be included in the text. Like Viv Herrett's diary, it provides an interesting picture of the life led by the hard working ground crews.

At 0755 twelve bomb-carrying aircraft from each squadron took off on an armed recce of the Pisida-Zuara area. Bombs were dropped on a landing ground at Ben Gardane with indifferent results, and they then attacked 100-plus M/T on the road. As they were heading back east over the sea, they encountered three SM79s escorted by ten MC202s on the way from Sorman to their new base at Gabes. Both squadrons attacked at once. F/Sgt. McQueen (FR419) damaged one of the Savoias, and PO Winn (FR341) shot down one of the Macchis.

Fl. Lt. Clabburn and PO Knox of 3 Squadron both damaged SM79s while Bobby Gibbes (FL334 CV-L) and Sgt. Hankey (FL292 CV-I) each destroyed an MC202. From the front quarter, Gibbes attacked a Macchi which was on the tail of FO Andy Taylor. As it broke away to the west, he delivered another attack on its rear starboard quarter from close range, and although he did not see any pieces fly off, or smoke, he considered it to be badly damaged and not likely to reach its base. His attack was witnessed by FO Taylor, who saw the Macchi making off 'for the land, losing height and flying in a manner that suggested it had been damaged'. Gibbes initially made no claim, but the aircraft was later found crash-landed, with damage to the cockpit and fuel tank. (Gibbes souvenired the top of the joystick.) *

F/Sgt.Ted Hankey's highly effective attack produced no more than a probable claim, in spite of some fairly compelling evidence pointing towards a 'destroyed'.

> E. OF PISIDA ABOUT ONE MILE OUT TO SEA. I was flying 'black 2' in a formation of 12 A/C and had just bombed M/T on the road, and were just forming up over the sea, when 3 Savoia 79s were sighted, escorted by 6/8 Mc202s about 500 ft. below at 2 o'clock flying in the opposite direction.
>
> I made an attack from rear quarter above on one 79 when a Mc202 crossed my path and I followed it around in a turn to the right, enabling me to fire four good bursts from approx. 350 yards closing to 100 yds. After my fourth burst I observed the hood fly off E/A upon which pieces of fabric flew out from the cockpit area. At this stage we were down to 2,000 ft. and I saw E/A flick quickly on to its back and go down in a slow spiral inverted dive.
>
> I watched E/A for 3/4 seconds when I was fired at from above and was forced to turn away from the E/A I was attacking.
>
> CLAIM - I Mc202 Probably destroyed.

F/Sgt. Gilbert reported a large splash in the sea as the Kittyhawks were re-forming. This should have been sufficient to up-grade Hankey's claim to 'destroyed', considering the difficulty a pilot would have had recovering from an inverted spiral dive below 2,000 ft. if he was still in a condition to try. In fact, the Italians actually *acknowledged* the loss of three MC202s from 13⁰ Gruppo, Magg. Viale and S.Ten. Maecci being wounded, and Ten. Savoia being killed.[27] Although F/Sgt

---

* There was a moving sequel to the events of 22 January, as Bobby Gibbes explained in his autobiography.

'I wrote to the Italian Air Force giving them particulars of the combat, and offered to present the joystick to either the pilot, if alive, or the Air Force. In May 1977 I visited Rome. . . I met General Pesce and we discussed the possible identity of the pilot whom I had shot down, and in 1983, he invited Jeannie and me to Italy so that I could personally present it. On arrival in Rome we were given V.I.P. treatment, and we were driven in an Air Force car to Brindisi for the "handing over ceremony".

The presentation was made at Brindisi Air Force aerodrome, and as I handed the joystick to Colonel Lorenzo Viale, who accepted it for the Air Force, there was terrific applause from the thousand or more people attending. I had learnt that my victim, Lieutenant Georgio Savoia, had died of wounds a month or two after being shot down, and I felt great emotion at this ovation from the crowd. What a wonderful greeting to an ex enemy who had been responsible for the death of their pilot who had won the Italian equivalent of the Victoria Cross in his final combat. Colonel Viale had been shot down in the same combat by Ted Hankey, who had claimed a probable that day. He had been badly burnt, and never flew again.'

(Ten. Savoia was awarded the Medaglia d'Oro for his defence of the SM79s, one of which was carrying the commanding officer of Squadra 5, a rank approximately equivalent to the command of a Luftflotte. Author)

Hankey is only credited with a probable on 3 Squadron's official list of victories, there can be no doubt that the aircraft which he attacked was destroyed.

The Australian squadrons did not escape unscathed from this encounter, however. The SM 79 gunners claimed one Kittyhawk shot down, and this was probably the aircraft of Sgt. J. Stoneley RAF (FR318) who was seen to crash-land at high speed, the aircraft breaking up. His name was the next to appear on the Boomerang Club shield. 3 Squadron lost Sgt. Alexander Willis (FL325), who was killed when his aircraft spun in after colliding with Sgt. G.R. Jones during the combat. Jones reached base safely with a badly damaged rudder and aileron.

Both squadrons were off again at 1240 to bomb and strafe the coast road either side of Zuara, with 3 Squadron as top cover. Bombs straddled the road, which was packed with M/T, and 450 then strafed for three miles towards Zuara. 'Two large fires [were seen] as a result of the strafing, presumed to be from tankers refuelling M/T'.

As 450's aircraft were re-forming, four Bf109s approached the top cover at 2 o'clock. These were seen by Sgt. Alan Righetti (FL367) who gave a 'turnabout right', but the leader did not hear him and the remainder of the flight continued straight on. Righetti now found himself the centre of attention of three 109s, and his port wing tank was set on fire by Maj. Muncheberg of JG 77. With fire in the cockpit, he baled out at 5,000 feet and landed with shrapnel wounds to both legs, his left hand and an eye.* Seeing this, F/Sgt. McQueen of 450 went down low and dropped his escape aid box, unfortunately to no avail, as Righetti was captured by Arabs and Italians, who took him to a field hospital.

Maj Muncheberg claimed two Kittyhawks in this combat, the pilot baling out from the first (Righetti) and the second was reported as having crash-landed with the wing breaking off.[28] FO Tom Russell (FL321) received slight shrapnel wounds in the arm, but returned to base with the others, so the validity of Muncheberg's second claim is difficult to establish. It is possible that he saw Righetti's machine crash, and believed that it was the second aircraft he had attacked. Another

Alan Righetti (left) with his friend Jock Steele, of 260 Squadron, who was killed in a dive-bombing training accident on 30 December 1942. (Alan Righetti)

* AWM 54 779/3/29

450 Squadron Mark III Kittyhawks at dispersal. The short fuselaged P-40K and the P-40M with its lengthened fuselage were both classified as Mark III by the RAF. (RAAF Museum)

possibility is that a Bf109 which streamed smoke when attacked by Fl. Lt. Ritchie may have crash-landed.

A third combined bombing operation took off at 1620, again with 3 Squadron as top cover. The intention was to bomb ships seen in Zuara harbour during the previous operation, but this time only one ship was present, without steam, and bombs were not dropped.

Leaving the harbour, 450 sighted five Bf109s approaching a landing ground, and carried out a near perfect bounce out of the sun. Three 109s were shot down, one by Fl. Lt Schaaf (FR341) who also claimed a damaged. Another was shared between Schaaf and Sgt. Devon Minchin (FR416), and the third fell to Fl. Lt. Johns (FL893) and Fl. Lt. Glendinning (FR254). Sgt. Keith Marrows (FR196) damaged another. Uffz. Werner Hennig of II/JG 77 was killed[29]; the other pilots survived.

450 Squadron did not fly operations on 23 January, and their ground parties, along with those of 3 Squadron left for Castel Benito, and were established there in time for operations the next day. 3 Squadron carried out an armed recce with bombs over the Zuara road, bombing M/T on the road near Zuara railway station, and aircraft on the nearby aerodrome.

23-25 January: "A" Flight left for Castel Benito after lunch. Flying Officer Marting arrived back with the squadron after escaping from Greece where he was a POW. We left for Castel Benito at 12.30 pm. It was very rough going over frightful desert as far as Beniulid - a fortified town forty miles north. We made fair time thereafter on a good gravel road that runs to Tarhuna. We camped seven miles from that town. We pulled out at 5.00 am and at Tarhuna came onto a bitumen road that leads to Tripoli. We finally arrived at our destination having been held up for several hours en route by a blown bridge. We passed through hilly but fertile country which grows grapes, olives, peaches, vegetables and barley mainly. A fair few Australian gum trees are in evidence. This 'drome is very nicely grassed and has hangars, workshops, billets and other facilities. Old bombing and straffing has wrecked most buildings however, plus over 200 planes. 26 January: Half the camp was in the grip of the grog last night as some of the fellows raided the town brewery and brought back gallons of plonk. (Viv Herrett)

Aircraft were flown to Castel Benito at midday on 24 January, and all four squadrons of 239 Wing took off between 1500 and 1530 to bomb and strafe Ben Gardane landing ground. This was the first attack by 239 Wing on a target in Tunisia, and was another success for 450 Squadron. Fifteen Bf109s were dispersed around the field, and 450's bombs fell amongst them. Sgt Crist strafed an unidentified twin engined aircraft which was taxying, and it promptly stopped. After re-forming, they strafed 100-plus west bound M/T, causing four large fires and damaging numerous vehicles. As they broke off the strafing, a solitary Ju88 of II/KG 30 was seen flying west at 3,000 ft. and this was attacked by Fl. Lt. Glendinning (FR419) and F/Sgt. McQueen (FL893) who shared its destruction.

PO Winn's aircraft (FR341) was seen to be trailing white smoke as he left the target area, and he failed to return, being taken prisoner.[*] F/Sgt. Nicholson (FR285) returned with Cat. II damage, thought to be the result of AA. 450 reported no E/A other than the Ju88 they destroyed, and 3 Squadron noted that no E/A were encountered. However, two Curtiss fighters were claimed by Hpt. Hackl and Ofw. Preinfalck of II/JG 77 during the day,[30] but which unit(s) these came from remains unknown.

PO Des Cormack of 250 Squadron, seven kilometres away from the best base enjoyed by 239 Wing during the Desert War. (Des Cormack)

The aerodrome at Castel Benito was like the Garden of Eden to the pilots and ground crews after the desert conditions they had endured for so long. Nearby houses were appropriated for the pilots' and Sergeants' messes, and some of the ground crew were also billeted in houses, while others had to make do with E.P.I.P. tents. Unlimited water was available, and the surroundings featured green grass, gum trees, fruit trees and fresh vegetables.

The stay at Castel Benito also had other advantages. A number of abandoned Italian aircraft were found, and both squadrons acquired two of these, which were put to good use in the months to come. 3 Squadron appropriated a Caproni 164 two seat biplane trainer and communications aircraft, and a more useful find was a Caproni Ca 309 *Ghibli* (Desert Wind) which was a light twin engined bomber, employed more frequently by the Italians as a communications aircraft due to its vulnerability. It was employed as a general squadron transport, ferrying beer and personnel.

---

[*] PO Winn's aircraft was hit by machine gun fire at 1500 feet while strafing. He flew east, rejoined the squadron and engaged a Ju88 which flew through the formation, but only one gun worked. Losing power, and with glycol fumes in the cockpit, he was too low to bale out and therefore crash-landed. (AWM 54 779/3/29)

450 Squadron secured a CR42, which seemed to become the personal property of Fl. Lt. Schaaf for a time, and a mysterious little biplane which the squadron thought was a Cant 100. Mr F.D. Hamilton, a former member of 450's ground crew, has an interesting tale to tell about this machine.

Word was passed around that no one was to touch the captured aircraft, as they had been booby trapped. But as soon as we had settled into our tents, we found that No. 3 Squadron had acquired a bright red aircraft about the size of a Tiger Moth, and which turned out to be the pick of the bunch. No.3 Squadron was directly under the control of the Australian Government, but No. 450 was under the Empire Air Training Scheme and because of this No.3 seemed to receive most of the lime light. Some of us in 450 were peeved that No. 3 could apparently have the authority to acquire an aircraft, seeing that they had earlier obtained a German ME 109.

I decided to go to the hangars to explore the situation. There was only one aircraft worth considering. It was the vintage of the two seater Gipsy Moth, but had a 6 cylinder engine instead of a 4 cylinder, and was an Italian Cant 100. *(Actually a Caproni 100 - author)* I inspected it closely, expecting it to blow up in my face at any moment, but it did not. Then I had to decide whether it was worth taking, as the enemy had made the aircraft unserviceable, almost severing the spar of one wing and the tip off the propellor (sic)by machine gun fire. Then there was the time factor, we would be on the move again in a few days.

However, a member of transport offered to tow the aircraft to my tent so that I could work on it and make it serviceable. While I checked the engine, some members of the squadron went on the scrounge to find parts to replace the damaged ones. They had some luck as they found two of the same vintage aircraft on a nearby landing strip. They approached the RAF officer in charge and asked if they could take parts from one of the aircraft. He said "definitely not". The party returned and asked the engineer officer of 450 if he could help them. He composed a letter to appear to come from higher authority. They tried their luck again, but the RAF officer saw through their stunt and again refused.

Next day a larger party went and they were in luck as the RAF officer was away. While a couple kept watch, the others set to work on one of the planes, removing the set of wings on one side and also the propellor. Removing the wings from one side caused the aircraft to tip over on the other side like a lame duck. They also had time to round up a few stray fowls and bring them back to be cooked by the squadron cook. I was offered half a cooked chook, but declined as my appetite was not the best. I was told later that I did not miss much, as the chooks had cooked down to mainly bones.

Our aircraft was soon made serviceable and was then test flown by our Squadron CO, Squadron Leader Barber, a South African from the RAF.

The aircraft was put to good use in the squadron. I was made responsible for the aircraft, but on one occasion I had to leave it with my counterpart in another flight. When he handed [it] over to me again he apologised for damaging the aircraft. It was really my fault for not explaining to him that the throttle opened the opposite way to our fighter-bombers.

Luckily the aircraft was moored by a rope under each wing to the ground, as he had set the throttle in the fully open position causing the aircraft to jump forward when started by turning the propellor. The mooring ring on one wing was ripped away causing the aircraft to chase my mate around in a circle until he was able to close the throttle.

When leaving North Africa, the aircraft was handed over to an American bomber squadron, as the sea hops to Malta, Sicily and Italy were considered dangerous and perhaps outside its range.[31]

Apart from circuits and bumps and ' air tests', the little Caproni was twice put to good use searching for pilots who had force landed, while the CR42 was used more for recreational purposes, frequently being 'tested', and once being actually recorded as flying aerobatics in the hands of F/Sgt. Vince McFarlane.

3 Squadron's *Ghibli* proved to be a faithful work horse, carrying essential supplies (beer) on numerous occasions, but it caused some apprehension during the early stages of its use.

On 2 February Gibbes flew it to Dufan to collect a new batch of pilots on posting to 3 Squadron. Nobody yet knew the capabilities of the Ghibli, and Gibbes decided to proceed by trial and error.

Change of ownership 3: 450 squadron's Caproni 100, captured at Castel Benito and restored to airworthiness by fitter F.D. Hamilton. (RAAF Museum)

'Put six in first time, which with myself and crew of one made eight,' he wrote. 'Trundled across drome but couldn't get off. Taxied back and suggested that two pilots get out to lighten the load. No trouble finding volunteers. Just got off the second time. When we got back I put the Ghibli in for a change of motors!'[32]

In spite of the feelings of luxury engendered by the exotic surroundings, and the interest aroused by the captured enemy aircraft, the war went on, and 450 flew as top cover to 260 and 250 Squadrons at 1202 on 25 January. The RAF squadrons bombed Medenine West LG and as they did so, two Bf109s took off and climbed away until they were in an attacking position. They made two ineffective attacks from long range, but none of the Kittyhawks were hit.

3 Squadron received reinforcements the previous day when six new pilots joined the unit, these being Fl. Lt. R.T. Susans, Fl. Lt. B.P. Eaton, WO P.M. Nash, WO R.P. Raffen, Sgt. J.G. Beer and Sgt. C.R. Laver. Sgt. Norm Caldwell, who was commissioned the next day, rejoined after being shot down on 14 January.

On 26 January twenty-two sorties were flown between the two squadrons in one operation, which was marred by heavy cloud. A brief skirmish occurred when two Bf109s attacked 450 Squadron, which was flying top cover to 3, but they quickly withdrew into cloud and were not seen again. 450 dropped bombs on scattered M/T between Medenine and Ben Gardane, and 3 Squadron strafed south of Pisida.

During the morning of 27 January, low cloud again hindered operations, and the two squadrons worked independently, 450 flying a rhubarb with four aircraft at 1111, which met with some success. The aircraft flew at zero feet out over the sea and found two ships of approximately 5,000 tons. These were bombed and strafed, one bomb finding its target, the aircraft then strafing in the face of some intense AA.

Change of ownership 4: on 23 January AVM Harry Broadhurst took over command of the Desert Air Force, and often used a captured Fieseler Storch to visit his units in the field. (RAAF Museum)

3 Squadron flew an armed recce with bombs, but found no worthwhile targets and returned to base without contacting the enemy. 450 flew another four aircraft rhubarb at 1230 and found two violently zig- zagging ships apparently heading for harbour. Fifteen 40lb. bombs were dropped, but no more than two near misses could be reported.

At 1520 ten aircraft of 3 Squadron took off with another eight from 450 as top cover to attack two ships north of Ben Gardane. These were probably the same vessels reported by 450 on their earlier op. The weather was still poor, 450 reporting 9/10 cloud in layers from 3,000 to 7,000 ft. Before the ships were found, six to eight enemy aircraft were seen low over the water four miles east of Zuara, almost certainly an escort for the ships, and Fl. Lt Clabburn detached Blue Section to go down and investigate. Bombs were then jettisoned and 3 Squadron's top section also engaged. 450 joined in, and several of their aircraft fired, but without effect. Fl. Lt. Clabburn and FO Taylor fired but made no claims. FO Dent saw a 109 heading west with a damaged aileron and its W/T aerial trailing, and managed to get in a burst at another 109, without result. It proved to be a costly and unsuccessful engagement, as Sqn. Ldr. Ron Watt (FL292) failed to return, probably the victim of Hpt. Ubben of III/JG 77. Watt was killed, and his death brought about an unexpectedly rapid promotion for Fl. Lt. Brian Eaton, as Watt had been expected to take over the Squadron from Bobby Gibbes, whose tour was soon due to finish. There had already been an attempt to ground Gibbes after his rescue of Rex Bayly, which he circumvented by some 'fast talking', but his time was nearly up.

3 Squadron had two days of rest on 28 and 29 January, some of the ground crew being given leave in Tripoli. 450 Squadron flew three operations on the 29th, totalling only twelve sorties, as larger formations were difficult to keep together due to the heavy cloud. Cloud base was at 2,500 ft, and the aircraft were compelled to fly under it, as it was at 10/10ths most of the time. They

bombed shipping and barges, claiming no more than near misses. 450 also stayed on the ground on 29 January and played Rugby Union against some New Zealanders, but they failed to trouble the scorer.

Four aircraft of 450 flew a recce at 0755 on 30 January, finding no shipping, so they went inland looking for M/T. They found a solitary truck, and Fl. Lt. Schaaf went down to strafe. A particularly adept, (or lucky) gunner hit his oil sump, which immediately threw oil over his windscreen. He 'advised rest of formation to beware of Breda, re-formed and came home by sea'. 3 Squadron sent eleven aircraft under Wg. Cdr. Burton to attack gun positions east of Zuara at 1435. The bombs all landed in the target area, and AA was only light.

450 had a day off on 31 January, while 3 sent twelve aircraft as top cover to 250 who were ship hunting off Zarzis. The leader of 250 Squadron lost his bearings and when the formation reached a point twenty miles east of Sfax, (a glance at the map will show just how lost they were) Gibbes gave 250 a bearing for the correct target, and then brought his own formation back to base.

On 3 February Winston Churchill visited the troops and was formally greeted by General Montgomery. The members of 239 Wing were part of the ceremonial occasion.

2-3 February: I spent another day in Tripoli. The shops are beginning to open up. We saw a dress rehearsal for Mr Churchill's visit tomorrow.

There was no flying today. We formed a guard-of-honour for Mr. Churchill at 3.00 pm and gave much lusty cheering as he drove by to his 'plane. (Viv Herrett)

The intensity of operations was not as great in the first week of February, a number of bombing and strafing sorties and weather recces being flown, often curtailed by cloud. On 6 February 450's Henschel was flown nine times, taking members of the ground crew for short hops around the local area. As the Germans continued to retreat, and construct road blocks around Zarzis and Ben Gardane, the Kittyhawks could barely reach worthwhile targets without drop tanks, and if they carried these the bomb load was restricted to 40 lb wing bombs.

Formal line-up of 450 Squadron Mark III Kittyhawks. George James, 450 Squadron Association's secretary added, 'an unusual sight, some big nob coming out!' (450 Squadron Association)

New bases were needed and on 7 February, 'advance parties of each squadron went forward to Sorman, forty-five miles west of Tripoli to establish a base nearer the frontier'.[33] On 8 February Fl. Lt. Dave Ritchie and F/Sgt. Reg Stevens flew to Sorman to carry out a recce. Ritchie landed and reported the LG as unserviceable, but in spite of this advice, the ground parties were forced to spend a fruitless week trying to make the marshy ground useable, until the attempt was abandoned and both squadrons' ground crews moved on to El Assa on 14 February, which was a further fifty-five miles west, and close to the Tunisian border.

450 Squadron had a brief clash with the enemy on 8 February, when twelve aircraft flew top cover for 112 Squadron, which had rejoined 239 Wing at Castel Benito. While 112 was bombing, two Bf109s approached in line astern from 5 o'clock, and the squadron turned into them. Sqn. Ldr. Barber (FR123) saw strikes on the wing of the leading aircraft and piece of aileron fell off, but he was forced to break off the engagement when he was attacked by the second aircraft.

450 flew another operation at 1258, dropping 40 lb. bombs on bogged M/T and five tanks. There were several 'hang ups', and pilots complained that bombs were dropping off up to ten miles away after bombing, a potentially hazardous situation should a hung up bomb be brought back to base.

Sgt. Davey of 450 Squadron had a hair raising experience later in the afternoon. At 1630 he took off to carry out an air test in FR314, and began a loop which took him into cloud. As he finished the loop, coming out of cloud at 5,500 ft. he noticed dense black smoke and flame from the right side of his engine, and carried out a hurried forced landing. He ended up in sand dunes about 200 yards from an Arab encampment, and his first conscious recollection after the crash was standing beside the aircraft with his parachute slung over his back and Arabs approaching him. He had struck his forehead on the gun sight, and was suffering from shock and concussion. At first the Arabs took him back to their camp, and suggested that he try to sleep, but this was impossible, owing to an open wound above his right eye, which was still bleeding. The Arabs then took him on a six hour donkey ride to 211 Group HQ near Castel Benito. They arrived at 0600 the next morning, and he was sent to the rear for proper treatment. The squadron feared the worst, as nothing was heard of his whereabouts until 1130, when the Orderly Room from 211 Group returned his parachute!

For the next six days, only twenty-one sorties made contact with the enemy, when M/T was bombed. For the remainder of this time, uneventful harbour patrols and weather recces were flown, or the squadrons were grounded due to bad weather.

A number of changes in the personnel of 450 Squadron took place during early and mid February. Fl. Lt. Schaaf completed his tour on 8 February and, with Sqn. Ldr. Barber and Fl. Lt. Clarke, was awarded a DFC. F/Sgt. Vince McFarlane was awarded the DFM. Sgt. A.W. Taylor and Sgt. George O'Neil completed their tours on 13 February and were commissioned before going to 73 OTU as instructors. Fl. Lt. Jack Bartle arrived from 1 Air Ambulance Unit as the new A Flight Commander, and F/Sgts. McFarlane and McQueen completed their tours and were posted out.

Chapter 11   The Tunisian Campaign

With the ground parties already in residence, the aircraft were flown to El Assa during the afternoon of 15 February. The war was resumed in earnest the next day, when sixty sorties from five operations were flown to the German landing ground at Medenine West, in support of ground troops, who entered Ben Gardane on 15 February. The raids provoked little reaction from the anti-aircraft defences, but 450 had another brief clash with JG 77 and some MC200s during their first operation at 0800.

After the bombing by 3 and 112, (which 450 classed as 'poor') the top cover was attacked by six Bf109s and three MC200s. Nine of 450's pilots fired and saw strikes, but as no pieces were seen to fly off, the only claim made was by Sgt. Marrows (FR417), a Bf109E probable.

PO Des Cormack's tour with 250 Squadron came to an end on 22 February 1943, when he left for 73 OTU and a spell of instructing. In 155 sorties he flew 203 operational hours. He is seen here with his ground crew and Kittyhawk III LD-A, identified by the protective shroud over the nose. (Des Cormack)

The following day 450 Squadron flew as escort for two Tac. R. Hurricanes. Heavy cloud with its base at 8,000 ft. did not prevent the reconnaissance, which was uneventful, but it was a sign of things to come. No operations could be flown for the next four days owing to the weather, although F/Sgt. McFarlane managed half an hour's aerobatics in the CR42 on 18 February.

The weather improved sufficiently for operations to resume on 24 February. 3 Squadron accompanied 112 to bomb the 'drome at Bordj Touaz at 0830, and although 112 dropped their bombs, 3 Squadron did not, owing to poor visibility. 250, 450 and 112 Squadrons went back to the same target at 1401, bombing gun positions and dispersal bays, but no aircraft were present.

At 0800 on 25 February, 112 and 3 Squadrons set off to bomb Gabes West LG, with 450 as top cover. When they reached the target it was obscured by cloud, so the formation continued further north and bombed M/T on the road. As they were returning, a double red Verey light alerted them to a crash-landed aircraft. Fl. Lt. Ron Susans took off at 1020 to search for this machine, and he found a Wellington which had belly-landed. He saw one member of the crew beside the aircraft, and the words "surface O.K. to land".

Gabes West was revisited in the afternoon, this time by 112 and 260 Squadrons, with 3 as top cover. The weather was clear and the LG easily located by the dust trails of aircraft taking off. The bombs fell in the dispersal area and an aircraft fire was later seen. 3 Squadron attacked four enemy aircraft, Fl. Lt. Ritchie observing strikes on the one he fired at. WO Nash also fired several bursts, but without result. The E/A withdrew beyond the landing ground, which was sending up every variety of AA.

After more than a month had passed since either of the Australian squadrons had made a definite claim against the enemy, the air war flared up with renewed violence on 26 February, when the Desert Air Force mounted a concerted series of attacks against the Axis landing grounds in preparation for Montgomery's next offensive. JG 77 responded with vigour, claiming an accurate total of fourteen Kittyhawks.

239 Wing made the first attack on Gabes West, taking off at 0730. 250 and 450 Squadrons provided twenty-three Kittybombers, with eleven from 3 Squadron as top cover. Twelve aircraft from 4 SAAF took off half an hour later, followed by another twelve from 260 Squadron at 0900. 239 Wing's bombs burst among the aircraft pens but did little damage, as most of the Messerschmitts were in the air.

Six aircraft of 3 Squadron engaged fifteen Bf109s six miles east of Gabes, and Sgt. McLeod[*] fired at a Bf109 which made off pouring black smoke. Four other pilots also fired at E/A without result, and two aircraft were hit by AA, causing Fl. Lt. Brian Eaton's undercarriage to collapse when he landed. [**]

450 Squadron also became embroiled with the Messerschmitts after dropping their bombs. FO Regan (FR254) attacked a Bf109 at point blank range over the sea. His four second burst shot away the starboard flap and the aircraft struck the water. FO Norton also found himself over the sea as he left the target, and saw two Bf109s at 1,000 ft. He selected the nearer of these and fired a five second burst, which caused it to blow black smoke. He was forced to discontinue his attack by the second Bf109, which followed him as far as Medenine East before breaking away.

The ORB mentions Sgt. M. McLeod in both its 'Summary of Events' and 'Details of Sortie or Flight' sections in its records for this date, acknowledging his claim for a damaged Bf109. However, his name does not appear on the list of eleven pilots who took part in this operation. It may be that he replaced one of those listed at short notice, but if so, there is no indication of whom this may have been.

** *Brian Eaton is recorded as a Squadron Leader from this point onwards, obviously having been promoted in anticipation of the completion of Sqn. Ldr. Gibbes' tour.*

PO Blackburn saw three 109s on his way back and fired at one of them, which shed pieces of its wingtip.

Two of 450 Squadron's pilots were lost during this operation. Sgt. Frederick Silk * (FR125) and Sgt. John Stoneley RAF (FR346) were both shot down and killed, most likely by Hpt. Bar, who claimed five of the Kittyhawks lost on this day.[1] Two aircraft from 250 Squadron, one from 4 SAAF and another from 260 Squadron also failed to return from the morning operation, and three German aircraft were claimed as destroyed.

239 Wing's next operation began at 1100, when twenty aircraft from 3 and 450 Squadrons, with 250 as top cover returned to Gabes West. Three large and twelve small aircraft were seen on the 'drome and in the dispersal area, but intense AA caused most of the bombs to fall wide, and only one aircraft was claimed as damaged. No enemy aircraft were encountered on this occasion, and all the Kittyhawks returned safely.

The same three squadrons took off together again at 1445, this time to attack Bordj Touaz, (Gabes South) with 3 leading, 250 in the middle and 450 as top cover without bombs. This operation proved to be most successful, but not because of the bombing, the results of which were not observed, as eight or nine Bf109s took off as the Kittyhawks approached.

Wg. Cdr. Burton (FL347) leading 3 Squadron, attacked one of these at an altitude of 200 ft; it crashed and burst into flames. The rest of the 109s managed to gain height and a general dogfight followed, in which the Australians enjoyed considerable success. WO Reg Stevens (FL265 CV-V) made the second claim.

8 miles S.S.E. of BORDJ-TOUAL drome. I was leading "blue' section of the leading squadron, and after bombing, the section was proceeding in a S.S.E. [direction] at speed when I observed 7 109s which had previously taken off from the drome, approaching from the rear. I gave a turnabout and the section attacked the 109s which immediately spilt up into two sections of two and a section of three.

Two 109s came in and attacked from about 500 ft. above, the leading 109 breaking away downwards, and I fastened on to him, and gave him a fairly short burst from rear quarter, at between 300 and 200 yards at a height of 7,000 ft. Although I observed no strikes on the E/A I had evidently shot his controls away as it went down in a steep dive from which it did not pull out and it hit the ground at approx Z3403.

Fl. Lt. Ron Susans (FL301 CV-I) made his first claims less than a month after joining the squadron.

I was flying as No. 2 to W/O Stevens in 'Blue" section. Immediately after bombing the section engaged 7 ME109s which had taken off from the drome on our approach. At approx 5,000 ft. I saw two 109s making an attack on a Kittyhawk (F/Sgt. Hankey - author) and I turned into the second from slightly below and nearly full beam. I fired a burst at approx 200 yds range and observed strikes just in front of the cockpit. I closed in to approx 100 yds and from rear quarter fired another long burst which blew part or all of the cockpit hood off the E/A. He flicked over and went down steeply from about 5,000 ft apparently out of control. I last saw this E/A going down steeply at about 4,000 ft. when I was attacked by another 109 and lost sight of the first E/A. Although I did not see the E/A crash, I consider that he was going down out of control, and, judging by the portion of the a/c damaged the pilot was badly wounded.

I later followed another 109 at about 5,000 ft. and turning in behind him, opened fire at about 300 yds, and gave him approx a 4 second burst. The E/A then rolled over on its back and dived steeply for the ground. I followed him down to 200 ft and opened fire again from about 300 yds. The E/A took no evasive action and headed straight back to his base. I pulled away just before I reached the drome and did not observe whether he tried to crash-land or not.

---

* 450 Squadron recorded Frederick Silk as a Sergeant at the time of his loss. The AWM Roll of Honour Data Base lists him as a Pilot Officer, which is most likely explained by the approval of a commission which had not come through at the time of his death.

F/Sgt. Jack Beer (FL356 CV-X) was another recent arrival who made his first claim. In a hectic introduction to aerial combat he displayed skill and determination worthy of a veteran, but perhaps not the same degree of judgement.

At 4500 ft. I saw one E/A evade a Kittyhawk by rolling on its back and diving straight for the ground. I followed and at approx. 1,000 ft. the E/A flattened out and headed for its base. My first burst appeared to fall short, but at the range of 300 yds I fired a second burst of one second from slightly below and almost astern, <u>observing strikes on tail unit and fuselage, giving off a dense cloud of black smoke which appeared to be more than that normally caused by boost, then a smaller cloud of white smoke which lapsed into a thin trail, the E/A began to lose height steadily from 1,000 ft. still heading for his base</u>. I followed right over the S. boundary of the enemy drome but at that stage turned to avoid the dense ground fire, and failed to observe the ultimate fate of the 109, <u>which I last saw at approx 500 ft. still losing height steadily and taking no evasive action</u>.

Returning to the scene of the engagement I saw four Kittyhawks 3000 ft. above me and whilst attempting to join them was attacked from port and above by 2 109s and immediately upon evading them, by a third from the starboard quarter. The three E/A made several attacks which were evaded by steep turns. I fired three short bursts which were not effective beyond causing them to take evasive action, and in consequence were longer in returning to the attacking position.

Whilst at a height of 1,000 ft. I saw a small camp consisting of two large and a smaller tent, and at some distance to the left a stationary truck. I dived on the tents and just before firing saw three figures outside them. After a long burst the entire assembly disappeared in a cloud of dust and smoke.

I turned to the S.E. and noticed a 109 flying to get into the sun and outclimbing me, and another was astern. After approx 5 minutes flying the astern E/A attacked and gained cannon strikes on my port wing and bullet strikes in the glycol tank. I turned and fired one burst, but the E/A dived and headed at high speed for its base. I did not follow and the E/A in the sun did not attack.

I flew for 30 minutes skirting the southern extremities of the Mareth Line. Reaching the 7 SAAF Wing drome, my engine was still running perfectly normal, (sic) and I decided to carry on to my base.

However soon after, the motor began to seize and my attempt to return was unsuccessful. I crash-landed the A/C approx 10 miles from this L.G. and was picked up by Army personnel who took me to the SAAF drome where I stayed the night and returned to the unit the next day.

The Messerschmitts did not reach the height at which the top cover was flying, so 450 Squadron was not involved in the engagement, but Fl. Lt. Alf Glendinning (FR269) took advantage of a rare opportunity when he saw one of them 3,000 ft. below him. He dived on it, firing two long bursts as he closed in to under 50 yards. The E/A went down vertically, pouring glycol and black smoke, and was last seen in this attitude 1,000 ft. from the ground. Glendinning's claim for a 'destroyed' was accepted.

239 Wing had much the better of this exchange with JG 77. 250 Squadron claimed a probable and lost one aircraft which crash-landed on the way home, its pilot returning on foot the next day. The Australians claimed three destroyed and Fl. Lt. Susans' probable, which was obviously badly hit. Reg Stevens' combat report summed up the combat concisely. 'it is significant that, at the conclusion of the fight, there were only two 109s left and these two dogged us without attacking for some 30 or 40 miles from their aerodrome, merely sitting some 1,000 ft. above us'. These might have been the two aircraft encountered by Sgt Beer.

Allied casualties amounted to fourteen Kittyhawks lost, with seven pilots surviving to return to their units. Hardest hit was the South African Wing, which lost seven aircraft and four pilots. 250 Squadron lost three aircraft, all of whose pilots returned, 260 lost one aircraft and its pilot and 450 lost two aircraft and pilots during the first operation. 3 Squadron's only loss was the aircraft of F/Sgt. Beer.

German losses at the hands of the Kittyhawks are harder to assess. They acknowledged the capture of one pilot, shot down by Spitfires, and two fatalities, one of whom, Oblt. Huck of Stab/JG 77 was the victim of either Wg. Cdr. Burton or WO Stevens. Typically, it would seem that

Flight Lieutenant Alf Glendinning of 450 Squadron, who claimed a Bf109 during the intensive fighting of 26 February. (Doug Norrie)

Pilot Officer Frederick John Silk of 450 Squadron, who was lost on his 41st operation on 26 February, aged 27. Tragically, his father, Private Frederick John Silk, 5 Battalion AIF, was killed at the same age in September 1917. (Jess Aldridge.)

aircraft whose pilots returned were not counted as losses, as pilots from the two Kittyhawk Wings claimed seven, four were claimed by Spitfire pilots and one by an American P-40 pilot.[2]

The next day's operations were less intensive, 3 Squadron flying an early weather recce, followed by a top cover escort to 250 Squadron bombing Bordj Tatalin at 1020. 250's bombs straddled the 'drome, but there were no aircraft present. 450's first op. at 0700 was as the middle squadron of a Wing formation to attack El Hamma LG. This target was obscured by cloud, so the formation attacked Bordj Touaz instead. The bombs from 260 and 450 Squadrons destroyed at least one aircraft, as a very large fire flared up after the attack.

At 1250 450 led the next operation, with 112 in the middle and 260 as top cover. They were unable to identify the landing ground at El Hamma, and bombed tents on a nearby escarpment instead. The top cover was engaged by four Bf109s before the bombing, and 450 Squadron noted the presence of four enemy aircraft above and to the west, which made no attempt to interfere with the bombing. As the Kittyhawks turned away from the target, four more 109s appeared and an engagement followed. At 2,000 ft. FO Norton (FR123) saw a 109 attacking a Kittyhawk 1,000 ft. below him, probably Sgt. Sanders' FL885, which returned with Cat. II damage. Norton dived and fired two bursts which blew off the canopy and produced a mass of flames from the cockpit. The Messerschmitt was probably the aircraft of Uffz. Egon Schluter of 1/SG 2, who was killed.[3]

No operations were flown for the next three days, until 450 carried out an uneventful armed recce on 3 March, which 'confirmed that the Mareth positions were being greatly reinforced'.[4] On 4 March the two Australian squadrons flew thirty-six sorties against road columns, but none on 5 March due to sand storms. 'It was appreciated that Rommel, having secured his western flank . . . now intended to attack through the Matmata Hills, seize Medenine and thus cut off the British divisions in front of the Mareth line'.[5] Rommel himself was unhappy with the plan, preferring to withdraw to stronger defensive positions far to the north at Enfidaville. However

His superiors in Rome and Berlin remained adamant. Arguments amongst the Axis high command led to disastrous delay, and Montgomery's Chief of Staff reported that 'by 5 March we were ready'. Rommel's attack began the next day. . . yet his units would drive directly into a carefully prepared British defence.[6]

The attack was a total failure, 'over fifty tanks being abandoned before they withdrew at nightfall'[7] and due to low cloud on 6 March, the Australian squadrons were called upon to fly only one combined bombing operation. The relative lack of air support made no difference on this occasion. By dawn on 7 March the Axis forces were gone, and the Kittyhawks went after them with bombs at 1145.

Six 3 Squadron aircraft flew as top cover for 260 and 450 Squadrons carrying 500 lb. bombs, which were dropped from 5,000 ft. through 5/10 cloud on M/T, without results being observed. While at 15,000 ft. 3 Squadron saw nine Bf109s 1,000 ft below, which were about to attack the Kittybombers. Sgt. Ken Goulder (FL288 CV-B) followed his No. 1 down to protect the bombers and

> got on the tail of one E/A, opening fire at 300 yds. He commenced to pour black [smoke] and much glycol, and flicked onto his back, diving vertically. I watched him going down for 2,000 ft but then my attention was transferred to another 109 which was 600 yds away and slightly above. I opened fire on this E/A from 500 yds., closing in to 150 yds., and saw strikes; he did a steep turn to the right thus offering me a splendid target, and I continued to fire until forced to pass above him. During this latter attack, I distinctly saw my strikes rake him from nose to tail. He rolled on to his back, and I last saw him in a vertical dive.

PO Knox saw Goulder's attack and watched the E/A until it disappeared in cloud. Shortly afterwards he saw a fire on the ground through a gap, which enabled Goulder to claim a destroyed. PO Knox and WO Reg Stevens both got in several bursts, each claiming a damaged, and WO Murray Nash (FL284 CV-C), another of the late January reinforcements, also made his first claim, a probable.

> I was just pulling up sharply in a climbing turn after a previous attack, when I saw a ME 109 approx. 600 ft. above at two o'clock and slightly ahead, moving in the same direction. The pilot was apparently unaware of my presence. I closed in to about 250 yds. dead astern on the same level, and fired a fairly long burst, seeing about six white flashes around the fuselage and wings. He turned slowly around to the right, spiralled steeply, and finally spun down, emitting a trail of black smoke, and apparently out of control.

450 Squadron was engaged by several Messerschmitts for twenty minutes, several of their pilots firing without making claims, and all the Kittyhawks returned safely. A month would pass before either squadron was able to make another claim.

Both squadrons flew another operation in the afternoon, 450 finding 100-plus M/T which were bombed accurately through heavy AA.

Another move forward was about to take place, and 3 Squadron's "C" Flight ground party had an interesting time during their journey.

8 March: Notified at 0900 to get ready to move forward 70 miles in an hour's time - passed through Ben Gardane about 1500 hrs arrived at Nafatia (sic) about 1700 hrs. Some Jerry A/C flew over our convoy but luckily didn't attack us - The truck close in front of us applied his brakes hard and we hit him hard in the rear, driving him forward onto another truck, his radiator etc was badly smashed but we got off lightly - A 260 Squadron A/C dropped 6 40 lb bombs about 100 yds from us on the road, luckily they didn't explode - he crash landed a bit further on. Passed large Jerry petrol wagons - Nafatia was raided seven times yesterday and 70 bombs dropped, one 3.7 gun post was hit one man being killed and every member received some injury.(Davidson diary)

The "B" Flight ground party of 3 Squadron was already established at Nefatia by the time Stan Davidson's group arrived, and the aircraft arrived in two flights in the middle of the day. 450

Squadron flew in at 1330. The new base was very close to the front line, and the ground crews were well aware of their exposed position.

9 March: no "ops" today - We had eight air raid alerts but A/C only came over our drome once - There are commandos stationed all round us, we are only 15 miles from Jerry's main forces. Guards are posted everywhere as we are expecting visits from Jerry raiding parties - Commandos have gone out to intercept them - The artillery can be heard plainly and the gun flashes are very clear. (Davidson diary)

In poor health, Rommel left for Rome on 9 March, and an audience with Mussolini. By next afternoon he was at Hitler's headquarters in the Ukraine, where he continued to argue his case for the shorter defensive line at Enfidaville. Hitler refused, insisting that the Mareth Line be defended by armoured units until it was in danger of being breached. He did concede that the infantry could withdraw to Wadi Akarit, thus shortening the Axis front by 160 miles. This was the best Rommel could do for General von Arnim, who now assumed Rommel's duties as C-in-C *Army Group Tunis*, under the overall command of General Giovanni Messe. Rommel wrote to Arnim: 'Unhappily, the Fuhrer has not granted my urgent request to be permitted to return immediately to Africa, but has ordered me to commence my treatment at once. My thoughts and fears will always be for Africa'.[8] He never returned.

On 10 March a combined armed recce was flown at 1330. Each squadron provided twelve aircraft, 3 Squadron carrying 40 lb .wing bombs while 450 had 500 pounders. The top cover was provided by twenty-three Spitfires. A good target consisting of two groups of tanks, armoured cars and M/T was located near Ksar Rhilane, and the two squadrons had one of their most successful ground attack days of the campaign. Wg. Cdr. Burton, leading 3 Squadron, sent 450 south to attack the second of these formations, ensuring that the weight of the attack was evenly distributed. AA was only light when the strafe began and none of the Kittyhawks were damaged. 3 Squadron claimed sixteen M/T burnt and eleven damaged, two armoured cars burnt and four damaged, and an ammunition carrier and a petrol bowser destroyed. As PO Arthur Dawkins passed over one of the trucks he had attacked, it blew up with such force that the canvas tarpaulin flew into the air and wrapped itself around his port wing tip, and when he landed, it was discovered that his air intake was full of packets of razor blades.

All of 450 Squadron's bombs fell in the target area, and then they went in to strafe, claiming seven M/T destroyed. As they left the target, numerous fires were seen, and one particularly large petrol fire was reported. So many vehicles were damaged that no attempt was made to count them.

This operation was in response to 'an urgent call for assistance from General Leclerc, who was leading a French contingent from Lake Chad to Tunisia. . . Arnim sent armoured units and dive bombers to ambush Leclerc's troops',[9] but they were forced to withdraw by the end of the day after the Desert Air Force's attacks. 112 Squadron met a force of Ju87s with a strong escort and in the ensuing combat lost six aircraft, with four pilots killed and two captured, a heavy price to pay for the rescue of the French force.

The next phase of the battle was about to begin. The Axis forces were now well entrenched in the Mareth line, and von Arnim had decided to make a stand there, as it was a strong defensive position, consisting of old French fortifications bordered by the sea on one side, and the rugged Matmata mountains on the other, 'which stretched westward to the apparently impassable Dahar sand wilderness'.[10] Montgomery prepared a two pronged attack, made possible by a Long Range Desert Group reconnaissance in December. This mission had found a gap through the Matmata mountains at Foum Tatahouine, and 'Montgomery now planned to despatch a force through this gap, along the edge of the Dahar, and then through the vital Tebaga Pass in the north which would open a way to the plain of El Hamma and Gabes - behind the enemy at the

Mareth Line'.[11] This left hook would be carried out by the New Zealand Corps under General Freyberg, while XXX Corps would attack the eastern front of the Mareth Line. Freyberg's forces began to assemble during the night of 11/12 March, and preliminary assaults by XXX Corps on outposts of the Mareth Line began on 16 March, with the intention of distracting enemy attention from the New Zealanders, as well as being a preparation for the main offensive,[12] which began on 20 March.

Before the main offensive began, the Australian squadrons were relatively inactive, 3 flying an uneventful recce on 13 March, followed by a rest from operations until 20 March. During this time 450 flew two uneventful bomber escort operations and a scramble without making contact with the enemy. The escort at 1030 on 16 March was led by Sqn. Ldr. Jack Bartle, newly promoted to the command of the squadron to replace Sqn. Ldr. Barber, whose tour was over.

During this period of inactivity the ground crews took the opportunity to make some modifications to the Kittyhawks' bomb racks, with good reason. Stan Davidson experienced his second close shave with 40 lb bombs within four days.

11 March: A 112 Squadron A/C dropped four 40 lb bombs in amongst our tents, but luckily we were all at the mess and no one was injured - had some New Zealand lamb for dinner and tea - it was a great change from the tinned stuff.

12 March: Started doing some of my own modifications on 40 lb wing bomb racks - successful too. All of them are to be done now.

17 March: Very heavy artillery from midnight onwards, our troops advanced and captured an important position. Worked all day making attachments for carrying 2 - 250 lb bombs on the American type carrier.(Davidson diaries)

When the main assault began on 20 March, the 239 Wing Kittyhawks were once again used to escort bombers, 3, 450 and 112 combining to cover eighteen Baltimores at 0820, with 3 doing another bomber escort in the afternoon. On neither occasion enemy aircraft were sighted, their absence being an indication of the success of the earlier airfield attacks. 3 Squadron now had at least seven Kittyhawk IIIs on line, evidence of a shortage of the much preferred Merlin powered Mk IIs.

After one further bomber escort operation by 450 and 112 Squadrons in the early morning of 21 March, 239 Wing was committed to the support of the out-flanking drive by the New Zealanders. This was a busy day for both the pilots and ground crews, each squadron flying two operations and moving to a new base.

21 March: The push started last night, plenty of heavy gunfire could be heard - Worked hard all the morning bombing up and re-arming. Repaired two U/S guns. Received orders to pack up at 1500 hours. Left soon afterwards and travelled 45 miles to Medenine arriving here in the dark at 1930 hrs. Had late tea and slept in the work shops - No sleep up till midnight. Jerry was over quite a lot but the AA kept him off the drome. (Davidson diaries)

3 Squadron flew their first ground support operation at 0730, bombing and strafing an enemy strong-point with rewarding results. They flew over the NZ column and saw their tanks, M/T and infantry preparing to attack. The bombs were dropped on an enemy anti-tank screen and gun emplacements, (two 250 pounders from each aircraft, using Stan Davidson's new centre line attachments), and then they strafed, destroying seven M/T, badly damaging three armoured cars and damaging several more vehicles. Sqn. Ldr Gibbes and FO Dent both had their aircraft holed by AA.

In the afternoon 450 gave top cover to 3 and 112 Squadrons in the same area, but the enemy had withdrawn and no suitable targets were found. They landed at Medenine Main.

At 1055 on 22 March twelve 3 Squadron aircraft took off on an armed recce of forces opposing the New Zealand Corps and found forty-plus Mark III and IV tanks and M/T in battle formation. The New Zealanders were notified of their position and four aircraft then bombed, damaging two tanks with a near miss which landed between them. Two more aircraft followed up with a strafing attack, damaging M/T and hitting two exposed personnel.

Wg. Cdr. Burton and Sqn. Ldr. Gibbes took off at 1320 to lead a formation of "Tankbuster" Hurricanes to the same target. 112 carried bombs and 250 Squadron flew as top cover. 250 engaged six Bf109s, which later caught up with 112 Squadron, forcing them to jettison their bombs, but the Hurricanes strafed successfully with their 40mm cannons.

On 23 March the ground support operations continued, 3 and 450 flying thirty-six sorties between them. 3 Squadron destroyed three M/T and a troop carrier, and PO Doyle brought FL715 back safely with a damaged reduction gear and oil all over his windscreen. During 450's second operation Sgt. Dick Rowe's aircraft (FR138) was hit by AA and he force-landed behind enemy lines. Later in the day Jack Bartle and Fl. Lt. Aitchison carried out an unsuccessful search for him, but with the assistance of some friendly Arabs he later returned on foot, to have his name recorded on the Boomerang Club shield.

Next morning, Jack Bartle and Sgt. A.F. Day added their names to the shield when they were both shot down by AA during the one big operation of the day. At 1009 forty-eight Kittyhawks from 112, 260 and 450, led by Wg. Cdr. Burton at the head of 3 Squadron, took off to escort Hurricane "Tankbusters" and attack gun posts and M/T south west of El Hamma. The strafe was successful, as two gun posts were knocked out, and five M/T and a troop carrier were claimed as flamers by 3 Squadron. Medium and heavy AA was encountered, Wg. Cdr. Burton and F/Sgt. Harbour receiving Cat. II damage. F/Sgt. Crist of 450 Squadron was slightly wounded, but returned safely. Less fortunate were Jack Bartle and Sgt. Day, both of whom went down in disputed territory between the New Zealanders and the Germans. F/Sgt. House remained overhead, attacking

Ruffled tail feathers: an unidentified 3 Squadron machine after a strafing sortie. Note missing trim tab.
(RAAF Museum)

enemy machine gunners who were firing at Bartle, until he was rescued by the Kiwis. For this determined defence of his CO, House was awarded the DFM. 450 claimed eight trucks, an armoured car and a jeep destroyed, as well as twenty-two trucks and three 88mm gun posts damaged.

The frontal assault on the right of the Mareth Line by XXX Corps was held up by determined German resistance and losses began to mount. Accordingly, Montgomery altered his strategy, deciding to shift the thrust of the main attack to the New Zealanders, who had reached the Tebaga Pass. Here the situation was little better. The Germans held a strong defensive position in a narrow defile, and when the NZ Corps had been reinforced by X Corps armoured units, a combined air, tank and infantry assault was planned for the afternoon of 26 March.

3 Squadron escorted Bostons bombing in the Tebaga Pass at 1110 on 25 March as part of the preparation for the assault on the following day. PO Stan Youl of 450 Squadron recorded his memories of the combined attack in his diary.

> At about 1200 hours today we were called over to Wing to be briefed on a special job. The A.O.C. of the Advanced Air Striking Forces was there, with other Commanders of the different groups of Americans, South Africans, including our 239, the crack Fighter Wing of the Western Desert. The A.O.C. gave us the dope on the whole scheme planned for the afternoon. . . The plan was for the Air Force to keep the fortified positions occupied while the Army advanced in full force. The Air Force was to bomb and strafe for about two hours to draw the fire of the 88s. The 88s being Anti-Aircraft, Anti-Tank, and also field pieces, are evidently the finest piece of ordinance (sic) in the Western Desert. They either fire at us or at the Army. If they fired at the Army they had to let us attack unhindered, or vice versa and let the army take the position.
>
> The attack started by a rolling barrage by the Army followed by tanks, armoured cars, and infantry, on a front of about half a mile. The air attack started with pattern bombing by two sections of twenty-four light bombers. Then came our role as dive-bombers followed by the Yanks strafing at ground level. After we had finished dive bombing, we went in again strafing at ground level. Was it fun, tearing in getting a bead on trucks, gun posts, guns, bodies and anything else that came into our sights. Climbing up, just missing the tops of the rocky crags, and then down again into the wadis, strafing the trucks hidden rather effectively. Flamers were going up all over the place. What a grand sight the whole scene was. After doing our worst for the quarter of an hour allotted to us, with clock-like precision, another formation took over from us. A few were missing after the whole show was over, but when the news came through that owing to our terrific attacks, the Army had overrun the position, and was streaming at full speed towards its objective, everyone in the squadron, and I am sure, in all the other squadrons, felt elated with the news, and that the action had been more than worth while. The army could go on according to schedule.[13]

Stan Davidson of 3 Squadron recorded his impressions of the day from the point of view of the ground crews.

No work this morning but during the afternoon we did very extensive "ops", the biggest air offensive of the Middle East was carried out today, 500 bombers and fighters pounded Jerry positions for 2 hrs - Two of our A/C did not return - At 18.00 hrs a Yank developed engine trouble in taking off, he dropped his bombs and they exploded 300 yds from "B" Flight mess, he crashed on the edge of the drome and later died from head injuries - Very hot winds blew all day.(Davidson diaries)

The two missing aircraft referred to by Stan Davidson were flown by Sqn. Ldr. Brian Eaton (FR457) and Sgt. Ken Goulder (FR286). Both were hit by AA. Eaton force-landed safely and returned the next day, and Goulder landed away from base at Nefatia Main with a damaged propeller and a flat tyre. In return for these losses the squadron claimed one troop carrier flamer, three M/T flamers, one tent burnt, twelve M/T damaged, four gun posts silenced and a number of personnel 'knocked over'.

450 flew twice, on both occasions six aircraft led two American squadrons from the 57th FG. The squadron's ORB recorded that PO Adrian Blackburn (FL729) was missing during the first operation,

however, Leonard Barton, 450 Squadron's historian, notes that he lost his life when he crash-landed with bombs still aboard. The pilots claimed five M/T flamers and twenty-seven damaged from their two operations.

The attack was a qualified success. Without the brilliant effort of the Desert Air Force it would not have succeeded. By dawn on 27th March the 1st Armoured Division was within a few miles of El Hamma, but here the Germans managed to hold the British advance long enough for the troops on the Mareth Line to withdraw before they were encircled, 'and once again the *Afrika Korps* slipped away - this time to Wadi Akarit'.[14]

On 27 and 28 March the two Australian squadrons flew a total of fifty-seven ground attack sorties against the retreating enemy, one aircraft of 450 Squadron, FR287, flown by Sgt. Frost, suffering Cat. II damage from AA.

29 March was an extremely busy day for both units, a total of eighty-one sorties being flown from four operations each. Having led the first operation at 0615, Sqn. Ldr. Bobby Gibbes missed the next at 0945, when his engine failed just after he had become airborne. He dumped his bombs, which did not explode, and landed straight ahead in a 'rough boulder-strewn wadi. He smashed through a maze of telephone wires and severely damaged the Kittyhawk before jolting to a stop'.[15] At 1240 he led the next operation in another aircraft, and the last of the day as well.

There were no operations from 30 March to 3 April, as targets were becoming harder to find, and another move of base was afoot. On 1 April the CO instructed F/Sgt John Hooke (who had recently returned from hospital after an attack of acute appendicitis) in the Ghibli. Fifty-five minutes was deemed to be enough for a twin-engined endorsement, and the next day John Hooke set off for Alexandria with LAC Wilhelm (Fitter IIE) as crew, and Fl. Lts. Ritchie and Clabburn as passengers, both of whom were tour expired. This journey turned into something of an epic. A trip to civilisation was not to be wasted, and the Ghibli was filled up with essential supplies.

Change of ownership 5: the booze bus - often referred to as *Gibby's Ghibli,* 3 Squadron's faithful Caproni Ca 309, captured at Castel Benito and subsequently used for 'communications'. (RAAF Museum)

"I didn't know anything about flying Ghiblis, or any other multi-engined aeroplane, so I said, when it came to petrol, 'fill 'er up' and I filled the inside of the aeroplane the same way, with bottles of grog. When it came to take off, I had an aerodrome, you could call it a scrape, which was a mile by a mile and a quarter, and I took off diagonally across it. I still wasn't airborne when I reached the other corner. It was damn nearly a mile and a half, and I still hadn't got airborne. However it was beginning to lift. I couldn't use the brakes because I knew if you applied the brakes you'd burst the fluid line in the cockpit, so in effect you had no brakes that you could use, except for parking. I was very nearly airborne as I bounced across the little humps of sand that had developed around the camel thorn, until finally the bloody thing got airborne, by which time one of the engines was beginning to overheat. I couldn't go over Halfaya Pass, which is what I should have done, so I had to keep low and hope the engine would cool down and I went out around Ras El Shaqiq and back, and by the time I got back to Gambut I'd used up enough fuel, and the engine had cooled down sufficiently to climb over the escarpment, which was 300 feet high. Then of course I had to land on Gambut and they'd had heavy rain and everything was awash, including the aerodrome. It wasn't too bad until I came to take off. You could feel the wheels going down as we raced along the strip, sinking into the soft mud. She carried on, bless her, and finally I got her into the air again. It was still quite a long way to take the grog. I had to take it half way up Tunis".[16]

The ORB faithfully recorded each take off and landing, From Idku at 1015 on 6 April, to Mersa Matruh, from Mersa Matruh to Gambut, from Gambut on 8 April, to Marble Arch, from Marble Arch to Medenine Main, and finally back to the unit at 1200 hours, with the all important cargo intact.

On 30 March, the ground parties had begun the move from Medenine Main to El Hamma.

Up at 0530 hours packed up and moved off in convoy at 0730 hrs, travelled slowly all day, camped about 8 miles past Gabes, the road is badly blown in parts - Came through the Mareth Line, some very grim sights here, dead lying all over the place, some of the bodies terribly mutilated - The road is heavily mined - we are camped right on the beach - At 2100 hrs 3 JU88s bombed and strafed about a mile from us, plenty of AA was sent up at them, one of them was hit.

By 3 April the new base was ready, and Stan Davidson noted the day's events.

At 0800 hrs the AA opened up on some lurking 109s - some Spits took off and they made off. Settled in our correct area by 1200 hrs - Our A/C arrived at 1330 hrs, we checked 20 of them in OK - Six Ju88s raided near us at dusk but our AA kept them off our drome - A lot of Jerry A/C over between 2300 and 2400 hours and dropped flares, HE and Anti P[ersonnel] bombs about a mile away - Twelve months overseas today-

4 April: From 0300 till dawn Jerry was over all the time dropping flares and bombs and doing plenty of strafing but never touched our area - Jerry started shelling the main road about a mile away at dawn - Had to de-bomb 12 A/C for a fighter sweep - At 1130 hrs 12 ME109s raided our area killing four chaps in trucks and injuring some of 260 Squadron's chaps, also started petrol fires - Two more raids by 109s during the afternoon, only slight damage - Jerry stopped shelling the road and started on us this afternoon - He landed about 30 shells in the area, some very near misses too but so far no damage - Had to "dedet" (remove detonators) all bombs on A/C at 2200 hrs. Jerry over again at 2300 hrs- (Davidson diaries)

The persistent shelling destroyed a 450 Squadron Kittyhawk and wounded three men, and the squadron withdrew temporarily to Medenine on 5 April. The Landing Ground was shelled again at 1730, several shells landing close to 3 Squadron's Operations Room. This stung the unit into taking some preventative action. At 0530 on 6 April, Bobby Gibbes, Brian Eaton, Murray Nash and Arthur Dawkins took off to search for the guns and found three likely locations which were strafed.

Another four aircraft led by WO Reg Stevens took off on the same task at 0705. They found some guns, but of course it was impossible to tell if they were those responsible for the squadron's

discomfort. The area was strafed thoroughly: three M/T and a 'Volkswagen' were damaged, with '30+ bodies in addition'.

There was no more trouble from the guns, but perhaps this was not entirely due to 3 Squadron's efforts. Jack Bartle, 450 Squadron's CO was

asked to stay on at El Hamma and, late that afternoon, two or three jeep loads of Gurkhas arrived at our mess; they were under the command of an English Officer and he declared it was their intention to move forward after dusk that evening to silence the 88's. This they did and very early next morning they once again arrived at our mess having suffered no casualties and wearing very happy grins. We were told that the 'Jerry' guns and their crews would take no further part in the war and this was borne out by a couple of the Gurkhas showing us a dozen or more bloody ears strung on two lengths of wire. Our aircraft returned soon after.[17]

450 Squadron ground crew taking refuge from the shelling by German 88s at El Hamma. Left to right: 'Scotty' Webster, George James, Eric Kershaw, Phil Kirkwood. (George James - 450 Squadron Association)

As well as 3 Squadron's private war with the German artillery, they flew an armed recce of the battle area at 1120, the 8th Army having begun its assault on the Wadi Akarit positions shortly before dawn. Gun positions were again attacked in the afternoon, but this time no doubt in support of the army's attack, when 3 Squadron flew as top cover for 260. 450 Squadron flew thirty-two bombing sorties from three operations, and had a scare during the first of these at 1022, when two bombs were accidentally dropped amongst British troops who had advanced into what the squadron thought were still enemy positions. The controller, 'Blackbird', was quick to tell them of their error, and there were no reports of casualties.

Twelve 3 Squadron aircraft led by Wg. Cdr. Burton took off on the day's last operation at 1530 with "Tankbuster" Hurricanes, 250 Squadron in the middle, and 260 as top cover. The task was to attack a reported concentration of enemy troops massing for a counter attack. As the squadron swept in at 2,500 ft. to bomb, there was no sign of the reported concentration, but the AA was intense and accurate, and Sgt. William Ward (FR271) was shot down and killed.

During the bombing dive, Fl. Lt. Ron Susans (FL270 CV-Y) caught sight of three enemy aircraft at 3 o'clock below, but lost them as he broke away after bombing.

Shortly after when at about 2,500 ft. I saw a single E/A heading N.W. and at about 800 ft. I dived behind him and closing to about 300 yds., fired a burst which I saw hit the E/A along top part of fuselage, and caused him to dive STRAIGHT AHEAD INTO THE GROUND. E/A was apparently unaware of my approach and took no evasive action.

Although much dust went into the air when he hit, I did not observe any fire. I did not stop to observe any further details, but continued in chase of my own formation which I could see 3/4 miles away heading for base .

I consider that the E/A was a Mc 202.

By mid afternoon the enemy line at Wadi Akarit had been broken, and over 9,000 prisoners taken. The enemy was in full retreat to the next defensive line, at Enfidaville, and advancing British patrols made contact with the US 1st Armoured Division on the Gabes road on 7 April. During the retreat the Australian squadrons of 239 Wing flew 149 sorties, claiming numerous vehicles destroyed and damaged. 450 Squadron had four aircraft damaged by AA and 3 another two, but no aircraft were lost or pilots hurt, and the damage inflicted on the retreating enemy more than out weighed the damage to the Kittyhawks.

A daily 'OPREP' from 3 Squadron for 7 April describes a typically successful operation.

3rd. Operation.

K.   7 Kitty II's and 5 Kitty III's
L.   NIL
M. i.   Bomb and strafe M/T on MAHARES-GASFA road S. of
            MESSOUNA. 450 Sqn. Top Cover.
    ii.   3,700 rds. .5 cal. 50% A.P., 30% Inc., 20% tracer.
    iii.   24/40 lb., 16/250 lb. G.P.
    iv.   1530 hrs.
    v.   Gained height to 6,000' and turned in over coast at
          CIKHIRA to bomb a concentration of 40+ M/T at Z0288,
          starting one fire. An excellent straffing target was
          found at Y8595 after our A/C had straffed target
          previously bombed. Straffing results:- 6 M/T destroyed
          16 M/T damaged, 20 bodies straffed.
N.   I A/C Cat. II, I A/C Cat. I.
O.   NIL. P. NIL. Q. 13.00 hrs.
R.   7/10 cloud at 8/9,000'.
S.   Med. heavy accurate from CIKHIRA, med. Breda from target.

"L" refers to enemy aircraft seen, "M i." to the task assigned, and any accompanying squadron(s), ii. to the amount of ammunition expended, iii. the quantity of bombs dropped, iv. the time the action took place, v. details of the route and events of the operation. "N" records details of damage to the squadron's aircraft, "O" to missing pilots, "P" claims against enemy aircraft, "Q" to the amount of flying hours the formation totalled, "R" to cloud conditions and visibility, and "S" to anti-aircraft fire encountered.

On 8 April the two squadrons flew seven operations between them. At 1125, 3 Squadron carried out an armed recce N.W. of Sfax. Brian Eaton, who was leading, had engine trouble and bombed a dispersal of M/T short of the intended target and then returned to base with his No. 2. WO Stevens took over the formation, which continued on to bomb and strafe M/T on the Sfax road. Sgt. Thomas strafed four M/T and was attacking personnel sheltering near a tank when AA from the tank hit his aircraft (FL318) and he 'force-landed just on our side of the bomb-line, extinguished a fire which started in his A/C after landing and "hitch-hiked" back to base'.

450 were off soon afterwards at 1142 and claimed three flamers and a number of other vehicles damaged, as well as destroying a mobile AA gun, but not before it managed to damage four Kittyhawks, two Cat. II and two Cat. I.

Sfax fell on 10 April, and Sousse two days later. The 8th Army was now rounding up a thousand prisoners a day. After 3 Squadron flew two escorts for Wellingtons 'delousing' mines in Sfax harbour on 11 April, the 239 Wing squadrons were rested for several days. The Squadrons'

Change of ownership 6: a captured Kubelwagen 'belonging' to 3 Squadron, probably at Kairouan.
(RAAF Museum)

ground parties left for El Djem on 13 April and the aircraft of 3, 112, 250 and 450 Squadrons flew in the next day. 260 Squadron remained at El Hamma, rejoining the Wing again at Kairouan on 18 April.

During their time at El Djem, 3 Squadron flew five operations without expending a single round of ammunition, while 450 flew only one unrewarding fighter sweep. On 17 April, 3 Squadron saw two cargo vessels covered by a MC202 and a twin engined aircraft, both of which left the scene before contact could be made. When they returned, they found that 260 Squadron had destroyed four Bf110s N.W of Cape Bon. Apart from this action, 239 Wing mostly found itself in the wrong place at the wrong time for the next five days. On 18 April all the squadrons moved to Kairouan, 3, 112 and 450 flying an early morning sweep before ferrying their aircraft forward shortly before midday. At 1645, 112, 250 and 450 flew a fighter sweep with Spitfires as top cover. They flew out to sea and followed the coast around Cape Bon. Three Bf109s were seen below coming from the east, but they dived away. They might have been the survivors of the 'Palm Sunday Massacre', which occurred when the three P-40 squadrons of the 57th FG, accompanied by the 314th Squadron, with Spitfires of 92 Squadron as top cover, intercepted a huge escorted formation of Ju52s. The aircraft were part of *Generalmajor* Buchholz's last desperate effort to keep the *Panzer Armee Afrika* supplied. Through 'Ultra' intercepts, the Allies were aware of these regular transport flights, and made particular efforts to intercept them. The Americans had taken off at 1700, and after patrolling for almost an hour were ready to turn for home when they caught the Ju52s low over the water off the Tunisian coast. Fifty-nine transports were destroyed, as well as nine Bf109s and a Bf110. The Americans lost six P-40s. (The SAAF Wing enjoyed a similar success on 22 April, destroying twenty-two ME323s.)

239 Wing's squadrons missed out on these bountiful targets, but 450 Squadron at least had the satisfaction of adding two more victories to their total on 19 April, during their second sweep of

the day. At 1333 they took off with 3 Squadron as top cover and 112 in the middle, led by Sqn. Ldr. Jack Bartle. Twenty miles east of Cape Bon a lone Ju88 was seen flying south at 3,000 ft. and several of 450's pilots attacked. It turned north and went into the sea in flames. 450's ORB did not record the names of the pilots involved, and the unfortunate Junkers was credited as a Squadron victory. Shortly afterwards five Bf109s were seen flying west and when 450 attacked them, they dived to 500 ft. A brief dogfight occurred, and F/Sgt. Devon Minchin (serial unrecorded) got in a burst which struck one in the starboard wing root. It went into the sea and was confirmed by Captain Saville of 112 Squadron. This was the Squadron's last confirmed victory of the North African Campaign.

19 April was also the day when Bobby Gibbes formally handed over command of 3 Squadron to Brian Eaton. Gibbes flew his last sortie in North Africa on 16 April, after being ordered back to Australia the previous day. He was bitterly disappointed not to be able to see the Tunisian Campaign to its end, but the decision was made. His appeals to be allowed to continue to fly until the end in North Africa were turned down. His tour had begun with the Squadron's first Tomahawk operation in the Syrian Campaign, lasting from 8 June 1941 to 16 April 1943. The only breaks were brief spells of leave, enjoyed on occasions by all pilots, and the enforced spell due to a broken leg when he baled out on 26 May 1942. He had flown 274 sorties and completed 472 operational hours.[18] With ten and one shared victories, he was the unit's second top scoring pilot. He was awarded the DFC in July 1942, the DSO in January 1943 and a Bar to the DFC on his return to Australia. There was a boisterous farewell party on 21 April, and he flew to Castel Benito in the Ghibli, thence to Alexandria.

On 20 April Sqn. Ldr. Jack Bartle led 450, 3 and 260 Squadrons on a fighter sweep to Cape Bon. Here they observed two SM79 hospital planes escorted by an Fw190, which made off when it saw the mass of Kittyhawks. In spite of the fact that the Germans had, on occasion attacked British ambulance aircraft, the Savoias were left alone, perhaps because of their nationality, and Jack Bartle's between tours employment as the CO of 1 Air Ambulance Unit.

3 and 450 Squadrons flew an armed recce together on 21 April in poor visibility. Although 450 was the leading squadron in the low position, they did not find any worthwhile targets, but 3's "Blue" section, which lost contact with the rest of the formation due to cloud, found movement on the road near Nabeul and claimed one 'smoker' and two damaged M/T.

3, 112 and 450 scrambled from standby at 0705 on 23 April in the hope of intercepting enemy transport aircraft, but nothing was found. Intense heavy and accurate AA came up from Menzel Bou Zelfa, and on the return journey FO R.V. (Rusty) Kierath of 450 Squadron called up to say he was going to force-land. There was some uncertainty as to whether his aircraft (FR477) had been hit earlier by AA, or whether he merely experienced engine trouble. Instead of force-landing, he baled out, and drifted out to sea, where he was picked up by a German air sea rescue launch. This sortie was the first of Rusty Kierath's second tour. Earlier he had completed an eventful tour, (first with 33 Squadron RAF, including an encounter with Marseille, when he was wounded by shrapnel) and then with 450, as one of its founder members. He completed a spell of instructing in Rhodesia, and returned to 450 Squadron for his second tour. After his capture he became a prisoner in *Stalag Luft III*. He took part in the 'Great Escape' and was murdered by the Gestapo on 25 March 1944, one of the fifty officers shot on Hitler's orders in retaliation for the escape.

On 25 April 239 Wing began a concerted anti shipping campaign to prevent supplies reaching the Axis forces in Tunisia. From this date, until the surrender in North Africa, most of the squadrons' efforts were directed against shipping, although there were a number of occasions when strafing and bombing sorties were flown.

At 0540, 250 and 260 Squadrons, with 450 as top cover took off on the first of these operations, and found a 5,000 ton motor vessel accompanied by a destroyer. The bombing produced either a direct hit or very near miss on the destroyer, which was seen to stop, and then move forward slowly.

3 and 112 Squadrons left at 0850 with a top cover of Spitfires. They found no ships, but discovered a Bf110 circling a large patch of oil one mile N.E. of Zembra Island. Sgt. Ken Goulder (FR485 CV-H) shared 3 Squadron's last North African victory with 112 Squadron.

> I was flying Green I in top cover led by W/O Stevens in a two squadron formation going out to bomb ships off CAPE BON. On nearing the target area an ME 110 was sighted some distance ahead and below. It appeared to be circling an oil patch on the water.
>
> S/L B. A. Eaton, the leader of our formation, ordered top cover to attack and W/O Stevens leading blue section ordered us into echelon right. At this stage I saw two Kittyhawks which I took to be blue 1 & 2 - actually they proved to be 2 a/c of 112 Sqdn.- diving on to the ME 110 on my left.
>
> As I closed into range - 300 yds - the E/A did a steep turn to the right endeavouring to evade the 112 a/c - which did not appear to have fired up to this stage - and thereby gave me the opportunity to fire a full deflection shot from 300 yds. I saw strikes on his fuselage, and pieces of fuselage & wing fall off. He also poured a lot of black smoke. I received no fire from the E/A and the pilot took evasive action, weaving violently and losing height right down to sea level.
>
> I followed him down and got in several bursts from quarter to line astern, from 200 to 250 yds. range. I saw further strikes on his fuselage and the amount of black smoke increased: also white smoke was observed from both engines. I then broke off, having exhausted ammunition and as I climbed away I saw 5 or 6 Kittyhawks attacking the E/A. Shortly after I saw it crash into the sea and disappear nose first.

Ken Goulder only received credit for *1/9* of the Messerschmitt's destruction, the rest being awarded to 112 Squadron, whose diarist recorded that the enemy aircraft 'sank . . . through sheer weight of lead'.[19] Goulder alone fired 1,000 rounds at it.

Later in the day 3 and 450 Squadrons attacked a destroyer at 1440, scoring several frustrating near misses. Fast moving naval vessels proved to be difficult targets.

The following day produced some success. At 1650 three ships were located steaming north in line astern, S.E of Zembra Island. By their estimated size, (5,000 tons) two of them were either heavy destroyers or light cruisers. The Kittyhawks attacked from 6,000 ft., releasing their bombs at 2,000 ft. The CO's bomb missed the first ship by 300 yards. Sgt. McLeod dropped his within 20 yards and F/Sgt. Hankey scored a direct hit. Five pilots obtained near misses on the second ship, and the third also suffered a near miss. Five minutes after the bombing a large explosion was seen on the first vessel. Medium AA came up from the ships. but none of the aircraft were hit.

On 28 April 3 Squadron flew as top cover to 112 and 250 on another shipping strike. As the lower squadrons were about to bomb a motor vessel and a destroyer, two Bf109s and an Fw190 made a pass through 3 Squadron's formation. Two turnabouts were given, and three pilots fired short bursts without making any claims. The German aircraft then climbed away out of range. Usually the Kittyhawk squadrons had a top cover of Spitfires for these shipping strikes, but on this occasion there were none present.

Spitfires were not present again when 450 Squadron gave top cover to 250 and 260 on 29 April. Two destroyers steaming towards Tunis were attacked by 250 and 260, several near misses being observed. During the bombing two separate sections of three Bf109s dived on the bombers, followed by one more, which attacked out of the sun. These were attacked and driven off by 450 Squadron. Sgt. Dick Rowe (FR490) attacked one from head on and saw pieces fly off the port wing. Rowe claimed a damaged. WO. Nicholson (FR491) attacked and chased another, observing strikes on the fuselage around the rear of the cockpit, but did not make a claim. Sgt. Austin also fired, but at the same time was attacked by another 109 and was hit in the starboard tailplane and elevator, returning with Cat. II damage.

100 hourly inspection of FL308, the last Kittyhawk to be flown by Squadron Leader Bobby Gibbes with 3 Squadron. It was taken over by Brian Eaton, who flew it regularly from 19 April until the end of the campaign in Tunisia. (Ken McRae)

On the following day, Spitfires flew top cover for all three operations. During the first, at 0545, led by Wg. Cdr. Burton in his personal aircraft HF-B, which probably carried the serial number FR451, a supply ship of 1,500 tons was attacked, the Wing Commander scoring a direct hit which set the ship on fire. 3 Squadron attacked a destroyer at 1135, scoring two very near misses. Three Bf109s were seen, but they made no attempt to attack and could not be engaged.

On 1 May F/Sgt. John Hooke and WO. Reg Stevens were commissioned. Readers will recall that they joined 3 Squadron from 239 Wing Training Flight in early June 1942. 3 Squadron's first operation in May took off at 0620. In the Gulf of Tunis a large Red Cross float plane was seen, but not attacked. No shipping was found, and bombs were dropped on a jetty. Two Bf109s were seen but did not stay to fight. 450 also bombed a wharf in the morning, starting a fire next to some buildings.

Two more anti-shipping sweeps were flown on 2 May, but visibility was poor due to low cloud and no targets were found. Similar conditions prevailed on 3 May, the one operation flown by 250 and 450 Squadrons finding nothing.

The weather was again poor on 4 May, but 3 Squadron took off at 0945 to patrol over the gulf and Cape Bon. Six Bf109s with long-range tanks were seen by Fl. Lt. Caldwell three miles east of the cape, but a good opportunity was missed when Caldwell pressed the trigger at a range of fifty yards, only to discover that his gun switch had not been turned on. PO Dawkins opened fire from 300 yards, but his attention was distracted by Fl. Lt. Caldwell's jettisoned bomb and the Messerschmitts got away. A stationary hospital ship with steam up was seen off the cape, but not attacked.

JG 77 was now the only German fighter unit still operating from African bases. The remainder of their fighters had retreated to Sicily, and were flying daily sorties with drop tanks, often landing on one of the few rough strips still in Axis hands to refuel and rearm.

Another inconclusive encounter with Bf109s took place early the next day when 3, 450 and 112 Squadrons carried out an armed recce of the Cape Bon area at 0645. Another hospital ship was seen, and eight Bf109s came out of the sun and dived straight through 3 Squadron's formation. 450 Squadron reported only two, and it seems that 112 as top cover noticed nothing. PO Forsstrom of 3 Squadron followed one E/A down but observed no results of his fire. It would seem that the Germans missed a good opportunity: the 239 Wing squadrons were lucky to avoid losses.

450 Squadron flew their first ground support operation for some time at 1046, bombing trucks and a bridge with 112 Squadron.

Perhaps in anticipation of the cessation of hostilities in Africa, PO Reg Stevens and a party of six men left by road for Algiers to purchase canteen supplies for 3 Squadron, and time was found to start a cricket competition, 'affording the airmen some well needed sport and relaxation'.

On 6 May 3 Squadron flew an armed recce over the Gulf of Tunis and the battle area, finding no worthwhile targets, but in the afternoon, with 450 as top cover, they bombed 100-plus M/T heading for Tunis. The pilots reported that accurate bombing was difficult owing to two formations of light bombers and their escorts being over the target at the same time.

The Army had begun its final offensive on this day. By midday on 7 May, British armour was close to the centre of the city of Tunis. American tanks entered Bizerta on the same day and by the morning of 8 May, both cities were under Allied control.

450 bombed a destroyer on 7 May, obtaining several near misses. 3 Squadron's third operation of the day at 1515 found a large vessel at La Goulette, which received a direct hit. On 8 May 3 Squadron took off on another shipping strike at 1335, bound for Zembra Island. Two Bf109s dived through the formation which was at 9,000 ft. and continued down to sea level. Four ships were sighted close inshore off Cape Bon, and these were bombed from 1,000 ft. A direct hit was scored on the leading ship. After the bombing a mixed formation of four Bf109s and MC202s came in from N.W. and attacked the No. 2s of the leading section. Sgt. Funston (FL229) got in a good burst at one E/A which immediately climbed steeply pouring black smoke, probably the result of boost, and no claim was made.

239 Wing was off again at 1650 and found three small vessels. Enemy aircraft were reported as 3 and 450 Squadrons bombed, and no results were observed. On this occasion the Axis fighters made a determined attempt to protect their shipping, ten Bf109s and MC202s engaging 250 Squadron, who shot one down. Twelve more Bf109s appeared 1,000 ft. below and 260 Squadron attacked them, claiming a probable and losing one aircraft, the pilot of which was rescued.

Each Australian squadron flew three operations on 9 May, independently of one another, and the main interest was the presence of numerous British destroyers operating off the coast.

At 1105 3 Squadron bombed a jetty, scoring two direct hits, and strafed along the east coast of the Cape Bon Peninsula, destroying a petrol carrier and damaging twelve more M/T. 450's third operation was an armed recce over Cape Bon. They bombed a road without hitting any vehicles, and then strafed, damaging fourteen M/T.

The Axis forces were now close to total collapse. By noon on 9 May their forces in the northern sector surrendered to the Americans. Two more days of desperate and futile resistance passed before the final surrender. 3 Squadron bombed and strafed over Cape Bon on 10 May, Sgt. Collier and Sgt. Funston each destroying one vehicle with direct hits. PO Dawkins and PO Leeds each produced a flamer by strafing and the rest of the squadron claimed a further ten M/T

Although this photograph was taken in Malta in July 1943, around the time of the invasion of Sicily, all of these 3 Squadron pilots took part in the campaign in Tunisia. Standing, left to right: FO Jack Doyle, F/Sgt. Arthur Collier, Sgt. Jack Beer, (on wing) F/Sgt. Peter Gilbert, F/Sgt. Ted Hankey, FO Jack Sergeant, PO Murray Nash, Fl. Lt. Brian Harris, PO John Hooke, Sqn. Ldr. Reg Stevens. Kneeling, FO Tom Russell. (Tom Russell)

damaged. 450 bombed forty-plus M/T with good results two hours later. In the afternoon Wg. Cdr. Burton led 112 Squadron as escort to Bostons bombing the small Italian held island of Pantelleria, between Tunisia and Sicily.

On 11 May 3 Squadron took off on its last operation of the campaign at 0520. They bombed a pier, scoring two direct hits, and produced a large explosion from a building at the base of the pier which received another direct hit. Seven M/T were damaged by strafing a nearby road. They were back on the ground at 0650.

450 took off at 0600 and bombed goods wagons in a rail siding, scoring two direct hits. They found a group of M/T dispersed under trees at the side of a road, and one section strafed, producing one flamer and two damaged. They landed at 0715.

3 Squadron's Operations Record Book tells the story of 239 Wing's last operational flight of the North African Campaign.

[At 1625] a recce of the area N. of ENFIDAVILLE, ZAGHOUAN, CAPE BON PENINSULAR, TUNIS and BIZERTA was made by W/C BURTON and S/L EATON. Heavy fighting found to be still taking place, but in all cases the enemy forces are entirely cut off from assistance or retreat, and no targets were found where it would be safe to bomb or strafe enemy positions without danger of hitting our own troops.

On 12 May von Arnim was captured, and the next day, Italian General Messe accepted unconditional surrender for all the remaining Axis forces in Tunisia. Over 250,000 prisoners had been taken. The persistent attacks on the *Luftwaffe's* transport aircraft and enemy shipping ensured that there would be no reverse Dunkirk. General Alexander's signal to the Prime Minister read 'Sir. It is my duty to report that the Tunisian Campaign is over. All enemy resistance has ceased. We are masters of the North African shores'.

The squadrons of 239 Wing celebrated the surrender with a pyrotechnic display of tracers and Verey cartridges, and in the case of 3 Squadron, by welcoming back the canteen committee from Algiers, who arrived with 'good supplies including wine, beer and eatables. For the first time in months the canteen was functioning at full pressure, much to the satisfaction of the whole squadron'. The South African Wing organised a "Grand Prix" of captured Axis vehicles and invited 239 Wing to participate. 'Among the entries was an Opel, a Volkswagen, a Peugeot, a Fiat, a Citroen and an Auto Union troop carrier. To the delight of 450 Squadron punters the race was won by the C.O., S/Ldr. Jack Bartle, in a Citroen'.[20] Leave was granted to all ranks and trucks took personnel into Tunis.

'A' Flight of 450 Squadron, Tunisia 1943. (RAAF Museum)

The CA 164 and the Ghibli worked overtime for the next few days, and three pilots left for the RAAF Liaison Office on the completion of their tours: PO Bray, PO Jones and PO MacKenzie. From 450 Squadron Fl. Lt. Aitchison, Sgt. House and Sgt. Marrows left, and PO Ellis, Sgt. Strom and Sgt. Shannon joined the unit as replacements.

Several shipping protection patrols were flown on 17 May, and 239 Wing then moved to a temporary new base at Zuara on 21 May, in preparation for a transfer to Malta, and the forthcoming invasion of Sicily. The African adventure was finally over.

3 Squadron's highly efficient engineering staff at work.
Sgt. Moore (left) and Fl. Lt. Ken McRae adjusting the
timing on the CO's aircraft.
(Ken McRae)

Country Boy

For a fighter pilot reported missing, Western Desert, 1943.

No need for maps, you'd recognise today,
This gold-reefed autumn day, this place,
Blue parachute of sky, delft range and still
Spitfire rosellas practising smart take-offs
And fuel-stop landings in the pyracantha,
Still, gold-eyed currawongs on fruit patrol,
Spinebills at honey in the banksia,
And watching magpies from the pine tree towers
Contentedly reporting on the weather -
"Warm warm warm, the yellow sun…"
I've had a thousand autumn days like this
Since your last flight,
Struck gold a thousand times like this
Here in your claim, the place where you began.
Still the debt compounds. Here in this Book-of-Hours
Brilliance of blue, and light, and trees,
What could I pay for all the autumn days
You have not known.
   Incredibly, so it seems now,
You asked no price at all, no price
For half a century of sun.

Jessica Aldridge

This moving poem, written by Jessica Aldridge, the sister of Pilot Officer Frederick Silk of 450 Squadron, KIA on 26/02/43, serves as an appropriate tribute to all those who failed to return.

It was first published in *Quadrant* in 1990. Her permission to use it here is very gratefully acknowledged.

APPENDIX 1

THE RECKONING

It should be understood that 3 Squadron RAAF and 112 Squadron RAF were both long established and successful units before they operated the Curtiss P-40 series of fighter aircraft, whereas 450 Squadron began its operational career flying the Kittyhawk I in February 1942, and continued to use the type for the duration of the war. 112 Squadron converted to Mustangs in July 1944, and 3 Squadron followed suit in November.

3 Squadron RAAF fought its first combat with enemy aircraft on 19 November 1940, when four Gladiators engaged eighteen Fiat CR42s.

The Squadron claimed sixteen victories while operating Gladiators, the last on 26 December 1940. They then converted to Hurricanes, and claimed thirty-four victories while flying them, the first on 15 February 1941, and the last on 15 April.

The unit was then withdrawn and began converting to Tomahawks, taking them into action for the first time on 8 June 1941 in the Syrian Campaign. The first victories came on 13 June, when they intercepted Ju88s attacking the British cruiser squadron supporting the ground forces in Syria. Twenty-four victories were claimed in Syria, and a further forty-one in North Africa while the unit was flying Tomahawks. By the end of 1941, a total of 115 enemy aircraft had been claimed.

The Squadron's first Kittyhawk victory was recorded on 1 January 1942, and by the end of the campaign in Africa the total had reached 189.5, the shared victory being with 112 Squadron. Seventy-four and a half of the Squadron's victories were claimed while flying Kittyhawks.

Like 3 Squadron, 112 began the war flying Gladiators, recording their first victory on 29 June 1940. They had already claimed seventeen Italian aircraft shot down before 3 Squadron entered the arena. The Squadron claimed seventy-one Gladiator victories, and one more when Fl. Lt. Charles Fry (RAAF) shot down a Bf110 in a Hurricane while flying from Crete.

112 began converting to Tomahawks at the close of June 1941, taking them into action for the first time on 14 September, when the first victory was recorded. By December 1941 the squadron had claimed thirty-six victories while flying the Tomahawk, bringing their total to 108.

The squadron began converting to Kittyhawks in late December 1941, and took them into action for the first time on 9 January 1942. The first victory came on 25 January, and by the end of the war in Africa, the squadron's total had reached 190.5, eighty-two and a half while flying the Kittyhawk.

In contrast to 3 and 112 Squadrons, 450 Squadron RAAF did not begin operations until February 1942, recording its first success on the 22nd of that month. The squadron claimed a total of forty-nine victories in North Africa, and if this total seems small in comparison to 3 and 112, it should be remembered that these two squadrons had a significant 'start' over 450, which is revealed by the table below.

All three squadrons had fewer opportunities to score victories after their change of role to fighter-bomber units. It can be seen that both 3 and 112 scored at a considerably faster rate when they were flying Tomahawks, and while the Kittyhawk was used as a pure fighter. From 26 May when Rommel's advance began, all the Kittyhawk units operated regularly as fighter-bombers, as well as being responsible for escorting the increasing numbers of medium bombers which the Desert Air Force put to excellent use.

Escorting the bombers was a difficult but rewarding task, and it can be fairly said that the Kittyhawk squadrons carried it out much more effectively than did the German fighter pilots during the

Battle of Britain. Losses were often heavy, as the fighters formed a screen around the bombers which was rarely penetrated, the German fighter pilots being content to increase their scores by the comparatively risk free procedure of dive and zoom tactics, which the Kittyhawk pilots found almost impossible to counter. Meanwhile, the bombers went about their task of attacking the Axis ground forces almost unhindered. The sacrifices made by the Kittyhawk pilots in carrying out their escort task should be fully appreciated as a most significant contribution to victory in North Africa. Few of the high scoring German *experten* could include significant numbers of bombers in their totals. Indeed, Marseille numbered only *three* bombers amongst his list of claims, *
a Blenheim over Tobruk on 28 April 1941, and two Baltimores of 223 Squadron on their first operation on 23 May 1942. These three aircraft all had one thing in common. They were *unescorted*.

> The natural rivalry among pilots meant that, with some *experten*, high scoring appears to have become an object in itself, while the hit-and-run tactics adopted to compensate for numerical inferiority meant that it was enemy fighter squadrons which tended to suffer. The bomber squadrons were rarely mauled, pounding both airfields and Axis communications almost unopposed, while the *Jagdflieger* pursued their private war, leaving the *Landsers* of all ranks cowering under enemy bombs.[1]

In contrast, the Allied fighter squadrons flew and fought as a team, as Nicky Barr explained in Lex McAulay's *Four Aces*: 'In 3 Squadron we were trained and had a sensitivity about flying as a squadron, not as individuals.'[2]

The inability of the German fighter force to support its ground forces effectively contrasted sharply with the evolution of the RAF's tactics and operational procedures as the Desert war progressed. The tactical use of medium bombers, and the highly effective Kittyhawks, which were able to offer direct support to the troops with their bombing and strafing, was never matched by the *Luftwaffe*. The fact that many of their fighter pilots ran up big personal scores was irrelevant to the prosecution of the war, and the undue emphasis placed on such achievements was an indication of the failure by the German commanders at all levels to understand the principles of air power.

At the end of the campaign in Tunisia, Allied air power was supreme. Almost 2000 sorties were flown between dusk, 5 May and dusk 6 May, the medium bombers laying what was called ' "Tedder's bomb-carpet", a moving barrage of air support along a line four miles long and three and a half miles wide, with concentrated artillery fire behind it'.[3] The *Luftwaffe* was powerless to prevent it.

By D-Day on 6 June 1944, Air Chief Marshal Sir Arthur Tedder GCB was Deputy Supreme Commander of the Allied invasion forces, and Air Marshal Sir Arthur Coningham GCB DSO MC DFC AFC was in command of the 2nd TAF. The greatest invasion force in world history went ashore in Normandy, protected by an umbrella of 14,674 offensive sorties, of which the RAF contributed 5,656.[4] The *Luftwaffe's* response was limited to pinpricks. It was in the Desert where these two great commanders established their principles of army/air cooperation and tested them successfully in the cauldron of battle.

---

* *Other sources list four. (His biographer Kurowski credits him with five: one of them supposedly a Maryland shot down in the morning on 24 September 1941, but his text disagrees with his appendix, the text mentioning a Maryland in the morning, and then describing in detail the destruction of **five** Hurricanes. The appendix for the same day lists two Marylands and two Hurricanes, and notes that this was the first time he had destroyed four enemy aircraft in one day. Fighters Over the Desert records four Hurricanes in the afternoon, and makes no mention of a Maryland earlier in the day.)*

COMPARATIVE VICTORY CLAIMS of 3, 112 AND 450 SQUADRONS

3 Squadron			112 Squadron			450 Squadron	
Gladiators	16		Gladiators (Africa)	25			
Hurricanes	34	(50)	Gladiators (Greece)	47*	(72)		
Tomahawks (Syria)	24						
Tomahawks	41	(115)	Tomahawks	36	(108)		
Kittyhawks	29.5		Kittyhawks	17.5			
Kittyhawks	45	(189.5)	Kittyhawks	65	(190.5)	Kittyhawks	49 (49)

The bottom line shows the number of claims made by 3 and 112 Squadrons *after* 450 became operational.

As Spitfires finally became available in greater numbers after Operation *Torch*, the future of the Kittyhawk squadrons was irrevocably decided. There would be no conversion to higher performance fighters. While some in the Air Ministry had lamented the lack of a dedicated dive-bomber after the initial success of the Stuka in 1939 and early 1940, it quickly became clear that it could only survive under conditions of total air superiority. Bomb carrying Kittyhawks on the other hand could defend themselves and then perform as fighters once the bombs had been dropped. No doubt many a Kittyhawk pilot may have longed for a Spitfire when fighting the 109s, but the Kittyhawk was a much more effective bomb carrier; they would always be available in quantity, and battlefield support from fighter-bombers had become an integral part of the Army's operational procedure.

By the time the Allies invaded Sicily and Italy, the *Luftwaffe's* fighter force had been reduced to insignificance, and the faithful Kittyhawks continued to do what they did best, relentlessly harassing the enemy at low level.

A study of the three squadrons' fatal casualties reveals a similar pattern to their victory claims. Before operating the P-40, 3 Squadron lost six pilots in action, while 112 lost the remarkably small total of two, although three pilots lost their lives in non-operational accidents. The following table shows the losses of pilots to all causes in North Africa after re-equipping with the P-40. Figures in brackets show losses which occurred in the same time frame as 450 Squadron's operations.

3 Squadron			112 Squadron			450 Squadron		
operational	accidental	total	operational	accidental	total	operational	accidental	total
34 (17)	7 (5)	41 (22)	38 (28)	9 (3)	47 (31)	28	3	31

Further details of all known Australian losses can be found in the Honour Roll.

* *Includes one Hurricane victory in Crete.*

APPENDIX 2

3 SQUADRON'S P-40 VICTORY CLAIMS: SYRIA - NORTH AFRICA

Details of claims for probable and damaged E/A can be found in the text. Claims over Sicily and Italy are not included.

W.S. Arthur	30/11/41 **Ju87** - 30/11/41 **Ju87** - 30/11/41 **MC200** - 30/11/41 **G-50**
M.G. Baillie	25/11/41 **Bf109**
R.H. Bayly	14/01/43 **Bf109**
A.W. Barr	12/12/41 **Bf110** - 13/12/41 **Bf109** - 13/12/41 **Ju88** - 01/01/42 **Ju87** - 01/01/42 **Ju87** - 11/01/42 **MC200** - 11/01/42 **Bf109** 11/01/42 **Bf109** - 08/03/42 **MC202** - 22/05/42 **Bf109** - 01/06/42 **Bf109** - 24/06/42 **G-50**
L.L. Boardman	24/06/42 **Bf109** - 30/12/42 **Bf109**
P.R. Bothwell	23/06/41 **D520** - 23/06/41 **D520**
E. Bradbury	22/01/42 **Ju87**
P.J. Briggs	13/12/41 *1/2* **Bf109** (shared Cameron)
A.C. Cameron	25/0641 **LeO451** - 12/10/41 **Bf109** - 26/11/41 **Bf109** - 13/12/41 **Bf109** - 13/12/41 *1/2* **Bf109** (shared Briggs) 01/01/42 **Ju87** - 01/01/42 **Bf109**
G.T. Chinchen	14/03/42 *1/2* **Bf109** (shared Packer)
G.E. Clabburn	15/09/42 **Bf109**
G.C. Coward	01/06/42 **Bf109** - 14/09/42 *1/2* **Bf109** (shared Jones)
V.F. Curtis	25/01/42 *1/2* **Bf110** (shared Reid) - 08/03/42 **MC200** - 08/03/42 **Ju87** - 15/03/42 **Bf109** - 26/06/42 *1/2* **Bf109** (shared Marshall of 250 Sqn.)
R. Dent	18/11/42 *1/2* **SM82** (shared Ritchie) *Originally considered to be a strafing claim and therefore not included in 3 Squadron's list of 'official' air to air claims.*
F. Fischer	19/11/41 **Bf109** - 01/01/42 **Ju87**
R.H. Gibbes	11/07/41 **D520** - 25/11/41 **G-50** - 25/11/41 **G-50** - 30/11/41 **MC200** - 22/01/42 **Ju87** - 07/05/42 **Bf109** - 22/05/42 **Bf109** - 01/09/42 **Bf109** - 28/10/42 **Bf109** - 17/11/42 *1/4* **Bf109** *(shared Ritchie / Smith of 112 Sqn)* - 22/01/43 **MC202** -
	On 18 November 1942, Bobby Gibbes shot down a Bf109 which had just lifted off from Magrun, deliberately waiting until its wheels had left the ground before opening fire. Wing disallowed his claim because it crashed inside the aerodrome boundary! It is therefore not included in any published lists of his victories, nor in 3 Squadron's 'official' list of air to air claims.
P.R. Giddy	22/01/42 **MC200** - 14/02/42 **MC200** - 14/02/42 **MC202** - 08/03/42 **MC200** - 08/03/42 **Ju87**
K. Goulder	07/03/43 **Bf109** - 25/04/43 *1/9* **Bf110** (shared with 112 Sqn.)
GROUP SHARE	20/11/41 **Bf110** (Jeffrey, Manford, Knowles, Gibbes)
E. Hankey	22/01/43 **MC202** *Initially claimed as a probable and confirmed post war.*

R.C. Hart	22/01/42 MC200 - 15/03/42 MC202
G.E. Hiller	10/07/41 D520
E.H. Jackson	25/11/41 Bf110 - 08/01/42 MC200
J.F. Jackson	25/06/41 LeO451 - 10/07/41 D520
W.E. Jewell	25/06/41 LeO451
P. Jeffrey	13/06/41 Ju88 - 15/06/41 M-167 - 25/11/41 Bf110 - 09/12/41 Bf109
G.R. Jones	14/09/42 *1/2* Bf109 (shared Coward)
E.K. Kildey	14/03/42 MC200 - 24/06/42 Bf109 - 12/07/42 Fi 156 - *by bombing: the aircraft was flying when attacked, but its destruction is not recorded in 3 Squadron's 'official' list of air to air claims.* 09/11/42 Bf109
L.E. Knowles	29/06/41 M-167 - 22/11/41 Bf109 (by collision)
E. Lane	10/07/41 D520
L. Lees	14/09/41 Bf110 *This aircraft was not seen to crash, and is therefore not recorded in 3 Squadron's 'official' list of air to air claims. Post war research by Russell Guest confirms that it crash-landed.*
W.H. Mailey	30/11/41 MC200 - 30/11/41 MC200 - 09/12/41 Bf109 - 09/12/41 Bf109 - 14/02/42 MC202 - 14/02/42 MC202
G.A. Neill	01/06/42 Bf109 - 14/07/42 Bf109 - 08/09/42 Bf109 - 08/09/42 Ju87
H.G. Pace	14/02/42 *1/2* MC202 (shared Thompson) - 08/03/42 MC200
T.E. Packer	14/03/42 *1/2* Bf109 (shared Chinchen)
J.R. Perrin	13/06/41 Ju88
R.P. Pfeiffer	08/01/42 MC200 - 08/01/42 MC200
G.H. Plinston	02/10/42 Bf109
A.C. Rawlinson	28/06/41 M-167 - 28/06/41 M-167 - 28/06/41 M-167 - 22/11/41 Bf109 - 22/11/41 Bf109 - 30/11/41 MC200
F.B. Reid	25/11/41 Bf110 - 25/01/42 *1/2* Bf110 (shared Curtiss) - 14/02/42 MC202 - 14/02/42 *1/2* MC202 (shared Duke of 112 Sqn.)
A. Righetti	30/12/42 Bf109
D.V. Ritchie	09/10/42 Bf109 - 17/11/42 *1/4* Bf109 shared Gibbes and F/L Smith of 112 Sqn) 18/11/42 *1/2* SM82 shared Dent (*See entry under Dent.*)
J.H. Saunders	13/06/41 Ju88 - 25/06/41 LeO451 - 24/09/41 Ju88
H.H. Schaeffer	08/01/42 MC200
D. Scott	22/11/41 Bf109 - 22/11/41 Bf109 - 30/11/41 MC200 - 30/11/41 Ju87
G.G. Scribner	08/09/42 Bf109
R.H. Simes	20/11/41 Bf109 - 22/11/41 Bf109 - 08/01/42 MC200 - 08/01/42 MC200 - 08/01/42 CR42
L.T. Spence	01/01/42 Ju87 - 14/02/42 MC202
R.N. Stevens	27/10/42 MC202 - 26/02/43 Bf109

R.T. Susans   06/04/43 **MC202**

B.M. Thompson   14/02/42 *1/2* **MC202** (shared Pace) - 27/02/42 **Bf109** - 27/02/42 **Bf109**

T. Trimble   30/11/41 **MC200** - 30/11/41 **MC200**

P.St.G. Turnbull   15/06/41 **M-167** - 28/06/41 **M-167** - 28/06/41 **M-167** - 10/07/41 **D520** -
                   10/07/41 **D520**

J. W. Upward   17/11/42 **Bf109** (by collision)

R.J. Watt   30/12/42 **Bf109**

G.H. White   14/02/42 **MC202**

R.K. Wilson   28/06/41 **M-167** - 25/11/41 **Bf110** - 25/11/41 **Fi 156** - 25/11/41 **Fi 156** -
                   01/12/41 **Ju88**

APPENDIX 3

450 SQUADRON'S VICTORY CLAIMS - NORTH AFRICA

F.W. Beste	08/03/45 **MC202**
R.G. Brown	19/07/42 *1/2* **Ju52** (shared Dyson)
R.D. Dyson	18/06/42 **Bf109** - 19/07/42 *1/2* **Ju52** (shared Brown)
A.D. Ferguson	19/07/42 *1/2* **Ju52** (shared Parker) - 19/07/42 **Ju87** - 01/09/42 **Bf109**
J.D. Gleeson	23/10/42 **Bf109** - 01/07/42 **Bf109** - 15/09/42 **Bf109**
A. Glendinning	22/01/43 *1/2* **Bf109** (shared Johns) - 24/01/43 *1/2* **Ju88** (shared McQueen) 26/02/43 **Bf109**
M.A. Jenkins	29/05/42 *1/2* **Ju87** (shared McBurnie)
G.E. Johns	22/01/43 *1/2* **Bf109** (shared Glendinning)
G. Lindsay	31/05/42 **Bf109** - 19/07/42 **Ju52**
H.F. Marting	15/09/42 **Bf109** - 20/10/42 **MC202**
D.H. McBurnie	08/03/42 **MC202** - 23/05/42 **Bf109** - 29/05/42 *1/2* **Ju87** (shared Jenkins) 29/05/42 **Bf109** - 01/07/42 **Bf109** - 04/07/42 **Bf110**
V.J. McFarlane	14/01/43 **Bf109**
D.N. McQueen	24/01/43 *1/2* **Ju88** (shared Glendinning) - *22/01/43* ***SM79*** *
D.G. Minchin	22/01/42 *1/2* **Bf109** (shared Schaaf) - 19/04/43 **Bf109**
I.A. Nursey	23/02/42 **Bf109** - 23/05/42 **Bf109** - 29/05/42 **Ju87**
G.H. Norton	27/02/43 **Bf109**
G.C. O'Neil	03/11/42 **Bf109**
E.P. Oakley	12/09/42 **Bf109**
F.E. Parker	19/07/42 *1/2* **Ju52** (shared Ferguson) - *19/07/42* ***Ju52*** *
F. Regan	26/02/43 **Bf109**
F.R. Schaaf	23/10/42 **Bf109** - 22/11/42 *1/2* **Ju88** (shared Winn) - 22/01/43 **Bf109** - 22/01/43 *1/2* **Bf109** (shared Minchin)
R. Shaw	22/02/42 **Ju88** - 08/03/42 **MC200** (or 202)
N.H. Shillabeer	27/05/42 **Bf109**
G.H. Steege	28/03/42 **Bf109**
J.E. Williams	18/06/42 **Bf109** - 05/07/42 **Ju88** - 12/09/42 **Ju87** 12/09/42 **Ju87**
R.W. Winn	22/11/42 *1/2* **Ju88** (shared Schaaf) - 22/01/43 **MC202**
I.C. Young	23/02/42 **Bf109**
Shared victory	*26/10/42* ***Ju88*** (Phelps, Cameron, Williams, Borthwick, Prowse, Schaaf)*
Shared victory	30/10/42 **Ju52** (Crouch, Markle, Jenkins, Reid)
Squadron victory	19/04/43 **Ju88** (twelve pilots)

* See notes below.

The list of victory claims for 450 Squadron was put together from a number of sources. The Operations Record Book provided first hand information for the majority of the units' claims, and a summary written on 28 February 1943 noted that the squadron had submitted claims for 47 destroyed, 18 probables and 26 damaged enemy aircraft up to that date. Two more victories were claimed before the end of the fighting in North Africa, bringing the squadron's total to 49, which is noted in the 1943 publication *RAAF LOG.*

Not all of these claims could be found in the ORB, but *Fighters Over the Desert* and *Aces High* were able to provide details of two probables which were subsequently confirmed; however, the elusive total of 49 had still not been reached.

Frank Olynyk, a respected American author and historian, very kindly came to the rescue with details from his own list of claims for 450 Squadron, and his information actually takes the total *beyond* 49, however, there are several anomalies which will probably never be cleared up with certainty.

Frank's list included two claims for Jack Gleeson which I had not found. These were a Bf109 on 1 July 1942, which was not mentioned in the ORB, but discovered by Frank in the 211 Group Operational Summary (OpSum) in Air 23/1805 at the PRO in England, and another Bf109 on 15 September, which the ORB recorded as a probable. (This was also found in the Group OpSum of 20 September.)

Frank had not included Sqn. Ldr Steege's Bf109 on 28 March, or Fl. Lt. Williams' second Ju87 on 12 September, as the ORB recorded them both as probables. *Aces High* noted that both *were* initially claimed as probables, but later confirmed as destroyed. The ORB later noted that *two* Ju87s were destroyed on 12 September, suggesting that Fl. Lt. Williams' probable was indeed upgraded. This agrees with the squadron's total of 47 at the end of February 1943.

Neither the ORB nor Frank acknowledged Fl. Lt. Parker's Ju52 on 19 July, but *Fighters Over the Desert* credits Parker with a Ju52 shared with Sqn. Ldr. Ferguson, *and* a Ju52 destroyed, quite unequivocally stating that the Squadron destroyed four Ju52s on this occasion.

Finally, Frank records 'a three engined aircraft' for Sgt. D.N. McQueen on 22 January 1943. This was a Savoia SM79, and did not originally appear in my list, as the ORB recorded it as damaged only. This claim, or the previously mentioned item, takes the total to fifty.

The mystery might lie with the Ju88 forced to land by six pilots on 26 October. The ORB did not claim this as destroyed, no doubt due to what appeared to be a reasonably successful forced-landing. All of the pilots ran out of ammunition due to having been on a strafing operation before they encountered the Ju88, and were unable to inflict any further damage. The ORB noted it only as 'claimed as damaged by the Squadron', even though it was forced to land. However, *Fighters Over the Desert* notes that 'six aircraft of 450 Squadron met and shot down a Ju88, which force-landed'.

Perhaps, if this Ju88 is included, fifty is, after all, the correct total for this fine unit.

APPENDIX 4

VICTORY CLAIMS OF AUSTRALIAN PILOTS FLYING WITH RAF UNITS

94 SQUADRON

M.M. Maxwell | 23/03/42 **Bf109**

112 SQUADRON

J.P. Bartle | 22/11/41 **Bf109** - 05/12/41 **Ju87** - 05/12/41 **G50** - 12/12/41 **Bf109** - 22/12/41 *1/2 Ju87* (shared Westenra) *Bartle also claims two further victories, a G50 and a Bf109, details of which were apparently not recorded due to moves of base.*

H.G. Burney | 20/12/41 **Ju88** - 08/02/42 **Bf109** - 08/02/42 *1/2 Bf109* (shared Humphries) - 14/02/42 **MC200** *(originally claimed as a Ba65 - see text)* - 13/03/42 **MC200**

C.R. Caldwell | 21/02/42 **Bf109** - 14/03/42 *1/2 MC202* (shared Urbanczyk) - 14/03/42 **MC202** 23/04/42 **Bf109** - *This victory was apparently not recorded by 112 Squadron.*

K.F. Carson | 20/11/41 **Bf110** - 21/11/41 *1/3 CR42* (shared Jeffries & Duke) - 21/02/42 **Bf109** *(Post-war research suggests that the last claim should have been for a damaged.)*

W.E. Carson | 06/06/42 *1/2 Bf109* (shared Adye)

R.A. Drew | 14/02/42 **MC200** - 14/02/42 **MC200**

R.J.D. Jeffries | 12/10/41 **Bf109** - 21/11/41 *1/3 CR42* (shared Carson & Duke)

R.M. Leu | 20/11/41 *1/3 Bf110* (shared Bowker & Christie) - 21/11/41 **CR42** - 30//11/41 **G50** - 05/12/41 **MC200** - 25/01/42 **Bf109** - 14/02/42 **MC200** - 14/02/42 **MC200**

K.R. Sands | 20/12/41 **Bf109**

R.A. Wild | 31/10/42 **Ju87** - 01/11/42 **Ju87**

250 SQUADRON

G.G. Buckland | 12/05/42 **Ju52**

W.O. Cable | 23/11/41 **Bf109** - 05/12/41 **Ju87** - 05/12/41 **Ju87** -
Only three confirmed victories could be located for this pilot, but as Aces High credits him with four, probables and damaged claims have been included: it may be that one of these was confirmed at a later date.
23/11/41 probable **Bf109** - 05/12/41 probable **Ju87** - 16/06/42 damaged **Bf109** *(NB: RAAF records credit Fl. Lt. Cable with three destroyed and six damaged)*

C.R. Caldwell | 26/06/41 **Bf109** - 30/06/42 *1/2 Bf110* (shared Whittle) - 30/06/41 **Ju87** - 30/06/41 **Ju87** - 07/07/41 **G50** - 16/08/41 *1/2 G50* - 29/08/41 **Bf109** - 27/09/41 **Bf109** - 28/09/41 **Bf109** - 23/11/41 **Bf109** - 23/11/41 **Bf109** - 05/12/41 **Ju87** - 05/12/41 **Ju87** - 05/12/41 **Ju87** - 05/12/41 **Ju87** - 05/12/41 **Ju87** - 12/12/41 **Bf109** - 20/12/41 **Bf109** -

D.J. Cormack | 15/09/42 **Bf109** - 01/10/42 **Ju87**

G.C. Coward	26/06/41 **Bf109** - 12/12/41 **Ju87** -
	'Charlie' Coward is also credited with four victories in Aces High. He later claimed one and one shared with 3 Squadron, which leaves us one half short: therefore his known probable and damaged claims have also been included.
	12/12/41 probable **Bf109** - 20/12/41 probable **Bf109** - 22/12/41 damaged **Ju87** (which was about to land - this may have been later confirmed.)
H.N. Humphries	27/09/41 **Bf109**
J.F. Kent	26/06/41 **G50** - *(PO Kent also damaged a Bf109 in the same combat, recorded by 250's ORB as 'last seen spinning in followed by a dense cloud of black smoke'.)*
H.C. Mayers *(Wing Commander 239 wing: his victories were claimed while leading 250 Squadron)*	12/05/42 **Ju52** - 08/07/42 **Bf109** - 20/07/42 **MC202**
R.H. Nitschke	20/11/41 **Ju87** - 20/11/41 **Ju87** - 09/12/41 **MC202** - 11/12/41 **Bf109** - 12/12/41 **MC202**
T.G. Paxton	08/06/41 *1/2 Z1007 (shared Hamlyn - ORB notes that it appeared to be about to make a forced landing when it was destroyed by shore batteries at 600 ft.)* 26/06/41 **Bf109** *('Aces High' credits this as destroyed, 250's ORB as probably destroyed)*
F.M. Twemlow	05/12/41 **Ju87** - 09/12/41 **MC202** - 12/12/41 **Ju87** - 22/12/41 **Ju87** 05/12/41 probable **Ju87** - 05/12/41 Probable **Ju87** - 22/01/42 damaged **Bf109** - 06/06/42 damaged **MC202**.
J.L. Waddy	09/12/41 *1/2 Bf110* (shared Bary) - 12/12/41 **Bf109** - 20/12/41 **Bf109** - 26/01/42 **MC200** - 12/05/42 **Ju52** - 12/05/42 **Ju52** - 12/05/42 **Bf110** - 12/05/42 **Bf110** - *(see text for details)* 21/05/42 **Bf109** -
R.J. Whittle	30/06/41 *1/2 Bf110* (shared Caldwell) - 30/10/41 **Bf109** - 20/11/41 **Ju87** - 20/11/41 **Ju87** - 20/11/41 **Ju87** - 23/11/41 **Bf109** - 05/12/41 **Ju87** - 05/12/41 **Ju87** - 05/12/41 **Ju87**-*(crash-landed & originally claimed as a probable: compare with 'Mac' Twemlow's claims on the same date.)* 13/12/41 **MC202** - 13/12/41 **Ju88** -

260 SQUADRON

W.R. Cundy	04/08/42 **Bf109** - 26/10/42 **Bf109** - 31/10/42 **Bf109** - 31/10/42 *1/2 Bf109* (shared Thomas) - 03/11/42 **Bf110** *(See text for details)* - 04/11/42 **Ju88** - 11/11/42 **Fi156** - 11/11/42 *1/6 Ju88 (Six pilots of 260 Squadron attacked this aircraft.)*
J.L. Waddy	31/05/42 **Ju87** -
	(31/05/42 Ju87 - 31/05/42 Ju87 - these two aircraft were originally claimed as probables. it was later confirmed by an AIF officer that three Ju87s crashed in this combat - see text. They are not included in his 'official' total.) 04/06/42 **CR42** - 12/06/42 **MC202** -

4 SAAF SQUADRON

J.L. Waddy	20/09/42 **Bf109**

APPENDIX 5

AUSTRALIAN P-40 ACES

The following pilots can all be considered as aces, if the definition of an ace includes shared victories. There are several different theories of what constitutes an ace, and how a pilot's score should be interpreted. As an example, Clive Caldwell's score has variously been presented as 28 1/2, (by combining two of his shared victories into one whole), or 30, (27 and 3 shared, on the basis that 30 aircraft at which he fired his guns were destroyed) or, more accurately, 27 and 3 shared, which indicates exactly what the pilot accomplished in terms of aircraft destroyed.

Claims for probables and damaged aircraft have not been included, and can be found in the text. The bold figures show P-40 victories claimed in the Middle East and North Africa.

Several pilots returning to Australia from the Desert also claimed P-40 victories in the Pacific, and these are noted. A considerable number of pilots, particularly those from 3 Squadron, scored victories while flying other types of aircraft, and the circumstances of these are noted. The pilot's final score is given in the last column.

PILOT		TOTAL
C.R. CALDWELL	**19, 3 shared** + 8 on Spitfires - (Darwin)	27, 3
J. L. WADDY	**12, 1 shared** (+ 2 unconfirmed) + 3 on Spitfires - 92 Sqn (Desert)	15, 1
A.W. BARR	**12**	12
R. H. GIBBES	**10, 2 shared** (+ 1 not officially recorded: see 18 November '42)	10, 2
R. J. WHITTLE	**10, 1 shared** + 1 & 2 shared on P-40s (Pacific)	11, 3
A.C. CAMERON	**6, 1 shared**	6, 1
R.M. LEU	**6, 1 shared**	6, 1
A.C. RAWLINSON	**6** + 2 on Hurricanes (Desert)	8
W.H. MAILEY	**6**	6
W.R. CUNDY	**5, 2 shared** (+ 1 not officially recorded)	5, 2
D.H. McBURNIE	**5, 1 shared**	5, 1
P. St.G TURNBULL	**5** + 4 on Hurricanes (Desert) + 3 on P-40s (New Guinea)	12
P.R. GIDDY	**5**	5
R.H. NITSCHKE	**5**	5
R.H. SIMES	**5**	5
R.K. WILSON	**5**	5
P. JEFFREY	**4, 1 shared** + 1 on Hurricanes (Desert)	5, 1
J.P. BARTLE	**4, 1 shared** (+ 2 not officially recorded)	4, 1
H.G. BURNEY	**4, 1 shared**	4, 1
V.F. CURTIS	**3, 2 shared**	3, 2
W.S. ARTHUR	**4** + 2 on Gladiators & 1 on Hurricanes (Desert) + 1 on P-40s (Pacific)	8
H.C. MAYERS	**3** + 1 shared on Hurricanes (Desert) + 8 on Hurricanes (BoB.)	11, 1
J.H. SAUNDERS	**3** + 3 on Hurricanes (Desert)	6
J.F. JACKSON	**2** + 4 on Hurricanes (Desert) +1 on P-40s (New Guinea)	7
T.G. PAXTON	**1, 1 shared** +2 on Hurricanes (Desert) +2 on Hurricanes (Ceylon)	5, 1
G.H. STEEGE	**1** + 3 on Gladiators & 4 on Hurricanes (Desert)	8
J.R. PERRIN	**1** + 5 on Hurricanes (Desert)	6

APPENDIX 6

DECORATIONS AWARDED to AUSTRALIAN P-40 PILOTS

Pilots who were decorated *before* converting to the P-40 are also included, in *italics*.

Name	Squadron	Award	Date
Fl. Lt. W.S. Arthur	3	DFC	26/12/41
Sqn.Ldr. M.C. Barber (SAAF)	450	DFC	Feb. 1943
FO A.W. Barr	3	DFC	20/02/42
Sqn.Ldr. A.W. Barr DFC	3	Bar to DFC	05/02/43
Sgt L.L. Boardman	3	DFM	06/10/42
Fl. Lt. C.R. Caldwell	250	DFC & Bar	26/12/42
Sgt. A.C. Cameron	3	DFM	Sept. 1942
Fl. Lt. G.T. Chinchen	3	DFC	18/09/42
Fl. Lt. D.H. Clarke	450	DFC	Feb. 1943
PO G.C. Coward	3	DFC	18/09/42
Fl. Lt. R.W. Cundy (as Sgt)	260	DFM	22/02/43
Fl. Lt. R.W. Cundy	260	DFC	09/02/43
F/Sgt. R.V. Dangar	450	DFM	18/09/42
F/Sgt. R.A. Drew	112	DFM	1942
F/Sgt. R.D. Dyson	450	DFM	06/10/42
Sqn. Ldr. A.D. Ferguson	450	DFC	05/02/43
FO F. Fischer	3	DFC	26/12/41
Fl. Lt. A Glendinning	450	DFC	1943
Sqn. Ldr. R.H. Gibbes	3	DFC	28/07/42
Sqn. Ldr. R.H. Gibbes	3	DSO	15/01/43
F/Sgt. E.C. House	450	DFM	Mar. 1943
Fl. Lt. J.F. Jackson	3	DFC	07/04/42
Sqn. Ldr. P. Jeffrey	3	DFC	13/05/41
Wg. Cdr. P. Jeffrey	No.2 Wing	DSO	12/12/41
Sgt. E.K. Kildey	3	DFM	06/10/42
Sgt. R.M. Leu	112	DFM	17/03/42
Sgt. W.A. Mailey	3	DFM	17/03/42
Wg. Cdr. H.C. Mayers DFC	239 Wing	DSO	28/07/42
Sgt D.H. McBurnie	450	DFM	28/07/42
Sgt V.J. McFarlane	450	DFM	Feb. 1943
Sgt. G.A. Neill	3	DFM	13/10/42
Sgt. G.C.W. O'Neil	450	MM	Jan. 1943
Fl. Lt. J.R. Perrin	3	DFC	01/04/41
Fl. Lt. A.C. Rawlinson	3	DFC	10/10/41
Sqn. Ldr. A.C. Rawlinson	3	Bar to DFC	26/12/41
Fl. Lt. F.R. Schaaf	450	DFC	Feb. 1943
Sgt. R.H. Simes	3	DFM	07/04/42
Fl. Lt. L.T. Spence	3	DFC	18/09/42
Fl. Lt. G. H. Steege	3	DFC	08/04/41
F/Sgt. B.N. Thompson	3	DFM	18/09/42
Fl. Lt. P.St.G. Turnbull	3	DFC	10/10/41
PO F.M. Twemlow	250	DFC	18/09/42
FO J.L. Waddy	250	DFC	02/10/42
Sgt. R.J. Whittle	250	DFM	13/02/42
Sgt. R.K. Wilson	3	DFM	20/01/42
Sqn. Ldr. J.E.A. Williams	450	DFC	Mar. 1943

Fl. Lts. W.O. Cable and D.J. Cormack were awarded the DFC after they returned to Australia and served with 457 and 452 Squadrons. Their achievements with 250 Squadron in North Africa were acknowledged in the citations for their decorations in Australia.

APPENDIX 7

THE FORMATION of 450 SQUADRON

Air Commodore Gordon Steege, DSO, DFC, (ret) was the first Commanding Officer of 450 Squadron RAAF, the first of the *Article XV* Empire Air Training Scheme Squadrons to become operational. This appendix consists of excerpts from a letter written by AC Steege to Professor Vincent Orange of the University of Canterbury in New Zealand (Air Marshal Sir Arthur Coningham's biographer) in August 1999, with some additional facts provided to the author from a recent interview, and correspondence.

> I left Australia with No. 3 Squadron in July 1940 for the Middle East and as a flight commander led it flying Gladiators and Hurricanes against the Regia Aeronautica in the Western Desert and Libya during Wavell's 1940 push to Benghazi and then in the "Handicap" when Rommel and the Luftwaffe pushed us back into Egypt. 3 Squadron was then deployed to "rest" at Lydda on air Defence of Palestine, and from there in June 1941, I was posted to command 450 Squadron (RAAF), the first of the Empire Air Training Scheme Squadrons which had just arrived from Australia at Abu Sueir, Egypt.

> 450 Squadron consisted only of ground staff, all recent war time enlistments, with corporal the highest rank, a Medical Officer, Adjutant, two Cypher Officers, a Ground Defence Officer and Equipment Officer. The Australia/UK EATS agreement provided that aircrew for such squadrons would be Australians to be withdrawn from those already serving with RAF squadrons, aircrew who had been trained and provided under the Empire Air Training Scheme. To provide some senior NCO experience on a temporary basis, I sought and was provided with a sprinkling of NCOs and a Ground Defence Officer from 3 Squadron.

Initially without aircrew, 450 combined with the pilots of 260 Squadron RAF, and served in the Syrian Campaign. When 260 Squadron joined their recently arrived ground staff:

> 450 [moved] back to Rayak. Here they were joined by three Flight Lieutenants, two from the training organisation in Australia and the other a pre war Australian in the RAF, badly burned when shot down in a Blenheim near Benghazi in 1940, nursed by Senoussi and carried by them back to the British lines in Egypt. With these three pilots, 450 acted as a conversion unit, converting pilots direct from training schools in East Africa onto Hurricanes. These were young Australian Sergeant Pilots with a couple of RAF.

> Towards the end of 1941 the first snow had appeared on nearby Mt. Hermon, the Hurricanes, instructors and trainees were sent away, and 450 Squadron ground staff moved by train from Rayak to Qassasin near Abu Sueir, Egypt, to equip with the newly arrived P-40 Kittyhawks and be manned with pilots.

> Here the same Australian Sergeant Pilots we'd converted onto Hurricanes at Rayak, and one of the inexperienced Flight Lieutenants from Australia, were posted back as the first of the aircrew with which the Squadron was to go into operations in the Western Desert.

> At this time Air Marshal Sir Richard Williams, who, as Chief of Air Staff RAAF for many years between the wars, had been replaced by Sir Charles Burnett, RAF, came through Egypt on the way to the UK, and in Cairo sent for me. I told him I had insufficient pilots, all these virtually straight from training schools in East Africa, with one inexperienced Flight Lieutenant, and that I was awaiting the balance, having pressed HQ ME for some with operational experience. I'd been a cadet at Point Cook in 1938 when he was CAS, he knew me, and said in very positive terms, "Steege, you are to accept only Australian pilots!"

> With a view to enlisting aid to get the required pilot strength, I flew a Kittyhawk out to Gambut to call on the Air Commander, but Air Vice Marshal Coningham was away and his Senior Administrative Staff Officer, Group Captain George Beamish saw me. I explained the requirement for the balance of pilots, some with experience, and Air Marshal Williams' specific instruction to me. George Beamish had been either a heavy weight boxer or a front row forward and was a big man - and unsympathetic about Air Marshal Williams' instruction to me. I later heard that following this meeting George Beamish said, "We can't have that feller Steege coming out and talking politics to us".

After returning to Qassasin, still pestering HQ ME Personnel Branch for the Australian pilots Williams had insisted on, I was telephoned to go to Cairo to see Air Vice Marshal Coningham. I flew a Kittyhawk to Heliopolis and as instructed, waited for a long time in an ante room outside a C in C's meeting he was attending. I had not seen him before, and I will always remember him as he came out alone, apologised for the wait, sat on the one seat with me, heard my situation, Air Marshal Williams' edict, and that in any case I needed a Flight Commander with operational experience. I found him a very handsome man with an engaging personality, of great natural charm. He said Australian EATS pilots in his RAF Squadrons were important to them. In the serious operational situation, withdrawing them to go to 450 would detract from those squadrons and his capability. As he was the commander responsible for air operations with what he had, I understood the position, but I explained my recent instruction from Air Marshal Williams. He said he would do what he could, and hoped 450 Squadron could move out to him soon. So different to George Beamish, I was eating out of his hand, and on return to Qassasin, when HQ ME offered a Canadian Flight Lieutenant with operational experience, I accepted. However, he and an Australian Sergeant Pilot with operational experience were both fatigued, and the Canadian didn't last long.

Sergeant R.V. "Rusty" Kierath was posted to 450 following my plea for some pilots with operational experience. He came direct from 33 Squadron flying Hurricanes in combat operations, and should have had a break before being sent in again with 450. When he joined 450 with other inexperienced pilots, he flew a total of 15 hours on the Kittyhawk getting handling and familiarity on type flying. This included formation flying and two 15 minute "gun tests" but not air to air combat training. The inexperienced pilots would have had the same 15 hours conversion and familiarity flying on the P-40, including formation flying and a couple of gun tests, but no air to air combat training. (recent correspondence)

Gordon Steege carried out some early comparison tests between the P-40 and the Hurricane. He liked the P-40's armament, but found that the Hurricane climbed faster and was more manoeuvrable. The P-40 was faster in level flight, and dived much faster. The US Air Attache, greatly concerned by the frequent landing accidents being experienced by the RAF, asked Sqn. Ldr. Steege to come to Cairo to discuss the problem. Steege recommended a steep approach, followed by a 'wheel' landing rather than a three pointer, and stressed that flying training should be adjusted to the standard of the least experienced pilot. One of 450's young sergeants ignored this advice, attempting a three pointer from a flat approach. The resulting ground loop damaged the undercarriage, and Gordon Steege immediately had him posted back to the Middle East Pool. Other pilots complained about this seemingly harsh treatment, but Rusty Kierath reminded them that '"Steegey" had made it clear in advance what was expected of them.' The recommended procedure was adhered to from that point on.

. . . . In January 450 moved to a rear LG near Haneish for a few days' final training. With good material, but inexperienced, I pressed his staff for a couple more days before moving out to operate from Gambut. *(Which was granted - author).*

Air Marshal Williams on his return from the UK, visited 450 at Gambut, and [while] inspecting the line up of pilots, came to the Canadian. Ignoring him, he said "Who is that?" I said, "Flight Lieutenant C......., Flight Commander, Sir." His only response was to ask "What is he doing here?"

In June 1942 when I received the signal of posting out, I drove up to Air Vice Marshal Coningham's HQ, and as was his practice with his Squadron Commanders, he saw me without fuss. He had recently signalled complimenting 450 on its performance.[*] I recommended against the appointment of the officer nominated to succeed me. He said it was hard to find an Australian to command, and did I have any suggestion. I said I believed a Flight Lieutenant Alan Ferguson, then commanding 451 EATS Army Co Op Squadron in Palestine, would be appropriate, but he would have to arrive and the other officer go elsewhere, urgently. 'Mary' instructed his staff officer to arrange this, and it was done in two days. He then asked where I would like to go and as I requested, sent me off to the Staff School at Haifa. I regret I never saw him again, for he was the most impressive man I ever met.

450 under Ferguson and others went on to a highly respected record through to the end of the war in Italy.

[*] *". . . the standard of fighting and bomber protection by your squadron has been quite exceptional. We are all impressed by the operational efficiency and keenness displayed. . . ." (Herington - footnote p.225)*

APPENDIX 8

A WORD FROM THE GROUND CREW

Ted Lawler was an Instrument Maker with 450 Squadron, and in this article, he explains the background to his training, some of the early vicissitudes which befell 450 Squadron, and the almost redundant role of an Instrument Maker in the Desert. He goes on to provide a detailed look at the tasks of the ground crew, cheerful and resourceful to a man, who laboured tirelessly under incredibly trying conditions to keep their pilots flying.

I welcome the opportunity to relate some of the efforts made by the Ground Staff in the desert.

To begin with, it must be noted that when squadrons were formed, no-one in Australia would have had any idea of man power requirements under war conditions.

I had applied to enter the RAAF as an Air Cadet and whilst awaiting call-up, which never came because of the war, I attended a course on aircraft instruments at Melbourne Tech. This was for nearly two years. After joining up I was in the first course for instruments at Melbourne Tech, with the same instructors, who admitted that they knew little or nothing about aircraft. All they could do was teach about instruments on cars, and that was very little, but one got the basics and learnt how to use different types of machinery to do with aircraft and their requirements. I came first in that course and from there was sent to Rose Bay where I learnt all about the Smith and the Sperry Automatic Flying Controls from the instrument men there (QANTAS). As I was the only one who completed that course, I was the only man in the RAAF who knew those controls.

From there I was posted to 450 Squadron, which, being a fighter squadron, and regardless of what type of aircraft flying at that time, they would not be equipped with auto controls. 450 left Australia with 7 Officers and 268 men, which included ground defence. This should give some idea of what I meant at the start of this note. 452 Squadron, a fighter squadron, was actually started at Williamtown after 450 had left, but went to England and was completed there with 14 Officers and 563 men, and it should be noted that all air bases in England had their own ground defence. Now, how did the powers that be work out how many men were required for a fighter squadron? The other squadrons in 239 Wing were near enough to the same as 450.

When we arrived at 102 Maintenance Unit at Abusueir in Egypt, possibly the biggest outside England for the RAF, we were all interviewed to see what we knew. When they found me and my knowledge I was put to work lecturing and demonstrating the Smith Auto Flying System. They even tried to get me transferred as they had no-one else to test this system and I was a gift from the Gods. Incidentally, the Smith was the British system and the Sperry the American. All the British large aircraft had the Smith System, but with the war aircraft were rolling off the supply line faster and faster, but there was no time to train staff on anything new.

To give an idea of efficiency, when we had been overseas for about four months, the CO sent a Corporal Dean to see if he could find any mail. First stop, RAAF Liaison. "450? Never heard of them! Who the hell are they?" Second stop, RAF Liaison. "Yes, we have heaps of it. Who are they, where are they, and where did they spring from?" At that time we and 260 (RAF) had been joined together. They had no ground crew, we had no air crew, so we formed an operational squadron in the Syrian campaign, half RAF and half RAAF, and neither Liaison Office knew about it.

Now to instruments in Egypt. There was no way in the world that instrument repair could be carried out in the Western Desert, for two very good and excellent reasons. Firstly we had no test equipment, and secondly, even if we had, we had nowhere suitable to put it. Instruments can only be repaired under extremely clean conditions, which we did not have: nor did we approach anywhere near that. We *did* have plenty of sand and dust, etc. So all one could do was replace, if we had spares, and most of them came from crashed planes. In reality, qualified instrument men were not required under wartime conditions. To qualify that statement, when I went into hospital, that left an offsider that I had gained, and one repairer in each of A and B Flights. I was not replaced and the repairer in A Flight remustered to an airframe fitter. That left two, and later one of them was sent home. Were instrument makers/ repairers really required?

But the main fact is that qualified instrument makers were not needed on fighter squadrons. Even on the RAF OTU that I was sent to after leaving hospital, there was only myself as the Corporal and three others, and we then had all sorts of aircraft, including bombers. All that was needed was someone who could remove and replace. Even the oxygen really only needed a strong person to remove and reinstall, mainly because of the weight factor. And the enormous roll over of planes should be taken into account. It is a sad fact of the war that many planes and their pilots did not survive their first and only sortie so there was even less chance of needing instrument makers.

When we were equipped with Kittys and I saw for the first time a rack used for filling oxygen bottles, I wondered what the hell it was. There were monstrous great cylinders weighing over 300 lbs that were used in conjunction with the rack to refill bottles from the aircraft. Each plane had two bottles, which in themselves were heavy, and the rack held twelve of these bottles so one could only do six aircraft at a time and the filling took quite some time. It did not take long to work out if we salvaged bottles from the prangs we could have these bottles ready to replace empties. Now don't tell me that the person needed to be a qualified instrument maker to do that job. Later aircraft had a different system of oxygen. They had a larger bottle but lower pressure and could be filled via a valve on the side of the plane, which made it much easier.

The Armourers' lot was, to say the least, very trying. When we found that sand and dust were going to be a problem we covered the gun nozzles with fabric as soon as the plane landed. No effort was spared in ensuring that this was done punctually, as sand in the guns ruined them very quickly, and a plane without guns: enough said. Then there was the lining up of the guns for accuracy. This, on the surface, seems easy but the first thing to do was put the plane in a flying attitude, and this was achieved simply by lifting the tail high enough to put the tail on an adjustable stand. After that was finished it had to be placed on ground level again. There is a case where an airman had used 'lifting the aircraft' as a reason for his bad back, to have his appeal rejected, because in the opinion of the interviewing officers, aircraft didn't need to be lifted. They apparently thought that all aircraft had a nose wheel and showed that they knew, as usual, nothing.

At a later date the 'powers that be' decided to use Kittyhawks as fighter-bombers and that naturally needed them to be fitted to be able to carry bombs. This was done on the Squadron, but no thought was given to getting the bombs on to the plane, so the only way to do that was to physically manhandle them. This was not so bad when they used 250 lbs but far more difficult when they used 500 lbs, and even worse when they started to use 1000 lbs. There were no lifting devices of any sort and because of space limitations under the aircraft only five men could get into position to load the large bomb. However, by using lengths of timber a sort of lever was devised to assist.

I could digress here a little to inform you that as ground staff we knew that the best we could do for the pilots was to make sure that their plane was 100% when they took off, and the various trades took pride in their work, making sure that no aircraft was less than 100%, and indeed all of the 450 Squadron planes were either 100% or they didn't take off, and that was very seldom. We had Sergeants in most areas who made sure that the work on the planes was right up to scratch at all times.

Engine Fitters. As soon as a plane landed, its ground crew swarmed over it to do an inspection and as soon as they finished wrapped it up in fabric to keep out the dust ready for the next take off. The engine men actually did changes in the desert. In some cases the exchange engine came from the Maintenance Units. Actually when we were near enough we went and obtained the engine rather than wait (it was faster that way). There were also times when aircraft came back so badly 'shot up' they were unflyable, but as the engine was good the fitters salvaged it. This of course took up time, but no one worried about whether they were doing more than someone else: as a job had to be done, so it was done. The main thing about the ground crew was that they didn't care what others were doing or not doing, but if they were on the crew of an aircraft they did their job 100%, or, as was the case with a very few, they were posted off the unit.

Electricians were essential for the starter motors and generators and ignition systems, and I must say that they worked with the engine men to make sure all was OK. These men, like most of 450, were highly qualified, many having been in businesses of their own, and knew their work. We all had to know how to start the engines to be able to check the work to see if it was OK, at least on the ground. During those run ups the one who was doing it always checked everything just in case something had gone wrong.

Then there were the transport drivers, who in most cases were motor mechanics, and had to look after their own trucks, doing all of the maintenance. They had quite a big responsibility, as they had to be ready to move at all times, and of course, move everything else. They were very well organised, each truck being allocated for specified work. That in itself was no mean feat, as 450 moved like a well oiled machine, and every man knew what truck he and any equipment that he used was going to be on. It was an education to see just how efficient the transport system was. When we had to evacuate a Landing Ground, everything went like clockwork, but I must admit they had plenty of practice, as we moved often. Anyone could become an emergency truck driver providing they could pass a test that would make today's driving tests look like child's play. Even the trucks were so varied: 3, 4, or 5 forward gears, some with high and low range, and left and right hand steering, and you had to be able to change from one to another at a moment's notice, (no cruise controls, auto, etc) but all were very well air-conditioned; dust came in both sides.

Cooks. Well, they didn't look after the planes, but what they did with what they had was absolutely tremendous. One cannot say enough about these men, who like the rest of 450 were of the Squadron, and were all good mates. To a man they were all cooks before they joined up, and really knew their work. One minor incident comes to mind, of a chap who wanted to be a cook and fronted up to the doctor. The question: "What do you know about hygiene?" The answer: "I don't know anything about hygiene, I only want to be a cook."

Of course there were many other trades. Storemen, most of whom had been in that sort of work: one at least had his own business carrying wholesale groceries and the like. Many of these men carried on in that capacity after hostilities ceased. All squadrons had the same set up: Carpenters, Fabric Workers, Telephone Operators, Painters and in our case at least we had two Coppersmiths. All of these trades functioned as one unit, and all played their part in the overall picture.

At one time we had sent to us some men from 3 Squadron to 'show us the ropes.' They did not last long, as our C/O found out that we were a very efficient unit. Just in passing, we had a reunion at Williamtown and were the guests of the C/O of 3 Squadron, who showed us what the Air Force is today, most interesting and greatly appreciated. But at our main dinner where the C/O and others were our guests, our President, in his speech, commented on how 450 had trained 3 Squadron those many years ago to be what they are today. This was taken in good part, and shows that the camaraderie of those days still exists.

The author of Appendix 8, Western Desert 1942.

(Ted Lawler)

APPENDIX 9

REPRESENTATIVE AIRCRAFT in PROFILE

1.   Tomahawk IIb AK446 of 3 Squadron RAAF.

2.   Tomahawk IIb AM392, *Nux Vomica,* of 250 Squadron RAF.

3.   Tomahawk IIb AK493 of 250 Squadron RAF.

4.   Tomahawk IIb AN413, *Nan,* of 112 Squadron RAF.

© Juanita Franzi

5.   Tomahawk IIb AN343 of 3 Squadron RAAF.

6.   Kittyhawk I AK772, *London Pride,* of 112 Squadron RAF.

7.   Kittyhawk I AK846, *VE,* of 250 Squadron RAF.

8.   Kittyhawk I AK961, *Snifter,* of 3 Squadron RAAF.

© Juanita Franzi

9. Kittyhawk I AK886 of 450 Squadron RAAF.

10. Kittyhawk Ia ET918, *Binkie,* of 450 Squadron RAAF.

11. Kittyhawk I AK778 of 3 Squadron RAAF,

12. Kittyhawk III FR305 of 3 Squadron RAAF.

© Juanita Franzi

13.   Kittyhawk IIa FL270 of 3 Squadron RAAF.

14.   Kittyhawk IIa FL272 of 260 Squadron RAF.

15.   Kittyhawk III FL885 of 450 Squadron RAAF.

16.   Kittyhawk III FR138 of 450 Squadron RAAF.

© Juanita Franzi

1.   Tomahawk IIb AK446 of 3 Squadron RAAF.

This was the aircraft flown by Flight Lieutenant Alan Rawlinson when he shot down three of six Martin 167s from Flotille 4F of the Aeronavale during the Syrian campaign on 28 June 1941. No squadron codes or individual marking letters were carried by the 3 Squadron aircraft at this time. The aircraft was also flown on numerous occasions by other pilots during the Syrian campaign, including Alan Cameron, Peter Turnbull and Bobby Gibbes.

2.   Tomahawk IIb AM392, *Nux Vomica,* of 250 Squadron RAF.

This was the personal aircraft of Sergeant Bob Whittle, one of the squadron's most successful pilots, who flew it regularly between 3 August and 30 October, when he used it to shoot down a Bf109 near Sollum. It was then withdrawn for maintenance, and later found its way to 3 Squadron, where it was flown by Nicky Barr on his first operation. Sgt. Rex Wilson belly landed it due to undercarriage failure, after a combat in which he damaged three enemy aircraft on 30 November.

3.   Tomahawk IIb AK493 of 250 Squadron RAF.

Pilot Officer Clive Caldwell was flying this aircraft as weaver for 250 Squadron on 29 August, when he was shot up by Werner Schroer. While flying it, Caldwell shared a G50 on 16 August, claimed a probable Bf109 on 28 August, and shot down a 109 the next day, although he was wounded, and the aircraft badly damaged.

4.   Tomahawk IIb AN413, *Nan,* of 112 Squadron RAF.

Taken on charge in September, this was the chosen aircraft of Pilot Officer Jack Bartle, although he did not claim any of his victories while flying it. It was lost on 12 December 1941, when Pilot Officer Robert Jeffries was shot down and killed.

5.   Tomahawk IIb AN343 of 3 Squadron RAAF.

This aircraft is typical of the unit's Tomahawks during Operation 'Crusader'. Note the mirror image camouflage pattern. It was flown exclusively by Sergeant Rex Wilson from 30 October, until it was lost on 25 November when FO Bruce Evans was shot down.

6.   Kittyhawk I AK772, *London Pride,* of 112 Squadron RAF.

This well documented aircraft has been illustrated before, but it is not generally acknowledged that it was flown by Clive Caldwell on 14 March when he shot down a MC202 and shared another with Sgt. Urbanczyk. It was more frequently flown by Sergeant Henry Burney, who shot down a MC202 while flying it on 13 March. It was lost with PO Burney, when he failed to return from a ground strafing sortie on 30 May 1942.

7.   Kittyhawk I AK846, *VE,* of 250 Squadron RAF.

VE, (apparently the initials of his wife) was the personal aircraft of Flight Lieutenant John Waddy, who used it to shoot down at least three, and probably four enemy aircraft on 12 May. He claimed another victory in it on 22 May when he shot down a Bf109.

8. Kittyhawk I AK961, *Snifter,* of 3 Squadron RAAF.

This hard working aircraft was flown on numerous occasions by John Hooke, several times by Keith Kildey and once by Tom Wood, all of whom are contributors to the narrative. Sergeant Danny Boardman was flying it when he shot down his first enemy aircraft on 24 June, a Bf109. Its last flight with 3 Squadron was in the hands of John Hooke on 7 July, after which it was withdrawn for maintenance. It ended its days with the 239 Wing Training Flight.

9. Kittyhawk I AK886 of 450 Squadron RAAF.

Taken on charge on 3 July 1942, Neil Shillabeer took it on its first operation on the same day. He flew it on at least thirteen occasions, and was its most frequent pilot. Don McBurnie flew it on 4 July, and shot down a Bf110 of 4(H)/12, his last victory with 450. On 19 July it was flown by Sergeant Gordon Lindsay, who shot down one of the four Ju52s destroyed by 450 squadron over LG 21. It flew one final sortie on 20 August, after the squadron's brief rest earlier in the month, and was then apparently withdrawn for maintenance.

10. Kittyhawk Ia ET918, *Binkie,* of 450 Squadron RAAF.

ET918 was ferried to LG 91 on 5 July 1942, and Squadron Leader Alan Ferguson flew it on its first operation the following day. It became his personal aircraft and he damaged a Bf109 on 18 July while flying it. Next day he used it to shoot down a Ju87 and share a Ju52 with Fl. Lt. Parker. It was flown on occasions by a number of the squadron's successful pilots, including John Williams, Ray Dyson, Frank Schaaf, Ted Oakley, Vince McFarlane, Neil Shillabeer, Gordon Lindsay and Don McBurnie. It was lost on 29 August when Sergeant Al Markle crash-landed after being attacked by Hpt. Homuth.

11. Kittyhawk I AK778 of 3 Squadron RAAF,

AK778 served with the squadron from 6 July until 14 September, and was probably refurbished and repainted during the first three weeks of August, while the squadron was on leave. It is shown here as it appeared in September. It was frequently flown by John Hooke and Tom Wood, and is in the log book of Keith Kildey. On 8 September it was flown by Sergeant Gordon Scribner when the squadron attacked a formation of Stukas and then became embroiled with a large number of Bf109s, which emerged from cloud cover. Scribner shot down a 109 and damaged another, as well as a MC202. Note the unpainted lower cowling panel, and the older style of fin flash, an indication of its age and original style of markings.

12. Kittyhawk III FR305 of 3 Squadron RAAF.

First flown by Flight Lieutenant Keith Kildey on 7 October, it was appropriated by the CO Bobby Gibbes as his personal aircraft, but was almost always flown by the formation leader when the CO was not flying. Thus it was used almost exclusively by Gibbes, Keith Kildey and Danny Boardman. Bobby Gibbes was flying it on 28 October when he shot down a Bf109 and claimed another as a probable, to bring the Squadron's apparent total to 200. (see main text) It remained on strength until 4 November, by which time the squadron was converting to the Merlin powered Kittyhawk IIa.

13.   Kittyhawk IIa FL270 of 3 Squadron RAAF.

On strength from 22 December 1942 until 11 April 1943, it was flown on more than thirty occasions by Flight Sergeant Reg Stevens, and could be regarded as his personal aircraft, as he rarely flew any other. He claimed a probable Bf109 in it on 14 January. Later in the day Flying Officer Rex Bayly used it to shoot down a Bf109, and Flight Lieutenant Ron Susans was flying it when he destroyed a MC202 on 6 April. After its withdrawal, it was transferred to the *Armee de l'Air*. It was also flown on one occasion each by Alan Righetti and Tom Russell, two of the book's contributors.

14.   Kittyhawk IIa FL272 of 260 Squadron RAF.

This drawing is provisional, as no complete photograph of a 260 Squadron Mk II Kittyhawk could be found. FL272 is recorded in Flight Lieutenant Ron Cundy's log book, along with numerous other Mk II Kittyhawks. He was flying this aircraft on 13 November while ground strafing at Gazala, when a machine gun bullet struck the perspex in front of him.

15.   Kittyhawk III FL885 of 450 Squadron RAAF.

On strength with 450 from 6 February 1943, it was flown most frequently by Sergeant F.C. Sanders. No victories were claimed in this machine, but two of the squadron's successful pilots, Flying Officer F.X. Regan and Sergeant Devon Minchin flew operations in it. It was apparently withdrawn for maintenance after its last flight with 450 on 27 March.

16.   Kittyhawk III FR138 of 450 Squadron RAAF.

A long tailed P-40M, FR138 was delivered on 27 February 1943 from 53 RSU (Repair and Salvage Unit) and first flown by Flight Lieutenant Jack Bartle on a training sortie on 3 March. It flew only nine operations with six different pilots between 10 and 23 March, when it was crash-landed by Sergeant Dick Rowe due to AA damage after a strafing operation.

APPENDIX 10

GERMAN VICTORY CLAIMS in PERSPECTIVE

As explained in the text, unintentional over claiming by pilots of *all* nations was common, and was brought about by a number of factors, the chief one being attacks by more than one pilot on the same target aircraft. Another factor, now well known, which probably contributed to the serious over claiming by the RAF over France in 1941 and 1942, was the basic evasive tactic employed by the *Luftwaffe*, a steep dive at full throttle, which produced a trail of black smoke from the Bf109's exhaust.

Nevertheless, there were numerous occasions in the Desert war when *Luftwaffe* victories could not be verified by documented Allied losses. They are discussed in the text when Australian pilots were involved.

The most spectacular of these occurred on 15 September 1942, when JG 27 claimed a total of *nineteen* Allied aircraft in a combat which began some time after 1715, when the three Gruppen of JG 27 took to the air to escort a Stuka raid. Marseille's biographer, Franz Kurowski, listed the following claims:
I Gruppe: eleven, II Gruppe: one, III Gruppe: seven.

Details from *Fighters Over the Desert* suggest that *twenty* claims were made, matching claims to names, several of which are omitted by Kurowski, who awarded Marseille seven kills in six minutes!

The true facts of this engagement are rather different. Sgt. Des Cormack of 250 Squadron took off at 1736, leading a section of 250 Squadron as top cover to 112, 3 and 450 Squadrons. PO Keith Kildey of 3 Squadron was airborne at 1725, leading eight aircraft. His combat report shows that the engagement began at 1800, at an altitude of 12,000 feet. Both pilots were heavily involved in the battle, submitting claims for a probable (later confirmed) and a damaged respectively, and both coming under attack from German fighters.

There was a total of 36 Kittyhawks in the 239 Wing formation. *Six* failed to return, and of these, 112 Squadron records show that Sgt. Young was shot down by friendly AA fire![1] Even if this is mistaken, a discrepancy of fourteen can not be adequately explained. Keith Kildey almost certainly ended up as a little white bar on someone's rudder after he brought home his aircraft with cannon damage to the tail. Sgt Ken Bee probably shared the same fate, returning with wounds in a damaged aircraft. 250 Squadron lost two aircraft, 3 Squadron two, 450 one, and 112 one.

Keith Kildey and Des Cormack were both interviewed as part of the research for this book, and both expressed shocked disbelief, followed by laughter, when told of the German claims.

The circumstances of this combat cast serious doubts on assertions that the *Luftwaffe's* system of dealing with the confirmation of claims was so reliable.

> Without a witness, a Luftwaffe fighter pilot had no chance to have his victory claim confirmed. Such a claim, even if filed, would not pass beyond group level.

> The final destruction or explosion of an enemy aircraft in the air, or the bail-out of the pilot, had to be observed either on gun-camera film or by at least one other human witness. The witness could be the German pilot's wingman, squadron mate, or a ground observer of the encounter.

> There was no possibility, *as with some RAF and USAAF pilots*, *of having a victory credited because the claiming officer was a gentleman and a man of his word.* * (Author's italics). The German rule was simply "no witness - no kill."

---

* See Bobby Gibbes' Foreword

The German system was impartial, inflexible, and far less error-prone than either the British or American procedures. *German fighter pilots had to wait several months, a year, or sometimes even longer for a kill confirmation to reach them from the German High Command.*[2] *(Author's italics)*

But such a waiting period apparently did not apply in the case of the high profile *experten,* as the following table listing the dates of their awards suggests.

Heinz Bar	RK 02/07/41, **27**; EL 14/08/41, **60**; S 16/02/42, **90**.
Adolf Galland	RK 01/08/40, **17**; EL 25/09/40, **40**; S 21/06/41, **69**.
Gordon Gollob	RK 19/09/41, **42**; EL 26/10/41, **85**.
Hans-Joachim Marseille	RK 22/02/42, **50**; EL 06/06/42, **75**; S 18/06/42, **101**; Br 02/09/42, **126**.
Joachim Muncheberg	RK 14/09/40, **20**; EL 07/05/41, **43**; S 09/09/42 **103**.[3]

Marseille made five claims on 2 September, (only 3 of which are valid) taking his total to 126, and was awarded the Diamonds (Br) on the same day, with 126 noted as his total at the time of the award.

Clearly, in the combat of 15 September, there could not have been seven accurate eyewitness reports, let alone *twenty,* but Marseille's seven victory claims were apparently accepted without question. 'After this outstanding victory, Marseille had brought his account up to 151 kills, meaning that he had reached third place in the absolute record list - behind Hermann Graf and Gordon Gollob.'[4]

Other recognised *experten,* Schroer, Homuth and von Lieres, submitted a total of six further claims between them.

Authors working in the 1990s have access to squadron records, and Chris Shores, writing in 1969, made it quite clear that 239 Wing's losses on 15 September 1942 totalled six.

The reader is referred to the comments made by Erhard Braune of III/JG 27, mentioned in Bobby Gibbes' Foreword.

Following is a list of other *Luftwaffe* claims, mainly involving Australian pilots and squadrons, and sometimes other squadrons of 239 Wing, when Australians were present. Many of these clearly could not be confirmed, because the targets returned to base, or definitely could *not* have been seen to hit the ground in the area where the combat took place, or were claimed by more than one attacking pilot, which, in the circumstances of close combat, is understandable.

	AUSTRALIAN & ALLIED LOSSES	GERMAN CLAIMS
12/10/41:	Roberts (3 Sqn) c/l inside Allied lines	Sinner 1 *(Parker)*
	Scott (3 Sqn) c/l LG105	Franzisket 1
	Parker (3 Sqn) s/d KIA	Marseille 2
	Whaits (2 SAAF) s/d KIA	
	One SAAF a/c damaged:	
	total 2	total **4**

Clearly, the two damaged 3 Squadron Tomahawks were seen to meet the rigid criteria required by the Luftwaffe.

30/10/41:	Cornall (250 Sqn) s/d captured	Schulz 3
	McInnes RAF (238 Sqn) s/d	Schacht 1
	Cole RAF (250 Sqn) damaged:	
	total 2	total **4**

12/11/41	Thomas SAAF (451 RAAF Tac R Sqn) s/d KIA Whalley RAF (451 Sqn) s/d KIA:	Dullberg 1 Krenske 1 Reuter 1
	total **2**	total **3**

two assailants for one target?

22/11/41	Lane (3 Sqn) s/d KIA Saunders (3 Sqn) s/d KIA Watson (3 Sqn) s/d KIA:	Redlich 2 Schneider 2
	total **3**	total **4**

two assailants for one target?

15/02/42	four a/c of 94 Sqn s/d McQueen (112 Sqn) damaged, landed at base:	Schulz 5
	total **4**	total **5**

*An Afrika Korps tank officer reported a cloud of dust behind
a sand dune, which was the 'confirmation' of his last claim,
(McQueen) bringing Schulz's total to 44.*

15/03/42	Unnamed pilot (450 Sqn) Cat. 1 damage	Schulz 1
	no losses	total **1**

22/05/42	Quirk (450 Sqn) s/d KIA Williams (450 Sqn) s/d KIA	Bendert 2 Steis 1
	total **2**	total **3**

Two assailants for one target?
*Bendert's second claim was **not** confirmed.*

22/05/42	Gundry RAF (112 Sqn) s/d KIA Rogerson RAF (250 Sqn) c/l return flight One 250 Sqn a/c missing:	Franzisket 2 von Lieres 2 Steinhausen 1 Stahlschmidt 1 Rosenberg 1
	total **2**	total **7** (5)

*Chris Shores noted that the second claims for
both Franzisket and von Lieres were **not** confirmed, thus
reducing 7 claims to 5, for a total of 2 actual losses.*

01/06/42	Wilson RAF (112 Sqn) s/d PoW Alderson (3 Sqn) wounded; a/c damaged:	Quaritsch 1 Stecher 1 Kronschnabel 1 Bf110 pilot 1(*Hurricane*)
	total **1**	total **4** (3)

*Kronschnabel's claim was **not** confirmed.*
Hurricanes were not present.

26/06/42	Cuddon RAF (112 Sqn) s/d KIA Barr (3 Sqn) s/d PoW	Kabisch 1 Schroer 2 (*1 Hurricane*) Rosenberg 1
	total **2**	total **4**

Hurricanes were almost certainly not present.

26/06/42	Wallis (250 Sqn) damaged	Korner 2
	Seabrook RAF(250 Sqn) damaged	Franzisket 1
	Copeland RAF (250 Sqn) s/d KIA	Stahlschmidt 3,
	Jones (450 Sqn) s/d baled out and returned:	*(2 of which were Hurricanes)*
	total 2	total 6

Again, it is unlikely that Hurricanes were present.

17/07/42	Stevens (3 Sqn) damaged	III JG 53: 2
	Weber RAF (145 Sqn) s/d baled out:	
	total 1	total 2

two assailants for one target?

01/09/42	450 Sqn:	Sinner 2
		Rodel 1
	no losses	total 3

According to Kurowski, Sinner and Rodel
made no further claims for the day.

01/09/42	Wood (3 Sqn) a/c damaged, landed at base	Fink (JG 53) 1
	no losses	total 1

03/09/42	*Although the two Australian squadrons were not involved*	
	in this combat, Ron Cundy of 260 Squadron was present,	
	and his log book noted the loss of PO Joseph Bernier.	
	Bernier RCAF (260 Sqn) s/d KIA	
	Powers RAF (145 Sqn) s/d baled out, wounded	Marseille 3 *(Curtiss)*
	Reyneke (2 SAAF) force landed; PoW:	Stahlschmidt 3
		(2 Curtiss, 1 Spitfire)
	total 3	total 6

03/09/42	Thomas (3 Sqn) a/c damaged Cat. 2 pilot wounded:	
	c/l base	
	Hannaford (450 Sqn) a/c damaged Cat. 2	
	pilot wounded: c/l base	Sinner 1
	no losses	total 1

05/09/42	two 145 Sqn Spitfires s/d *(3 Sqns airborne at 1125)*	Marseille 4 *(1148-1200)*
	Thomas RNZAF (112 Sqn) s/d PoW	*(all Curtiss)*
	Oakley (450 Sqn) damaged Cat. 2	Stahlschmidt 2
		Rodel 3
	total 3	total 9

08/09/42	one 145 Sqn Spitfire lost	Schroer 2 *(Spitfires)*
	Freer (3 Sqn) c/l in minefield (damaged):	Stumpf III/JG 53. 1
	total 1	total 3

12/09/42	Hogg RAF (112 Sqn) damaged Cat. 2	Stumpf JG 53. 1
	3 A/C of 450 Sqn damaged Cat. 1	Nairz JG 53. 1
	no losses	total 2

15/09/42	Donald (3 Sqn) s/d. PoW	Marseille 7
	Scribner (3 Sqn) s/d KIA	von Lieres 2
	Young RNZAF (112 Sqn) s/d c/l (flak?)	Homuth 1
	Thorpe RAF (250 Sqn) s/d PoW	Borngen 1
	Strong RAF (250 Sqn) s/d PoW	Schroer 3 (incl. 1 Spitfire)
	Ewing (450 Sqn) s/d PoW	Krainik 4
		Gruber 1
	No Spitfires were present.	Stuckler 1
	total **6**	total **20**.

16/09/42	Wood (3 Sqn) damaged, wounded: landed at base	Schroer 1
		Schofbock 1
	no losses	total **2**

01/11/42	Agnew RAF (112 Sqn) force-landed Allied lines	Unterberger 1*
	DeBourke RAF (112 Sqn) wounded in shoulder,	Rodel 1
	normal landing at base.	Berres JG 77. 1
	(two Australians of 112 Sqn. were involved in this action)	Bar JG 77. 1
	* The pilot was reported to have baled out.	
	no losses	total **4**

09/11/42	Blades RAF (92 Sqn) s/d KIA	Muncheberg JG 77 1
	Borthwick (450 Sqn) s/d wounded.	Hackler JG 77 1
	3 a/c of 450 Sqn damaged Cat. 1:	JG 77: 3 further claims
	total **2**	total **5**

18/01/43	Prowse (450 Sqn) wounded:	Bar JG 77. 2
	c/l near army dressing station behind own lines.	Weidlich JG 77. 1
	Palethorpe RAF (250 Sqn) A/C damaged	
	*Bar's claims were **not** confirmed.*	
	total **1** (*Prowse - if observed*)	total **3** (1)

Notes

1. German pilots are all from JG 27 unless otherwise noted.

2. Allied pilots listed are all Australian unless otherwise identified.

3. Allied losses grouped together under a specific date all occurred in the same combat, and the German claims listed in the next column are all for that particular combat.

4. German claims have been linked to the Allied losses in each specified combat by Shores and Ring in *Fighters Over the Desert,* or Franz Kurowski in *German Fighter Ace Hans Joachim Marseille - The Life Story of the Star of Africa.* Times and locations of German claims were compared with Allied losses in the same time frame and location.

5. Shores and Ring either state that a German pilot 'claimed' an aircraft, or that an Allied pilot was 'shot down' by a specific German pilot. If a claim was *not confirmed,* (eg. see entries for 22/05/42) they make this clear in the text.

6. Given the statement by Tolliver and Constable that 'Such a claim (*without a witness*) even if filed, would not pass beyond group level' it follows that the claims reported in *Fighters Over the Desert* were subsequently 'confirmed' and included in the claimant's total.

7. In the combats described by Kurowski, there is no mention of claims which were *not* confirmed.

8. According to Kurowski, all claims made by Marseille can be regarded as 'confirmed'. This would appear to include four of seven victories claimed over the Channel in 1940, which Kurowski, Constable and Toliver acknowledge were *not* witnessed at the time. (See quotation [2] above.)

9. Claims for Hurricanes and Spitfires, when they were not actually present, can generally be assumed to be cases of mis-identification.

APPENDIX 11

POSTSCRIPT

Readers might wonder how some of the major participants in the story, and contributors to the narrative fared, after leaving North Africa. It is hoped that the following brief notes will serve to satisfy any such curiosity.

'Woof' Arthur, DSO, DFC, MiD, returned to Australia and served with 76 Squadron before becoming CO of 75 Squadron on 21 January 1943. With this unit he shot down a 'Betty' and claimed another as a probable. He was awarded a DSO for his part in an interception of a large force of Japanese aircraft over Milne Bay, when he attempted to drive a Japanese aircraft into the water after his guns would not fire. He commanded 2 OTU in 1944, and led 81 and 78 Wings, during the latter part of 1944 and 1945. He became a Group Captain at the age of 24.

Nicky Barr, OBE, MC, DFC & Bar, was captured on 26 June 1942, and spent considerable time in hospital recovering from his injuries. En route to a prisoner of war camp near Milan, he escaped, almost reaching the Swiss border before he was re-captured. He escaped again from a train taking prisoners to another camp and spent two and a half months with Italian partisans, before being captured again. Once more he escaped from a prison train, and this time he contacted a Special Operations Executive group operating behind enemy lines. He worked with them for three and a half months before contracting malaria, so he was taken through the German lines to the Allied ground forces. He was awarded the Military Cross in recognition of his action against the enemy on the ground. He returned to Australia and became Chief Instructor, Fighter Training at Mildura. In November 1944 he went to New Guinea to gain experience of operational conditions and flew four sorties before returning to the OTU. Lex McAulay's excellent book *Four Aces* covers his career in great detail.

Rex Bayly, DFC & Bar, later served with 451 Squadron, returning to 3 Squadron for a second tour. He became CO in Italy from April to October 1944.

Dave Borthwick, MiD, began to recover from his injuries in Cairo and was invalided home to Australia. After a period of convalescence, and an OTU course at Mildura, he joined 78 Squadron on Kittyhawks in New Guinea, where he was twice mentioned in despatches. He ended the war as a Flying Officer, and spent the next five years flying with ANA, before becoming a farmer.

His victor on 9 November 1942, Obfw. Heinrich Hackler, stayed with JG 77, claiming fifty-six victories before his death over Antwerp during Operation *Bodenplatte*, on New Year's Day 1945. By this time he was the *Staffelkapitan* of 11/JG 77 and a Knights Cross holder.

Dave Borthwick - I secured a photo of Hackler, and when I showed it to my wife, she said, "What a very good looking young man." I had to remind her that I did not clean up too badly myself at that age. I am sorry not to have had the opportunity of trying to drink him to death, having failed the other way.

Eric Bradbury did not fly with 3 Squadron again after his nightmare experience with the German tanks. He later served at 2 Fighter OTU at Mildura with Alan Rawlinson and Peter Jeffrey.

Bill Cable, DFC, returned to Australia after a tour with 250 Squadron which lasted exactly one year, and joined 457 Squadron as a Flight Lieutenant on 26 October 1944.

Clive Caldwell, DSO, DFC & Bar, Polish Cross of Valour, returned to Australia and instructed at 2 OTU. In January 1943 he became Wg. Cdr. Flying of 1 Fighter Wing at Darwin, where he destroyed eight Japanese aircraft. Awarded a DSO, he was rested and became CFI at 2 OTU. He returned to operations in May 1944 as Leader of 80 Fighter Wing on Spitfire VIIIs. As there were few Japanese aircraft left in the area, the Wing was occupied with ground attack operations. He

and a number of other senior officers, including Wilf Arthur, attempted to resign their commissions in protest at what they saw as a waste of resources, and mismanagement of the RAAF's fighter force. The resignations were not accepted, but nor did the gesture achieve a change in role of the fighter squadrons.

Des Cormack, DFC, instructed at 73 OTU for almost a year and returned to Australia at the close of 1943. From 14 August 1944 he served with 452 Squadron at Darwin as a Flight Commander, and was discharged on March 28 1945, to resume his teaching career. He and his wife Mary- taught in the Northern Territory and remote parts of South Australia before settling in Adelaide. The close associations with the pupils and parents of their small rural schools are amongst his most satisfying memories.

Ron Cundy, DFC, DFM, returned to Australia and joined 2 OTU at Mildura as an instructor. In October 1943 he joined 452 Squadron as a Flight commander, where he served until September 1944, after which he instructed again at 8 OTU until the end of the war. He regarded the Mark VIII Spitfire as '*a glorious aircraft to fly [with] absolutely no vices. Unfortunately I did not have a chance to try it in combat'.*

Victor Curtis returned to Australia and served at 2 OTU. He was killed in a flying accident on 6 January 1943.

Brian Eaton, CB, CBE, DSO & Bar, DFC, American Silver Star, later commanded 239 Wing in Italy. After thirty-eight years in the RAAF he retired with the rank of Air Vice Marshal. He was part of the evaluation team which chose the F111.

Alan Ferguson, DFC & Bar, later returned to Australia and commanded 81 Wing in 1945.

Frank Fischer, DFC, ended the war as a Squadron Leader, having served at No. 2 OTU on his return to Australia. After the war he flew with ANA and TAA.

Bobby Gibbes, DSO, DFC & Bar, returned to Australia and led 80 Fighter Wing from October 1944 to April 1945, without ever seeing another enemy aircraft in the air. After the war he formed Gibbes Sepik Airways in New Guinea, and later established coffee and tea plantations before retiring in Australia after spending twenty-seven years in New Guinea. Subsequently, he and his family sailed a catamaran called *Billabong* from England to Australia, and he later built a twin-engined microlight aircraft of French design in his lounge room, which demonstrated the tolerance of his wife Jean, as much as his skills as an engineer. He published his autobiography, *You Live But Once,* in 1994, which has been a valuable source of information during the preparation of this work.

Jack Gleeson, DFC, completed a tour with 450 Squadron, and then served with both 451 and 3 Squadrons before taking command of 450 on 15 June 1944. He held this position until 25 October.

John Hooke, OBE, DFC, completed his first tour with 3 Squadron in Sicily and later returned to the unit after a spell of testing with 132 MU at Helwan. He also flew with an Anti Aircraft Cooperation Unit (26 AACU). He completed his second tour with 3 Squadron as a Flight Lieutenant, and then, with the acting rank of Squadron Leader, became a forward controller, 'Rover David', with 1 MORU (Mobile Operations Room Unit), which operated on the front line in control of close support fighter-bomber operations. After the war he flew with ANA for six years before returning to farm at Beaufort, near his home town of Buangor, in Victoria.

John Jackson, DFC, returned to Australia and led 75 Squadron in its heroic 44 day defence of Port Moresby during March and April of 1942. He destroyed a Zero on 28 April, and was killed in action in the same combat. The Seven Mile strip at Port Moresby was renamed in his honour. His exemplary leadership of 75 Squadron gave him almost legendary status.

Peter Jeffrey, DSO, DFC, after his return to Australia, was the original Commanding Officer of both 75 and 76 Squadrons, being responsible for their formation and training. He later commanded 2 OTU, and 1 Wing at Darwin, returning to the OTU for the rest of the war. After the war he was discharged and became a farmer, but returned to the RAAF upon the outbreak of the Korean War. He became Deputy Director of Operations, and later served as Superintendent Air at the Weapons Research Establishment in South Australia, where he renewed his association with Alan Rawlinson. They maintained a life long friendship until Peter Jeffrey's recent death.

Keith Kildey, DFM, returned to Australia and served at 2 OTU Mildura, surviving a head on collision between two Wirraways when the student flying the other aircraft broke in the wrong direction. He then served as CO of the Port Moresby Air Defence HQ until the end of the war. Leading a group of Victory Bond fly past aircraft to Tasmania in a Mustang, he carried out a solo beat up of Devonport for his parents' benefit, and the impromptu display was enthusiastically reported by the local paper, causing an outcry from other Tasmanian towns, which missed out. This came to the unwelcome attention of AVM Walters, who was inclined to court martial him, until Peter Jeffrey intervened in his favour. He then left the Air Force to farm in Tasmania, resuming his RAAF career in 1950. Retiring as the Wing Commander in charge of air traffic control, he took up a successful career with ICI.

Ian 'Joe' Lyons, MBE, was another whose low flying career almost caught up with him. At the conclusion of his training, he carried out a spectacular beat up of his home town at Eaglehawk near Bendigo, in the only all yellow Hawker Demon at Point Cook. The Eaglehawk primary school children wrote him numerous letters of congratulations. Others were not so impressed. The subsequent court martial did not prevent him from going to 3 Squadron. After recovering from his hearing loss, he also served with 2 OTU, later flying Kittyhawks with 82 Squadron in New Guinea. He was part of the Occupation Forces in Japan with 76 Squadron, and subsequently served with 77 Squadron as Operations Officer in Korea. He also acted as personal assistant to AVM Walters, with whom he shared a passion for horse racing. Joe later owned a successful race horse, called *Kittyhawk*.

Alex Markle, the Canadian with 450 Squadron, ended up in Camp P.G. 78 (*Prisonierra de Guerra*) in Italy. When Italy surrendered in September 1943, the occupants of the camp left it, living from hand to mouth by their wits in the Italian mountains and valleys. Al Markle and his group were given shelter by a farming family, narrowly avoiding capture when their hosts' home was looted by a German patrol. They took to the mountains again, finally making contact with a Sikh regiment of the British army in early 1944. He wrote of his war time experiences in the privately published work *Memoirs of a Fighter Pilot,* which was made available by George James, secretary of 450 Squadron Association.

Murray Nash, DSO, DFC, succeeded Brian Eaton as CO of 3 Squadron on 22 February 1944, remaining in command until 18 April, when he left to command a ground control unit attached to the US Fifth Army. He resumed command of 3 Squadron on 29 October 1944, remaining with it, except for a short break in March 1945, until the end of the war in Europe, when the Squadron was disbanded..

Jock Perrin, DFC, returned to Australia and commanded 5 and 24 Wirraway Squadrons, but he also spent some time at 1 OTU at Nhill, where he won the respect and gratitude of Eric Bradbury and Tom Wood, being the only instructor with combat experience. He later commanded 76 Squadron in mid 1943 and went on to become the Deputy Director of Operations at RAAF HQ in 1943-4. He was SASO RAAF Overseas HQ from 1944 to 1946.

Alan Rawlinson, OBE, DFC & Bar, AFC, returned to Australia and was posted to 2 OTU on its formation as Chief Instructor. With Peter Jeffrey, he wrote the 'Syllabus of Training for RAAF Fighter Pilots' sitting on the bare dusty floor boards of Jeffrey's office floor. 'Woof' Arthur was his

Chief Flying Instructor and Eric Bradbury was Chief Ground Instructor. He later formed and commanded 79 Squadron, the first RAAF Spitfire unit to serve in New Guinea. He took up a permanent commission in the RAF after the war, and became Wing Commander Flying of the Vampire Wing at Odiham. In 1953 he formed and commanded the first guided weapons trials unit of the RAF, and tested semi-active beam riding missiles at Woomera. Initially known as 'Blue Sky' the missile was later called 'Fireflash' during its acceptance trials. Returning to England, he commanded RAF Patrington and worked on the integration of Bloodhound guided missiles with fighter aircraft. In January 1960 he became Sector Commander and OC RAF Buchan in Scotland. As part of the NATO defence network, Buchan linked up with Norway to the East and Iceland to the west. He retired from the RAF in 1961 and returned to Australia, where he took up a position with Hawker de Havilland, responsible for Missiles and Military Systems. In 1969 he bought a vineyard and planted 10,000 vines, which gave great satisfaction to the family until they retired after the 1984 vintage.

Alan Righetti was wounded when he was shot down on 22 January 1943, and spent several months in a prison hospital in Naples before being transferred to an Italian PoW camp. After the Italian surrender he was taken to Germany, where he was sent to *Stalag Luft 3* after brief stays at other camps. He had not been in residence long enough to be a direct participant in the 'Great Escape', but he did act as a 'stooge', giving signals about the movements of the guards. Security was so tight that he never knew who received his signals. The camp was evacuated in the face of the advancing Russians. He and many others were released by the British Army on 2 May, and he managed to drive to Brussels in an acquired Mercedes Benz. He was flown to London on 7 May. He chose to stay in England and studied at Leeds University, before returning to Australia in 1946, when he was discharged with the rank of Flight Lieutenant. He graduated as a Bachelor of Agricultural Science from Melbourne University in 1950, and farmed in Victoria until 1960, when he became head of the School of Sheep and Wool at the NSW Department of Technical Education. He later put his skills to use in the world of commerce, retiring in 1983.

Ken Sands, DFC, became CO of 450 Squadron from 6 December 1943 to 7 April 1944.

Frank Schaaf, DFC, returned to Australia and was attached to 104 and 111 Fighter Sector HQ in 1943-44. He commanded 82 Squadron from 7 July 1945 until 15 February 1947.

Lou Spence, DFC and Bar, US Legion of Merit, US Air Medal, returned to Australia and commanded 452 Squadron in Darwin from 3 February 1944 until 4 June 1945. He commanded 8 OTU later in 1945, and became CO of 77 Squadron (Mustangs) in Japan on 28 February 1950. He led the unit with distinction from the beginning of the Korean War until his death in action on 9 September 1950.

Gordon Steege, DSO, DFC, returned to Australia in December 1942 and commanded 73 and 81 Wings in the SW Pacific during 1943-44. He also commanded 77 Squadron in Korea from August to December 1951. As an Air Commodore, he commanded RAAF bases at Amberley, Butterworth and Edinburgh. He retired as SASO, HQ, Operational Command in 1972. In 1983 he became Australian consultant for Lockheed Martin Overseas Corporation.

Ron Susans, DSO, DFC, commanded 79 Squadron and 80 Wing in 1945, remaining in the Air Force to command 77 Squadron during 1947 and 1948. He later commanded the unit again during the Korean War, from December 1951 until July 1952, when the Meteors were mainly involved with ground attack operations.

Reg Stevens, DFC and Bar, took command of 3 Squadron in mid 1943 while Brian Eaton was ill, and later became CO of 451 Squadron, from September to December 1943.

Tom Trimble returned to Australia and led 457 Squadron from 2 February to 18 December 1944.

Peter Turnbull, DFC, joined 75 Squadron with John Jackson upon his return to Australia. He was one of the few pilots with combat experience, and he put this to good use in the defence of Port Moresby, destroying three Zeros in March and April of 1942. He took command of 76 Squadron and led the unit with distinction in the defence of Milne Bay, until he was killed in action while attacking a Japanese tank on 27 August 1942. Turnbull Airfield at Milne Bay was named in his honour.

Frank Twemlow, DFC, completed his tour with 250 Squadron in July 1942, with a total of 200 operational hours. He was posted to 107 MU, where he tested newly repaired aircraft. He returned to Australia on 7 February 1943, and instructed at 2 OTU until discharged on 20 December 1944. He flew with Qantas from 1946 to 1960, when he resigned to take up charter work.

John Waddy, OBE, DFC, flew Spitfires with 92 Squadron before leaving North Africa. After his return to Australia he instructed at 2 OTU Mildura until July 1944. He then commanded 80 Squadron from 15 September 1944 until 1 June 1945. He ended the war as a Wing Commander, and was awarded the US Air Medal.

Bob Whittle, DFM, finished his tour with 250 Squadron on 30 December 1941, rated as 'an exceptional fighter pilot.' He instructed at 73 OTU in Aden until June 1942, when he returned to Australia. He joined 86 Squadron in early 1943 and flew operationally from May 1943 to June 1944. During his time with the unit he destroyed a Zero and shared in the destruction of a 'Betty' and another Zero. He spent the remainder of the war instructing at an OTU. After the war he resumed his career as a pharmacist. He was a founder member of the Murwillumbah Aero Club, and instructed there for many years. In 1999, due to community demand, the Murwillumbah airfield was renamed the Bob Whittle Murwillumbah Airfield in his honour.

Tom Wood spent time in various temporary holding camps until being transferred to Italy on 27 October 1942. By December 1943 he had been transferred to *Stalag Luft 3* at Sagan, and was part of the security organisation for what became known as the 'Great Escape'. He also spent some time working as a tailor, altering the appearance of uniforms for the escapers. Perhaps fortunately, the recently arrived prisoners from Italy were not included in the escape, and he remained at Sagan until 28 January 1945, when the camp was evacuated in the face of the approaching Russian Army. A 98 km trek brought them to a *Marlag* at Tarmstadt, where they stayed until 9 April. This camp was also evacuated, and the prisoners trekked 149 kms in nineteen days to Trenthorst, within 11 km of Lubeck, frequently sleeping in the open, with the occasional luxury of a barn or stable. After five days living in stables with 'rats as big as cats', the British Army arrived. They were taken by truck to Emsdetton, thence to the airfield at Rheine. There they were loaded into Lancasters and flown back to Dunsford in England.

As we got off the aircraft, each of us was taken in hand by two WRAFs, taken to a delousing machine (an air compressor with a long spout which blew a white powder up our trouser legs and sleeves - looked great on Air Force blue!) and were looked after by the girls until we were taken by truck to Horsham and then by train to Brighton where we were quartered in the Metropole Hotel and issued with a full kit.

After a few days in Brighton, four weeks' leave was granted, and Tom Wood was able to visit relations in Leeds. He returned to Australia on the *H.M.T. Andes,* via the Panama Canal and New Zealand, and was discharged on 9 October 1945.

APPENDIX 12

SQUADRON ROLLS OF AUSTRALIAN P-40 PILOTS: 1941 - 1943

AUSTRALIAN PILOTS SERVING WITH 94 SQUADRON, 1942

408001. Maxwell, M.M.

AUSTRALIAN PILOTS SERVING WITH 112 SQUADRON, 1941-43

402782. Allison, G.F.
406171. Bartle, J.P. (2nd tour to 450 Sqn.)
402343. Burney, H.G. + 30/05/42
402107. Caldwell, C.R. DFC & Bar
404233. Carson, K.F. PoW 16/06/42
404168. Carson, W.E.
402307. Cassell, S.D.
407415. Drew, R.A. DFM + 17/06/42
404618. Elliott, P.T. + 09/03/42
404542. Ferguson, A.H. + 20/12/41
406179. Jeffries, R.J.D. + 12/12/41
404504. Johnson, S.C. + KIFA 02/01/42
404178. Leu, R.M. DFM PoW 21/06/42
407005. McBryde, L.
404181. McCormack, E. + KIFA 16/09/41
402530. McQueen, D.N.
404183. McWilliam, C.F. (to 250 Sqn 28/10/41)
404180. Mills, E.H. + KIFA 31/08/41
406260. Parker, F.E. (to 450 Sqn.)
406265. Sands, K.R. (to 450 Sqn.)
402987. Simpson S.O. (to 450 Sqn 13/03/42)
403209. Stinson, J.L.
404186. Stirrat, I.H. + 04/10/41
404188. Taylor A.W.J. (to 450 Sqn Feb /42)
407884. Wild, R.A.

AUSTRALIAN PILOTS SERVING WITH 250 SQUADRON, 1941-43

400613. Adams, M.
400642. Buckland, G.G. + 30/05/42
404495. Cable, W.O. DFC
402107. Caldwell, C.R. DFC & Bar
(to 112 Sqn as CO.)
407412. Cormack. D.J. DFC
402317. Cornall, C. PoW 30/10/41
404004. Coward. G.C. (to 3 Sqn.)
402114. Gale, D.R. + 26/06/41
407427. Hannaford. H.R. (to 450 Sqn.)
400089. Humphries, H.N.
402124. Kent. J.F.S. + 30/06/41
77976. Mayers, H.C. DSO, DFC. 239 Wing
PoW 20/07/42 + (see text)

402004. McCullough, J.M. + 18/08/41
404183. McWilliam, C.F.
407247. Mortimer, A.T.L. + KIFA 03/07/41
402130. Munro, D.A.R. + 18/06/41
407180. Nitschke, R.H. + 20/12/41
1053584. Paxton, T.G. + 07/04/42 Ceylon - Ops
402022. Pike, G. A. + 25/05/42 illness
402806. Power, J. + 10/07/42
404008. Ryan, M.E.
402684. Twemlow, F.M. DFC
402685. Waddy, J.L. DFC (to 260 Sqn.)
406269. Wallis, R.T.A. + 10/07/42
404009. Whittle, R.J.C. DFM

AUSTRALIAN PILOTS SERVING WITH 260 SQUADRON 1941-43

402732. Cundy, W.R. DFC, DFM
402893. Tregear, F.W. + 24/04/42
402685. Waddy, J.L. DFC

3 SQUADRON PILOTS MAY 1941 - MAY 1943

402838. Alderson, E.H.T. + 20/10/42
565. Arthur, W.S. DFC
411726. Austin, A.N. + 14/01/43
407070. Baillie, M.J. + KIFA 11/04/42
250774. Barr, A.W. MC, DFC & Bar. PoW 26/06/42
400035. Baster, A.R. + 08/01/42
407416. Bayly, R.H.
402717. Beard, W.A. + KIFA 16/04/42
403854. Bee, K.C. + 21/12/42
10634. Beer, J.G.
402718. Biden, R. + 16/06/42
402787. Boardman, L.L. DFM
250696. Bradbury, E.A.
782. Bradbury, L.H.
404234. Bray, H.J.
270699. Briggs, P.J.
407780. Bullwinkel, J.H.
703. Burbury, D.J. PoW 14/09/41
695. Bothwell, P.R. +. 25/11/41
407781. Caldwell, N.R.
404085. Cameron, A.C. DFM PoW 11/01/42
400788. Cashmore, F.H.
80. Chapman, D.R.
250704. Chinchen, G. DFC PoW 14/06/42
(later escaped)

401103.	Churchill, J. PoW 27/10/42	400092.	Lees, L. + 22/11/41
205745.	Clabburn, G.E.S.	400095.	Lyons, I.A.
61180.	Collier, A.H.	402375.	Mailey, W. DFM
404004.	Coward, G.C. DFC. (from 250 Sqn.)	404345.	MacDiarmid, C.S. + 30/05/42
400039.	Curtis, V.F.	403376.	MacKenzie, R.J.
416328.	Dawkins, A.W.G.	742.	McIntosh, J.A. + 22/01/42
411294.	Dean, N.J.	408752.	McKernan, N.G.
412118.	Dent, R.C.	406943.	McLeod, M.
412049.	Diehm, W.G. + 14/01/43	405752.	McTaggart, J. + KIFA 18/08/42
402231.	Donald, J. PoW 15/09/42	401708.	Manderson, J.J. + KIFA 06/08/42
403324.	Dougall, G.A. + 15/07/42	290488.	Manford, J.G.
404604.	Doyle, J.C.		(on attachment from 450 Sqn.)
133.	Eaton, B.A.	411933.	Matthews, R.L.
20761.	Eggleston, F.F.H. PoW 12/12/41	400101.	Nash, P.M.
713.	Evans, B.A. + 25/11/41	404773.	Neill, G.A. DFM + 22/10/42
402113.	Evans, N.A. + KIFA 05/06/41	407751.	Norman, H.A. PoW 27/05/42
401280.	Finlason, W.D.S. PoW 21/12/42	824.	Pace, H.G. + 13/05/42
250626.	Fischer, F. DFC	407453.	Packer, T.E. (to 450 Sqn.)
411692.	Forsstrom, C.F.	402391.	Parker, T.D. + 12/10/41
406838.	Fox, P.W.	260226.	Pelly, B.
403577.	Freer, K.H.	380.	Perrin, J.R.
400040.	Funston, N.J.	407130.	Pfeiffer, R.V.
400002.	Furniss, J.K.	37419.	Plinston, G.H.F. RAF
260714.	Gibbes, R.H.M. DSO, DFC	407183.	Raffen, J.P.
715.	Giddy, P.R. + KIFA 12/03/42	407080.	Randell, M.P.A. + KIFA, Ops.28/06/41
416168.	Gilbert, P.D.	386.	Rawlinson, A.C. DFC & Bar
404337.	Glendinning, A.	402137.	Reid, F.B. + 15/02/42
403693.	Goulder, K.	403604.	Richardson, A.J. PoW 25/10/42
260717.	Gray, R.H.S.	401151.	Righetti, A. PoW 22/01/43
411022.	Hankey, E.	405262.	Ritchie, D.V.
401808.	Harbour, K.	406082.	Roberts, H.G. PoW 22/11/42
411321.	Hardiman, L.G.	401669.	Roediger, I.H.
416333.	Harris, B.G.	264812.	Russell, T.L.
260719.	Hart, R.C.	833.	Rutter, D. + 09/12/41
407075.	Hiller, G.E. + 02/12/41	403149.	Ryan, F.J. + 16/06/42
401443.	Holder, J. PoW 02/11/42	471.	Saunders, J.H.W. + 22/11/41
401216.	Hooke, J.H.	260835.	Schaeffer, H.
411914.	Howell-Price, J.F.	402147.	Scott, D. PoW 14/12/41
416119.	Howie, R.H.	411392.	Scribner, G.G. + 15/09/42
270530.	Jackson, E.H.B.	407593.	Sergeant, J.C.
493.	Jackson, J.F. DFC	402259.	Simes, R.H. DFM + 09/01/42
145.	Jeffrey, P. DSO, DFC	408015.	Smeeton, H.
404509.	Jennings, R.M. + 27/02/42	270839.	Spence, L.T. DFC
260725.	Jewell, W.	465.	Springbett, K.
401644.	Jones, A.N. PoW 03/11/42	407648.	Stanley, K.W.
402938.	Jones, G.R.	404672.	Stevens, R.N.B.
280726.	Jones, R.S. PoW 11/01/42	407463.	Stapledon, B.T.
	(later escaped)	260758.	Stratten, J.K.
400766.	Kildey, E.K. DFM	280760.	Susans, R.T.
650.	Kloster, W. PoW 22/11/41	403080.	Taylor, A.B.
2762.	Knight, D.E. + 14/12/41	406120.	Teede, E.
456.	Knowles, L.E.S. + 22/11/41	761.	Threlkeld, T.L. + 16/02/42
405742.	Knox, T.M.	407465.	Thomas, W.W.
406002.	Lane, E.H. +22/11/41	400944.	Thomas, V.M.
405484.	Laver, C.R.	408060.	Thompson, B.M. DFM.
411499.	Leeds, W.	401200.	Tonkin, A.E.H. + 14/01/43

260652.	Trimble, T.
481.	Turnbull, P. St. G. DFC
406966.	Ulrich, R.Y.
402896.	Upward, J.W. + 17/11/42
411622.	Ward, W.B. + 06/04/43
273.	Watt, R.J. + 27/01/43
845.	Watson, M.H. + 22/11/41
405892.	Weatherburn, L.J. PoW 14/01/43
406101.	White, G.H
401873.	Willis, A.J. + 22/01/43
407088.	Wilson, R.K. DFM + 09/12/41
411423.	Wood, T.G. PoW 20/10/42
400402.	Young, I.C. (On attachment from 450 Sqn)

450 SQUADRON PILOTS
FEBRUARY 1942 - MAY 1943

J8387.	Aitchison, E.G. (RCAF)
405169.	Austin, R.M.
80027.	Barber,M.C.H. (RAF) *(South African)* DFC
406171.	Bartle, J.P. (from 112 Sqn & 1 Air Ambulance Unit.)
412646.	Batten, J.E.M. (RNZAF)
403307.	Bell, J.T.
406312.	Beste, F.W. PoW 05/07/42
403210.	Blackburn, A.J. +26/03/43
401099.	Borthwick, D.W.P. MID
R84508.	Brown, R.G. (RCAF). PoW 20/07/42
401406.	Cameron, G.H. + 14/01/43
	Cantrell, E.T. (RAF) Canadian
R84072.	Chittenden, W.J. (RCAF)
407411.	Clarke, D.H. (RAF) DFC
R93426.	Crist, B.V. (RCAF)
404237.	Crouch, T.E.N.
401368.	Cummins, J.L. MID
404545.	Dangar, R.V. DFM
1314003.	Davey, C.N.V.
402321.	Davidson, D.McK.
400916.	Davidson, R.G.
413035.	Day, A.E.W. (RNZAF)
40296.	Dean, J.N. + 29/05/42
401106.	Devlin, H.W.+ KIFA. Ops.22/05/42
403660.	Downes, R.F.A. + KIFA at I METS 07/10/42
84666.	Downey, C.P. (RCAF)
406234.	Dyson, R.D. DFM
408676.	Ellis, J.F.
406196.	Evans, J.D. PoW 22/10/42
403582.	Evatt, J.W. + KIFA. Ops. 05/04/42
403326.	Ewing, P.A. PoW 15/09/42
394.	Ferguson, A.D. DFC
401490.	Forsyth, T.J. + 27/07/42
412674.	Fourneau, S.J. (RNZAF)
R82779.	Fox, W.R. (RCAF)
R90247.	Frost, L.A. MID (RCAF)
411882.	Gillard, T.A. (RNZAF)

400221.	Glancy, A.N. + 17/06/42
404796.	Gleeson, J.D.
404337.	Glendinning, A. DFC (from 3 and 92 Sqns.)
407422.	Goldberg, R.G.
404629.	Gray, E.J. + 27/02/42
402695.	Gregory, A.H.
406244.	Halliday, W.J. +13/06/42
407427.	Hannaford, H.R. (from 250 Sqn.)
408093.	Harrison, M.C. + 14/01/43
401506.	Hast, R.A.
R79022.	Holloway, R.D. (RCAF)
406274.	House, E.C. DFM
R78724.	Hughes, R.C. (RCAF)
400645.	James, J.R. + 08/06/42
407241.	Jenkins, M.A.
45543.	Johns, G.E.
402240.	Jones, M.J. PoW 26/06/42
402090.	Jones, R.C.
404785.	Jones, T.E. + 26/06/42
401238.	Jowett, H.A.C.
400203.	Kelsall, A.
404341.	Kennedy, D.L.
402364.	Kierath, R.V. PoW 23/04/43 + 29/03/44
401517.	Lambie, H.T.
403140.	Law, D.R.
400720.	Lindsay, G.
40723.	Longmore, W.J.M. (RAF)
R86820.	Markle, A.G. (RCAF) PoW 08/11/42 (escaped)
400812.	Marrows, K.
J4919.	Marting, H.F. (RCAF) MC PoW 23/10/42 (escaped)
106150.	Mackay, W.J.A.
290488.	Manford, J.G.
407441.	McBride, K.M. + 23/02/42
402523.	McBurnie, D.H. DFM
41517.	McConnochie, W.G. (RNZAF)
403360.	McFarlane, V.J. DFM
403484.	McPherson, G.D. + KIFA. Ops. 05/04/42
402530.	McQueen, D.N. (from 112 Sqn.)
400151.	Metherall, W.J. + 16/05/42
404546.	Minchin, D.G.
406402.	Murdoch, K.A. PoW 26/06/42
404980.	Mylne, A.D.
R86113.	Nicholson, A.D. (RCAF)
89308.	Norton, G.H. (RAF) (to 112 Sqn as CO 17/05/43)
402389.	Nursey, I.A. + 30/05/42
401143.	Oakley, E P.
401078.	Officer, G.J. PoW 03/11/42
403475.	O'Neil, G.C.W. MM
403369.	Osborne, J.C. PoW 10/07/42
407453.	Packer, T.E. + 29/05/42 (from 3 Sqn.)
406260.	Parker, F.E. (from 112 Sqn.)
411562.	Payne, R. (RNZAF) + KIFA. Ops. 22/11/42

R80093.   Phelps, J.S. (RCAF)
403443.   Prowse, R.J.
404770.   Quirk, E.J. + 22/05/42
402998.   Read, W.T.
400833.   Reid, H.B. + 31/10/42
 J8155.   Regan, F.X.J. (RCAF)
400486.   Robertson, C.W.
414681.   Rogers, A.J.C. (RNZAF)
   269.   Rose, I.F. D'A.
411400.   Rowe, R.
R89523.   Rushton, H.F. (RCAF)
416155.   Sanders, F.C.
406265.   Sands, K.R.
  3288.   Schaaf, F.R. DFC
412715.   Shannon, A.F.
402139.   Shaw, R. + 29/05/42
407459.   Shillabeer, N.H. + 29/08/42
401676.   Silk, F.J. + 26/02/43
402987.   Simpson, S.O. + 05/07/42
402810.   Sly, E.L.
   213.   Steege, G.H. *DFC* (from 3 Sqn.)
1258632.   Stone, R. (RAF) + 13/06/42

1067420.   Stoneley, J. (RAF) + 26/02/43
412278.   Strom, E.H.
404188.   Taylor, A.W.J.
404066.   Thompson, C.M.T. PoW 23/02/42
404069.   Thompson, E.T. + 31/05/42
R72057.   Wallace, W.H. (RCAF)
400850.   Watt, R.R.
401019.   Williams, A.L. + 22/05/42
 40652.   Williams, J.E.A. DFC
           PoW 31/10/42 + 09/03/44
409624.   Wilson, R.E.
403776.   Winn, R.W. PoW 24/01/43
401334.   Youl, S.C.
400402.   Young, I.C. + 12/06/42

Notes. Ranks are not included, as many pilots were promoted several times. Decorations recorded are for the time span of the narrative. A number of the pilots listed above were awarded decorations during the Sicilian and Italian campaigns, and these will be listed in the next volume. Similarly, those who later became prisoners of war, or were lost in action, will be listed in the second volume.

APPENDIX 13
'RUSTY' KEIRATH

F/O R.V. KIERATH.
AUS. 402364.
RAAF.

7th. May, 1943.

Dearest Mother — Well, what do you think about me being here in Germany as the guest of the Government? I can truthfully say that it was no wish of mine, however I'm quite alright and apart from being a P.O.W. am quite happy. Doing a patrol one morning my aeroplane was hit by anti aircraft fire — the engine seized up & stopped while we were over the sea well inside enemy territory. I decided to "bail out" & so stepped over the side, pulled the rip-cord and had a very pleasant journey down to the water. I spent about 2 hours in the water during which time I drank a flask of brandy (which Mrs. Swift had given to me) and then a boat-load of Germans came & picked me up. I didn't get a scratch or hurt myself in any way but I was really cold, that was soon put right in a German Hospital and I'm none the worse for my experience. At present I am in a temporary camp awaiting a transfer to a permanent camp, consequently you cannot write to me here – I will send you my duration address at the first possible opportunity – My love to all the families & lots & lots for yourself.

P.S. I will endeavour to number my letters. xx.

Reg.

APPENDIX 14
ROLL OF HONOUR

3 SQUADRON RAAF, JUNE 1941 - MAY 1943

1. Sgt. NORMAN EVANS 05/06/41   (Training accident.)

2. Sgt. MICHAEL RANDELL 28/06/41   (Engine failure on take off after refuelling at forward base when returning from combat.)

3. Sgt. DUDLEY PARKER 12/10/41   (Shot down by Lt. Sinner of JG 27.)

4. FO ERIC LANE 22/11/41 (am)   (Shot down by Oblt. Schneider or Hpt. Redlich of I/JG27.)

5. Fl. Lt. JOHN SAUNDERS 22/11/41(am)   (Shot down by Schneider or Redlich in same combat.)

6. FO MALCOLM WATSON 22/11/41(am)   (Shot down by Schneider or Redlich in same combat.)

7. FO LAWTON LEES 22/11/41   (Shot down by one of six JG 27 pilots in afternoon combat.)

8. Fl. Lt. LINDSAY KNOWLES 22/11/41   (Collision with Bf109 of JG 27 in same combat as above.)

9. FO BRUCE EVANS 25/11/41   (Shot down; probably by Obfw. Espenlaub of I/JG 27.)

10. FO ROY BOTHWELL 25/11/41   (Shot down by AA while attacking ground forces.)

11. Sgt. GEOFFREY HILLER 02/12/41   (Shot down by Hpt. Redlich of I/JG 27.)

12. FO DAVID RUTTER 09/12/41   (Shot down by Oblt. Homuth, Oblt. Schneider or Uffz Grimm of I/JG 27, who claimed three Tomahawks: Sgt. Alan Cameron force-landing safely.)

13. Sgt. REX WILSON 09/12/41   (Shot down in same combat as FO Rutter)

14. FO DONALD KNIGHT 14/12/41   (Shot down by Lt. Stahlschmidt or Oblt. Unterberger of I/JG 27, who claimed two Tomahawks, Sgt. Derek Scott surviving as PoW.)

15. FO ALAN BASTER 08/01/42   (Shot down in combat with large group of Italian and German fighters: no specific claim identified.)

16. Sgt. RONALD SIMES 09/01/42   (Shot down by Oblt. Homuth of 3/JG 27.)

17. FO JAMES McINTOSH 22/01/42   (Shot down by Lt. Stahlschmidt of I/JG 27.)

18. Sgt. FRANK REID 15/02/42   (Shot down by Lt. Marseille of 3/JG 27.)

19. FO THOMAS THRELKELD 16/02/42   (Shot down by Oblt. Keller of I/JG 27.)

20. Sgt. ROGER JENNINGS 27/02/42   (Shot down by Lt. Marseille of 3/JG 27.)

21. PO PETER GIDDY 12/03/42   (Killed in flying accident: aerobatics.)

22. Sgt. MERVYN BAILLIE 11/04/42   (Killed in training accident with RAAF Conversion & Refresher School.)

23. Sgt. WILLIAM BEARD 16/04/42   (Killed in training accident.)

24. FO HAROLD PACE 13/05/42   (Shot down by Lt. Marseille of 3/JG 27.)

25. Sgt. COLIN MacDIARMID 30/05/42   (Shot down in combat with Bf109s of JG 27 or JG 53, seven German claims for six losses.)

26. Sgt. ROSS BIDEN 16/06/42   (Force landed with engine failure, possibly as a result of attack by Oblt. Tangerding or Fw. Fink: bomb still on board detonated.)

27. Sgt. FREDERICK RYAN 16/06/42   (Shot down by Tangerding or Fink of III/JG 27: same combat as Sgt. Biden.)

28. FO GEORGE DOUGALL 15/07/42   (Shot down by AA during ground attack sortie.)

29. Sgt. JOHN MANDERSON 06/08/42   (or 16th - Training accident.)

30. FO JOHN McTAGGART 18/08/42   (Training accident.)

31. Sgt. GORDON SCRIBNER 15/09/42   (Shot down by one of eight claiming German pilots of JG 27.)

32. PO EDWARD ALDERSON 20/10/42   (Shot down by either Lt. Kientsch or Uffz. Vavra of II/JG 27.)

33. PO GARTH NEILL 22/10/42   (Shot down by one of three possible German pilots: Fw. Gruber III/JG 27; Lt. Harder III/JG 53 or Hpt. Rodel II/JG 27.)

34. FO JOHN UPWARD 17/11/42   (Killed in collision with Fw. Buter of II/JG 27.)

35. F/Sgt. KENNETH BEE 21/12/42   (Shot down by AA during strafing attack on airfield at Hun.)

36. FO WILLIAM DIEHM 14/01/43   (FOs Diehm and Tonkin were flying two of eleven aircraft shot down by JG 77 for a total of fourteen claims: Maj. Muncheberg 3, Hpt. Bar 3, Hpt. Ubben 2, Oblts. Laube, Freytag and Omert 1 each, Ofws. Brandt and Neiderhagen 1 each and Fw. Michel 1.)

37. FO ALLAN TONKIN 14/01/43   (See above.)

38. FO ARTHUR AUSTIN 14/01/43   (FO Austin was lost in a later combat in the afternoon, but is included in the total of fourteen German claims for the day.)

39. Sgt. ALEXANDER WILLIS 22/01/43   (Collision with Sgt. Jones of 3 Squadron during combat.)

40. Sqn. Ldr. RONALD WATT 27/01/43   (Shot down by either Oblt. Freytag or Hpt. Ubben of II & III/JG 77.)

41. Sgt.. WILLIAM WARD 06/04/43   (Shot down by AA while searching for ground target.)

450 SQUADRON RAAF, FEBRUARY 1942 - MAY 1943

1. Sgt. KEITH McBRIDE 23/02/42

(A/C damaged in combat with Lt. Sinner of I/JG 27. Crashed landing at base.)

2. Sgt. EDWARD GRAY 27/02/42

(Shot down by Hpt. Homuth of 3/JG 27.)

3. PO GORDON McPHERSON 05/04/42

(Lost control, spun and crashed during combat patrol.)

4. PO JOHN EVATT 05/04/42

(Lost control, spun and crashed during combat patrol.)

5. Sgt. WILLIAM METHERALL 16/05/42

(Crashed during combat as a result of his A/C being struck by another Kittyhawk which had been abandoned due to battle damage.)

6. Sgt. ELSTON QUIRK 22/05/42

(Shot down by Obfw. Bendert or Uffz. Steis of II/JG 27.)

7. Sgt. ARTHUR WILLIAMS 22/05/42

(Shot down in the same combat by one of the above two pilots.)

8. Sgt. HENRY DEVLIN 22/05/42

(Crashed on take off for combat mission.)

9. Sgt. JOHN DEAN 29/05/42

(Shot down by Hpt. Maak, Lt. Korner or Lt. Stahlschmidt of I/JG 27 in the same combat as Sgts Packer and Shaw, each pilot claiming one Kittyhawk.)

10. Sgt. THOMAS PACKER 29/05/42

(See above.)

11. Sgt. RAYMOND SHAW 29/05/42

(See above.)

12. F/Sgt. IAN NURSEY 30/05/42

(Shot down by Hpt. Maak or Lt. von Lieres of I/JG27, or Oblt. Borngen of II/ JG 27, who claimed three victories between them; two other aircraft being lost.)

13. Fl. Lt. ERIC THOMPSON 31/05/42

(Shot down by Bf109s; probably from III/JG 53.)

14. Sgt. JOHN JAMES 08/06/42

(Shot down by ground fire while strafing during return from fighter-bomber escort mission.)

15. PO IVAN YOUNG 12/06/42

(One of two 450 Sqn A/C shot down by Obfw. Clade and Uffz. Gierster of II/JG 27, F/Sgt. Beste surviving.)

16. Sgt. WILLIAM HALLIDAY 13/06/42

(Shot down by Lt. Marseille or Lt. Remmer of I/JG 27. Four aircraft were lost, for four claims by Marseille and one by Remmer.)

17. Sgt. ROY STONE (RAF) 13/06/42

(Shot down by Lt. Marseille or Lt. Remmer in same combat.)

18. Sgt. ALEXANDER GLANCY 17/06/42

(Shot down by Lt. von Lieres or Lt. Korner of I/JG 27: one claim each, Sgt. Hooke of 3 Squadron returning.)

19. FO THOMAS JONES 26/06/42

(Shot down by Bf109s of III/JG 53.)

20. F/Sgt. STANLEY SIMPSON 05/07/42 — (Shot down by ground fire while strafing LG106.)

21. PO THOMAS FORSYTH 27/07/42 — (Shot down by Lt. Stahlschmidt and Oblt. Unterberger of I/JG27.)

22. PO NEIL SHILLABEER 29/08/42 — (Shot down by Uffz. Schneider of I/JG 27.)

23. Sqn. Ldr. JOHN WILLIAMS 31/10/42 — (Force-landed while strafing on this date and captured. Subsequently murdered by Gestapo on 29/03/44.)

24. Sgt. HAROLD REID 31/10/42 — (Shot down by Obfw. Ludwig of I/JG 77.)

25. Sgt. RONALD PAYNE (RNZAF) 22/11/42 — (Apparently lost control in storm cloud and crashed.)

26. Sgt. GILBERT CAMERON 14/01/43 — (Sgts. Cameron and Harrison were shot down in the same combat by pilots of JG 77 - see 3 Squadron entry on same date for German details.)

27. Sgt. MAXWELL HARRISON 14/01/43 — (See above.)

28. Sgt. FREDERICK SILK 26/02/43 — (Shot down by JG 77, probably by Hpt. Bar, who claimed five of JG77's thirteen victories for an actual loss of fourteen Kittyhawks.)

29. Sgt. JOHN STONELEY (RAF) 26/02/43 — (Shot down in same combat as above, Hpt. Bar again is the likely victor, as all other German claims except one were made in the afternoon.)

30. PO ADRIAN BLACKBURN 26/03/43 — (Shot down by ground fire during ground attack sortie.)

31. PO REGINALD KIERATH 23/04/43 — (Baled out due to engine trouble: captured by enemy ASR launch and made PoW. Murdered by Gestapo on 29/03/44.)

239 WING

Wg. Cdr. HOWARD MAYERS 20/07/42 — (Shot down by JG 53 and captured during raid on Fuka. Lost during transfer to Italy as PoW. See p.148)

112 SQUADRON RAF, AUGUST 1941 - JUNE 1942

1. Sgt. EVERARD MILLS 31/08/41 — (Lost control and crashed during training flight.)

2. Sgt. EDWARD McCORMACK 16/09/41 — (Engine failure on take off. Spun during attempt to regain airfield.)

3. Sgt. IAN STIRRAT 04/10/41 — (Shot down by Oblt. Rodel or Lt. Schacht of II/JG 27, who both claimed a victory.)

4. FO ROBERT JEFFRIES 12/12/41 — (Shot down over Tmimi, possibly by Oblt. Graf von Kageneck of JG 27.)

5. Sgt. ARCHIBALD FERGUSON 20/12/41 — (Shot down by Lt. Remmer or Obfw. Schulz of II/JG 27, who claimed 3 A/C between them, actually shooting down five.)

6. Sgt. STANLEY JOHNSON 02/01/42 — (Lost while flying through dust storm near Halfaya Pass.)

7. Sgt. PHILLIP ELLIOTT 09/03/42   (Lost during combat mission, but probably due to oxygen or mechanical failure, diving from 8-10,000 ft. without apparent cause.)

8. PO HENRY BURNEY 30/05/42   (Lost during ground attack sortie. One of seven allied A/C lost around 1500 hours, for seven German claims.)

9. PO ROY DREW 17/06/42   (Lost during ground attack sortie: it is considered that he may have been Oblt. Marseille's 100th victim.)

250 SQUADRON RAF, MAY 1941 - JULY 1942

1. Sgt. GEORGE PIKE 24/05/41   (illness)

2. PO DONALD MUNRO 18/06/41   (Shot down by Oblt. Redlich or Uffz. Steinhausen of I/JG 27, who claimed three A/C from 250 Sqn. between them. *See text for details.*)

3. Sgt. DAVID GALE 26/06/41   (Shot down by Oblt. Franzisket or Obfw. Kowalski of I/JG 27, who shot down two A/C of 250 Sqn.)

4. PO JAMES KENT 30/06/41   (Shot down by Oblt. Franzisket of I/JG 27.)

5. Sgt. ARTHUR MORTIMER 03/07/41   (Lost control, spun and crashed during training dogfight.)

6. Sgt. JOSEPH McCULLOUGH 18/08/41   (Shot down by Obfw. Forster of I/JG 27 - shipping patrol.)

7. PO RICHARD NITSCHKE 20/12/41   (Shot down by Lt. Remmer (I/JG 27) or Obfw. Schulz (II/JG 27) who claimed 3 A/C between them, actually shooting down five.)

8. PO GRAHAM BUCKLAND 30/05/42   (Shot down by Oblt. Marseille. Buckland is reported to have baled out, possibly with wounds.)

9. Sgt. JOHN POWER 10/07/42   (Shot down by Lt. Schofbock or Obfw. Rosenberg of III/JG 27, who accounted for three A/C between them.)

10. Sgt. ROY WALLIS 10/07/42   (Baled out into sea after combat with Bf109Es and MC202s. Not found by ASR owing to presence of enemy aircraft. Sgt Wallis was flying a borrowed A/C of 3 Sqn, (ET837) and as a result, is incorrectly recorded on 3 Squadron's Roll of Honour at the AWM.)

260 SQUADRON RAF, APRIL 1942

1. Sgt. FRANK TREGEAR 24/04/42   (Lost during ground attack sortie: probably caught in explosion of M/T he had strafed.)

They shall not grow old, as we that are left grow old,
Age shall not weary them, nor the years condemn.
At the going down of the sun, and in the morning,
We will remember them.

Laurence Binyon

NOTES

INTRODUCTION

1. Group Captain A.C. Rawlinson OBE, DFC (Bar) AFC. *A Narrative of Service as a General Duties/Pilot with the RAAF and RAF 1938 - 1961.* p. 34 (Unpublished memoirs, 1991)
2. ibid, pp. 13-15.
3. Ray Wagner, *The Curtiss P-40 Tomahawk,* p.10, Profile Publications Ltd, ND.
4. Robin Brown, *Shark Squadron - The History of 112 Squadron 1917-1975,* p.38, Crecy Books, 1994.
5. Neville Duke, *Test Pilot,* p. 58, Grub street, 1992
6. Bob Whittle, correspondence.

P-40 INTO BATTLE - 3 SQUADRON in SYRIA

1. Rawlinson, op. cit., p.35
2. Operations Record Book - 250 Squadron.
3. Frederick A. Johnsen, *P-40 Warhawk,* p.74, MBI Publishing Company, 1998.
4. John Herington, *Air War Against Germany and Italy,* p.88 footnote, Australian War Memorial, 1954.
5. Johnsen, op. cit., p.74.
6. Rawlinson, op. cit., p.37.
7. Christopher Shores, *Dust Clouds in the Middle East,* p.199, Grub Street, 1996.
8. Wg. Cdr. (RTD) Bobby Gibbes, DSO, DFC & Bar, *You Live But Once,* pp. 44-5, Privately published, 1994
9. Shores, op. cit., p. 215.
10. Anthony Robinson, *RAF Fighter Squadrons In The battle Of Britain,* pp. 169-173, Arms and Armour Press, 1987. (for details of 85 Squadron claims)
    Alfred Price, *Battle of Britain: The Hardest Day 18 August 1940,* pp. 204-207, Macdonald and Janes, 1979. (for details and times of German losses)
    John J. Vasco and Peter D. Cornwell, *Zerstorer - The Messerschmitt 110 and its units in 1940,* pp. 136-139 & 183-185, JAC Publications, 1995. (for details of RAF claims and details and times of German losses)
11 Shores, op. cit., p.224.
12. Ibid, p.229.
13. Ibid, p.236.
14. Rawlinson, op. cit., p. 39.
15. Christian J. Ehrengardt and Christopher Shores, *L' Aviation de Vichy Au Combat-La Campagne de Syrie 8 Juin - 14 Juillet 1941,* pp. 138 - 9, 141, Lavauzelle.
16. Gibbes, op. cit., p. 47.

TOMAHAWKS in the DESERT.

1. John Terraine, *The Right of the Line,* p.341, Wordsworth Editions, 1997
2. Shores, op. cit., p.180.
3. John Herington, *Air War against Germany and Italy,* p.104, Australian War Memorial, 1954.
4. Ibid, p. 104.
5. John Rawlings, *Fighter Squadrons of the R.A.F. and their Aircraft,* p.355, Crecy Books, 1993.
6. Christopher Shores and Hans Ring, *Fighters Over the Desert,* p. 48, Arco Publishing Company Inc, 1969
7. Christopher Shores and Clive Williams, *Aces High,* p.632, Grub Street, 1994
8. Herington, op. cit., p.105.

9. 3 Squadron Operations Record Book, RAAF Historical Section, (hereafter referred to as ORB)
10. Brown, op. cit., p.42.
11. Terraine, op. cit., p.356
12. ORB
13. Wing Commander John Watson and Louis Jones, *3 Squadron at War,* p.35, D.A.F. 3 Squadron Association, 1959
14. ORB.
15. Shores and Ring, Op. cit., p57.
16. Franz Kurowski, *German Fighter Ace Hans Joachim Marseille - The Life Story of the Star of Africa,* p.94, Schiffer Publishing Ltd., 1994.
17. Shores and Ring, op. cit., p. 55
18. Herington, op. cit., p.197.

OPERATION CRUSADER

1. Adrian Gilbert (Ed.) *The Imperial War Museum Book of the Desert War 1940 - 1942,* p. XIII, Sidgwick & Jackson, 1992.
2. Herington, op. cit., p.196.
3. Ibid, p.197.
4. Duke, op. cit., p.60.
5. Herington, op. cit., p.201.
6. Rawlinson, op.cit., p. 47
7. 11 Squadron ORB
8. 45 Squadron ORB
9. Rawlinson, op. cit., pp. 48 - 52
10. Neville Duke, *Test Pilot,* pp. 190 - 191, Grub Street, 1992
11. Rawlinson, op. cit., p. 52
12. Russell Guest, *3 Squadron List of Victory Claims*
13. Shores and Ring, op. cit., p.66
14. Kurowski, op. cit., p.112.
15. Rawlinson, op. cit., p. 53
16. ibid, p. 53
17. Gibbes, op. cit., pp. 75-6
18. Brown, op. cit., p.46.
19. Rawlinson, op. cit., p. 56
20. ibid, pp. 56-7
21. Clive Caldwell, quoted in Herington, op. cit., p.207.
22. 112 Squadron Combat Report.
23. Shores and Williams, op. cit., p.355 & 421.
24. Herington, op. cit., p.209.
25. Christopher Shores, *Aces High Volume 2,* p. 147, Grub Street, 1999.
26. Bob Whittle, Log Book.
27. Correspondence with Eric Bradbury
28. Shores and Ring, op.cit., p.79.
29. Robert Grinsell, *Messerschmitt Bf109,* p. 22 Janes Publishing Company Ltd 1980.
30. Shores and Ring, op. cit., p. 81.
31. 112 Squadron Combat Report
32. ibid, supplementary to above
33. Shores and Ring op. cit., p.82.
34. ibid p.82.
35. Shores and Williams, op. cit. p.163.

ENTER THE KITTYHAWK

1.   ORB, op.cit.
2.   Combat report of Alan Cameron, in Herington, op. cit., p 211.
3.   Brown, op.cit., p.52.
4.   Interview with Ian Lyons.
5.   Brown, op. cit., p.53.
6.   Gibbes, op. cit., p.107
7.   Shores and Ring, op. cit., p.89.
8.   112 Squadron Combat Report (Sgt. R. Leu)
9.   Herington, op. cit., p.216.
10. Brown, op. cit., p.58
11. 112 Squadron Combat Reports (various) and summary
12. Duke, op. cit., p. 71
13. Chris Dunning, *Courage Alone. The Italian Air Force 1940 - 1943* Hikoki Publications, 1998
14. Herington, op. cit., p. 217.
15. Bernd Barbas, *Planes of the Luftwaffe Fighter Aces, Vol. 2* p.151. Kookaburra Technical Publications Pty Ltd. 1985.
16. ibid, p. 151.
17. Kurowski, op. cit., p.137.
18. Rawlinson, op.cit., p. 55
19. Brown, op. cit., p. 60.
20. Clive Caldwell's Log Book.
21. Brown, op. cit., pp. 60-61
22. Shores and Ring, op. cit., p.99.
23. ibid, p. 99
24. Tom Wood : unpublished papers, *A Few Recollections of my Air Force Life.*
25. Leonard L. Barton, *The Desert Harassers,* p.14, Astor Publications. 1991.
26. Peter Firkins, *The Golden Eagles,* pp 184-5. St George Books. 1980.
27. Air Chief Marshal Sir Kenneth 'Bing' Cross, *Straight and Level,* p. 151. Grub Street. 1993.
28. Terraine, op. cit., p.285., and *The Illustrated Encyclopaedia of Aircraft, Vol. 4.* p.825. Orbis Publishing 1982.
29. Terraine, op.cit., quoting Denis Richards, p.285.
30. Encyclopaedia, op. cit., p.881.

WAITING FOR ROMMEL

1.   Herington, op. cit., p.231
2.   Shores and Ring, op. cit., p.109
3.   ibid. p.110
4.   ibid. p.109
5.   Kurowski, op. cit., p.148
6.   ibid, p.145
7.   ORB 450 Squadron.
8.   ibid.
9.   Kurowski, op. cit., p. 149
10. Shores and Ring, op. cit., p.112
11. Brown, op. cit., p.242.
12. Herington, op. cit., p.231
13. Lex McAulay, *Four Aces,* p.24, Banner Books. 1998.
14. ORB 450 Squadron.
15. Terraine, op. cit., p.370.

16. ORB 450 Squadron.
17. Shores and Williams, op. cit., p. 431
18. James Sinclair, *Sepik Pilot* , p.16. Lansdowne Press Pty Ltd., 1971.

KITTYBOMBERS

1. Sinclair, op. cit., p.31.
2. ORB 3 Squadron.
3. Shores and Ring, op. cit., p.114 and Shores and Williams, op. cit., p. 610
4. Alexander Markle, *Memoirs of a Fighter Pilot,* (unpublished autobiography, courtesy 450 Squadron Association)
5. Shores and Ring, op. cit., p. 115
6. Shores and Williams, op.cit., p.113.
7. Herington, op.cit., p. 234.
8. ibid. p.234.
9. McAulay, op. cit., p. 25.
10. ibid. p. 25.
11. Barton, op. cit., p.14
12. Shores and Ring, op. cit., p.118
13. Terraine, op.cit., p.373. (The quote within a quote is from the Luftwaffe Historical Section, quoted in Richards and Saunders. p.202 (see page 752 of Terraine.)
14. Shores and Williams, op. cit., p.610
15. Conversation with John Hooke.
16. Shores and Williams, op. cit., p.610.
17. Herington, op.cit., p.240
18. ibid, p.241.
19. ORB No. 3 Squadron.
20. McAulay, op. cit., p.29
21. ibid, p.29.
22. Shores and Williams, op. cit., p. 249
23. Conversation with John Hooke.
24. Herington, op. cit., p. 242.
25. Wood papers, op. cit.
26. Barton, op.cit., p.17.
27. Shores and Ring, op.cit., p. 132.
28. McAulay, op.cit., p.33.
29. Shores and Ring, op.cit., p.133.
30. Herington, op.cit., p. 244.
31. George James, quoted in *OK - Recollections of the Desert Harassers,* p.37. 450 Squadron Association, 1996

THE STAND AT EL ALAMEIN

1. Alan Moorehead, *The Desert War - The North African Campaign 1940 1943,* pp 174 -5, Hamish Hamilton Ltd., 1965.

2. Roger Parkinson, *The War In The Desert,* p. 118, Granada Publishing Ltd (Hart Davis, MacGibbon Ltd) 1976

3. Fred Majdalany, *The Battle of El Alamein,* pp. 42-3, Weidenfeld and Nicholson, 1965

4. Lex McAulay, *Against All Odds - RAAF pilots in the Battle for Malta 1942,* Hutchinson, 1989, and AWM Honour Roll

5. Shores and Ring, op. cit., p. 148

6. Gilbert, op. cit., p. 115
7. Terraine, op. cit., p.3778
8. Markle, op. cit., pp 33-35
9. Sinclair, op. cit., p. 35
10. Newspaper clipping provided by Tom Wood
11. Heinz W. Schmidt, *With Rommel in the Desert,* White Lion Publishers, 1973.
12. Terraine, op. cit., pp 383-4
13. Shores and Ring, op. cit., p.176
14. ibid, p. 177
15. ORB 450 Squadron
16. Kurowski, op. cit., pp 202 - 3
17. Shores and Ring, op. cit. p.178
18. Wood papers: op. cit.
19. Gibbes, op. cit., p. 139
20. Shores and Ring op. cit., p.180
21. Barton, op.cit., pp 19 - 21
22. Shores and Ring, op. cit., p.182
23. ibid, p.183
24. Gibbes, op. cit., p. 139
25. Shores and Ring, op. cit., p.184
26. ORB 3 Squadron
27. ibid
28. Wood papers, op.cit.
29. Herington, op. cit., *foot note* p.370
30. Anthony Cave Brown, *Bodyguard of Lies,* p. 103. Comet Books, (W.H. Allen & Co. Ltd.) 1986
31. ibid, p. 103
32. David Irving, *Rommel: The Trail of the Fox,* p.180. Wordsworth Editions, 1999
33. Majdalany, op. cit., p.74

THE BATTLE OF EL ALAMEIN

1. Schmidt, op. cit., p.175
2. Herington, op. cit., p.370
3. Shores and Ring, op. cit., p.194
4. ibid. p.194
5. Schmidt, op. cit., pp 176 - 177
6. Gibbes, op. cit., p.143
7. Shores and Ring, op. cit., p 197
8. Gibbes, op. cit., p. 143
9. Shores and Ring, op. cit., p. 197
10. Markle, op. cit., p. 42
11. Shores and Ring, op. cit., p. 199
12. Shores and Williams, op. cit., p.637
13. Brown, op. cit., p.78
14. Parkinson, op. cit., p.148

BREAK-THROUGH

1. John Weal, *Junkers Ju87 StukaGeschwader of North Africa & the Mediterranean,* p.64, Osprey Publishing, 1998
2. Christopher Shores, *USAAF Fighter Units MTO 1942 - 45,* p. 4, Osprey Publishing Ltd. 1978

3. Sinclair, op. cit., p. 38
4. Shores and Williams, op. cit., p.201
5. Schmidt, op. cit., p.177
6. Barton, op. cit., pp 23-4
7. Markle, op. cit., pp. 44-5
8. Shores and Ring, op. cit., p. 206.
9. Barton, op. cit., p.28
10. Shores and Ring, op. cit. p. 209.
11. Correspondence with Ron Cundy.
12. Russ Snadden, *Black 6. The extraordinary restoration of a Messerschmitt Bf 109,* p. 171, Patrick Stephens Ltd. Somerset 1993.
13. Gibbes op. cit., p.155
14. Barton, op.cit., p. 28.
15. J.E. Johnson and P.B. Lucas, *Courage in the Skies,* p.168, Leopard (Random House) London 1996.
16. ibid, p. 169.
17. Barton, op. cit., p. 30.
18. Vincent Adams Winter, *Noble Six Hundred. The Story of the Empire Air Training Scheme.* p.64, Privately Published, Brighton 1982.
19. Shores and Ring, op. cit., p. 216.
20. Christopher Shores, Hans Ring and William N. Hess. *Fighters Over Tunisia,* p. 127, Neville Spearman, London 1975.
21. Watson and Jones, op.cit., p.97.
22. Parkinson, op. cit., p.171.
23. Shores, Ring and Hess, op. cit., p.151.
24. Sinclair, op. cit., pp 43-45.
25. Schmidt, op. cit., pp. 193-194.
26. Shores, Ring and Hess, op. cit., p. 158.
27. ibid, p. 168.
28. ibid, p. 168.
29. ibid, p. 168
30. ibid, p. 177.
31. RAAF Museum: correspondence from Mr. F. D. Hamilton.
32. Sinclair, op. cit., p. 47.
33. Herington, op. cit., pp. 401-402.

THE TUNISIAN CAMPAIGN

1. Shores, Ring and Hess, op. cit., p 224
2. ibid, pp 223 - 224.
3. ibid, p. 226.
4. Herington, op. cit., p. 403.
5. ibid, p.403.
6. Parkinson, op. cit., pp 180 - 181.
7. Herington, op. cit., p. 403.
8. Irving, op. cit., p. 260
9. Herington, op. cit., p.404.
10. Parkinson, op. cit., p.183.
11. ibid, p. 183.
12. ibid. p. 185.
13. Barton, op. cit., pp 34 - 36.

14. Parkinson, op. cit., p.188.
15. Sinclair, op. cit., p. 49.
16. Conversation with John Hooke.
17. Jack Bartle, quoted in *OK - Recollections of the Desert Harassers* . pp 31 - 2.
18. Sinclair, op. cit., P viii.
19. Brown, op. cit., p.99
20. Barton, op. cit., p.39.

APPENDIX 1

1. E.R. Hooton, *Eagle in Flames - The Fall of the Luftwaffe,* pp 214-5, Arms and Armour Press, 1997
2. McAulay, *Four Aces,* op. cit., p. 9
3. Terraine, op. cit., pp 399-400
4. ibid, p.632

APPENDIX 10

1. Brown, op. cit., p. 72
2. Trevor J. Constable and Col. Raymond F. Tolliver, *HORRIDO! Fighter Aces of the Luftwaffe,* pp 15-16, Arthur Barker Ltd. 1968
3. Ernst Obermeier, *Die Ritterkreuz Trager der Luftwaffe 1939 - 1945, Vol.1, Fighters.* Dieter Hoffmann, 1966
4. Kurowski, op. cit., pp 202-3.

SOURCES and BIBLIOGRAPHY

Official Documents

Public Records Office - England

Air 27/157   11 Squadron Operations Record Book

Air 27/455   45 Squadron Operations Record Book

Air 27/873   112 Squadron Operations Record Book

Air 27/877   112 Squadron Combat (Fighter) Reports

Air 27/1501   250 Squadron Operations Record Book

Air 27/1503   250 Squadron Diary

Air 27/1504   250 Squadron Combat (Fighter) Reports

Air 27/1537   260 Squadron Operations Record Book

Commonwealth War Graves Commission

Debt of Honour Data Base

RAAF Historical Records

3 Squadron Operations Record Book

450 Squadron Operations Record Book

3 Squadron Combat (Fighter) Reports

3 Squadron Postagrams - Daily Operations Reports-1943

RAAF Graves Registration Records

RAAF Honours and Awards Citations

3 Squadron lists of combat claims, based on : (i) The Book of Original Entry & (ii) Russell Guest's revised list

Australian War Memorial

Roll of Honour Data Base

PR00514 - Log Book and personal papers of Group Captain C.R. Caldwell, 250 and 112 Squadrons

PR88/037 - Log Book of Flight Lieutenant H.R. Hannaford, 250 and 450 Squadrons

PR84/364 - Personal papers of Group Captain J.L. Waddy, 250 and 260 Squadrons

AWM 54 81/4/77 - Records of RAAF personnel serving with the Royal Air Force overseas

AWM 54 779/3/129 - Interrogation reports of evaders and released prisoners of war

Personal Documents - RAAF Museum

Stan Davidson (3 Squadron armourer) *War Diary*

Mr. F.D. Hamilton (450 Squadron fitter) *Correspondence*

Personal Documents and Interviews

Eric Bradbury (3 Squadron) *correspondence*

Dave Borthwick (450 Squadron) *letter to 450 Squadron RCAF*

Des Cormack DFC (250 Squadron RAF) *personal interview, Log Book*

Ron Cundy DFC, DFM (260 Squadron RAF) *Log Book, correspondence*

Bobby Gibbes DSO, DFC & Bar (3 Squadron) *correspondence*

Viv Herrett (450 Squadron) *War Diary.* (Courtesy of 450 Squadron Association)

John Hooke OBE, DFC (3 Squadron) *personal interviews, Log Book*

Max Jenkins (450 Squadron) *interview, Log Book extract*

Keith Kildey DFM (3 Squadron) *personal interview, Log Book*

Ted Lawler (450 Squadron) *correspondence*

Ian Lyons MBE, (3 Squadron) *personal interview*

Alexander Markle (450 Squadron) *Memoirs of a Fighter Pilot* (Courtesy of 450 Squadron Association)

Alan Rawlinson OBE, DFC (Bar) AFC (3 Squadron)

A Narrative of Service as a General Duties/Pilot with the RAAF and RAF 1938 - 1961

Alan Righetti (3 Squadron) *War Diary, correspondence*

Gordon Steege DSO, DFC, (450 Squadron) *interview, correspondence*

'Snow' Swift DFC (272 Squadron) *correspondence*

Bob Whittle DFM (250 Squadron RAF) *correspondence, Log Book, contemporary newspaper articles*

Tom Wood (3 Squadron) *personal interviews, private papers - A Few Recollections of my Air Force Life, Log Book*

Published Works

Bernd Barbas, *Planes of the Luftwaffe Fighter Aces, Vol. 2,* Kookaburra Technical Publications Pty. Ltd., 1985

Leonard L. Barton, *The Desert Harassers,* Astor Publications, 1991

Anthony Cave Brown, *Bodyguard of Lies,* Comet Books, (W.H. Allen & Co.), 1986

Robin Brown, *Shark Squadron - The History of 112 Squadron 1919 - 1975,* Crecy Books, 1994

Trevor J. Constable and Colonel Raymond F. Tolliver, *HORRIDO! Fighter Aces of the Luftwaffe,* Arthur Barker Ltd. 1968

Air Chief Marshal Sir Kenneth 'Bing' Cross, *Straight and Level,* Grub Street, 1993

Chris Dunning, *Courage Alone: The Italian Air Force 1940 - 1943.* Hikoki Publications, 1998

Christian J. Ehrengardt and Christopher Shores, *L' Aviation de Vichy Au Combat - La Campagne de Syrie 8 Juin - 14 Juillet 1941,* Lavauzelle

Peter Firkins, *The Golden Eagles,* St George Books, 1980

Wing Commander (Rtd) Robert H. (Bobby) Gibbes, *You Live But Once,* Privately Published, 1994

Adrian Gilbert (Ed.) *The Imperial War Museum Book of the Desert War 1940 - 1942,* Sidgwick & Jackson, 1992

Robert Grinsell, *Messerschmitt Bf109,* Janes Publishing Company Ltd., 1980

John Herington, *Air War Against Germany and Italy,* Australian War Memorial, 1954

H. M. Stationery Office, *Prisoners of War Naval and Air Forces of Great Britain and the Empire 1939 - 1945.* (1945)

Reprinted by J. B. Hayward & Son *in association with* The Imperial War Museum, 1990

E. R. Hooton, *Eagle in Flames - The Fall of the Luftwaffe,* Arms & Armour Press, 1997

David Irving, *Rommel: The Trail of the Fox,* Wordsworth Editions, 1999

George A. James (Ed.) *OK, Recollections of the Desert Harassers,* 450 Squadron (R.A.A.F.) Association, 1996

Frederick A. Johnsen, *P-40 Warhawk,* MBI Publishing Company, 1998

J.E. Johnson and P.B. Lucas, *Courage in the Skies,* Leopard (Random House), 1996

Franz Kurowski, *German Fighter Ace Hans-Joachim Marseille - The Life Story of the Star of Africa,* Schiffer Publishing Ltd, 1994

Fred Majdalany, *The Battle of El Alamein,* Weidenfeld and Nicholson, 1965

Lex McAulay, *Four Aces,* Banner Books, 1998

Lex McAulay, *Against All Odds - RAAF Pilots in the Battle for Malta 1942,* Hutchinson, 1989

Alan Moorhead, *The Desert War - The North African Campaign 1940 1943,* Hamish Hamilton Ltd., 1965

Ernst Obermeier, *Die Ritterkreuz Trager der Luftwaffe 1939-1945, Vol. 1, Fighters,* Dieter Hoffmann, 1966

Roger Parkinson, *The War in the Desert,* Granada Publishing, (Hart Davis, MacGibbon Ltd.) 1976

Alfred Price, *Battle of Britain: The Hardest Day -18 August 1940 ,*Macdonald and Janes, 1979

John Rawlings, *Fighter Squadrons of the RAF and their Aircraft,* Crecy Books, 1993

Anthony Robinson, *RAF Fighter Squadrons in the Battle of Britain,* Arms and Armour Press, 1987

Heinz W. Schmidt, *With Rommel in the Desert,* White Lion Publishers, 1973

Christopher Shores, *Dust Clouds in the Middle East,* Grub Street, 1996

Christopher Shores, *USAAF Fighter Units MTO 1942 -45,* Osprey Publishing Ltd., 1978

Christopher Shores and Hans Ring, *Fighters over the Desert,* Arco Publishing Company Inc., 1969

Christopher Shores, Hans Ring and William N. Hess, *Fighters over Tunisia,* Neville Spearman, 1975

Christopher Shores and Clive Williams, *Aces High,* Grub Street, 1994

Christopher Shores, *Aces High Volume 2,* Grub Street, 1999

James Sinclair, *Sepik Pilot,* Lansdowne Press Ltd. 1971

Russ Snadden, *Black 6, The extraordinary restoration of a Messerschmitt Bf109,* Patrick Stephens Ltd., 1993

John Terraine, *The Right of the Line,* Wordsworth Editions, 1997

John J. Vasco and Peter D. Cornwell, *Zerstorer - The Messerschmitt 110 and its Units in 1940,* JAC Publications, 1995

Wing Commander John Watson and Louis Jones, *3 Squadron at War,* D.A.F. 3 Squadron Association, 1959

John Weal, *Junkers Ju87 StukaGeschwader of North Africa & the Mediterranean,* Osprey Publishing, 1998

Vincent Adams Winter, *Noble Six Hundred, The Story of the Empire Air Training Scheme,* Privately Published, 1982

INDEX

Personnel - Allied

Personnel - Axis

Places

MILITARY UNITS & OPERATIONS

ALLIED

AIR FORCE

AXIS

AIR FORCE

French

German

Italian

ALLIED

ARMY

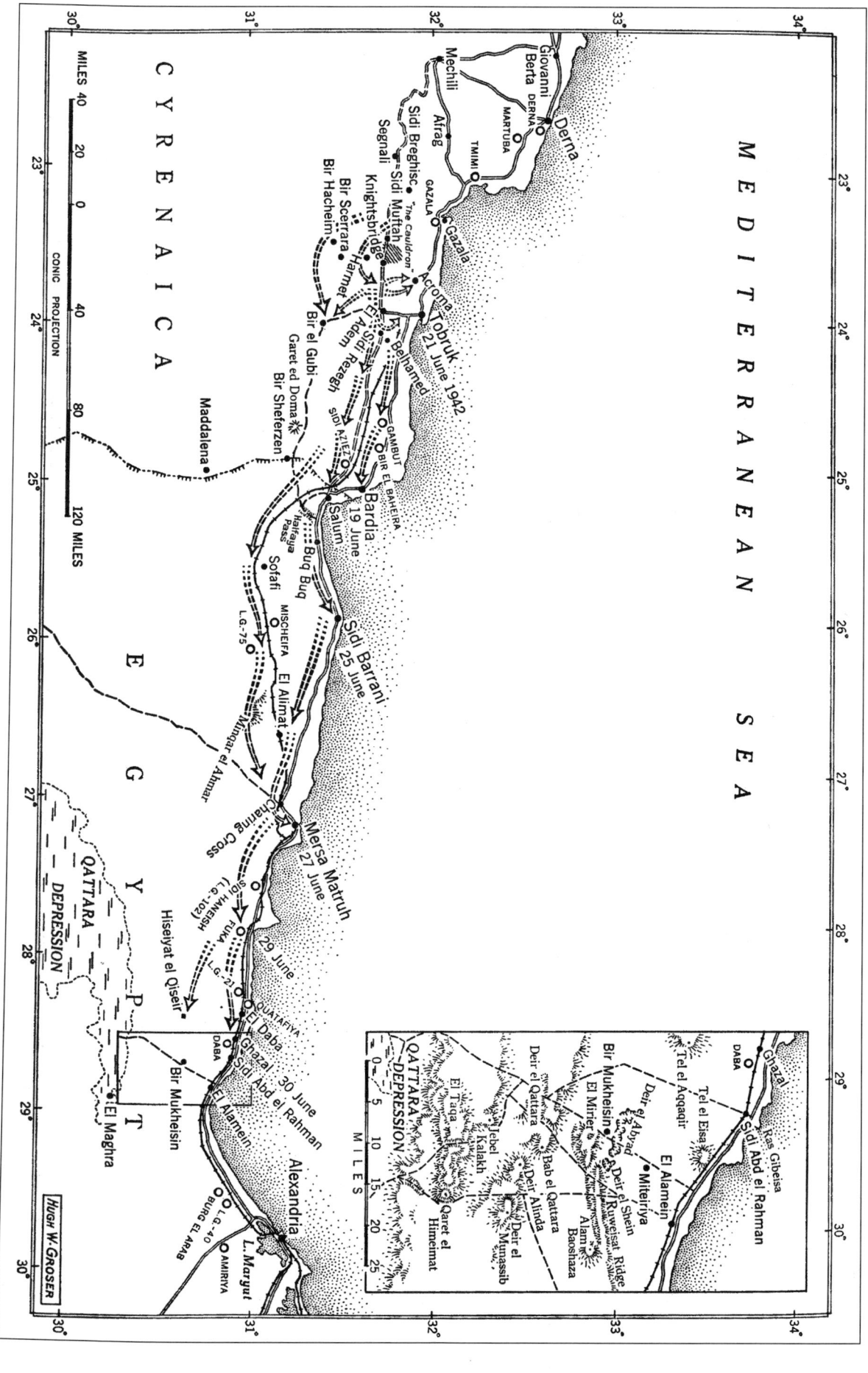